I0592105

C. A. (Cyrus Augustus) Bartol

Principles and Portraits

C. A. (Cyrus Augustus) Bartol

Principles and Portraits

ISBN/EAN: 9783744652551

Printed in Europe, USA, Canada, Australia, Japan

Cover: Foto ©ninafisch / pixelio.de

More available books at **www.hansebooks.com**

THE RISING FAITH. By Rev. C. A. BARTOL,
D.D. One volume, 16mo. Cloth. Price $2.00.

From the Boston Advertiser.

The book in its drift is a sequel to the "Radical Problems" published last year; though it deals less with the mysteries of faith and opinion about which thinkers and teachers, earnest and thoughtful like himself, differ widely. . . . With a dash of his pen he strikes at forms of belief and worship which to him are nothing, or worse than nothing, but to many millions of the human race have been a savor of life unto life, and have opened the way of spiritual illumination, the reality of which no man living has the right to question. But after all, the reader, whatever his religious experience may have been, if he reads to the end, will find the religious philosophy of Dr. Bartol resting on the deep and unchangeable foundations of faith in God, — the foundation on which all creeds and all systems must be built to be eternal.

From the Liberal Christian.

His book may not define the creed of the future, but it does better. It inspires us with "the rising faith." What a glorious faith it is! Faith in God, in man, in immortality. Faith in reason, in spirit, in character. Faith in the past, in the present, in the future. Faith in law, in order, in beneficence. Faith in human nature, not as a finality, but as "a becoming." Faith in man's environment as admirably adapted to develop him into " the stature of a man which is that of the angel." Faith in liberty, but not in license. Faith in the pure marriage of coequal hearts and minds. Faith in forbearance and self-sacrifice as better than divorce-made-easy to solve the social riddle of the time. Faith in educated labor as the best solution of the problem of labor. These are a few of the " notes" of "The Rising Faith" which Dr. Bartol blends in his wonderful *Fantasia.*

From the Christian Leader.

It is the faith that Mr. Bartol has attained to as the result of his studies, observations, reflections for more than sixty years, following the apostolic direction to try all things and hold fast that which is good. And certainly a great part of what he with his constant trying has held fast to will be called good by the large majority of those who are esteemed right-minded and sound-thinking men. . . . But above all things, the writer is true to his own convictions. These he states positively, clearly, unhesitatingly, but with all gentleness.

He is certainly a Liberal Thinker, but in sweetness, candor, fair-mindedness, love of his fellow-men, patience with their errors and infirmities, shrewd observation of their weaknesses, purity and spirituality, he should be taken as an example by all the Liberal Thinkers of our day. The book has a long life before it, if for nothing else but its literary excellencies. . . . It will be cordially welcomed by all the best intellects of our day as a valuable contribution to human thought, and be the text of many an essay for a long time to come.

Sold everywhere. Mailed, post-paid, on receipt of the price, by the Publishers,

ROBERTS BROTHERS, BOSTON.

RADICAL PROBLEMS. By Rev. C. A. BARTOL, D.D. One volume, 16mo. Cloth. Price $2.

CONTENTS. — Open Questions; Individualism; Transcendentalism; Radicalism; Theism; Naturalism; Materialism; Spiritualism; Faith; Law; Origin; Correlation; Character; Genius: Father Taylor; Experience; Hope; Ideality.

From the Liberal Christian.

What a wonderful, wonderful book is the "Radical Problems." We are not a third through it yet, and Heaven only knows where and how we shall find ourselves at the end of the journey. Already are we so shocked, stunned, bewildered, edified, delighted, — in short, thoroughly, thoroughly bewitched, — that we have no words to express ourselves. . . . That this book has a long life before it who can doubt, or that it will cause a grand commotion in the theological world? It will be impetuously attacked and vehemently defended, but will survive alike the onslaught of its assailants and the intemperate zeal of its defenders; and will be the fruitful source of many a brilliant essay and inspiring discourse and stimulating and suggestive club-talk, long, long after its gentle and gifted author has left us to receive a most cordial welcome by his brother thinkers in brighter spheres.

From the Commonwealth.

Spirituality, purity, gentleness, love, child-like simplicity, bless and sanctify him; but he is spirited as well as spiritual. In his gentleness there is a quick vivacity, and he sometimes exhibits a keen incisiveness as of whetted steel. His aim is not so much to solve as to suggest. He is no dogmatist, nor is he an expositor or judge. He finds open questions and delights to leave them open questions still. Meantime he looks into them with the eyes of his inmost soul, discerns much, throws out a profusion of glancing and irradiating suggestions that open the questions farther instead of closing them, then retires to look elsewhere. . . . This man carries eternal summer in the eyes, and sees beds of violets in snowbanks. His own climate is his world, and he can make no excursions out of it. A pleasant world it is, with no deserts, jungles, reeking bogs, foul, ravening creatures, and poles heaped with ice. As some will see only with the physical eye, so he with the spiritual only.

From the Globe.

It contains seventeen chapters, honestly representing the individual spiritual experience of the author, and at the same time indicating some of the intellectual tendencies of the time. It is "radical," not in the usual sense of the word, but in its true sense, that of attempting to pierce to the roots of things. Many of the opinions and ideas expressed in the book may be repudiated by the conservative reader, but its spirit and aim cannot fail to charm and invigorate him. Dr. Bartol, indeed, is one of those men who have religious genius as well as religious faith. . . . The book is a protest against popular theology, made from what the writer considers the standpoint of true and pure religion. We have considered it from a literary point of view, and, thus considered, its wealth of thought and imaginative illustration entitle it to a high rank among the publications of the year.

Sold everywhere. Mailed, postpaid, by the Publishers,

ROBERTS BROTHERS, BOSTON.

PRINCIPLES AND PORTRAITS.

AND

PORTRAITS.

By C. A. BARTOL,

AUTHOR OF "RADICAL PROBLEMS" AND "THE RISING FAITH."

BOSTON:
ROBERTS BROTHERS.
1880.

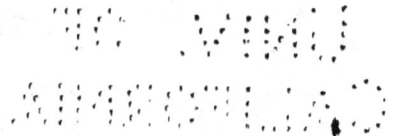

UNIVERSITY PRESS:
JOHN WILSON & SON, CAMBRIDGE.

CONTENTS.

Part I. — PRINCIPLES.

		PAGE
I.	DEFINITION	3
II.	EDUCATION	32
III.	DEITY	66
IV.	SCIENCE	108
V.	ART	134
VI.	LOVE	157
VII.	LIFE	178
VIII.	BUSINESS	202
IX.	BEASTS	228
X.	POLITICS	263
XI.	PLAY	292

Part II. — PORTRAITS.

I.	THE PERSONALITY OF SHAKSPEARE	315
II.	CHANNING, THE PREACHER	342
III.	BUSHNELL, THE THEOLOGIAN	366
IV.	THE GENIUS OF WEISS	386
V.	GARRISON, THE REFORMER	413
VI.	HUNT, THE ARTIST	435

272901

PART I.

PRINCIPLES.

PART I.

PRINCIPLES.

I.

DEFINITION.

IN a scientific age, requiring that every thing shall be clearly observed, conceived, and described, it concerns us not to overlook what no sphere of definition can include. Exact discovery, like the projection of a map or chart and the figures in a picture, needs its undefined background. The atoms that combine in definite proportions, the imponderables of light and heat, — which Goethe said change bleak and brown winter to the green and blooming landscape, — proceed from and refer to somewhat immense. We can define a proposition, but not that germinal ocean of life from which Agassiz thought come all animal and vegetable forms. Definition is limitation within measures of weight, space, and time; but how much cannot be put in pound or notched on any scale! Definition is discrimination; but are we not able to contemplate the whole? Yes, if *universe* be a lawful word.

We belong to one or another school of philosophy according to our tendency to emphasize the unity or diversity of things. Plato, Spinoza, Leibnitz, Hegel, care for discrimination, but they aim to trace the universal thread on which every bead or boulder is strung. Aristotle, Francis Bacon, Locke, Comte, and all the modern experimentalists aim to divide and distinguish the whole into elements and parts. Neither of these intellectual dispositions can dispense with the other. If the last be extreme, we have the materialist; and the mystic when the first prevails. But the unobservant fail alike of special information and of communion with the One in all. To the ignorant and moon-eyed the world is but a bright blur: they dwell in the vague and void. To the truculent dissector and exclusive analyst the world is a series of dots or lines under his lens or heap of ashes from his retort. The doctrine of evolution is an attempt at justice at once to matter and mind; and the evolutionist is an idealist in seeking connection and consequence everywhere. Darwin and Spencer — one unfolding the physiological, the other the social side of the same theory — are no teachers of chance and a mindless origin, but contributors to a worship wider than can be held in the church-walls, as are those French naturalists who have shown that human society only repeats and furthers the economy, justice, and orderly government of insects even lower down than the ants and the bees. " In my Father's house are many mansions ; " and it is sublime to see in what huts and chambers of minute cells begins the housekeeping which legions of angels in the Master's thought carry out. It is the prime delight of reverent study to trace analogies and variations of one tune throughout the vegetable and animal sphere. The three green needles in one sheaf and five in another of two species of pine-tree, the edging of the leaf in the red oak and rounding of it in the white oak, — as though the same scissors took pleasure in varying the pattern in a similar cloth, — are parallel on a lower plane with the shifting and turning of one melody in a symphony of Beethoven, and intended for like satisfaction. The pismire, hauling a worm ten times as big or bit of gravel ten times as heavy as itself to construct and provision its sandy tenement, has a strange similarity with the hunter taking home his heavy game from the desert or jungle and the captain dragging a ship with his little tug. What a mirror of humanity in the airs of the peacock, cunning of the opossum, turtle, and fox, motherly cluck of the hen and proud rooster's strut, cruel hug of the bear and saving goodness of the Newfoundland and Great St. Bernard dog! We are implicated with the beasts, be we their descendants or not. Likeness or difference, the definable and indistinguishable, these are the poles of the world; men and nations are classifiable as they incline to one or the other. The German genius, for example, would discover the centre all comes from or pivot on which all turns, and the French would find and formulate the facts. The vast and misty implications of the German tongue tell of the Black Forest and mountain mirage; the French language is clear and sunny as their climate and soil. It is the dialect of narrative, conversation, description, and wit; and it is impossible, when a *double entendre* is not intended, to mistake what a Frenchman means to say. The speech he uses may be lied in, but is too precise itself to lie; and Brown-Séquard found English

a looser and easier language for a lecture than his vernacular. The German mind is a quarry; the French, a
foundry. The French drops its bucket after the truth,
but does not roil the well; the German digs deeper,
that the water may not fail, or may gush through
an artesian spring. The questions Where from and
Where to the Frenchman postpones to that of Where,
— getting the most out of the present, while the
German would decide if there be for us a future or
not.

Both scales, finite and infinite, are in every soul; the
point to consider is how the balance inclines. The
philosophy to which only the finite exists shuts out
God and heaven, and duty save as a calculation of
profit and loss. We, in its view, are booked for a
journey, we have taken a berth, we are at an inn, but
soon to leave for ever carriage and bed and board. The
relation of sex for a limited term loses in the light of
utility its charm; and business becomes a game of
sharpers, if conscience be but convenience and no
reckoning exist beyond the ledger in the safe.

But my thesis is that there is no strict definition possible of the meanest thing. A railway sleeper runs
farther than across the track, — even to the timber,
tree, acorn, or pine-cone, earth, water, air, sun, and the
immemorial nebula which has been successively the tomb
of an old world and cradle of a new one, till imagination staggers on the trail. The iron rail dates from the
bowels of the earth and elements preceding the fiery
throes which shot up in liquid streams the metallic
mines and veins. The ant-hill reared over night, which
the thundering train shakes down in the morning, was

provided for in a balloon of fire-mist bigger than the solar system. The very foot, well shod, which I plant on the gravel, is a dance of shifting atoms to and from the ends of the earth. There is somewhat transcendent in the origin and orbit of every particle, and a conscious infinity in the soul they serve.

"Imperial Cæsar, dead and turned to clay,"

is a clownish conceit. I and my neighbor survey our adjoining fields and drive iron bolts for bounds, but we cannot measure ourselves. We know not when we began. Nobody has grown wiser than David, who only knew he was "curiously wrought in the lowest parts of the earth." The elements flew to clothe in me what they did not make. Neither can we tell how much we occupy of space. My body is of a certain size, but not my mind. I am where it is, — in the sky, primeval chaos, or paradise. Its travelling has no chart. It concentrates itself through a microscope on a dot a thousand times too small for the naked eye, and seizes with its speculation a protoplasm a thousandth part of the dot, or expands to the size of Sirius the spheres which are but ethereal motes. It gathers through a hole two-thousandths of an inch wide the light of the planet Mars. An attendant at church said, "I took in the service with the millionth part of my mind." An idea or feeling has indeterminable scope. We never went round our own heart, gauged a sentiment, or expended it in any ebb or expression of word or deed. What is the last time your trained terrier would run for the ball you throw? He would run till he dropped. Where will your ardor halt? You may make a study of your mate and offspring, as does Mr. Darwin of his infants; but there is in them something you are aware of, but can neither observe nor describe. The woman dear to you is a piece of flesh, — no doubt belongs to the animal kingdom in the order of mammals. She is fitted to reproduce and nurse her like. But with her fleshly organism she includes something else, — a personality which forbids her being made an instrument or tool. She is abused when she is tyrannized over, and dies to your thought and heart when she is defined. Still less can we define God. Say, boldly, he cannot define, for he cannot measure, himself. Religious people are startled by the idea that he is not conscious of himself. But he were self-measured and finite, not infinite, did even any self-consciousness fully take his own being in. If he be nowise forgetful of himself, he would be devoid of the finest virtue which his creatures display. He is conscious of and in his offspring and work rather than in and of himself; and we are the process of his mind as well as fashion of his hands. He is from everlasting, yet he were blind and dumb and dead but for what he does; and should he rest on a Sabbath day, or *strike* work for a moment, he would commit suicide by ceasing from the labor which is his play. He is not abstract, but concrete, and rushes for ever into the action which is his only speech. He is good, but never stops to think how good he is; and for his own glory, of which the tradition of selfish ages says he is jealous, he cares not a jot. It is as pure a fiction when we apply arithmetic to him and call him threefold as when we speak of a quarter of the world.

This doctrine of infinity is the ground of liberty, or

unlimited room to put forth our powers. The reason a generous soul will not trespass is because it is not restrained. Titian, the Venetian painter, was trained in his youth to treat religious subjects only, till he was pursued by the ascetic spectres he had portrayed. So when Alphonse, Duke of Ferrara, engaged his pencil at court, Titian said to him, " You have seen nothing but saints and church tableaux from my hand." The wise duke referred him at once to themes of his own taste and inclination, which led him not to skeleton figures and monkish gloom, but to all that is alive and happy in this earthly scene. Before long, however, Titian himself proposed to paint a *Christ*. " I thought," said the Duke, " such was not the subject you would prefer." " True, it was not," answered the master, " when I was forced to it; but since you give me my liberty I am eager to use it well, and henceforth I promise that the churches and convents shall have as much from me as the city and palace. I have let my hand run too much after my fancy, and I should be vexed not to repent." How many have had a lifelong disgust, if not actual hatred, for the Bible, which they were compelled, as a task or penalty, in their childhood to read ! A pious kinsman of my own confessed with shame that he preferred Shakspeare on this account, and went secretly into the barn to read the plays all by himself. Yet the Scriptures are poems too.

But it is objected by many philosophers of mark, that no positive idea of the infinite is possible to the human mind. I reply, that no such idea of the *finite* is possible. The infinite relation of every thing determines its finite constitution. Every thing has an immense ancestry and posterity, and every person is, coincident if not coextensive with God. We can draw no circle, however large, in which any thing can be contained. Every thing refers to something else, and immeasurably more, as a wave to the sea. Moreover, every thing is eternally derived, and the history of a particle would be the history of the universe. In what mineral formation, vegetable soil, animal frame, or human organism and substance prior to all these, who shall tell what part any particular atom has played ? What soul or spirit has it served, what emissary has it been of the Holy Ghost, or what journey taken longer than that of the Wandering Jew ? How it perspires from a pore, exhales in a breath, finds room in a sigh with a million of its mates, yet is more solid than iron, tougher than steel, more palpable to a finger fine enough than marble or granite, more potential than catapult or battery, while with such soft impartiality and invincibility it nurses the skin of a man or a plant, constitutes the root underground and leaf on the bough, and is primordial germ of all nature's growth ! We cannot catch it, more than, as Socrates told his disciples, they could overtake his soul ; and what this trowel or chisel of an atom has yet to do, what prophet shall tell? All that lives will fade, but it will hold over and survive. If the world be burnt up, this asbestos will remain, — no fire it does not work in, or ashes it is not raked from. •It is the unmelted, safe, and unfailing bond of value, angel of an endless errand, and messenger that punctually arrives. Being the least we can conceive, it yet has, through the largest we can imagine, its scope. In the lightning it is swifter than an arrow and heavier than a cannon-ball. In every form of giant powder fulminates its imperceptible grain. It is the force in the frost, whose hoar rime on an autumn morning turns every blade of grass to a silver spear. It has picked for ages at the Atlantic cliffs, and promises to come again. 'It cracks the granite with slight, repeated, unnumbered blows. It drills the hole, plants the charge, and blasts the rock with explosions too noiseless to hear and too far-reaching to compute. It is in the colors of whose rates of diverse velocity only a mathematical term is the gauge. With fine penetration to paint, it has a strength as vast, too, as the gravitation that heaves the orbs. Its artist-touch is resistless in every dot. What its quality is, no science can define. We can appreciate it only as we stand with wonder and worship at the gates of an inscrutable Presence to which it brings, and leaves us to our prayers.

When this mysterious property becomes a living monad in a man, he becomes immortal, and, like Jesus, feels commissioned to lay it down and take it again, being conscious of power to rebuild himself from his own sepulchre. It is the distinction of every great soul to be aware of this survival, and not depend on any apparition or promise, but say, " I am the *rising* and the life." So David felt he could not be left in the tomb, although, as has been maintained, there was no revelation of future being to the Jews. Mohammed, without the Christian camp, and Swedenborg, an aeronaut above it, had on this point no doubt. If it be said paradise has as much credit with the vulgar as with the wise, the answer is, real belief in immortality as an article can arise only from consciousness of it as a fact. Many desire and perhaps expect continuance of their carnal existence with all its coarse delights. Even churchmen lay on the resurrection of the body supreme stress, as the degenerate Mohammedans thought of beautiful houris for the recompense of the faithful, as for them, in a finer than Indian hunting-ground, a sort of heavenly prey. But the Master's sense of transcending the grave and cradle alike, before he lay down in either, was simply the extraordinary unfolding in him of the spiritual germ necessary to constitute in the divine image our humanity, and it will be awakened in whoever in heaven or earth shares the growth into such extraordinary proportions. For such a personality no definition or measure can be found.

But on the prejudice or presupposition of our origin in the elements, so many and small, has been based a spurious philosophy of accidental being. We are told, if the very same couples had not met through a long progenital line, or a young man had not been touched with a passing fancy for a young woman, if a chaise had not stopped or been overturned, or a ribbon fluttered, or an accident almost fatal had not happened to make a romantic rescue in season, but for some whim or pastime to occasion an encounter of two persons, it amuses the minute philosopher to assure us, we should never have seen the light; no Moses or Solomon or Son of Joseph and Mary would ever have been! What fine sport of speculation thus to hang human society on hairs, and make the originators and founders of states and churches, the revolutionizers of empires and religions, themselves the creatures of a trivial accident or ephemeral caprice, carrying the fortuity of atoms to higher stages than Lucretius imagined, and deriving the moral as well as material creation from a throw of the dice, a romping game, a running from the track or rut in the road! But we should sooner think the mountain-ranges, spinal columns of the continental globe, to be pieces of luck, than Cæsar, Dante, or Shakspeare. Could the bed of the sea not have been scooped, or starry firmament not reared? It is less credible that Milton or Job might have been passed by! World or no world, before or after Abraham, Jesus knew that God could not dispense with or man do without *him*, and so he was bold to assert his own necessity. In the prophet's phrase, space and time were a bed too short and narrow for him to lie down and stretch himself in. For, when the mind opens, its difference from matter is not only actual but enormous. *No life out of death*, is an axiom with the scientist. There must be a pre-existing seed or egg. The nebula is a star-egg with the star-plan in its amorphous mist, as the acorn holds the plan of the oak. From a fine tracery comes animation of plant or man. Yet, how inconceivably close together are the living and what we call lifeless, the rapid insect generation shows. Is there any refuge from the puzzle of these same buckets, full or empty as they rise and sink, but that all must be alive somehow and that there is no death?

Look at nature with science as a lens. The rock swarms, the clod dances, the mineral is but the vegetable stepping down and the animal an ascending plant, and the man a beast extended and the angel a developed human soul. To make an absolute partition of organic and inorganic, and deny an immaterial principle, is to have two kinds of eternal *matter*, and to have naught eternal else. What a lame and impotent conclusion for the intellect by which it is made! But is it not a self-contradiction for science to suspend all on hap-hazard concurrence, ruling out original intent or final cause? It seems, indeed, that we see and hear and speak at last; but all was blind and dumb and dead at first! To common-sense what is this but the bottom of the universe dropping out? Despite the Scripture, He that formed the eye and planted the ear, himself never heard or saw!

Note, too, this confirmation of our thought, that a mind that dwells on diversities instead of correspondences is uninventive. By seeing likeness in difference, such men as Newton, Kepler, Oken, Goethe, and Swedenborg made their discoveries. The man who in public life is taken up with the interests of his village or section, and not with the commonweal, will be an unpatriotic local politician and greenback demagogue, not a true statesman or financier. He will be not a Webster or Sumner, but a Calhoun or Hayne. The ecclesiastic or theologian, who splits hairs of dogma and stickles for peculiarities of form, who rends the Church and binds not up its wounds, is a schismatic and heretic, undoing the atonement the Master wrought. The conjugal companion, enslaved to his own view and temperament, keen for a point of dispute, and stoutly and stubbornly self-committed to a selfish judgment once expressed, builds but that house divided against itself which Jesus says must fall. The legal counsellor, who has made a microscope of his eye to magnify out of all proportion the conflict of phrases and facts, will not broadly survey his case or truly serve his client, however he may worry the plaintiff or defendant on the other side. Two astute lawyers settling the exact terminology of a deed or conveyance, and consuming a month of time on the mode, while the substance of the property wastes, and only the fees increase, form a spectacle for angels and men. There is an intellectual pleasure in discriminating; but, as different notes in music are sweet only for the harmony they combine in producing, and are but barren apart, or jangling discords together when they fail of that, so, if we miss the concord and rest only in the oppugnance of our opinions, life will be a battle-field of clash and collision, and barren as the plain ploughed with cannon-balls. When we call a man acute, we give him the property of a knife. It is a better gift to heal the breach.

Let me add that the notion we have of infinite duration or extent is inseparable from an idea of infinity in the mind by which such notion is entertained. Our soul is that circle which has no beginning or end. Herschel or Proctor does not pretend to describe or enumerate the stars which stretch off beyond imagination of mortal ken; and as new planets are discovered sailing into the port of knowledge, or as a more potent telescope reaches other of the stars which we so ignorantly and incorrectly call fixed, even so gradual and endless is our revelation to ourselves. When Mr. Gough lectures to the farmers among the White Hills, their surprise is in the sensations and conceptions of which they had never supposed they were capable, but which arise from their unconsciousness into conscious states, as submarine volcanoes push islands above the surface of the deep. No memory or experience can surround the mind, and no prophecy equal or antedate our destiny.

There are worse than Chinese limitations in any meta-physical map of our powers, and how all outward prog-ress is but figure of this fact! Travel had come to an end of its fancied possibilities in the old stage-coaches over the hilly roads, till the wondrous panorama unrolled turnpikes and tunnels, and Menai and St. Lawrence River bridges, with pillarless spans, and lo-comotives with steel and iron rails. Something like a Baltimore clipper to outstrip the Dutch galleon and Chinese junk was once the paragon, without a dream of Fulton's day, with screws and paddles driven by steam, to make the waters bubble and boil. Her Majesty's mail was quick enough transit for a letter till the lightning bore the message with a different sort of post-haste. What shall we say of the phonograph's or microphone's record and vocal or instrumental restora-tion, or the telephone's transmission of sound? We have not explored our physical situation more than a ship's keel has traversed every rood of the sea. But what an impiety to confine our thought to the outward utility of these earthly developments, when they are also such hints of a spiritual advance, and cipher-despatches whose meaning can be divined only in new and loftier affections of mankind! Are not these easements and furtherances signs of a goodness for us to copy and carry out?

Especially we may infer that criticism, or estimate of merit or fault in a book, picture, or character, must al-ways fall short of the subject, as an inventory of house-hold goods will leave out something, at least the house-hold gods, especially if what we judge is a personal or social growth, as of a youth bursting his clothes. We have historians, but no history was ever written.

The Bible is as indefinable as the assimilation of food. We may take exception to its learning or logic or moral standard, varying as it does with the ages it represents; but in its divine touches on human souls is somewhat escaping every solvent or probe, and so wrought into its old texture that no Scripture anthology will preserve it or Bible of to-day take its place. The Coliseum is precious in the ruins and clambering vines that tell its story, which any architectural restoration would miss, and a modern structure on the same spot unravel. "A piece is gone from that old English Boston church window," said my friend, "but we will put nothing in its place." Nature is a quality and quantity that cannot be defined, outlined by any draughtsman, or seen by Argus with all his eyes. As reasonable creatures we own functions and processes which reason neither accurately notes nor performs. Could Alexander have beheld his interior, other worlds for him to conquer would have been disclosed. Could Humboldt have seen the cosmos as a microcosm of the mind, he would not have called himself an insect crawling on the face of the earth. It was an uninspired theology that tried to sing, —

"What worthless worms are we!"

The planet is our plaything, and smaller than we. As explorers try for a northwest passage to a circumpolar sea, we seek a shoreless ocean, but have not got out of our human straits. We are like an infant slowly discovering its own limbs, for our spiritual members are still hidden from our eyes, while our "glassy essence" for ever escapes. We cannot learn too much, and the

2

thirst for knowledge must be slaked, not rebuked; but
we may be and are too *knowing*, and it is a questionable
compliment New England pays to itself of being the
brain of the land.   This nasal tone of ours, the string-
music of the head, needs tempering and softening with
wind-instruments, the flutes of feeling.   Let us have
respect for the concrete and established, and rely less
on those abstractions which are air-plants without historic roots.

Definition itself, I conclude, must be with strict limits
defined.   What is it but a cutting off or dissecting, for
convenience, of things which are not severed after all?
We speak of *kingdoms* in nature; but is the mineral
strictly one of them, with its flint on the edges of the
sworded grass, and its gravel the white spheroid of a
bird's egg, its lime in a turtle's shell, cattle's horns,
beetle's wings, claws and hoofs of animals, bones and
teeth of men?   Is it *mineral* when every atom of it is
pervaded with thought or feeling, moving with will and
sensitive to pleasure or pain?   Therefore not for the
indefinite, but a quite other thing, the infinite, I plead.
Covenants and articles have their value, but are not in-
valuable, any more than is articulate speech.   After the
clatter of tongues in the market or the hall, I find good
society in my dog.   He has the excellence and advantage of being dumb.   He makes observations, but no
remarks.   He is silent, but how attentive!   He understands from a look or motion, without a word.   He does
not pester me with conceits of wisdom or reproofs of
my behavior, and is the first of all flesh to forgive my
sins.   He is a piece of nature, and does not try to perceive how much he weighs or girts.

But the metes and bounds that man sets and perceives in the outward aspects of things, and from which the Romans took their hint for a god of bounds, by their contrast with the illimitable they offset, give to man such a sense of the infinite as no beast can be supposed to possess. Some feeling of it the bird may have in its flight, but how far short of the sailor's as he puts forth from port, or of the poet's imagination, soaring " from earth to heaven, from heaven to earth," or of any person's as he loses himself in reverie or is dissolved in wonder that washes out all care and fever from his mind, till he feels like an angel as he comes out as from a bath in the actual sea. No human act or expression can be rigidly defined. Our look, caress, or kiss is not the same for a different person, although no physiology can denote or geometry measure the lines of change. Love is indefinable. It cannot stand still to have its measure taken for any garment of words. While present it withdraws into the past, projects itself into the future, retires to the closet with God, or rises into heaven after angels unseen. It glows in the face and hides in the breast. It opens a drawer or rifles a grave of what cannot crumble or decay. Seeing itself in the glass of memory, it is transformed into the image of hope, and in this little figure of a mortal vessel it coasts along the immense. But we have this treasure in an earthen vessel which the love is ready to cast away for any ideal object, for companion or country, God or Christ, on which it is fixed. We feel that our love is more and greater than ourselves, even an infinite spirit that enters upon our mortality as its lawful estate and heritage, and uses us as servants for its own ends;

for he is a stranger to the sentiment who fancies that love means his own pleasure instead of another's welfare and universal good.

We are related to the infinite in every way; and we should not question so much and long about the Buddhist Nirvana, but for its real sense. There is a bliss, not indefinite but indefinable, yet clear and vast as a cloudless atmosphere, as we "are laid asleep in body and become a living soul." When ordinary slumber approaches, and is just about to touch in their healthy fatigue our waking powers; when, after long listening to its holy sound, the last vibrations of the bell in some cathedral-tower faint away from the ear, perhaps in a foreign land; when in a quiet hour on the sea-shore the waves softly lap the sand, or with just-heard sob and melodious murmur leave the crevices of the rock; when the rustle of leaves on the tree dies by as gentle degrees as does the wind that had stirred it; when some expert performer, after a touching air, draws out with his bow on the string the note so fine we cannot tell, for the ghostly echoes, at what time it ceased; above all, in some hour of devoted love or spiritual communion, when our cup of content is full to overflowing, and we are, like the sun, as calm as we are warm, — then our being blends with the divine, we share the blessedness of God, and feel secure as he.

> " Those storms must shake th' Almighty's seat
> Which violate the saint's retreat."

But this ecstasy is a sort of death: it is dying to one's self, to all action or distinct volition; it is annihilation of the separate will, a trance of every feeling and faculty, — not knowing, like Paul, whether we are in the body or out of the body, only that we are in "the third heaven." As scientists say, the higher up in the sky the more serene it is, so this is the tranquil firmament of the soul. The hour of action will strike, but the season of rest is also wholesome and good, when

> " Not a wave of trouble rolls
> Across our peaceful breast."

But our science tends to points of matter, and the demand now is to be definite. Define your opinion, position, objection ! Exact information is the order of the day. So much has been accomplished through the microscope and telescope and all other nice instruments of modern investigation, that we hope at length to detect God and heaven through an object-glass, or resolve them in a crucible. Have we not ascertained the speed of light, and different rates at which its diverse beams travel, the number of particles or vibrations in a given space, and the protoplasmic tile which is the only substance used or using itself to build "this universal frame"? I have to say, what is real in this world is not discovered so. Dr. Wayland wrote with great wisdom on the "Limitations of Human Responsibility," but they were never found. Who can tell just where the penumbra of a planet ends? So indeterminate is the shadow into which all our ideas go or come. Our affections alike refuse to have their measure taken or field staked out; if restricted, they are destroyed, whether it be a divine or human person on which they are fixed. If we cannot have unbounded confidence in our com-

panions, parents, partners, children, customers, friends,
we cannot have any. This, shall I say in passing, is
the sad feature in our social life, that our offspring
as they grow up so often cease to confide in father
or mother, and that members of the same family so
strangely withhold the expression of the love for each
other they feel. What shame or distrust so hinders
the outlet of nature, and becomes the heart's bane, so
that .young people open their breasts more freely to
those they are but half acquainted with than to any
kindred or co-mate under the roof? This imperfect
sympathy is the chief evil and main suffering in our
domestic state. But we starve without love, and the
supply will be sought elsewhere that fails at home. A
great affection is the true sacramental bread and wine,
and how much ground it covers who could ever tell?
But, if it have no boundaries, it has tests. This is the
criterion, that it seeks its object, but not its own
pleasure in that object; it rubs not round it to come
back; it interferes not with any other affection or lawful relation more than a bird with an engine over which
it flies. It never robs one person to pay another. It
enriches every worthy regard, and throws its flood into
all the channels of feeling, as the Nile or Mississippi
spreads into wide or manifold mouths. He may question his devotion to one who is not good to all. If one
says she cannot visit her mother in her age and infirmity because she is married, and, like the person in the
parable, cannot come, all love is attainted by the word.
How really valuable to her husband can be a love so
pinched? Sentiment is never a cistern that can be
reckoned, but a stream or spring which it might puz-

zle any surveyor to gauge. The disciple asked the Master how often he should forgive, and the calculation was refused. Numberless times, Jesus answered, in his poetic form of " seventy times seven." It has been said, error is manifold and truth is one ; but I say, error or evil is finite and truth or good infinite. No devil is God's rival ; and it was in the East a false and infantile theology that equalled the Destroyer with the Creator. When Religion leaves its cradle and becomes of age, it learns that good affections alone hold of the infinite, and bad dispositions, storm and rage as they will, are feeble and doomed to defeat. You may define your denials and doubts ; but objections to any real affirmations proceed commonly from weak self-importance or a foolish pride and revenge. It is the mistake of our education to make the understanding, which is always a limited faculty, sharp at the expense of that whole nature whose artless charms, as it basks in the sun of being, are ill exchanged for over-conscious and ambitious intellectual gains. Men lose truth in adroitness, and women may be accomplished and unsexed. There is such a thing as going to school too much, and excluding from the store-room of the brain what is more precious than the Greek or geometry put in.

In religion, moreover, and no less, let us beware of sacrificing the infinite to the finite. All the piety is not in the Church, more than all the coal and oil in Pennsylvania, gold in California, cotton in Carolina, water in the reservoir, or money-value in the mint. We must not put doctors of divinity and ecclesiastical institutions for nature and history, man and God ; for *God's acre* is no burial-ground of past existence, and we can insulate but a few particles of his electricity in the glass jar of a creed. Every author has his own limitations; why should I escape mine? Fortunate chick that leaves its shell with no broken bit or unabsorbed drop on its back! Not unfortunate, if it can chip its way into the sunlit sphere. My friend with the incubator leaves such as have not strength for that to perish in their stony womb.

The intuition or apprehension of the infinite limits alike the logical and the scientific sphere. The pure logician fancies that truth will come out at the end of his process like a toy from a turning-lathe.

Truth is no such product, but a perception identical with what is perceived and a creation to those in whom the perception does not exist, be it wisdom or beauty which the seer may show; and natural science, which professes to deal only with what has a beginning and an end, owns only phenomena and the laws under which they can be arranged. Only the faculties of sense and understanding does it employ, while there are other powers of affection, imagination, conscience, and worship as deep at least as sense and understanding in the soul, and not amenable at their bar, which Infinity alone can draw or feed. If the scientist confine himself to what begins and ends, and the man put himself wholly into the scientist, he abdicates his manhood and takes his crown of divinity off. But the greatest scientists communing with a kindred and knowable One in All still wear the diadem that sparkles in the light of God's countenance. I know a mathematician who has weighed the sun and stars without being weighed by them, but whose mind remains for the solar system and the whole material universe an overweight, as it must be whenever the soul is in the other side of the scale.

Therefore, only as a pure abstraction can religion be defined. The Christian religion, as a life and world movement, may be held in our heart-strings and beheld in vision, appreciated and obeyed, but not intellectually quite understood. Christ was never rejected, only misunderstood and mortally slain. Can the sun, air, and water-spring, can goodness, gentleness, and truth, be rejected? Christ not only indoctrinated, but with his incision inoculated, mankind. Certainly, we exaggerate his individuality when we confound it with the infinity to which it relates. When, like the wise men, feeling nothing is too good for him, we bring the gold, frankincense, and myrrh of every rich thought, tender and glad or troubled feeling, to his feet, and say, *It is all yours*, we rob the Being whom alone he came to reveal, and whose alone it all is. But his religion is not a dogma: it is a growth; and to reduce it to a set of articles, or arrest it in any old Romish or other sect, is as if we should relegate the animal or vegetable realm of all beauty and fragrance and vital grace in the garden, field, earth, and air, to the huge saurians and the early gigantic ferns. He is an automaton in theological schemes and an idol when made an end, no better in principle than a savage fetich when he is a finality; but in this social line along which as live traditions we are handed down, he shot the gulf and made the connection between the human and divine. Little threads had been passed across the roaring chasm before, but he was the cable drawn after. As reason to us, he answers to reason in us, and so far as Rome withstands reason she does not represent or continue him. A French caricaturist represents the priests as burning the books and extinguishing the lamps in an open hall, while they cry out, "Quick, quick! let us kindle the fires and put out the lights," certain shadowy crosses rising in the background to hint the light-bearers' fate. What responsibility for such perversion lies with the Author of our religion? He is belied by such as identify with any intolerance his mind. Christianity is rooted in and grows out of the seed he planted, of which no persecution is a blossom, and which is yet no air-plant, but runs without a break or fault through or under all the monstrous and cruel superstition back to his birth. Is it better to humanize than to Christianize? This is a catchword question. For is not all, if not humane, yet in some sense human, that human creatures are and do? The Turks are men; yet an English traveller, observing their atrocities, said, "If a Bulgarian could vomit any thing it would be a Turk." Christianity is in no conclusion but what it tends to become. The man Jesus cannot be put back into Mary's babe, and Judæa is too small now for Christ's cradle, which he can no more return to than the old nebula could resume the sun. Let ambitious theorizers put their ideas into a show-case; we must have some bread of life to eat. Each sect is but a pigeon-hole, from pale Radicalism to scarlet Rome; but true religion, according to the old Greek phrase, is an everlasting flow. Jesus was but a germ; and what a borrower from heaven and earth is every germ that succeeds.

But Christianity is no denial of liberty, rather its security and pledge. How many a soul it has released to rush into action and receive good! In Faust's chamber one corner of the mystic triangle had to be loosened to let the evil spirit out; this same religion makes a road for the good one in. Freedom we want and ask. We breathe the atmosphere and tread the globe. Nests of birds and lairs of beasts are open to the day. Every thing pines in a cage. The sea-lion taken from his Pacific swimming-school and carried round in a showman's tank snorts out his wrath and disgust; and we find only a prison in the largest domain of fact and rule. When the scientist can reckon how far a musical vibration may reach, he may try to render this other thrill of countless chords in the human heart. God goes when we fill the space with physical laws. Make out your list of things *not* to pray for, — health, rain, the dead, or a better temper in yourself, — and when you have finished your catalogue you will cease to pray. A young girl was sick as unto death, and there was no virtue in medicine for her case; but all the rest of the house gathered around her in soft watch day and night, fed her from their life, with the cords in their bosoms held her to her moorings, and prayed back her flitting ghost; and I said to the mother, "But for such devotion your child would have died." She answered, "It is so!" I met my neighbor moping about his ailing horse, which he said he must lose. I said, "Do not let him know your opinion; it will kill him if you do: carry not your wretched face into the barn, but speak cheerfully to him; pat him, tell him he has a good chance, be trustful and he will get well," as he did; for the tame and wild creatures partake our feeling and share in the diffusion of knowledge. The cat understands whom to trust, the old rat shuns the trap, the bird or squirrel measures a different distance from different persons according to its confidence or fear. A like sentiment to what is above us is our support; and is there not for a man in the catalogue a place as much as for a butterfly or a bug? What are his characteristics and evident notes? Not only to argue or observe, but to hope and wonder and love and pray. The flash in the eagle's eye, the color on the flamingo's wing, is not left out in the list of their traits; why omit those of my properties, affections, and aspirations, which are the best arguments of my origin and end? Please, O naturalist, in your collection put me down! The text is venerable, the tradition noble, and the resurrection somehow took place! Yet I believe in my soul not because of the book; I believe in the book because of my soul. Books and institutions may be riddled with criticism, but there is a mark in me no arrow can reach. A simply ritual or biblical religion with an ever-growing number of persons can no longer meet the case; yet despise not the office it has done. How much service has been performed by that cast-away, wrenched, and rusty railway-coupling which no one deigns to pick up! Some spiritual bond we must have; but scorn not the ancient while you fashion the new! May the fresh chain draw as much treasure, and more, over rumbling bridges, along gloomy defiles and the edge of precipices of peril, into places of safety and peace! A reasonable radicalism is always in order, as a *strike* may sometimes be in place. But healthy division and subdivision are for reunion. Not logic, but love, made the world, and language was invented both to distinguish and unite. Lord Bacon says dry light is the best; but the natural beam is yellow in the sun, blue in the sky, gray or azure in the sea, hazy in the horizon or on the hills, a Joseph's coat in the rainbow, and a chameleon in the clouds; and truth is not pure white, but many-tinted, and like a changeable silk or gem. Those who veiled their political designs were once called *obscurantists;* and there are religious folk of that kind. But there is an honest *clear-obscure* in nature, in art, and in the human breast. There is a charm in the darkling as in the transparent stream.

Understanding alone cannot suffice. Pure intellect is the past, instinct is the present tense. Intelligence is a store, not the first perceiving power; and new apprehension must keep knowledge alive, else it becomes a bank whose circulation has ceased. Abstract reason must be fed by other faculties, otherwise, as an army without forage, it starves. Sap the ground of instinct with sceptical doubt, and you endanger the superstructure of faith, as the gay city of Paris is undermined with quarries ready at an earthquake to yawn. All our theories are held in check by the never quite comprehended facts, — the fish breathing water, the bird swimming in air, the toad's heart beating in the rock, the human frame resisting polar cold by laws we imperfectly trace but can nowise comprehend. All statistics are defied by the simplest act. A look, caress, kiss, for a different person is not the same thing; and in every thing life alone can instruct. It has been said we must learn science of the scientist, art of the artist, and theology of the theologian. But we shut the door of improvement and belittle every branch of knowledge when

we confine it to itself. As well give the cubic contents
of Burrampooter or the Nile as of the river of the humblest life. We cannot dissect ourselves. How ghostly
we are to each other, and what a phantom slipping from
us is the world! The freedom we must affirm on our
passage through time is for all. Pope Pius pretended
that Italian independence made him a prisoner at Rome.
It is a proper confinement if the common liberty puts
an individual in jail! What is sacred is not peculiar
to any one person or place. Your bottle of water for
a baptism from the Jordan has contracted a soil and
stain; the neighboring brook is more clean. The present soul alone is great; all its sin or sorrow is superficial as a flesh-wound. From the adobe-house it now
occupies it looks out to the firmament's fiery wheels.
It heals itself of all injury from whatever hostile or
friendly hand, as the wounded whale, plunging away,
cools in the broad Atlantic its bleeding flanks. Faith is
latent if not professed. As a creature's horn does not
bud to be blasted, so the horn of our hope shall be exalted with honor. "Some faces," says Goethe, "have
but a date; others a history." Let me add, there is a
prophetic countenance. Men are low, but on an ascending grade that goes out of sight. Once the now
human being may have been a howling beast. Afterwards, "Thus saith the Lord" issues from his lips. At
last he absolves his brother and himself. Pope or papa
is the Real Presence in any soul.

Let us not lose or oppose discrimination. Things are
discrete, and must neither be divided nor confused, but
properly distinguished as they branch from their hidden
and indescribable root. Adam gave names, and the

nominalist has with the realist still a place; nor has the time come for Christian and other denominational titles to be dropped. Without nomenclature, poorly as its office is done, we should not know where we are in belief, philosophy, or life. Give to the anti-Christian, it has been said, a Christian position in pulpit and church, as on the same subject he only takes a different point of view. In the fire on Fort Sumter the secessionists took a different point of view with their guns, but were not invited to trail them within the manned and defended walls. Religious faith has become superficial when we can unship it from our minds as a temporary affair or Æolian attachment, and kick it like a footstool away to carry on theological discussions by which its virtue and value are even for a moment disallowed. A great genius like Spinoza, solving Hebrew and Christian ideas in some vast generalization, should have welcome among all thoughtful men; but to an antagonist of our religion as such, why should the ribbon and cross of moral or intellectual honor, as in a holy war, be assigned? When liberality becomes liberalism, and liberty libertinism, and all questions are open, conviction has deceased, and the time has come, in the fundamental and fatal indifference, for *euthanasia* or the Japanese official suicide and happy despatch. That season in this world arrives timely, sooner or later, to nations and denominations that have had each a worthy mission, as it does for suns to set and for the morning star, that saluted early risers or guided belated wanderers, to fade in the blazing day.

II.

EDUCATION.

" HE has splendid talents; what a pity he had not been educated!" said Taylor, the Bethel preacher, of Channing, the famous divine. The strong and supple man of the street and the sea, who could row and reef and steer and order, and meet men, from the sailor to the president or king, on their own terms; head of the table in all companies; graduate of the university of the world; his fluent body a piece of music; his manners a flattery of mankind, as he touched with Oriental courtesy his head, his heart, and his lips at once, and even out of his wife's funeral carriage greeted every acquaintance with a shining face; the cosmopolite, yet idolater of Boston, knowing and known of all, that never had an unhappy day in his life; this child of Boreas and the north star, who, like the ship he loved, had taken his shape from every wind and wave in the world, yet had an unquenchable supernatural light in the cabin of his brain and ever-heaving love, as of a thousand horse-power, in his beating heart, — this man found something stiff and angular in his great scholastic contemporary, a certain planetary distance hard to overcome, an unsmiling solemnity, and a fearful foil to his own playful humor and perpetual wit. How partially educated, with all our *degrees*, most of us are! Not one in a million has ninety degrees every way, like the sphere. My friend mourns over her dog, a handsome collie, that by reason of a neglected education he remains so untrained. When he could be taught to mind, she says, at a word or wink, to fetch and carry, follow or stay at home, bark at pedlers, watch the wagon, open his eye and the flap of his ear at every sound in the night, and to distance every burglar and offensive beast with his growl, he can in fact only give his paw, whine and drop his tail when he is sorry, or leap up into her face with untimely and excessive show of his love. But how many children, not to say men and women, are as undeveloped as this puppy of a year old ! We have our town school, our academy, and college ; and the reading, writing, and ciphering, and languages withal, in the preparatory course for Harvard or Yale. The four-years' curriculum, porch and entry of a profession, supposes a perfect unfolding of some sort. But who is an educated person? A liberal education must go beyond any specialty of Latin, Greek, mathematics, physics, metaphysics, or of expertness in medicine, divinity, or law, which is scarce better than an apprenticeship to a trade ; and it must draw out all the faculties, so that the man, after his minority, shall take possession of his estate with a cultivation that tries its resources. An educated person adds grace to knowledge. He never interrupts, or cuts another's sentence in two, never storms, swears, laughs obstreperously or makes a noise. " He shall not strive or cry, neither shall any man hear his voice in the streets." Turner was a great painter ; but if he was coarse in his habits or gruff to strangers, so far, despite his canvas, he was a brute and a boor. If Goethe touched his hat to the civil power, and Beethoven, like a Quaker, nailed his to his head, the poet evinced more culture than the musician. We may be revolutionary, but we must not be rude. We speak of an educated face and voice. What unredeemed wastes and deserts in some countenances! What dissonance as of savage tom-toms and monotony as of Chinese gongs in much human speech! Form, posture, and gesture are so many witnesses or detectives to demonstrate a full and round instruction, or disproportion and deformity worse than of statue or building. Webster was a matchless advocate, but the Fugitive Slave Law discovered a hole in his head.

But what are the powers whose appearance in the frame we thus hint? Chief or only, as some construe, are the senses and understanding, purveyors of fact and arrangers of phenomena under laws. This is a simple and superficial process, which makes the universe a row of pins or so many hills in a potato-field. Animals can count; and the learned goat in Victor Hugo's "Notre Dame" spells out "Phœbus," the name of Esmeralda's hero, sorting the letters with his hoof. But has not Science a right to the van, with the crowd of her triumphs in these modern times, tracing the one organic thread on which worm and man are strung, hunting up in all things our relations, establishing the derivation of every earthly mine and quarry from the sun by observation of the metals in his beams? Admirable industry and success; pertaining, however, to structure and surface alone. But are not these investigations deep, while other pursuits and abilities are comparatively shallow and on the outside? I answer, as materialists we arc on the outside, for matter has no inside. That is its definition. The abyss, the core of the planet, is as external as the top of the ground. A thought or feeling may have depth, but an atom or a constellation has not. Not space or ether is fathomless, but the soul. God inhabits not, but includes the sky; and that is not a man who carries not the heaven he goes to in his heart. "In this place is one greater than the temple," said Jesus; marble temple at Jerusalem, or the one not made with hands, mattered not. "Out of the depths have I cried unto thee," sang David; but he meant no pit or gulf under the sun. His *miserere* rose from his troubled breast.

The scientist may fancy that the artist is trivially engaged in an ornamental business; but the ornamentation is as near as is the skeleton to the centre and secret of the creation. Shall I do or see aught deeper than this morning's sunrise? Color rides as far as doth the chariot of form in which it is borne. God is an artist; whether he be scientist, who shall say? Beauty plays on the features of persons and things, as does the soul in expression; but our cutting through its lines, so inconceivably thin, leads to nothing more profound. The sense of beauty and the native disposition to reproduce it, and to figure the leagues of a landscape on the inches of a panel or bit of woven cloth, indicate a faculty as legitimate, as interior and immortal, as any tendency to explore Nature and study her mechanical, chemical, or vital operations, though the scholar be a Columbus, Harvey, Newton, or Darwin.

Our best sign in education at present is industrial art. To learn and know how things should be done, and especially how to do them, is to know as near as we can how they are. Jesus tells his disciples, doing the will informs with the doctrine. " If ye know these things, happy are ye if ye do them." The world is *will and forth-setting*, says the German Schopenhauer. Who understands any enterprise like those engaged in it? The creation we are part of is no finished plan to be surveyed in its completeness, but a vast excursion and undertaking we cowork in with God, which would have failed and floundered had he ever paused one day in seven self-complacently to call it good. He is the miscreant who thwarts instead of running to further this design.

It is therefore an over-speculative genius that puts the idea first. " In the beginning was the word," or the thought. In the beginning, adds Goethe, was the *act*, which is wisdom and love, evolution and revelation, falling into line with which by our active powers is the way to discern the truth as well as to become acquainted with ourselves. The sculptured Phidian Greek Jupiter ter is an active rather than a reflective figure. God does not know himself *theoretically*, but in his offspring and his work. He comes to consciousness in what he inspires and brings to pass, and were else a mystery to himself! Our intelligence is not abstract and absolute : it waits on our performance, without which, as the universe is a grand performance unconcluded, we shall never see where we are in our neglect of what we have to do ; for it is a false proverb, that action is narrow and thought broad, and a true one, that our first duty done clears up the second. So the world, made in six or in six millions of days, is not ended or ready to be burned, but needs many a stroke and touch yet ; and the Japanese that takes a bit of metal and spends his life on one vase whose solid bronze beauty all Europe cannot match, is more on the discharge of an earthly mission and the direct road to heaven than the sectarist in religion with his scheme of salvation, or the disputer in the schools. Creator is the divine chosen name, or Evolver, as we shall soon say; and the test is what we have done in the way of betterments of the poor imperfect fashions to which alone nature and human nature have been equal as yet.

But that we may not misdo or undo, we must have the well-considered plan. To accomplish, not simply to consider it, is the everlasting object in view. No earthly business prospers without its *runners;* and the highest name for the immortals is angels, — messengers that, if they did not fly on their errands through earth and heaven and hell, ought to be stripped of their wings. For the sake of the intellect, if that be not only eternal but supreme, we should favor the handiwork. *Industrial* is the true adjective for education. *Developing schools* is no misnomer. We shall never understand our Author or ourselves save in our work, and that is the best of detectives; for be it a piece of joinery, a garden, poem, picture, in all by a law the man will put himself or his spirit. What nonsense that we do not know what sort of a man was Shakspeare! Does Michael Angelo need other biography than that autobiography of which his brush was the pen? Who wants or can have a better history of Washington Allston than he relates in his Rosalie, Lorenzo and Jessica, Jeremiah, and Belshazzar's Feast? The French Millet in his wooden shoes tells with his pencil his sympathy with toil; and Corot's painted sky and air and transfiguration of the landscape predict paradise. Said the veterinary doctor, "You must trot out your horse; how can I tell what the matter is with him while he stands in the yard?" Action discloses health or disease in body or mind.

But "where is no vision the people perish." Must not some idea of our nature and situation fit and furnish us for our stint of laborer, farmer, carpenter, cabinet-maker, machinist, artist, or artisan? The philosophic faculty is, indeed, one to be educated. It is imperial and reigns, while the sciences are but prefects that govern with local rule and must always justify their administration at the central bar. But philosophy should beware of formalism, as reality can be caught in no net of phraseology, nor the world put like stray cattle in pound. Every perception is precious; but truth is an endless game, and no one word will bear being repeated and pressed on. Beyond a certain point it becomes an idol, a substitute for the fact. No final statement is possible. "He has overworked the participle," was Rufus Choate's complaint in court of a witness who recurred with suspicious frequency to an expression he had evidently committed to memory and learned by heart, to use as a trump-card. Logical and learned terms have no magical import or illumination, and are so overworked by metaphysicians that plain people guess they are dealing with a black art, or with apothecaries' labels, unintelligible and hard either to read or pronounce. Every system is but a staging or step. The city of God is but in part surveyed or built; and not a few who are neither color-blind nor deaf-mutes are devoid of the philosophic, as many lack the mathematical capacity. .I learn that the class of a certain competent Harvard lecturer on Immanuel Kant fell down to one. All the explanations of that nature, which is a projection of supernature, are provisional and no ultimate accounts. I explore my own talents, members, and desires, but cannot quite get my hand underneath myself. I try to hoist the infinite. The roots of the tree of knowledge run too deep, and its fruit hangs too high, for me to dig to the tendrils or reach the topmost bough. I have to temper my Eve-like curiosity by sticking to some calling of teacher, preacher, architect, engineer, or other stint by which I can serve the little set I live in, giving up the ambition to circumnavigate that larger world than tempted the sails of Captain Cook. Poet, singer, painter, saint, you can be, but not comprehender of your origin or end. I can do my duty, but not measure my doom. It pleases me to have my destiny of immortality, including a personal consciousness in the universal soul, planted on principle as well as instinct, or on actual resurrection or revealed promise. Whatever may become of the fuel in me, I feel the undying flame. Yet my fate is a mystery I go to and cannot without experience extend or bound. What a debt we owe to philosophy for grappling with subjects in which, beyond our dress and dinner and dickering, we are concerned, while by no science of matter are the questions entertained which we thank God we can ask! To positivism life is a riddle and creation a conundrum which it gives up. It is despair of knowledge. But philosophy examines the manifesto of the vessel and voyage we are on. It at least hun-

gers and thirsts for information. It is not content with
bread and water; and by its expectation more than its
argument establishes for us an eternal claim. It is
proof itself of what it cannot prove. But quarrel
among the philosophic as among the scientific class is
aggravated and made inveterate by an intellectual
ingredient which keeps every passion alive, on its feet,
and armed for the fray. Meantime, how well and
wisely the immense secret is kept! God knows too.
much to undermine the humility of his children by letting them know all. Wonder and worship are effectually provided for. Every experiment fails to reduce
sentiment to understanding, like that first one in the
garden. The higher we climb, the deeper into the pit
of amazement, like some slipping and stunned adven-
turer, we are flung. Let not religious people dread any
devastation of their domain; nor need the Pope try
to fend the Church from wreck with any *buffer* of syllabus, encyclical, or Vatican decree. Nature herself is
greater security than a college of cardinals against any
swamping of the soul in its own acquisitions. Our
astonishment will recur and still have its revenge. Its
fountain is too deep to be drained. Under the probe of
our analysis gushes an artesian well; and all our syn-
thesis turns out to be but a gathering of sticks for
kindlings to this interior fire we call prayer, of which
our closet is the hearth.

If, however, it be presumption to affirm possible
knowledge of the whole, it is worse mistake to set
limits or specify aught we cannot know. When a philosopher talks of the *unknowable*, the adjectives and
epithets he applies to it are absurd and have no gram-

matical sense. He had better hold his tongue and his
pen. None can say how far knowledge will go, but it
cannot overslaugh the religious sentiment; for that is a
faculty to be educated, which the constructive one cannot outrank. In the mental stratification nothing is
more substantial or profound. Is not its impulse like
the molten jet rather of the precious metals, silver and
gold, through the coarser layers of the globe; and its
secrecy the hiding of diamond and pearl in the earth
and the sea? Yet sensuous curiosity, in our time so
active, is held to be the only channel of import, and
claimed as a monopoly for the mind; and this trade-
wind so blows that a deeper faculty encounters discredit
and contempt. With us it is all to be a scholar and
naught to be a devotee. But that devotion cannot be
crowded out which is no easy luxury of the vestry or
conventicle, like the puffing of a shoal of porpoises off
the cape or spouting of a whale in mid sea, but a holding of the breath for effort and effect, beyond force of
wind, stream, or vapor. Yet the idea of it has gone
out of fashion. We peer and do not pray! On what
a strong diet of decrees, election, native corruption,
danger of hell-fire, promise of heaven to the faithful as
a bait dropped by those apostolic fishers of men, our
elders were fed! Fifty years ago in New England the
divine Being could not be ignored more than an iron
pillar or the tent-pole over the patriarchs' heads. But
now an atheist is as good as anybody. Having filed
away all the old points, what strong meat of doctrine
instead have we left? Miscalled freedom or radicalism
in religion puts God into the category of a *perhaps*. In
our seats of education nothing is so odious to the boys

as *prayers*, which they miss or scramble to, half dressed; and, one night in the college that bore me, the college-bell was ungeared, lowered to the ground, and thrown into the Androscoggin River. One of the strange icono-clasts had his shoulder hurt, and his soul, I doubt not, still more. Our Harvard inscription of "Christo et Ecclesiæ," if still read yonder on the wall, how many a sluggard and profane truant is conspiring to chisel out! Why not, if materialism, with a dozen so-called sciences at its beck, be right? Mr. Tyndall's irony of a prayer-gauge means that there is nothing to measure in this unmeaning prayer. Let him bring a sky-gauge, a star-gauge, or a heaven-gauge, or with his sinker touch bottom in his own soul; then we will try his patent for hospitals, applying our petition to one ward and passing by another to see what difference it will make! New infidelity, indeed, which proposes to cable the deep of spirit as well as the Atlantic bed! "I weigh a hundred and forty pounds, but when I am mad, a ton," said one. There is tonnage of a ship and of a freight-car, but what is the burthen of a man? Has Moses, Napoleon, David, or Paul yet got into the scales? Not alone for its intrinsic enchantment and charm, but for its stimulus to the intellect and as the secret of genius, is it in order to insist on veneration as a power. If the mind be a debtor not simply to abstract study but also to art, so is it to worship; and the whole ecclesiastical establishment, bating nuisance of insincer-ity, might well be kept up simply to illuminate. "The Lord shall light my candle," said the Psalmist. "Thy word is a light unto my feet and a lamp unto my path." Lowly waiting at the gates and door-posts of the One

who will not fail with his love and lustre to appear, shall
serve our thought more than any ambitious will-worship
for success. But how men stand on tiptoe and strain to
get their eyes above heads in a crowd! How we run
neck and neck, and get overstrained! Neuralgia, paral-
ysis, and consumption await selfish aspirants who burn
the midnight oil when they should be asleep. They die
at forty or fifty, and we say they have worked too
hard! Indeed they have, hindering God's work in and
through them, and never opening that humility which
is his only door. Delicious awe before the Highest
is worth all the discoveries of cotton-gin, mill-turbine,
patent reaper, and field fertilizer, purely as an economic
force. The Romans reared massive aqueducts, filling
valleys and crowning hills, not understanding the law
by which a flood would run with all inequalities of level
through a little pipe. All we want for a nobler efflux
is that head of power in the breast which genuine owning of Deity will supply, and which makes men as fresh
and young at eighty as at twenty, with feeling virgin
and untouched. If, after the Latin motto, prudence is
a great revenue, so is reverence. How men sweat and
toil to beat in the arena or to distance in the race! But
when I tie to that Will which is a perpetual going forth,
I feel like a skiff towed at a steamer's stern; for we can
use up gravitation sooner than God. My neighbor got
tired pumping water into the tank at his house-top, and
he put a van on his barn, over the well, so that it now
furnishes kitchen and table and hose-sprinkler, with a
fountain in front of his lawn into the bargain, while
from his siesta he looks on. Doubtless we must work
as well as wait; but there is no work like subduing our
own selfish will.

> " At anchor laid, remote from home,
>   Toiling I cry, ' Sweet Spirit, come !
>   Celestial breeze, no longer stay,
>   But swell my sails and speed my way.' "

Cowper's prayer and its answer had the same source.

Of this vital agency let us apprehend all we can ; but the fatal destitution is to be without the conscious push which set the planets in their orbits and brought our progenitors to these shores. Bow to and nurse the motive power but for which the mightiest reflective brain is a hulk, a machine out of order, a train helpless and in the way, or an engine without stir ! The talents and acquirements of many men are like those cones or pyramids of cannon-balls rusting useless in the armory yard ; for ammunition there must be powder and shot. Persevere, and let us have your last speculation, O formulator of the world, while we return to you our no better critique ! The formula does not hold water yet, hard though it may be, as in a roof or boat, to find the leak. The proof of progress will be the reducibleness of your terminology to some clearness of common parlance and common sense, enlarging the circle of light beyond which still retreats the unknown and irreducible x ; for what a calamity were it to have the horizon really lifted and destroyed !

In this ascending series of faculties, after their values or complementary colors, what but an offshoot of the religious sentiment is the moral sense, it being to Kant that proof of Deity which philosophy could not provide. All else may be illusory, but not this whisper of right and ought ordering duty even at the cost of death. Was calculation of social advantage the root or occasion of conscience? We only know that of all worthy history conscience is the cause; and when we delight in the beauty and fragrance of the blossom, we care not to analyze it into the compost of rotting kelp malodorous on the soil. Our business is not with our genesis or the unreachable origin of aught in us; it is with our bidding and task. Grandly indecomposable are the Ten Commandments, however the rock crumble on which they are writ! What is authority but whatever voice can rebuke for sin? The preacher needs no pulpit, cassock, apostolic succession, or ordination vows, if he be, like Garrison, the imperative mood of a nation to which all the indicative, subjunctive, and potential moods yield, unwilling statesmen dragged, big politic brains capitulating, and the armies of the republic obeying at last what was but a solitary cry of *Repent*, in the wilderness, at first. The American conscience has had such tuition on questions of freedom and slavery, peace and war, temperance and strong drink, that the wonder is, so much dishonesty, selfish deceit, and benevolent lying are left, to accuse our laying stress on wit and cleverness rather than justice in our schools, with the natural consequence of a brood of politicians and churchmen who postpone truth to management and cunning, and with strange insensibility count it no dishonor, if they can carry their plans and save their traditions, to be insincere. It is " the abomination in the holy place" to-day, that the clergy cling to what has been handed down, however it contradict the new conclusions. We have not arrived, with advance of the whole line, beyond the notions of a six-days' creation, universal deluge, bodily resurrection, turning of water into wine, multiplication of loaves and fishes; why not add the gridirons, ovens, and earthen pots? Sad show between worship and thought of an ever-deepening, widening gulf; yet how matched and offset by the spectacle of the supercilious belligerents against the clerical cloth, who care but to deny or criticise, and fling with right good-will from their sling, unlike David's, the stone of denunciation, while they tender not the bread of life and truth. Give us the cobwebbed cathedral-windows through which some light struggles, give us food mixed with gravel, rather than empty fighting and barren conceit! Philip de Neri travelled far to see a famous saint, and directed him to pull off his muddy boots, which the reputed holy man in his cell refused. "It is not a case," said Philip; "there is no sanctity where there is no humility." To the theological reformers we must offer this test: Bring us your regiment of saints; this is the only argument we cannot resist! If you be sensual, self-seeking, sour and contentious, like the rest, you are not in the host of God. The child rebuked for playing with his tin soldiers on Sunday, answered, "Oh, mother, this is the army of the Lord;" and it was a better troop than radicals or conservatives contending for emolument, office, and honor in Church or State. "Your money is orthodox," said the beggar to my friend who waived the appeal for aid, and wanted to get off on the ground of being a heretic. Is there any schism or heresy or heterodoxy in being candid and pure?

But character halts without aid of imagination, which our classes in Shakspeare and Browning, music and drawing, recognize not only as amusement and by-play of the mind, but a co-ordinate power. Its work is unhappily styled fiction; for to idealize is to realize. Build, we are told, on the facts; apply the scientific method strictly and universally to all the conduct of life. But the facts are low! They are a history of the decline and fall of more than the Roman Empire. What are the facts but cinders and scoriæ from the great Providential furnace of the world?· "Facts are stubborn things." They are angry, wrathful, sensual, swindling, deceitful too. No; rather build on the principles, matters of imagination. That it is all imagination, makes nothing a proper subject of contempt; for what is imagination but the eye of the soul to see on planes and in directions never open to understanding and sense? Shall we apply the scientific method to the American flag or to the cross? Shall we be entitled to no freedom or religion that we cannot get out of the microscope, dissecting-knife, and crucible? The scientific method was applied to the black man, and he came forth an ape, with some modern improvements and some characteristics dropped. Haeckel would apply the scientific method to the German schools, in the form of materialistic evolution for the basis of instruction; but his elder and master, Virchow, objects. Haeckel says every atom of carbon has a soul, only without memory, — a great lack, for that is to be without love, faith, worship, or hope; and the burning of millions of such souls every morning in our grates were no cause for regret.

There is, then, not only the scientific, but the philosophic and poetic method. Does it put the air and the clouds for the ground? The Montgolfier ascension has added to practical service and promises useful knowl-

edge as much as digging and delving after Symmes's
hole. Nothing would be more tyrannical than logic or
science, if allowed exclusive sway; confining us to outward observation and inference, what a prison it would
build for the mind! Nor could all the inward psychologic
generalizing dispense with that fresh vision and living
inspiration which forbid any final inventory. We cannot take account of stock in the store where, like so
many clerks, we are employed. Liberation for new
enterprise the spirit asks and gives, and to material
processes it must not be confined. Said a witty woman
of her niece's sketches, "I suppose they are good; they
give me the same disagreeable feeling I always get from
nature." When external things are pressed upon us,
our refuge is language, letters, literature, as the child's
escape from drill and routine is into the fairy-tale.

But the main use of the imagination is to promote
morals. It alone enables us to take another's point of
view, to put ourself in his place, and look out of his
eyes; without doing which, how can we obey the golden
rule? Jesus, looking at himself without self-pity out of
his murderers' eyes, surveying his own crucifixion, not
from the cross but the ground, and begging God's forgiveness for their ignorance, was a poet without writing
verse. "He was," says my pianist, "the greatest musician that ever lived." Only a sympathetic imagination
begot such prayers or sublime assertions. "Before
Abraham was I am." "He loved me before the foundation of the world." "I and my Father are one."
"In this place is one greater than the temple." "I
am the resurrection and the life." Homer, Dante, and
Shakspeare shrink before such an investiture of the

soul. That was a drama; the sun itself a candle which the play was worth.

Before an educated imagination, cruelty to our fellow-creatures will disappear. There is good business in our fisheries on the Grand Banks, but fishing is a detestable sport. Is that a fine and well-dressed woman I see baiting her hook and drawing in her victim to bleed with regular spasms to death? All her silks and gems shall not persuade me of her graduation. Cruelty is her bracelet and ring. · Nor are men more cultivated in their savage hunt for game. The world is wax to spirit. Imagination is our retreat from hard fact, — that staple of science, under the axe of whose guillotine not only much that is false and superstitious, but somewhat noble and beautiful falls.

On our scale of faculty the next mark is love. But can love be educated? Yes, if it be more than a propensity. Men try in vain, with poor prospect which does not brighten, to build society on any opinion of God, man, or nature. No creed is broad enough. We must build on that yearning toward and longing for each other which we call love, and which many a brute may teach. The horse in willing obedience and the shepherd-dog in self-forgetting love, and both in uncontainable desire to please and do what the master they worship wants, are better Christians than half the people one meets going to church. Love slurs the difference, sinks dispute, seeks concord, will compound and compromise quarrel, and yield every point but honor and truth. But is not this like having none of the backbone of which we are so conscious and proud? I fear that obstinate folk, planting themselves on their propo-

4

sitions, sometimes miss the best uses of a backbone! A backbone is not a ramrod or crowbar, and a man with the choicest specimen of it is not a granite Bunker-hill monument standing high or a dummy-engine moving through the street. The spinal column is not perfect when any intervertebral is ossified. It was made not for erectness only, but to bow with. Leaning on and to one another as neighbors and friends, we are personally strong, and. a community exists! Amid censors and critics, foreign and domestic, searching for one armor-joint, and ready to light and draw blood from each bit of exposed flesh, ingenious to find the unprotected point, foes of that peace which is the mind's repose, like the insects that disturb our natural sleep, and well figured by William Blake in his painting of an enormous human flea, we have all had experience of some piece of mortal goodness, most likely in a woman's shape, — some dear sister, some living and blessed sacrifice in a mate or aunt, — by her presence dispersing thoughts of suicide, restoring us from despair, refreshing us for duty, and convincing us, beyond all arguments in the schools, of the being of God. There is a light in some human eyes that reveals him, and a tone of voice that is his speech. We touch him in the pressure of a hand! All may be ashes to-morrow save that by the sister so expressed. It is no congenital gift or grace of *Benevolence large*, as the phrenologists say. Much pining by herself for the sympathy which the *lady*, or bread-giver, affords, and sore heart-break for lack of good cheer, have gone for savory ingredients into the spiritual bill of fare, and spread that diviner board. She invites us to what at some well-remembered period of her life she never got, but knows the full value of, and means that nobody in her circle, if she can help it, shall want. We speak of the *God-man;* she is the *God-woman*, and that particular Virgin Mary is the one I would have the prayers of, and myself worship as part of Deity, even that essence which outward nature is not moral enough to disclose. But can this quality be taught in any academy? We do not desire a professor of the heart. But if the mercy be left out of the curriculum, if the old sacrifice be not repeated as a daily offering, and if what, when over-demonstrative, we laugh at as sentiment be not everywhere latent and implied as a magnetism that animates and unites, all the expert schooling is vanity and naught.

The affections may be unfolded; but is there any training of the *will*, or indeed is there any will to train? What shall the power be called that binds and wields all the rest, that enables the man to fix his object and repeat his blows, and persevere to the end in his aim, and fling himself — the most resistless and effectual catapult — against intrenched wrong? Is the soul, as a science spurious to some of us would hint, only an automaton, like Mr. Huxley's frog, that, with the slow turning of the wrist, crept as slowly from the palm to the back of Mr. Huxley's hand? A little more weight of determining, from a motive without determination in one scale or the other, does it make Richard by turn in the lists the black sluggard or to the Saracens the all-dreaded knight? Did *circumstances* make Cromwell, whose portrait tells us he had made up his mind? Did the stirring and piping times with the mother, as

she was about to become, cause Napoleon to be rather
the child of Revolution than her own? and did an accidental confluence of agitated particles produce thus the
mightiest modern force?   I must leave the debate between the Necessarians and the dictionary, — which
contains *will* and its equivalents in all tongues, — or
rather between them and the Maker of all, if language
be, like its organs, divinely produced, only suggesting
that it concerns the credit of our seminaries of learning to turn out *doers* as well as scholars with their
premature baldness, untimely spectacles, indecisive
characters, and incompetent limbs.   We have the kin-
dergarten, which owns the active and executive in us;
let us have *menschengarten*, too.

What we do well in this world we must do, as the
shipmaster bids his crew, *with a will*.   Deeper than this
ego-note of a separate self is the wonderful ME, deriving from which rids us of our individualism, — it being
not ourselves, but our *self*.   Our selves are doomed to
perdition.   They are fugitive slaves that find no rest
or home.   Our Self is the Eternal, whom we adore and
serve.   When you touch my body I say, as did the
Lord respecting the woman, "Who touched me?" because my will possesses and unifies every fibre and
nerve of the moral property I am trustee of and must
account for to my and your self.

In this schedule of education the fact of sex, bisecting
our constitution, must not be overlooked.   Man has
more brain than woman, but also more body and beard;
and woman has more fineness, if less strength.   She is
more angel, and he more animal.   Proportion and quality are the main things; and if many a woman has

desired to be a man, and no man to be a woman, it is that our sisters have more love and respect, and think too well of us, while we have not done justice to them. Yet from their inspiration and society we get more than from all the pictures and books. Is any power on the list left out of their frame; or is one missing from the chest of tools God gives us to sharpen and use? It is the stigma of our relation to them thus far, and flagrant proof of wrong in the past, that even a common moral standard has not been allowed. A man's honor and a woman's have not meant the same thing. Purity has not been considered a virtue equally binding on him; nor, by the code of custom in some quarters, is truth as strictly required of her, but cunning or concealment suffered as a weapon in default of force, as some beasts defend themselves with tooth, claw, and horn, and others, in their weakness, — such as the fox, hare, and mole, — with craft, flight, and burrowing. The author of that interesting story, "Far from the Madding Crowd," says, no woman but would lie for her lover, to protect him on occasion of need. I have inquired in successive companies of women, and been uniformly assured it is so. But shall the scale of right be shaken and changed by sex, and virtue not be virtue, the very same on both sides and in either part of that one image of God which it takes man and woman together to make? Whatever, with him or with her, the variations and derelictions may have been, and however winked at, yet in the coming man and the coming woman we swear these diversities and contradictions of a double scale shall not continue to exist; but rectitude, sanctity, and veracity be the same with both as in God!

If there be deference, let it be from him, the mightier mate. It was the supreme charm in Abraham Lincoln, and one thing fitting him to be the patient and provident President of the quarrelling United States, that he could endure injury in private without sign or sound of complaint. What a shepherd that calm, noble, all-enduring, unirritated, and high-uplifted head became to our huge, straying, bellowing, and recalcitrating flock! Can you, without resentment, let your hair be pulled, your flesh beaten or bruised? You are qualified for office.

Education in every branch not for the other sex? In what line have not their laurels, while men talk of spurs, been already won? Who are among the great modern singers but Lind and Sontag, and chief actors but Rachel and Bernhardt? George Sand and George Eliot are by some judges put on a level with Balzac and Scott. In the arts of painting and sculpture the promise in this country is with young womanhood, and the performance as well. In eloquence there are womanly patterns for preachers and lecturers to admire. In the theory and practice of medicine and surgery, unless you pick with care your male combatants, some women will bear off the palm. Woman's sphere is a hemisphere, half of man's; and no collegiate or other culture which she asks should be denied.

If education take in all qualities, both mystic and athlete, in its span, and a retiring of the agitator in favor of the educator be the millennial sign, who is the educator but the one in whom all the powers are trained? None can teach but the taught. The single point of religion raises doubt, as of a kingdom to pass away. Is religion then, as Shelley said, a curse? But the

faculty is intrinsic and universal. Without its exercise
and activity we have but the moiety of a man. It
were a pseudo-radicalism to consider it a specialty of
each individual instead of a common property, or that
it can be parcelled out among sects, more than the sun,
rain, and air; it being a spirit devoid of which any
specimen of human nature is more defective than one
born or become deaf or blind. In our civil war it was
held a fatal objection to disunion that the Mississippi
River could not be divided. Religion is the Mississippi
of the soul. It is water of life for a country and for the
world. Unbelief springs from the notion that it can be
monopolized by denominations or spent in forms. But
the more one has of it, the less possible is it for him to
be strictly Orthodox, rigidly Episcopalian, a bigoted
Catholic, tame Liberal, or Free Religious in the sense
of putting freedom from it for freedom in it. For your
articles, Unitarian or Trinitarian, I care not; but a
reverent Romanist rather than an irreverent Protestant
should have my child in his hands. The man — for
such a *woman* I never knew — who stands not lowly and
awe-struck in this wonderful world; who has got over
or never had any surprise in being here; who laughs
at human pretension to the divine breath, and makes
the elements not our servants but the ground of our
being, alike our womb and receiving tomb, and construes
existence as no share of infinity, but the toy and trifle
of a day; or, in mood more sombre, however sincere,
bows his neck to fate as an officer and annihilator to
execute the sentence of the law, abjuring the Father, by
Pagan and Christian adored, — can have no lot in that
liberal education which would be a misnomer without

the central love. Leaving out that, your physical sciences are but grave-clothes, and the metaphysical, as the Bethel minister said, " fire-flies in the swamp, — flash, flash, and all dark again."

But our feeling of the measureless and all-measuring cannot be quenched. We have motive and courage to our task if we develop what time cannot devour. Lo! how the germs wait to be quickened in the youthful breast, however weeds have the start and get ahead! I have been disheartened by the thrifty thistle and bull-brier in my field. But cutting with scythe the hollow stems of the first, ere the wind wafts the downy seed, lets in the rain to rot the roots; and clearing with a hedge-bill the wiry brambles of the last permits oak and sassafras to spring up in their place. I have the delight to see the vegetable enemies vanish, like bears and wolves, before a better progeny and growth. The *fittest* in or out of us, O Mr. Darwin, will survive, not by a material or mechanical law, but with help and by the will to redeem the soil of nature and the mind, — to drain, plough, harrow, plant, prune, check the caterpillars, and scare the crows. Agriculture is a cipher for spirit-culture; and freedom, though blood-bought, is worthless without fruit. Freedom is room for virtue, a way to truth, door of the temple, porch of the heaven of love; yet let freedom go to the winds if it be not *that!* We have freedom enough, and enough of nothing else. The clamor for it is a baby-cry. Would you have it for its own sake? Then it is your idol, not your God.

Therefore the educator must distinguish between evil and good. The tiller of the land is no optimist

to put brambles and deadly nightshade on a level with
corn and wheat. If the yellow wax-wood and white-
weed are among the quarter of a million of plants whose
"uses have not been discovered," the farmer, despite
such transcendental notion, thinks extermination the best
service, nevertheless, to which they can be put, and
discredits their potential virtue in hating their actual
vice; and the moral cultivator cannot regard drunken-
ness, adultery, lying, and cheating as materials of goodness, a way to heaven or means of grace. No, they
are at least and at best but lost ground! The thorns
and the apple-peru occupy room, and suck up the juices
of the soil as thoroughly as the lily and the rose; and
human dissipation turns to waste the territory that
might abound in beauty and fruit.

No doubt we learn from our sins; for there is naught
God cannot get somewhat out of for our improvement.
But it is a false notion that without the negative the
positive cannot be taught. Must love go to school to
hatred, and shall falsehood be the instructor of truth?
From what deception did the faithfulness, and from
what malignity did the beneficence, of the Deity come?
Experience of transgression is but the second or third
best, rather the worst way by which obedience can be
reached. "In all these hard times," said the preacher,
"the wages of iniquity have not fallen a jot;" and
those wages are misery and want, postponement and
delay, bitter reflection and cautery of hell-fire.

Let us arrest the days for their dues to us, and seize
the angel's blessing from every one. We are on the
sea of life which they make; let us not suffer them to
slip as waves under the boat which they ought to bear

on, nor gliding and treacherous to drift us upon the rocks. Let us trim our sail to calm or storm, and be ready for the gale while in halcyon weather we court and catch the breeze. Surveying the smooth and smiling main, a shipmaster, who had suffered losses on the deep, said with bitter jest to the sea, "You want, do you, another cargo of figs?" Let us have a freight and bark that cannot be cast away.

Much is said of the waste of means and life in empty sloth of the non-producers, in flame of rum that goes down, and smoke of tobacco that goes out; but all these are leaks and ruins of the uneducated or miseducated man, of the drone, or the slave bound to his cup or hoisted on the end of his pipe or cigar. He is not quite educated yet. His habits are not accomplishments. Vulgar boys can imitate them all. They hanker after his dregs and drippings, and go round picking up the stumps he throws away, as he corrupts the rising generation with his mature vice. A mechanist said, Niagara could turn all the machinery of the world; but what a cataract of intellectual power runs to nothing from those indulged and injurious appetites, which education would prevent or cure! As the Greek sage said, "I am temperate because I follow my desires." Let us live close to spirit, and to its offspring, nature! That is a teacher holy and wise, and by a process deeper than mechanism or chemistry it keeps the world clean, taking up every atom of waste or filth into fruit and beauty; from the mud bringing the pond-lily, making drain-pipes of the air and sea, setting man an example to utilize the ordure and offscouring of great cities, till marsh and desert blossom as the rose, and orchards and vineyards displace the brier and the bog. Let us imitate her growth and newness, her repentance and reform, perceiving that no substance of mind or matter is evil, and that only by misdirection and excess we sin. Our *naughtiness* is our nothingness, and our being is the amount of our virtue and joy.

To educators with such aims, all-hail! How infectious with youth is every sort of quality in the elder and guide! What mental photographs unfading remain of those Bowdoin officers at whose feet I sat, — Cleaveland with his zeal over human skeletons, and minerals, the earth's bones; Packard's glow at the Greek roots; Smythe's ardor for mathematical theorems at the blackboard; Upham's meekness, more impressive than his expertness in the Latin tongue, — Upham the mystic and lover of peace, who, when Fort Sumter was under fire, told the young men consulting him he had not deserted his principles, but, if they must fight, they would never have a better chance! These men's souls did for the successive classes in their charge more than all their understanding and acquirement. They were unconscious of their best.

But no amount of special or universal information, though one had encyclopædias by heart, will fit one for an educator without that knowledge of human nature which makes him, if not a divine, yet a diviner, with a divining-rod for the springs in the scholar's mind, a true fortune-teller, from traits and for destinies deeper than the flesh. Custom-house appraisers, engine inspectors, sealers of weights and measures, calculators of steam and of water-power, should be no better versed than he with the stuff he is to judge of. He should be a discoverer of inclination, a magnet of enthusiasm and curiosity, a detective of secret inclining or indisposition, a tempter of talent, and justifier and fulfiller of the type every soul is born with, to make the best and most of it, revealing to the student — what so often he is most ignorant of — himself. Louis Agassiz put his point strongly, that every pupil should have an instructor all alone. Several in a class may compete with and complement each other; yet how it concerns the commonwealth, more than its mines and quarries, that riches of individual genius be not hid! You influence and unfold others less by what you know and say than by what you are, less by the argument which makes people remark what a good lawyer you would have been than by the worthy act; and the act reacts on the temper to confirm and expand. The historian says that by the terrible French and English wars in the Low Countries the foreheads were flattened and the occiputs bulged. What a sober lesson we get from the fact of mutual likeness between those who live long together! This common growth of men and women unawares comes not of talk, more than do plants or vegetables in a bed. Through your silence your disposition radiates, and your affection descends like the rain. After all your reasoning and remonstrance, your patience, or the stillness you retreat to, works on your pupil or your child or any mate more than your nice discrimination or eloquence, so abundant and comparatively cheap. The stars do not expostulate with the comets which they draw! The college boys tell the truth to the professor and dear pastor who is their friend, but hate spies and informers, and meet trick with trick. How contagious is deceit, a game that will never lack partners on either side! In a certain institution, near fifty years ago, two students were out in the yard in the edge of the evening, trying to fix the places of the constellations with the help of a celestial globe. One of the Faculty made upon them a stealthy descent. Seeing him approach, and at once perceiving his suspicion of a bonfire, then a favorite amusement with the undergraduates, they maliciously so handled their lamp as to fetch him rapidly to the spot. Fancy his disappointment, mortification, and discomfiture, in the full volley of his expected discovery of their crime, when they presented only their innocent and quietly upturned survey of the heavens to his astonished gaze! With an involuntary exclamation of disgust at himself, if not admiration of them, and a doubt in their minds whether his satisfaction might not have been greater to have found them in fault, he withdrew. Let the teacher never set a snare! He may catch or be caught. To educate in lying he is sure.

Education is liberation from narrowness. Some exclusive notion of intelligence is the lure of every vocation. I have known one who thought painting alone supremely worthy of a man. Simon Stylites judged, it was to pray. How often preaching the gospel to prepare for another world is called the only proper business of this! With many, philanthropy swallows up other pursuits. But natural science has cut so wide a swath in our day, and mowed down so many superstitions, that, like kings planting their flags on new shores, and claiming continents for their own, it would cut off all rivals, and assert over the whole planet eminent domain, as if dissection of the globe and its contents were the royal avenue to truth. Is the structure of things the single subject of inquiry, and is appearance all there is of reality?

Education implies personality, and that our powers do not evolve by a law apart from our own and others' will. In the crude substance of our nature, some things of more worth are to be brought out, the animal left, the man or angel delivered; and this under some superior or supernatural lead. As we extricate mineral, metal, or gem from the earth's bowels, and prize it above gravel or dirt, as one tree, oak, or elm is chosen and cherished more than another, a poplar or birch, — so we have comparative valuation of human traits. Every religion is from some prophet, every government has a founder, forms of society have their fathers, and instructors are indispensable to schools.

Education must not leave the body out. Is he educated who, like a clown that sits for a picture or enters fine company, knows not what to do with his hands — "these pickers and stealers," as the poet calls them — but to pick and steal, whose mouth has cunning and his right hand none? The man that can swim, resuscitate a drowning person, hoist a sail, hoe corn, kill potatobugs, stop a runaway horse, confront a burglar, carry an invalid, make or mend, has a culture, not of muscle only but of brain and mind, of which the do-nothing's impotent spine and fingers are devoid. He may be learned, but he is not trained. What a nuisance he is in a civil crisis, incompetent defender of the injured, and cipher in a mob! He may speak the vernacular correctly, and understand many a dialect; but what save paper-currency, irredeemable greenbacks, are his words not backed up with deeds?

Some debate has arisen over a recent proposition that the only essential point in a lady's or gentleman's education is to speak well the mother-tongue. The qualification of such a statement is, that it is as indispensable to *do* as to speak. "Beauty is its own excuse for being;" but "handsome is that handsome does." In any author is somewhat more important than his art, namely, the will, in whatever word or deed, to serve God and his fellow-men in any task to which hand or tongue beyond or within his calling may be lent.

We Americans are too haughty, too sure of our pre-eminence among the nations, and too confident in our destiny, to own our deficiencies or repent of our sins. We look at the melancholy wrecks of fortune caused by ignorance and transgression, and only a few monitors faintly whisper their regrets! We consider as fate what was choice. The dishonest man was our neighbor, and we are tender, and hesitate to point the moral for the young to take note of; while Scandal with her busy tongue and Rumor with her thousand trumpets can noise abroad matters of taste and social relations of minor consequence, tithing the mint, anise, and cummin of propriety, and overlooking the weighty presumptions of the law. But let us understand, appeals to conscience fail, unless indorsed by development of the mind. A true biography would tell the story of men who have fallen to disgrace and poverty from high places of riches and power, because they refused to learn, and thought they were such wiseacres that they could not be taught by others in their own line of business, and refused to think there was in the community any such thing as common-sense to which they should open their eyes and ears, but wore blinders of pride and conceit, and could look only in one way. Nothing lives but can teach us something, — a dog by his quicker scent or sight; a horse by his hearing or by an instinct of danger, making him turn in the right direction, or stop, in a dark night, on the brink which we behold not.

A true history of our own country would calculate losses incurred from want of that generous culture which inspires good judgment even in worldly affairs. Avarice alone does not accumulate, nor acquisitiveness acquire, nor haste to be rich enrich. Look at the enormous squandering on premature schemes of roads and mills, for which there was no need or use proportioned to the outlay of means! We could have nursed the liberal arts which we have so neglected, and saved our superfluous energy, so injuriously spent, and had more property. Had we educated the affections, which moderate the propensities, we should have, for beauty and bounty and all charity, the vast sums lavished in the burning of tobacco and the making of alcohol to burn us. An uneducated people will not, by force of prohibitory laws, or of societies and agents armed with statutes against the circulation of indecent books and prints, be either temperate or pure. An uneducated nation will not, if it be strong, keep the peace, but vent its animal passions; like England, still hinting a name half brute and half man, as she rushes to butt and gore in Afghanistan and Zulu-land, with reasons of policy, and for excuse the rectifying of frontiers thousands of miles away.

An uneducated man will not be a better soldier or civilian, nor an uneducated woman a nobler wife or mother; and the animals will be too truly our next of blood, and the angels our far-away cousins and unrecognized relations, a sort of pictures and figures of speech, while we remain, as we are, an uneducated race.

5

III.

DEITY.

IF we have no logical proof to offer of God, it is because a derived were a secondary Divinity, and so
the proposition were prior to him from which he could
be inferred, as Saturn preceded Jupiter in the heathen
myth. But what we worship must be as much in the
premise as in the conclusion, *Alpha* as well as *Omega*.
His case would go by default, could we bring him into
court. He *is* not, if he be left at the mercy of our argument. If he exist not in self-demonstration to the soul
humbly owning itself as his offspring, he will never appear in the world. Constellation or protoplasm, upper
or under firmament, will be searched for him in vain.
Only to some hints of his presence do we venture to
point.

Whether we affirm or deny him, we cannot get rid of
his *idea*, which the atheist assumes while he contradicts.

"Himself from God he could not free,"

is true not alone of the cathedral-builder, but of the
hod-carrier, and even of the profane swearer that takes
the holy name in vain. "O God, though he believed
not in thy being, he obeyed thy law," prayed Theodore
Parker beside a professed atheist's bier. Must not a
lawgiver for the conscience have been needful, had the

atheist analyzed his thought? He cannot be seen in
nature with the naked eye; but "all physics lead to the
sea of metaphysics;" and of this question no denial
will ever dispose. But we have, in this age, such a
childish pleasure in breaking into and discovering the
springs of this great toy of the material world, that the
physicists have come to indulge themselves with holding
the metaphysicians in unmeasured scorn. Yet, as the
philosophic Dr. Walker said, if these latter are to be
tried, "let them have the privilege, common to all English blood, of a jury of their peers."

It is, however, the modest ground of ignorance on
which the modern atheist sometimes takes his stand.
We are, he says, on board a vessel whose ports of entry and of discharge and the fortune of whose voyage
are alike unknown, and with whose commander we are
unacquainted. All to our mind is uncertainty, and all
in fact is doom. But I have learned in crossing the
ocean that this illustrative commander is no gossip.
He may be stowed away in the cabin or walking on the
paddle-bridge, absent from sight while we saunter and
talk in sunshine and calm, and awake while we sleep in
the tempestuous night; not communicative of his plans,
allowing no conversation with the man at the wheel,
and having in the lower regions, where the furnace is
fed, servants as unseen and taciturn as himself.

Sensuous observation does not discover God. But
truth is not made out of microscopic particulars. It is
an order and connection implying an ordainer and con-
nector. What were a stone to Lyell, plant to Linnæus,
star to Kepler, or human soul to Plato, without the
thread on which kindred natures are strung? Action,

however private, is always in actual concert, and debate
is in committee; a "third party" appointing the first
and second is taken for granted to decide in any difference of judgment or plan.   Inspiration is a reality, however stated ill.   Did any flesh and blood ever exist more
truly than his *daimon* to Socrates, Jehovah to Moses,
or the Father to Jesus, or than does a Holy Spirit to him
by whom it is asked?   The mountain itself is a mirage,
and the sea but a vapor, and the wind a figure of speech
for this ghostly force.   We catch a whiff of its breeze.
What the prophets blazed with is a spark in us or latent
heat, from which comes many a despatch for our conscience, pallor on our face, and quiver to our nerves.
Let me note in several directions signs of the superhuman in the lawful and ordinary working of the human
mind.

First, what we in a true metaphor call the thirst for
information.   Why or whence this curiosity insatiate,
whose eagerness a dog's barking at the hole in the wall
poorly signifies, whose game in the secret of the universe is never reached, yet whose pursuit never stops?
How delightfully we are tantalized and put off!   We
want to know, and never know enough.   For every
question closed, like the old hydra-heads, two open, —
about health and disease, beasts, insanity, organic and
inorganic life.   I heard a mathematician say, "We must
get to the constellation Hercules some time for a better
observation of what is now hid from us in the star-strewn
space."   Where or whence the motive for such search
but in a supreme intelligence and its counterpart of a
boundless field?   We are little children looking around
wistfully in our father's factory, who timidly venture to

handle some of his tools. We are mocked and cruelly handled ourselves if driven out, or told we can never understand. Not only to investigate but to love the truth, and stand by it at all costs of the stake or the cross, is an impulse that signifies the Deity from which it comes.

In devotion to the right is evinced the same infinite force. Does not the cashier, refusing to unlock the safe, and choosing to die rather than betray his charge, draw on an immense energy beyond any reservoir of private will? The St. Lawrence River no more communicates through a chain of lakes with the clouds and sea and old deluge that drowned the world, than such a conscience is derivative from God. No utility or calculation can furnish for it any gauge. When you will find the end of the root of the tree of life, and can lay your axe to it or tear it out of the soil in which it grows, then you can tell by weight and measure this moral sense.

In love we also get beyond any Atlantic-cable soundings. He is ignorant who doubts pure affection, or affirms that our object is our own pleasure, twist it how we will. We admit disinterested friendship betwixt some men; but we sink ourselves to the last degradation as we deny it betwixt man and woman. We base our unbelief on a thousand false stories of spies with whom gossip is gospel, and we overlook ten thousand untainted ties. Nothing is more common than mutual faith and devoted love. A hundred painted pieces of flesh and blood pass in the panorama of life. Why on this one figure do my eyes fix, and why for it are my faculties pledged " till death us do part"? I know not.

God knows. It is so only because he is! Will one say it is nature, not God? But nature means what is *born*, and implies the principle that bears and begets. In it alone the one and universal are at peace. Matter is multitude and a mob of elements, that hustles its votary while he lives and will push him till he dies. It is a cage which the soul like a bird must escape from to soar and sing. If our spirit were but an oaten straw, it will make music when the Holy Spirit blows. However ingeniously we build our earthly schemes of comfort and knowledge, an earthquake is coming to us and to all we hold dear, to shake the ant-hills we swarm in. Only on the Rock of Ages can we rest. Materialism is no foundation, but a swamp. Some centuries since, the magnetic pole diverged from that of the earth's axis, but, unable to swing beyond a certain point, it afterwards began to return. The human mind may wander from, but must go back to coincide with, the divine. Christianity is our best social mark of this celestial inclination away from all declination of error and declension of sin. For radical and free religious speculation let there be room. But before it can displace established religion, it must have positive electricity. It must become a leaven in the lump of this world's dough, turn its criticism to enthusiasm, spread among the people, and plant a church. Long blowing among the ashes and raising clouds of dust will not come to so much in house-warming as one coal of fire that may kindle a great matter; and some altar of sacrifice alone can furnish the live coal.

But, say the atheists, there is no knowledge of God in all this fancy and faith. What is knowledge? If it be absolute and complete comprehension, then we know nothing of ourselves or of our neighbors, of a clod on the earth or of the oxygen that has been discovered in the sun. But if knowledge be *apprehension*, — the realizing of subject or object to our thought, be it of fellow-creature or our Creator, — then we know as certainly as we are. But how do we know? The scientific process is to observe facts and put them in rows which we call laws; and God is no arrangement or fact, but supreme factor prior to both. Knowledge is not sensuous alone. It cannot be so altogether, and may not be so at all. By every affection and power the prehensile soul in us seizes and clings to that which answers to itself, and whatever it grasps, so far it knows. The eye grasps one way, and the ear another. Touch, taste, and smell are spies and informers. But there is, beyond their scope, an imaginative, wondering, loving knowledge. Sensible knowledge stops with the surface, and matter is all surface. But detection of tendency or analogy penetrates the shell to the kernel of nature. We truly call this *divining*. It is genius and the germ of all knowledge that is deeper than we have in common with the beasts. It is the same process in natural philosophers like Newton and Kepler, and in pious sages such as Thomas à Kempis, Tauler, and Jacob Behmen. If the former know nature, the latter know God. Do they only dream? But this phantom or phenomenon of nature, which night blots and morning restores, may be illusory and transitory, while I cannot conceive of thought as a passing show. Sense and understanding could not know or care to know aught, were they insulated from the rest of the mind and could they explore, apart from

any feeling of trust, any joy in discovery, any aspiring
to perfection, or any poetic rounding into picture of the
living classes and kingdoms and the landscape in which
they are contained. Have we knowledge in a map or
chart, as by Mercator's projection, or in the varnished
paper and plaster of an artificial globe? But beside all
of the planet that any instrument can represent or
parchment record, is there not a knowledge of art, not
alone of form and color but what they mean to the
mind? Is it a misnomer to speak of a *connoisseur*, or
knower of pictures and statues, or of design in a soldiers' monument, a temple, or tomb? Is there not
knowledge in that capacity, deeper than the ear's
curious chambers, by which deaf Beethoven listens to
choirs in heaven for the musical message and oracle of
sound he must translate on earth? Is it stretching
language to speak of a knowledge of the heart? The
lover, in comparison with what his acquaintance reaches,
justly counts all the metaphysics and mathematics but
a court of the gentiles and porch unfit to live in. How
much in nature cannot be reduced to tape-line, cubic
contents, and avoirdupois weight, but transcends the
multiplication-table, and makes an emblem of the shining diagrams in the evening sky! How genius always
makes nature its ladder! Says Michael Angelo: "My
eyes greedy of beauty, and my soul of its salvation,
have only this one virtue of contemplating noble forms
in order to mount to heaven." Did he never get there
on those painted rounds which are more real than Elijah's
chariot of fire? A noble woman, borne up-stairs to
die, and playing with death as did Sir Thomas More
when he took away his long beard from the executioner's

axe, said, "The ascension has begun." Was not her
humor as good as a prayer? A friend said to me of his
wife, "Her last effort was a smile." In communion
with God we ask nothing. When people die well, you
may read the liturgy if you please, but there is nothing
to pray for! When I saw, at a certain funeral, no
coffin, earth having already gone to earth, every shutter
open, and the sunshine streaming in on a cheerful company, while one could not tell whether to condole or
congratulate on the vanishing of a saintly soul, I said,
These people believe in God! Is knowledge only of certain dimensions? The great Florentine sculptor says
to his friend Marcile Ficin: "I see, by my thought, in
thy face what I cannot relate in this life: the soul still
clothed in flesh but already ascended to God." No
artist's pride in his profession or pleasure in any
accomplishment prompted him to vainglorious words.
"Painting or sculpture, at my hand, cannot suffice to
appease that divine love which, in order to strain us to
its embrace, holds open its two arms on the cross."

We are told to wait for science to justify the idea of
a God; and material science can give us but a coroner's
inquest over the dead. Another method that master-
student used, whose marbles live while populations perish, and who hung the Sistine Chapel ceiling with shapes
of such awful grace. "Let down to me, O Lord, that
chain of faith which holds all celestial gifts." So spake
no nominal saint, or servant of the Church or of the
Pope, whom he dealt with on manly terms while he meted
out justice alike to Paganism and Christendom with his
canvas and stone. "Tried with good and bad fortune,
I ask pardon of God to myself. Succor with thy supreme

pity me, so near to death, so far from thee ! " Did he, properly speaking, *know* nothing about it? Such piety is the normal and only genuine knowledge of God. In it the *object* is conscious *subject* too. What and how much can you intellectually know of your friend or mate? Must you furnish statistics, make an inventory, and give a tabular statement of their traits? A rational judgment may tally with or wait on your feeling. But the essence of this knowledge is no computing of quantities or report of committees. It is direct and inalienable property of love, any precise defining of which were laying it out in coffin and shroud. Certain dry dialecticians of sentiment remind us of the skeletons suspended by a string and turned around in the anatomist's lecture-room. When they speak, we hearken to a rattling as in the valley of Jehoshaphat. We ask, "Can these dry bones live?" Certainly a man reduced to his logical understanding, with only its quarters for the accommodation of truth, and without affection or adoration, is the chief augur of death. He seems continually engaged on an autopsy of himself. He whom you can define as three persons or subsistencies, or anywise put into your arithmetic, is not the living God. We know ourselves and one another not by distinction of number but by action and co-operation ; and, beyond curiosity, co-efficiency with him is necessary to know God.

Woman is supposed to have less understanding than her masculine mate. How does she know men better than they do each other? How does a woman discern a man's feeling ere he is quite aware of it himself ; or how imagine a return, but that love, instead of being blind, is a searching sagacity and the quickest wit; and she has more of it, to even the scale against his argument and stronger arm? I think it is not for lack of vision, if our sisters be deceived; for with one lifting of their lowly eyes they look us through! More loving, they need more love; and they are more loyal too, and less able to imagine that love should ever cease. I have known men grow cold in friendship, but women never. Others may have found them fickle: the witness of my experience is to a fealty in them which no time, absence, or discouragement could cool or change. My thanks to God are for relations with them in which is nothing to regret. By members of my own sex I have sometimes been cheated, deserted, and deceived. The woman does not found her affection on facts. Is material information needed for a basis of the love of God? What did Jesus know of the round globe, the western hemisphere, geologic formations, starry systems, ether, telegraph, telephone, phonograph, atoms, or orbs? Yet who from all this has learned more than did he of Him? The sun is self-luminous, and love is self-intelligent. It gives no reason, being its own, and needs no justification, and is the best form of that knowledge of which it is the means and end. While lust blinds the parties to it, and makes victims of them both, love imparts that perception of its object with which, beyond any lynx or argus, it is born; and such a sentiment for the human implies the divine. Can I love not only kith and kin and my own lovers, — which is but decent equivalent and scarce more than *quits*, — but the man, too, by whom I am insulted, gazetted, and maligned? 'T is no accident or work of my will. To

no such miracle am I equal. It is a beam of the sun,
a well from the soil, a balm on the wind. Amazon or
Missouri must have a source; and from a spring never
fathomed must come this feeling that *unselfs* the soul,
that flies to suck no flower, and runs to grind no grist,
and contemplates no mortal issue, but rests in its object instead of coasting round it to come back. This
feeling cannot make of what it seeks its instrument or
tool. It inspires and uses us, and merges all separate
selves into that self of nature we branch from, and of
which space and time are but accidents and modes. It
is the knowledge of God, and it is God himself in the
human breast. From its personality we cannot part.
Not three but all persons are in it. Impersonality is a
husk, a negation, and a void. Who can live on denial,
breathe in a vacuum, or feed with the swine? To be
personal is to be positive, to draw and sustain.

Once more, we know God so far as we know the
truth, which is infinite, and of which all the exact sciences are but illustration and effect. When Geoffry
St. Hilaire, Oken, Cuvier, Agassiz, and Darwin detect
in the lowest creature the organism of the highest, or
when we speak of correlation of life and force, can the
Correlator be left out? Radical thinkers would substitute truth as the object instead of God. But truth is
only one of his names, and we know as much of him as
of it. There are things the angels desire to look into,
but will never find out all; and there were no truth
or God if they could! But if truth be a relation,
unsearchable in its beginning or end, then God is our
relation, and only by loving all our relations we come
to know him and them. What were the earth but a

receiving-tomb, if the millions of our race, if martyrs and confessors, in sore extremity have, groaned out their spirits ignorant of him by whom they were refreshed or in whose cause they gave their life; the generations but withering leaves, melting snow-flakes, or stiffening flies, with no appeal to heaven which the deaf and dumb firmament did not mock, while we their descendants in these lees of time and ends of the earth still wait, as for an experiment in chemistry, for our ingenious logicians to demonstrate the being we may trust; but, till the evidence is all in to establish the divinity or explode it, the bench of science with judicial decree must say *down, down* to all aspiration, look for comfort, faith of Socrates, or prayer of Christ! There *must* be some other than this dismal way. Expert lawyers admit no truth but such as can manage to get through the corkscrew of their cross-question. But it shines in at every window, and rides on every ray which cannot be too small to be the chariot of a god.

Yet again, so far as we know beauty we know God; and do we not know it in nature and those human features from which it beams more than in the landscape? But of beauty no science can be the picture-frame, talk learnedly as we will of its laws. The strokes are too broad, the form and color too vast and nice, the scale too extended on rounds of land and sea and sky, the touches in flesh too fine, and the reaching to our sensibility too soft and various, — from a sunrise to the dawn of expression on a human face, — for any verbal propositions to contain. One may make a patient and faithful sketch; but in laying on the color is a moment of ecstasy. Just how he does it the artist cannot tell. By

some live beauty of holiness he comes into half-uncon-
scious knowledge of being *helped*. We say an orator
or preacher is *assisted* when he surpasses himself. "Unless above himself he can erect himself, how poor a
thing" is the artist as well as the man!

We know God, but not all about him. Do we know
all about each other, or our situation on this rolling ball,
touching but at points the spheres of our neighbors, as
we sail in an offing away from the secret of our own
breasts? Do we know all about a blade of grass, that
far-off cousin of the sun and blood relation of the rain?
Huxley and Tyndall are no more aware than we of the
ultimate physiology of the automatic frog or undulation
of the light they so curiously dissect and trace. If in
no demonstration or intuition, yet in some intimation,
we know duty and immortality. So we know God.

Furthermore, I know my duty, and for anybody
to doubt my knowledge of it were the last insult.
But how? Not by science, but *conscience*. Yet I
know it as well and somewhat more dearly and deeply
than I do the composition of air or water or the
constitution — which science makes such proud pother about — of the sun. Is not obligation revealed
as clearly as an acid or alkali, or as the solar light
divides in the spectroscope the metallic lines? According to Immanuel Kant, it reveals an *obliger* too.
Faraday served God by turns in his oratory and laboratory, not confounding their offices, as he said.
There are diverse theories how and by what increments grows this crystal or diamond of conscience by
which all the paste of compromise or glass of convenient expediency is cut. But nothing conceivable is finer

than its final edge. God, duty, and immortality are all of them *intimations*, and we have their proof in their possession. Love and beauty answer every question of their own reality or eternity. But, before they can be preached as doctrines, they must be experienced as facts. We cannot believe these *points* till they are produced as *lines* in our conscious purpose and faithful deeds. But their evidence is in their recurrence, periodical as the planets, inextinguishable as the morning and the evening star. In denying such *knowledge* the candid and profound Mr. Spencer already knows too much. Why does he say so much about the unknowable, and qualify it with the definite article, and regard it as the background of all observation, substance of what is manifest and fountain of that law which Hooker calls the bosom of God? Why make it worthy of a capital letter, like *Him*, a plan from which all order is designed and pigment of which all nature is paint, if, after ascribing to it such qualities and powers he is to deny that aught of it can be known, and make the universe stop bolt upright in man with but a precipice over which into an abyss of nothingness he is to plunge? When, in an educational convention, a long generation ago, some gentleman from the South expressed his pleasure that to the subject of slavery no allusion had been made, Horace Mann replied that the honorable member of that body had already said too much! If the *unknowable* so contradict itself as to have all these mighty attributes which its affirmers so innocently assume, it is high time, and the only safety for them, to resign their professors' chairs, and lecture no longer on this particular subject, but be quite still and let it alone;

for never did the Scotch proverb, " Least said is soon-
est mended," better apply. If you say something is unknowable, we ask what; and, if you know *what*, then
't is unknowable no more. " What do I know? " asked
Montaigne. " What do *you* know? " inquired Socrates.
We know nothing completely. But if we know any
thing, it is the image we were made in, and have no
name for but God.

It is a case for testimony of such as, like Jesus, say
they have known God, and by their witness have moved
the world more than all discoursers on the elements,
from Lucretius down. Why should not saints and
seers and experts in piety, at the tribunal which is to
pass on the facts in this court of knowledge, be heard
as well as observers of equinoctial precessions and
planetary conjunctions, of a transit or an eclipse?
There are other transits than of Venus, different conjunctions more truly celestial, but no eclipse of God.
" True science," saith the poet, " is the reading of his
name." Is it not on record that the most convinced of
heavenly things have been the keenest discerners of
earthly ones? — such as Swedenborg, equally at home
among facts and spirits; Linnæus, father of botany, who,
like Moses, saw the *Sempiternal Omnipotent passing by*,
as his garments rustled their skirts; and William Blake,
most ideal of English painters, who conversed with
the apostle Paul, and although ill-treated and meanly
lodged on earth, knew, as he told his visitors, the Lord
had a splendid palace for him to enter by and by. Her-
der, the spiritual naturalist, was found dead at his desk,
the hand which had just been writing cold and stiff.
On examining the paper, his friends perused these lines :

"Transported into new regions, I cast around me an inspired look. I see the world reflecting the glory of the Sublime Being who has created it. The heaven seems a tabernacle of the Eternal. My feeble intelligence, bent to the dust, unable to sustain the spectacle of these august wonders, arrests and hushes itself, stops and is still." Did the intelligence stop with the pulse?

Faith is the pioneer and main constituent of knowledge. Said an artist: "I am going to treat that subject better than it was ever handled before: I know I shall not, but I believe I shall." Doubtless his panel held the record of his belief; for there is an *upper* as well as under-standing, an observatory to gaze from as well as a house-window or ship's deck. When I saw how riding through Boston on a car-top gave me, by opening every yard and attic, a new city, I had a lesson on the importance of elevation of view.

We are getting better ideas of God. As Agassiz found the stakes he drove into the glaciers changing their place, so the old dogmatic heaps steadily advance to melt as they are exposed to the sun. But justice will never be outgrown or left behind. In Bulgaria, a thousand years ago, King Bogaris inquired of Methodius, a Christian monk who was an artist, "Hast thou any picture to rival those of the terrible deeds of my men with which my galleries are filled?" The painter answered, "I will show you the event most dire a creature's eye shall ever behold," and he uncovered his canvas of the "Last Judgment." This missionary with his brush converted the pagan monarch and all his subjects, and the seed was planted of the church which now in a death-grip closes with the Mohammedan faith. Not long ago hun-

6

dreds of Greek Christians in the presence of Turkish officials were cut down for refusing to recant. "Infidel," so
each one was addressed, "wilt thou save thy soul by following God and the prophet?" "No!" answered the martyr, and at the word his head dropped under the sword.
To one youth, whose beauty pleased the executioners,
the question was put thrice; and the reply was, "By God's
help, *never!*" till he too fell under the fatal blow. Had
he no knowledge of that to which he appealed? We have
gauges and meters for light and heat and rain. Earth,
sea, or air has no unfathomable depth. But what quicksilver or spirit-tube, what deep-sea line or astronomic
reckoning, has told to what degrees piety may attain?
What opportunity of temptation or charming attraction
could find, in Joseph's or in St. Anthony's purity, a shallow point or possible end? I know a poet who says,
the wave-washed crags shall be flown away with on the
wings of time, but love shall outlast such transitory
things. Only by experience of love could the poet be
taught. "It is well," said James Walker, "to speculate
about prayer, but how much better to pray!" I imagine
that, as Daniel Webster told the farmers they would
learn more from conversation than from books, so one
real address to our Author is more instructive than
much metaphysical reading. Some students in college
said that the professor talked about electricity, but
never gave them a chance to feel the electric shock! I
appreciate the argument for Deity from necessary ideas
or actual works; but I do not reason when a sense of
his being touches me, and his beauty and benignity fill
with joyful assurance the channels whose emptiness
alone is my doubt and fear. When I saw the ocean's

inlet up to the brown hills and woodland brooks swell with the rising tide; when the wind of the spirit, like the south breeze on the fainting flowers, listed to revive me out of all my discouragement and grief, — I cared not for other demonstration, more than for proof that my helpmate was alive by my side. There may be a congenital incapacity for communing with God. In favor of the second commandment Charles Sumner would wipe out the first; but without the first, in the long run the second would fare hard. Abou Ben Adhem's curiosity to know if he were among the Lord's lovers was no sin; and the love of fellow-men would not last if from no height of worship its stream should fall. The saying travels concerning certain famous English writers, " Three positivists and no God." But how find him?

I find him, first, in his name. Is it answered *that* is only a word? But what are words? People do not forge and utter words as they please. They cannot be made or unmade by the votes of assemblies or edicts of kings. They are chronic. They come into existence by a law of nature. They are carved out of unstable air by a supernatural power. To call God's word or name "priestcraft" is itself cant. A set of priests could no more have created it than they could an ocean or a mountain-range. Duty is twin with adoration, and without its nurse of devotion pines and droops.

> " The stars shine not in their houses,
>   But o'er the pinnacles of thine,"

writes the poet to his mistress, making the celestial posts stations and sentry-boxes for what he loves. His figure, in the way of knowledge, is worth all the astron-

omy through the confounding stretch of constellations
which Mr. Proctor describes.

> "The hosts of God encamp around
> The dwellings of the just."

If not, what is their use? There might as well be no
hosts! 'T is the only standing army I respect. "The
glimpses of the moon" were none too big a candle to
show to a son his father's ghost. Leave the heart's
meaning out, and there were no loss in folding the heavens as a vesture or rolling them together as a scroll.
"If there be gods, 'tis pleasant to die; if none, it is
not pleasant to live:" for who then would care how
soon this farce of matter were played out and the tent
of the universe struck? Matthew Arnold says, "God
means the Brilliant in the sky." But what makes it to
shine and to wear the blue firmament for a robe? There
could have been no name if no Lord, — as no names for
plant, beast, earth, sea, but that these *things* were, and to
do aught in his name is to do it by his strength and for
his honor. "After all, God bless you," I said to a
good-natured atheist, as we parted; and he rejoined with
a smile, "I know what you mean!" If there be no
God, where did he get his title? Who performed the
baptismal service for him, and at what font did he
stand? Cæsar may be a myth, and Eve in the garden
a tale, but no appellations can overrate the Eternal.

Secondly, I find him in his work: what he does, shows
what he is. All the phrases which sceptics think so
lightly of, concerning him, are but the labels of his wonders. "But all the Bibles," says the denier, "are human compositions written in time: show me sacred books

that existed before the men did, I will admit they were from God!" But did the penmen indeed originate the *subject* of their books? Was not their stint set? We do not affirm a God out of us. What is out of us is not so easy to say. The whole creation is somehow in our thought. I have a feeling that fetches down Orion. I draw him to me by a thread of light. My imagination girdles the Pleiades. Sirius, that more magnificent sun, a thousand million miles away, minds my arithmetic, revolves in the space of my bosom, quivers, and pours out volcanic floods of light as my little telescope includes him within the walls of my throbbing clay. God is not less because to me he exists not externally but in the consciousness of my own bosom, and I cannot dismiss my guest. If no characters by him were ever entered on a paper leaf, stone tablet from Sinai, or Egyptian column, do we not find his engraving in living organisms and on the vast layers of the globe?

Providence is one of these obstinate, indestructible words in the daily discourse of mankind, — whether general or particular, the schools dispute. But a great, forthreaching, unbaffled, and unending plan, a purpose through the ages, one must be worse than color-blind not to see, with a steady accomplishment, — style it fitness, adjustment, design, as you will. But "a power that makes for righteousness" must know what it is about. Can a sightless archer every time hit the mark? Could that expert shooter who cracks a glass ball with a lead one in the air, rarely missing his aim, perform such a feat without an eye? But does not *Providence* miss? To our partial vision so it may sometimes seem. But when we look at the target and know the object, we find the centre touched. It is only because we assume an intent to make virtue always happy — as a cheap novel ends with a successful match — that we question if there be a Providence at all. If our being and position, however, on the whole be not a boon, we could not find God in any testimony of other folk. Nature must show him before I can accept him on that great hearsay of the Bible; and famous names of psalmist and seer, heading the list, cannot settle the matter, unless the answer of experience indorse the verbal God. In addition to the creeds, which are other people's deposits, I must have funds of my own. Would any poet's description suffice to me for nature's charms? Must I not find true his inventory or memorandum of the beauty that has been my bath as I gazed at the grass and flowers, climbed the hills, heard the gurgle of the brooks, felt under my boat the lift of the seas, and surveyed through my lens or window the procession of the stars? So, unless God be my personal acquaintance, antique letter and solemn sacrament are in vain. Does he inhabit a dedicated house, sanctify a seventh day, become incarnate in one human form, enter the communicant's digestion in a consecrated crumb of bread and drop of wine, appear in a picture or carved crucifix? Can we touch him in holy water, smell him in altar incense, hear him in a collect for the Supper or High Mass, and behold him in the elevation of the Host? Must I worship him in an only-begotten Son, a Virgin mother, or an immaculate Mary's mother, in the canonical saints, ministering priest, or infallible pope? No, not so only: my body, too, is a temple of the Holy Ghost; and the universe is no refuge for foundlings save a few elect.

God had no partiality for Jesus; through what an unsparing school that Captain of our Salvation was put! The Most High has no cabinet. Not a nook of nature but is his workshop, not an event without his procedure. Persian sun-worshipper, Buddhist self-anihilator, Egyptian pyramid-embalmer, Mohammedan saint, Red-man sacrificing to the great spirit, or Ethiopia outstretching her hand in prayer, is as dear to him as lowly Christian or devout Jew, as a martyr Stephen or Nathanael without guile. As all lands are woven together by the cables and wires that thread the air or undergird the sea, so every communication of Deity to which I accord significance must terminate in myself, and I must feel of every message the tingling touch. Perhaps I can be so at home in another's heart as to feel it there! To live in the heart, which we cannot live without, is love! Lovers, says Shakspeare, like Ferdinand and Miranda, *change eyes*, each looking with the other's sight; and I suppose sympathy can be so intense that the friend's state of mind passes more swiftly than a flash and becomes ours. Hence a fellowship removing all individual bounds; and on this rock is built the spiritual church. *Communion of saints* is the life-boat that cannot be swamped in the materialistic sea.

*Thus, thirdly, I say we find God not only in his name, and his work which gives him his name, but in his nature or image. Had he left no sign-manual of his authorship in our frame, all else were to us a dumb show. Why do beasts and insects not perceive the drift of the plot on this broad external stage? Because, even in their innocence, they cannot yet come to themselves, and in themselves find their Father.

But what features of his face are unveiled to us?
First, of sincerity, the open look. Why can we not be
free from this candid bond, but that the Divinity reveals
within us his essence of truth, as a claim beyond convenience or uses of the hour, so infinite that no liar can
be content till he has confessed? After what long and
stubborn perjury, from at last being convinced by some
co-conspirator that falsehood is kindest and best, a
quickened conscience forces the wretched deceiver, man
or woman, in mutual crime, to own at last even the forswearing, and throw off the disguise that hinders peace
with God! The very clothing of the soul is on fire to
burn and consume while it persists in untruth! Next,
the line of rectitude in this countenance we pray God
to lift upon us, and which he never quite withdraws.
Truth is right speech, and righteousness is true conduct. .
If your neighbor will not rest in any wrong you do him,
you will be the last to be satisfied with your own unfairness, because Deity is equity in your vital parts. There
is one more lineament in that face whose glance we cannot escape; it is goodness. But the goodness must be
more than doting on one person, however winsome and
dear. I know an earnest love; but God save me from
an exclusive one, and keep me from wishing or enduring
the monopoly of a human heart! We may be partial to
one person, like the sun flattering some mountain-top
or blazing back from some windowed tower as he rises
or sets; but be we also impartial as the sun, making
the whole earth his reflection and flinging his radiance
through the sky. The most devoted particular affection can be but one direction of the rays that embrace
all our fellows and find no limit in any border of the

world. The obligation of this triune truth, justice, and love hints the divinity without which it could not exist.

Is there deformity in nature? Nature's over-abounding beauty makes the apparent deformity its foil. Is there ugliness in human nature? "The beauty of holiness" offsets and chases it away as a sea-fog or flitting cloud. We may know what progress a man has made by the importance of Satan in his creed. If the devil have a large place, the man is low down in the valley where all the depravities cluster and flock. As the man rises, the demons flee. As he unfolds, they disappear. God does not recognize them, nor do they exist to him.

Once more we find God in the healthful exercise of our powers, not in one faculty of reverence, but in all our labor and study and human service, as much as in the order of the sanctuary, or a grace at table, or in musing, like David's, on our bed, or Isaac's meditation at eventide. We find him in innocent pleasures as in solemn forms, as parents are as much pleased with their children's gambols as with their deferential requests. The little orthodox boy, repeating his prayers so punctually in his country cot, said one morning, "Good-by, God! I am going to Boston to stay a fortnight;" he not having been taught how that sublime Presence would smile on him amid all the sights of the city as when the soul was commended to him in sleep. The small girl was pious in a more rational way, who, going home from her first dance, ere she put off her pretty dress, fell on her knees to thank God for the pleasure he had given her at the children's ball.

We expect to find God in a future state, which we await patiently.

> " In this close body pent,
> Absent from thee I roam."

But we may not expect to see him in heaven quite otherwise than on earth. As these outward heavens have a like constitution with the material earth, in whose dark bowels below are the same metals which the spectroscope detects in the rays of the sun, so true celestial or terrestrial life and happiness agree. We have been admonished by the preacher, in view of eternity, to despise and postpone the passing hour.

> " The present moment flies,
> And bears our life away."

But the *present* of a man is not like that of a beast. It is not limited to the tick of the clock, or imprisoned in walls of space. It is made up of memory and hope. It is the focus of yesterday and to-morrow, of a thousand experiences and anticipations. A cultivated man is like the chronometer, constructed to measure months and years as well as seconds of time ; or like the dial, the shadow of whose gnomon cuts by degrees the whole circle of light. Every instant act or immediate enterprise is characterized by what wide contemplation ! The eyes of Abraham or of Abraham Lincoln stop not with the object before them, but have a far-away look at country and posterity, at what is past and to come. The soldier for liberty and native land thinks less of the blow he gives or takes than of the issue of the fight. Satan is not the god even of this world more than of that to come. But for the true God, the world, in all its parts and ongoings, were a house without a builder, a train without a conductor, a procession without a head, a sepulchre and not a home, or an asylum for orphans instead of one mansion in a larger house. To a gloomy theology its fabric looks like a vast block which disaster or disease has emptied, and which is not haunted even, though it may have "To let" hanging over its doors.

What was that hereafter we call heaven invented for but for love to live in, — the shrine of its pilgrimage, the altar for renewal of its vows, the opportunity for fresh greeting, with room for everlasting accommodation? What promissory note so good as God's writing on our heart of this hope! "Ye are our epistle," says Paul to his Corinthian converts. Nay, we are God's epistle, and what he has inscribed on these fleshly tables he will answer, and never deny his responsibility for the instrument he has drawn. Science is a witness of his work; but love is a voucher for his purpose. Science deals with the successions and transformations of matter, and never goes beyond what has a beginning and end; but love declares *it* was before the world's foundation, and shall be after its end. It is the fire itself, and not that which is or can be consumed. It is God in us. It is the soul of honor and virtue. Policy of what is for our advantage may in smooth sailing keep us straight; but, storm-tried, what stately reputations, with all their streamers of fame and influence, go down! Yet, as no drouth can drink up the fountains, nor frost quench the flames, nor sirocco burn the atmosphere, nor cyclone reach to the stars or overset the hills, so there is, even in these tabernacles, a worth in which whoso finds God cannot lose his own soul.

In doctrine one may be materialist, but not in practice. Things do not fill any mind in proportion to their qualities of weight, color, or size. Does the big globe occupy any such room on your premises as the little figure of your companion or friend? One house may take up more space than the street or continent. A soldier who fought for liberty and native land said he would not shed a drop of his wife's blood, even for his country. What horror arose on the proposition to save the old slave Union by sending brother or mother into bondage! How we pack the annals, geologic or historic, of the earth, into a corner of our brain! How a passion for one man or woman will sweep the board, wipe the slate, break down all partitions betwixt heart and head, and penetrate our being to its roots! See the lovers, tingeing all nature with their thought, seeking the lonely path, the high tower, deep wood, or desert shore, that they may not be disturbed by alien subjects or other forms! By what profound topic or knotty question could they be so absorbed? Are they interested in science or art? Surely not on Newton's gravitation, or Darwin's selection, or any picture of Titian or Tintoretto, are they engaged! A theme for argument, a great affair, would divert them from each other and from their track; and any trifle is enough to give vent to the feeling it is so painful for them to suppress, as a little wire discharges the thunder-cloud.

Men have many interiors, and in storing their apartments make many mistakes. With some, pleasure only is admitted, till happiness is destroyed. With more, business is supreme tenant, driving all others out; and when the capacity or opportunity for that fails, how the

man of native strength, having no love of beauty, or
taste for society, or relish for books, or affectionate enjoyment even of his home, flounders like a stranded
whale, empty of comfort in his age, the eye now lack-
lustre that was once so keen at a bargain, and at last
gazing fixedly and sourly at the death which is the only
refuge from a miserable life! Can the mind be a warehouse, with no attic or garret even to entertain the
idea of a God? Shall the atheist answer, It is a superstition which science has outgrown? I will rejoin,
Large as his sensible understanding may be, his unbelief
is a vacuity in his own head! Like one in whom some
bodily member or organ is wanting, he has not the
usual equipment and outfit. With the propagandist of
scepticism I find no fault; only I find him empty, and
cannot feel anger, but only pity for his defect. By
congenital want or artificial mutilation one entire side
of his proper nature has been lopped off or left out. All
men and nations are not in error, while he, with his
handful of fellow-deniers of spirit and devotees of the
clod, is sound and right. Destitution is of divers sorts.
It is bad enough to be short of an eye, hand, or foot,
to be deaf to music, or color-blind. But all else is a
slight privation compared with the lack in the human
bosom of a sense of the divine.

Well guarded by conscience as one may be, his
morality is at risk if not backed with responsibility to
an unquestionable witness and infallible judge. What
trustworthiness is there in a moral sense that has no
root? If I cannot tap for my refreshment the resources
of an infinite strength, temptation may increase till all
worldly motives and restraints give way; and tempta-

tion, as the novelist-preacher Thackeray tells us, is om-
nipresent in wilderness and town. " It is an obsequious
servant, that has no objection to the country," and pursues us into the most inaccessible retreats.

Certainly an idea of God cannot be arbitrarily imposed. Our respect is summoned to all the results of
free thought, although the elimination of Deity should
be one. But when thought commits suicide, and
starves itself by disowning the breast it is nursed at
and cannot be weaned from, the death is no ground
of jubilee. The obsequies are sad. If no one thought
of me, how could I be? If I am accident, and the
gods save in fancy do not exist, then I do not wish
even to think, and am ready for my decease. Fetch
straightway my coffin and my shroud !

Whether Deity be personal or impersonal is a question whose solution in any way cancels not the inward
sense. His personality is not ours raised to the highest
power, but ours is his reduced to the lowest terms.

Surely he will reach us in some way. If the calm
fails to persuade us of his presence, the demonstration
will be completed by the storm, as when the steamer
and the iceberg meet. Some neighbors met a year
ago to talk of horses and cattle in a country-barn.
The tempest had been up all night and all day, like
a moving and bursting water-spout, which seemed at
last, having turned the roads into rivers and the plains
into ponds, to have spent all its store. But from a
little reserve or remnant of cloud which the horizon sent
up swiftly like a " Monitor " with its hidden battery, fell
a sudden bolt to wrench out the corner of the building,
and in a moment set its contents on fire, bringing all

in it with the shock to their knees, and scarce failing to
crush them to the ground. What is this business-firm
and partnership and executive department of the lightning and the fire? Light as a feather and buoyant as
a balloon seems the cloud out of which the electricity
" slips so smoothly that a sense of beauty mingles with
our fear." But where lurks the potentiality which no
heavy enginery can match, and what is the quality of
force whose quantity might not spill over the hollow
of our hand, but which, when hurled from the Divine
finger, rends mortise and masonry apart? If it be a
lever, where is the fulcrum? if a hammer, what is the
hold? if a chisel, how is it whet? and if it be mother
of all the mechanical powers, who ever saw the terrible womb that perpetually brings it forth? " In thunder and lightning and rain," the structure these men were
in, an awful bonfire, shrivelled and crumbled, its beams
and rafters for a while a blazing web in the air, and
then dissolved in smoke. The human and animal creatures were one tumultuous group on the greensward
that steamed with the heat, all of them feeling alike the
resistless sway. A heap of red cinders, soon turning
to damp gray ashes, remained, while the flying artillery
of the air, like a white wreath of vapor, rolled on with
concealed yet resounding wheels to strike elsewhere
again. But earth and sky are righted by what leaps at
once from both! It is the quiver on the shoulders of
the Most High; and they on whom the bow has been
once drawn covet not the launching of another shaft. In
the flash and stroke together is " the vision of sudden
death." *Jupiter tonans* the Deity was called by the
Greeks, and in Hebrew poetry " the Lord thundereth

marvellously with his voice." But when on the fury
and the noise rises the morning-star, serene as if
nothing had occurred, comes the chief impression of
strength. The elemental strife is but a "dreadful
pother;" but the quiet order is an unfathomable deep;
and in the soul is an energy, akin to its Author's, which
no clamor of land or sea or sky can overcrow. How
lightly and at once, like ants busily restoring their sand-
hills on the track, the human creatures rear out of
ashes their ruined abodes, and plan new and greater
barns where they may bestow all their fruits and their
goods!

But while the old unfathomable energy lasts, and
defies alike our comprehension and our gauge, the worship of the race can never be uprooted by any doubt.
No axe can be laid at the root of this tree; for the
treasures of the wind and rain and hail have not run
out. The banker in this institution can always resume!
His notes may be issued on long credit, but they are
paid punctually and are never overdue. The blinding
bolt is not itself blind which fetches us in prayer to
our perhaps unused and forgotten knees; and "prayer
without ceasing," signified or not by any bodily attitude,
is the true posture of the mind. Till God goes into
bankruptcy and the heavens fail, we shall depend on
and draw from what was never put to our credit in any
vault or iron safe. "Thanks and use," Shakspeare
adds to Christ's admonitions and to David's psalms.

Scientists speculate and practical men talk as if
there were in some cycle of time a slackening at nature's forge, the snows not so deep, or summer days
so warm, or tides so high as before. But the axle

turns, and lo, the dog-star again rages, the coast is once more submerged, the thick winter-fleece clothes the earth, and all precedents are surpassed, to spoil memory, confound calculation, and cover us with confusion, till, in another lull of nature, as if to take breath, the deficits and queries return. But adoration, like every sentiment, will not miss its food.

No philosophy of materialism or mocking temper can overcome faith. The scorner, as with a jet of water, may put out the jet of flame in his talk, or fling a vitriol which burns and gives no light. The divine influence, as well as human love, is shut off by contempt. How easily we can think of men whose genius has been hindered by the smartness of their wit! "A haughty spirit goes before a fall" in our intellect no less than in our lot. Rabelais, whose learning was matched by his acuteness alone, seeing in all things a ludicrous side, and making a coarse jest of that womanhood which is the chief revelation of Deity to every true man, when he expired, could only say, "Draw the curtain, the farce is played out;" and when he received extreme unction, he remarked that they had greased his boots for the great journey, and that he went to seek the grand *Perhaps*, while he made a pun on the robe put on him for the last agony, as he declared, "Blessed are they who die in Domino!" He sat in the seat of the scornful.

But how credulous is such an unbelieving man! What astonishing *credit* he gives to the theory that there is a fate to baffle all human desire, and that the world is but a big apple of Sodom for its inhabitants to eat! Only by incredulity, running to the extreme, can we question that this spectacle, so vast and fair, this splendid frame

7

for the human picture, means only vanity and death. It
is a confidence overweening, indeed, that, after a little
playing and short ciphering, the board is to be swept
and the slate wiped, and that this whole humanity is but
a series and succession of forms trying in vain to get their
chins above the flood. What an inanimate phantasmago-
ria were the creation; what a dark lantern the Creator
must carry, and with phosphoric display of false fire
write on the wall, or cast figures for a moment's amusement on this screen of time, with but unreality before
it or behind! "We are but empty shadows," will
the preacher say? If there be *in us* no substance,
then there is *no substance* at all. We can only behold
through our idea, as by his telescope the astronomer
beholds a star; and if his instrument be incorrect, it is
not a constellation but straw-spangle he beholds.

What God is, who shall say? When the *far-off*
beckons us, as we sit on the hillside or by the shore,
and the inmost in us impels us to go, is not the prospect and the impulse too Himself? When we regret
our deed or decision, and should lament the opposite
had that been made or done instead, what causes us to
waver, but this Infinite Being, which is content with no
definite and arrested result? I do not know who God
is; but I do not know any more who I am! He is no
greater mystery to me than I to myself. The objection
that I cannot sound or comprehend the existence I
affirm, applies to that of every creature that breathes.

An argument especially for faith is its contribution to
life. How we live on each other, and how distrust
plants the seeds of disease! Withdrawn confidence
weakens us centrally, like taking away fit soil from a

plant or loam from an apple-tree, food from a beast, or lime from our own bones : and then sickness, in whatever shape of diphtheria, meningitis, or consumption, seizes on the frame thus laid open to its attack. One's *constitutional* malady we may call it; but want of kindness will be a malady in any constitution! We smile at one's dying of disappointed love, and perhaps any single rejected affection is seldom fatal to life. But we shall very surely, if not quickly, die of not being loved at all; and this should be the *post mortem* record in how many a case! If the guest be not welcome in the company, he will leave the room at an early hour. If nobody wants me here, I am ready to depart! *Abandoned woman*, we say : by whom among men? The sin against her, if the expression be correct, is greater than she can have committed herself. Said the Bethel minister, of an incorrigible transgressor, " He is an expensive machine, but *I will never give him up.*" Let us not give each other up, by all our hope of not being given up by God !

Faith in him is indeed more indispensable than in each other; for it is the essence of life. How often the thought of him is the only resort! Who has not known some woman of superior gifts and graces, yet without companionship, or only a partner that was a cross on which she was crucified body and soul, with none but the Unseen for the mate of her mind? Yet in that communion she could have peace and joy. Are such sublime issues from an imaginary source? We go to it empty and come away full. Goethe is not accounted religious in the church, yet he portrays in the " Fair Saint " or " Beautiful Soul " one whose petitions never failed of reply.

In the divine justice is our escape from human wrong. There are chambers of the Inquisition which Catholic Spain never opened, and in which no German conclave ever met, to which we are summoned by those ever ready to touch what is painful and make the unpleasant remark. The thumb-screw and iron boot have gone out of fashion, but how the wedge of more refined torture is driven by domestic examination that does not spare! " When I see a certain person coming to console me for the death of my child, I want," said a bereft mother, " to run away." Let us thank Him to whom we can always run !

God is the problem whose last and clearest solution is in the corollary of duty, which, as Kant says, is the practical reason piecing out the ladder to climb to him where the speculative ends. In this transparency of conscience all the vexing riddles conclude. With a dogged satisfaction, in dire extremity, it helps us to stand at our post and do our office, as the old " Cumberland " still fired her guns when sinking to her gunwale. There was something in those sailors, as in all faithful unto death, not going down !

For the being of God it is the custom to use diverse arguments, one from necessary ideas, the other from design. Let us take from beauty a third. It is not strange that men should find it difficult to believe in a living goodness who are insensible to natural charms. Emile Gebhart says that Rabelais had a feeling of moral truth and beauty, but the grand poetry of visible things never awoke in that doubter's heart. Lake Leman and Mont Blanc could not touch with one tone of softer color Calvin's terrible style ; no wonder he made such a hard monster of God! If Bacon said aright, "better than think ill of God, not think of him at all," then how much of our theology is naught! We judge of men and women largely by the simplicity and good taste of their dress; and though some singular fashions have been adopted and set to hide personal deformities, no costume can quite conceal what is fine or unhandsome in the proportions of the human shape. But if nature be the *apparel* of God, what intrinsic benignity must be his! Struggle of an evil principle with a good? How the grisly phantom of this second supposed adversary flies before the torch of science, and one beneficent power appears on every hand! However we may explain suffering, nothing malign can be detected in the magnificent spectacle so ever-varying in this everlasting theatre, and whose stage-properties a kindly manager must arrange. What a solace this great show affords for our grief! Surely the beauty that still shines on death-beds and coffins and all that moulders in the tombs, which it springs up to cover and adorn, is full of comfort and hope; and when we look on the face of the dead, — so composed, every distortion of disease removed, and even the wrinkles of age smoothed away, while so commonly a smile seems stealing back to the lips on the third day, and the features of a little child are so sweet we can scarce bear to drop the lid on its bier, — sorrow as we must, we cannot despair. What a true hint, moreover, in the Hebrew phrase, " the beauty of holiness;" for how ugly it is to be impure! Many a bird or beast loves and cares to be clean; but there is an idea of sanctity held by man alone. The horse greedy for his oats, and the dog biting whoso

meddles with his bone, find for their sensuality no rebuke in the surrounding scene. Human creatures alone
are *sensual*, because they can imagine what cleanses or
pollutes. What a speechless reproof lights on our drunk-
enness from the steadfast orbs ; and how the spotless
heavens look down grieving at every sinful excess!
To instruction in French and music let us for our children add some lesson of beauty every day, to prevent
and moderate the passions, which there is so much in
our social habits to stir. No fear of base incentives
can there be for those by whom this nobler stimulus is
felt.

If we do not clamor to insert the name of God in any
written instrument after that most venerable Declaration
of Independence, in which the nation, yet unborn, made
its appeal, it is because in our real constitution no word
is engraved so deeply ; and should any legislature presume to *enact atheism*, what a tornado of wrath, which no
other issue could stir, would arise to hurl the legislators
from their seats ! God is in man. The German Heine
may be a good witness that, if we do not confound
Christ with, we must not part him from God, and that
our judgment of the Divinity must have sentiment
rather than criticism for a test. "Christ," he says,
"is the born Dauphin of Heaven, and has democratic
sympathies, and delights not in costly ceremonies, and
is a modern God of the people, a citizen-God." He
adds : "From the moment that a religion seeks the aid
of philosophy, its ruin is inevitable. It must not attempt to justify itself. The instant it ventures to print
a catechism supported by arguments, it is near its
end." We are not first in this case. The God whom

we are after was up before us, and must wake us with that light of his countenance which the morning is, or we could never be stirred. Atheism serves us by provoking to a better theism. We can no longer worship the God of the old articles, — a being jealous of his own glory and dooming his children to eternal woe. Our God is one who has no time or disposition to remember himself. He remembers us, and finds himself in his children's breasts. He is blessed in their happiness, conscious in their persons, and parentally careful for their good. He rushes into action and measures not his course, nor broods over injuries nor avenges his wrongs. Only the harm we would do ourselves he cancels and corrects.

It is a curious circumstance in the scripture chronology of the idea of God, that while Job knows not where to find him and David cannot flee from him anywhere, Jesus blends with him in one being. What a progress of millennial steps, and what a stride from that Hebrew monotheism to which Mohammedanism reverts! In every one he is. With all the gasping or bleeding to death, yet the greenwood thicket, unfrequented desert, or solitary shore, where in single combat men seek to stab or blast out each other's life, and the field or open sea, where armed hosts or battleships meet in deadly shock, — are full of a grandeur and grace which no anguish can obliterate or ploughing of cannon-balls either merge or uproot. To the atheistic argument drawn from suffering who but the sufferer replies? After an exhausting illness, away from home, I was put, on my journey through a great city, alone in an upper chamber under the eaves, there being no other room in the inn. I crept to a dormer-window, open because the air was mild, and gazed out into the starlit firmament and on the illuminated street. As I felt the soft breeze cool my fevered nerves, and hearkened to the stroke toward midnight of every city-clock, and as I held to life with a grasp so weak and an attachment so loose, I was stirred with a sensibility to the glory without me never felt before. It was but a repetition of the ecstasy that had lifted me once before, as I lay for a week in bed, with the north-wind blowing at the glass panes and the billows foaming and resounding over the rocks hard by. Was there for any figure of health and strength that ran and leaped along the crags, or rocked and sped on the billows, transport comparable to my pervading peace? Who that has ever got up from a couch of chronic sickness or of violent disease but will remember the rapture of his first ride in the open air, perhaps among melting snows and springing grass and budding trees? There is no measure for this faith. Agassiz and other Alpine explorers found they could not hold even a glacier in their stakes. By a motion of the frozen particles, for which no meter has been invented, so the long and monstrous mass of ice flowed imperceptibly with all its serpentine windings, and over its ever-shifting and uneven bed, down the hills, keeping every slope and valley full, and carrying the stakes the philosophers had driven so fast in its course. Thus all your stiff articles to fix a tide of life which is fathomless and far diverse from any glacier, will inevitably be borne along, and found, if at all, in different places from those where, as finalities of doctrine, they were put; and no sledge-hammer strokes will suffice for their arrest.

Atheism would seem, in denying any demonstration of God, to strike all the oracles dumb, and silence in conventicle or cathedral every chant and prayer. But it were easier to fasten on the volcano a safety-valve, to hold back the geysers of Iceland, to check the sea's steaming into clouds, or the warmer currents of air from rising into ether farther than any thermometer can follow, than to stop these risings, which we call anthems and supplications, from the human heart. When you have prevented the weather itself with any particular gauge of its phenomena, then you may hope with your prayer-gauge to abolish this meteorology within.

Religion in our schools is called a sectarian thing. Is the wind sectarian because it is used for a particular man's van, or vane, or sail of his outgoing ship? Is the water sectarian because it irrigates his garden, or on the Merrimack or at Niagara is turned on the wheels of his mill? Is the earth sectarian because little bits of its surface are by special ownership turned into fenced fields? Is the light sectarian because it is possessed and employed for your private purposes as it streams in at your window-panes? If not, then is not religion sectarian because, in the precincts of one or another denomination, it is embodied, appropriated in certain articles, and set forth in peculiar forms; and God does not belong to any party because his nature is construed in some especial way. He is the truth of things. The thread they are strung on, as a necklace, is alive. He is beauty, which is expression in nature as in a human face. He is the goodness which all good implies, as it puts the receivers under that necessity of thanks which is the best proof of a Deity; for it is so needful

to be grateful for what we enjoy that we should make a
fetich could our soul have no other vent. Not only an
argument has to be answered, but an *instinct* must
become *extinct* before atheism can prevail. Does the
denier expect to quench the pious flame? An innate
reverence in the human breast withstands and forbids.
Religion is the unfailing bequest. We have protective
societies for children, to guard them against the cruelty
sometimes even of parental hands. Let us in churches
and schools of every sort defend them against atheism
and unbelief. "A strong tower is our God," sang Luther. It is a fort we well can hold. The atheist is a
man against God or the idea of God in the human mind.
Whence, I ask him, did this adversary of his come? Is
the unseen opponent that he assails a fiction or invention
of the priests? The cup of real life is not only full to
overflowing, but well-nigh broken by the glory poured
into it, sometimes almost too great to bear.

Let us admit progress of the idea of God. If Job could
not find him, and David could not flee from him, Jesus
was one with him. He so chanted him that my fine
pianist affirms that he was the greatest musician that
ever lived, adding, "I might be laughed at in Boston
for such a sentiment, but should be understood in Leip-
sic or Berlin." "Without God," he continued, "all
our thoughts are as colors in the night." "But," says
the last radical paper I read, "God is but a figure of
speech!" Is he not the speech itself? While we search
after God, he searches after us. He becomes aware of
himself, as the German philosopher said, in the human
mind. While we, like Job, are hunting for him, he
finds himself not on a throne, in a palace, with crown

on his head or sceptre in his hand, but in our contrite and obedient heart. For humility alone makes room, ánd lifts up its gate, that he may come in. He accepts no lodging, and can get no accommodation in our pride. In mountainous regions the valleys take in more of the sun than do the hills ; and our lowliness is his reception.

IV.

SCIENCE.

NO knowledge of human nature can be exact or complete. Man is a whole, and cannot be dissected till he is dead, has left to the anatomist and undertaker what he has no further use for, and can be more entire without. If then we accept the definition science gives of itself, as dealing only with appearances that begin and end, there is in it no more religion than in a squirrel's stowing away of acorns, a bee's economy of wax, or the building of a beaver's dam; and if Mr. Buckle's doctrine be correct, that to know more is the only progress, then knowledge is of no use and scarce worth the time and pains. For even philosophy were a poor pursuit if it did not lead to love and service of God and man. A student who had made metaphysics his college elective said he liked it, "but it led to no place." It is but the crooked log through which the pig tried in vain to get into his pen, if it stop in speculation. It is full of promise only as a way-station, and it is good if it enlarge our heart. Open questions are the mind's unclosed windows, excellent for ventilation, and a final theory is not to be desired. The notion of evolution is for the animal organism a beautiful fit, as of a shoe to the foot or glove to the hand: but what is evolved must have been involved; and, like the boy's lead whirligig, the wheel is found to turn back in many a vegetable and animal race, and the interior principle of the process is all the while undisclosed. The world finds a type in the jelly-fish which expands and contracts with its tentacles its transparent sphere; nor can any one tell which was first, the nebula or the star. Darwin cannot demonstrate that man is an ascended beast, any more than could Swedenborg that beast is a descended man. Only this category holds, that the universe could not have come from a vesicle, there never having been a time when a universe must not have been. Everlasting together are the plan and planner and thing planned, and Agassiz's ocean of germs is as satisfactory as a single bulb to start nature with; but what was the primary and is the perpetual push we have yet to inquire. The raw material escapes in its minuteness, and the Architect in his infinity. Tile and tiler are hid; and the scientist is a charlatan, a shoemaker who has dropped his last, or a watchman off his beat, if he pretend in any scheme that all which *is* can be understood. The great philosophers are distinguished from the small ones in affirming that no philosophy can cover the ground. Newton, Kepler, and Swedenborg exceed Laplace and Humboldt in genius and fame. Faraday and Davy abroad and Henry and Pierce among us bear witness to the Rock of Ages underlying all beside. Till the mountainous reputations are blasted and blown away, science must serve and not rule; and the specialist will not help or prosper, unless the *universal* set his stint.

There is a saintly as well as a scientific knowledge; and if scientists say it is feeling and not knowledge, they can be pushed on this point as much as they push the saints. What is it to know facts, and what fact do they know? Their apprehension of any process or element, as of light, gravity, motion, electricity, or magnetism, is so shallow and slight as no more to merit the name of knowledge than the devotee's communion with that immense soul of which he is a part. A Deity external and separate from the worshipper cannot be found in any depth of earth or sky; but he is revealed in our conscience and heart. Beyond all the demonstrations from necessary ideas or actual works, is the proof by prayer. When we listen to a real petition, or read its genuine words, or are moved to put it up, a conviction rises of the object it is inspired by and goes to, which deserves the name of acquaintance no less truly than any rational deduction or observation of the outward world. Let us drive the logician or experimenter to his intrenchments, charging him with sciolism if he presume to indict us for superstition! Strange ecstasy of the mystic, from which we cannot withhold our respect! The artist's aureola did not create, but came from the halo around his head. In his transport he cannot keep his feet on the ground. Live coals seem to have touched his lips to eloquence beyond oratory of the senate or the court. Naught so resistless as the contagion of his sympathy for the human heart. The dead that lie on the bier have a resurrection to every hearer in the uplifting of his speech.

The saint, says Mohammedan piety, does not admit that he is afflicted. Suffering itself seems to waken a consciousness that it is wrong to reproach God. Job's wife, not Job, wants to curse. Those not smitten by a calamity take the great name in vain; but "though he slay me, I will trust in him." If he be almighty, he cannot be all-good, says Mr. Mill. But may we not have a false notion of power? It does not consist in harmonizing the contradictory or doing the impossible. Is it in the power of God to make mountains without valleys, or seas without waves? It is alike beyond the compass of his ability to make character without discipline, or by arbitrament abate for our final welfare a jot of what we endure. No doubt he does for us the best he can! This counterweight for the sceptic's argument is in the confession of such as by the Lord are sorely grieved. "Oh no, you shall not say any thing against him," cries the victim; and surely no voice has more right in this matter than his own. What miracle, more than to multiply bread in the desert, or at a wedding turn water into wine, is wrought in the agonizing breast? Not till we become its subject can we know; but its experience in others we cannot gainsay. There is an evolution not on the earth or in the succession of its animated tribes. We are ourselves astonished at the sentiments toward our Author that in the hardest passes and over the most bitter cups rise to the surface and come to the front. Are they knowledge, or fancy and a makeshift for refuge when we are in a corner and hard pressed? No one in whom they exist allows their illusiveness! The wisest are most earnest to insist that from these sensibilities of a resigned and adoring soul their best information comes.

Meantime to how many queries science cannot reply! Is the earth a ball or a shell? Is there a Northwest passage and a circumpolar sea? Will the magnetic and planetary axes or the ecliptic and equator ever coincide? Is electricity the same as motion, and lightning as light; or have all the species unfolded from one germ? Is the atomic or the nebular theory true, or has the beast a human origin or a future life? But such questions stir a moderate curiosity, in comparison with these other inquiries, whether I am begotten and born of a greater than mortal thought and love, which will do right by me, and answer all my queries before I decease, — in which case I am sure I can never die, — and justify the aspirations that have their vent and bubbling fount in a bosom whose jet does not slacken, but gets more warm and lively as I grow more old.

Science adds to the uses of life, but its prompter and precursor is faith; for without prior belief that the world is a form and series of permanent relations, we should lack all motive to investigation, and no less all reason for action; for who, without crediting that what he discovered must abide, would think it worth his while to explore the heavens and the earth? The writer to the Hebrews gives us a long list — Abraham and Noah and Moses and Abel and other sublime names — of such as proceeded, without knowledge, by faith. How easily we could make out a modern score! By faith Columbus sailed for a Western world. By faith Newton beheld in the apple a little globe, and in the sun, moon, and stars but falling apples. By faith Franklin and Kane put forth after open channels at the frozen pole. By faith Benjamin Franklin lifted his kite to the cloud, to verify a suspicion that lightning and electricity are the same. By faith Morse foresees a pen that reaches over land and under sea. By faith

Goodyear predicts a substance, whose utilities he has to guess at before he can make good. By faith Morton risks murder in an operation, to learn if continued life be consistent with insensibility to pain; and ether becomes the physical savior of mankind. By faith Leverrier is put on the track of a new planet from observed perturbations of the old. From the same faith, now laughed at, men will travel and fly in the air from shore to shore, by and by.

Knowledge has not only its origin, but its end in faith. But for faith's ministry to the joyful exercise of our moral and affectional nature, how imperfect a satisfaction it were to know! Without the marvelling, which I have heard called moonshiny and moon-eyed, our perceiving would come to a barren pause. As I look from some headland, betwixt islands, out upon the main, and detect that curve in the planet which no plain is broad or smooth enough to hint, as the vast ball rounds itself to my imagination beyond my sight, and I think of it as in the stellar universe but an insignificant mote, the thrill comes not in what my eye comprises, but in what my thought suspects. My transport is in the inward launch into amazement of my mind. I have a lift which no vessel, heaving on the surge, can feel. Is it said, Let the brute fear and wonder, it is man's province to know? I reply, Man knows more than the beast, but only to wonder more. His astonishment deepens and widens with his survey; and one cause for his hope of conscious personality after death lies in his judgment that no continuance, through whatever mortal obstructions, can surprise him more than being and living at all. The voyage, but that he

has taken it, were as incredible as any salvage from
the wreck! Shall I not. therefore, take myself as I am,
and make an inventory of the contents of my own
soul? If I find a migratory instinct in it, why not
obey it like an emigrant bird, and, as did those men of
old, " seek a city which hath foundations, whose builder
and maker is God"? Must I justify my spiritual
frame to a syllogistic expert? I should as soon think
of making out to his contentment my title to a sanguine or nervous temperament, to the cubits of my
stature or the color of my eyes. Let him stay in his
phlegm, and stoop to his hole in the ground, to affirm
it must cover all! I shall not be balked at the dead
line because he balks. My native instinct is to picture
and aspire, and to believe that my canvas of a New
Jerusalem means something, however poorly my pencil may draw. I must value what I know, as serving
for what I would reach, like the legs of a horse, wing
of a bird, or fin of a fish. Why care for knowledge if
it be not strength? The end of a man is not a thought,
but an act; as no idea, but an ever-evolving universe, is the end of God. In the Greek marble what
I admire is the blowing out of Jove's beard with his
breath! Every invention in the arts of life has secondary and higher advantage for the mind. In itself
science is a pursuit and prosecution, not peace. It is
an unsettled trial in a moot court. How the old theories are disturbed by new ones, — of light, electricity,
gravitation, the tides, above all, of life, in its nature,
origin, and extent. Ixion rolling his wheel was not
more restless, or Tantalus more athirst. The race we
run is noble, the competition exhilarating; and what

riches drop by the way! But no conclusions are reached. Peace passeth understanding : the Scripture is true! In the motions of the soul alone is rest. In an organism, says Immanuel Kant, all the means are ends. We may add, a spirit is that in which affection is satisfaction, and flight is ease. Most men are like travellers in haste for some unseen point ahead. What they see or where they are, passes for naught; they are wretched till they arrive at the city, mountain, waterfall, or dell. But at last, with a sense of beauty for our eye-salve, we discern Nature's equality in all her parts ; that she pitches her tent in no chosen place, that land and overarching sky are God's pavilion, and we are arriving all the time. He whose heart is stayed on principle has love for his breath, and, conscious of rectitude on the journey, never leaves the inn. Heaven is not a goal, but a way, which is its own object and delight.

Yet all material inventions unseal or illustrate spiritual things. If planetary perturbations can be accounted for only by the action of an unseen orb, do not the perturbations of human life require another world? Is not a swifter converse through wider tracks the suggestion or prediction of the lightning's antipodal talk? Does not the telephone hint that all the extraordinary and supernatural hearings reported may be natural too? Shall not the phonograph say what a huge record-book is the universe? You may tell me I am but a blossom of matter, a handful of dust scooped out of the earth. I present you the whole globe, *per contra*, as my camel, by this telephonic trick, harnessed for my idea or my affection to ride, and kneeling like llama or dromedary to lift the burden of my thought. Shall the rider be trampled into ashes at the end? As Rarey tamed the horse, we tame the orb with its myriad horse-power. Paul Revere rode fast; Greek hilltops flashed out the news; torches, passed from hand to hand, have been mediums, balloons and carrier-pigeons communicators, in peace and war. The American Revolutionary spy sews a letter into his dress, or Stillman, in Hungary, hides it in the heel of his boot; an ice-boat outstrips the locomotive; and, more swift and reticent errand-bearer, a wire is now taught to hear as well as see. Particles of matter, or centres and lines of force, are our vessels and transportation-companies; and, suspended in air, career freight-trains and baggage-cars. Light, sight, sound, and hearing are all motion; motion is force; and force is God. The earth has shrunk to a spinning-top or a shining pin on the floor. Space and time, made, as one said, to keep us apart, are annulled to bring us together. Our voice goes, fast as our purpose, into an iron ear hundreds of miles long. There shall be no secrets; all nature is an escritoire, every drawer of which may be unlocked.

But this is all figure. What a better telephone is that memory through which come the rebuke and love that saluted the morning of our life! A grown man in my neighborhood tells me how fresh to him are the friendly words I spoke when he was a little boy. The ringing of the church-bell at Ruel moves Napoleon, the powder-stained captain, to tears, as its chime sets all the old belfries rocking again. Once familiar spectacles may be far away; but *sounds* are the same as ever, from the church-tower, from the wind rattling the panes, from the thunder crashing overhead, so near, into bolts of splendor and sheets of rain that stirred to awe and worship the boy, as over the country road he went home from school. Hark to the old *intonations* of our kindred, repeated fifty years after by strangers who know not why with wet eyes we love their persons so! I hear still the neighbors' chat in my far-away birthplace, and my own voice in my father's parlor reciting to them the seventeenth chapter of John, or Cowper's lines after his mother's funeral, which almost broke my heart, children being often hurt by not being understood. I seize the peculiar and exact accent in the family doctor's laugh sixty years ago, breezy and nasal as it was, with a strong New England flavor, more from his head than his chest or throat. The brooks I played by still gurgle with endless laughter, and the wooden rockers of the chair with whose monotone my mother hushed me to sleep resound hark on the sanded floor. The brass cannon stuns me; and I yet shrink and shiver at its sharp discharge at Freeport Corner, on the soldiers' parade, the War of 1812 having just passed away, leaving its smoky field-pieces and remnants of ammunition behind. Commander and troop are dead, —

> " Their bodies are dust,
> And their good swords rust ; "

but I hear the order given and the steady tramp of the men. I passed by the house where, a young man, I was entertained. Host and hostess were dead, their epitaphs moss-grown, their children scattered whither I knew not ; but the strains of welcome, as of yore, issued at

the gate. Where and how shall the hospitality be returned? O upper friends, hear at least my thanks!

So there is not an atom but answers to a thought.
Shall not the telephonic apparatus end or prevent misunderstanding, make diplomacy a conversation, and
among hostile or jealous nations put peaceful greetings
for bloody cartels? The telephone is to the criminal a
threat. He cannot fly with the lightning, more than a
dog can run with the train. This sharp gossip of the
magnet he shall not escape. There is a *second hearing*
as well as a second sight. When the voice was heard
from heaven saying, "This is my beloved Son," some
said it thundered, others that an angel spake to him.
What the voice was no science more than ignorance
can decide. The man of coolest head in Boston told
me, that, musing in his chair one night, words came to
him in distinct articulation, "There is another world."
What is music but a score which the composer over-
hears, — celestial harps or voices from afar, like ord-
nance at long range, delivering even to deaf Beethoven
the tune and to Mendelssohn the "songs without
words"? I know not if "the cloud of witnesses"
ever break for us into speech. But our yearning is
prophecy, echoed by every prophet, that they will. "I
thought," said a mother, "my dead boy would speak
to me, and I held my breath to hearken. As we sailed
over Lake Lucerne, I believed if I could but get rowed
on to the horizon, he would appear!"

Faith incites to knowledge, and knowledge returns **to**
faith. We *live* in a circle, if we do not reason in one.
Faith and knowledge are alternate buckets of the water
of life. Could we know absolutely, we should not be

content with knowing! We know but this, that naught can be quite known ; and Hegel can scarce persuade us that " *nothing* is the equivalent of *being*." For we can *absolutely* love, trust, and hope. There is no sure opinion. The only certainty is in what we feel. In us more than out of us is the miracle. What sound so strange as our own recollection! A friend saw in a store where she went to buy meat for her sick husband a box of pansies, which at once brought back the face and voice of the woman who tended and fed her in a garden when she was a little girl. The reminder swept her away from the provision-dealer's stall, from her present home, from her gray hairs and the age of the world she lives in, to the long-passed period and distant spot where the pansies bloomed and the motherly guardian nourished. Again she saw, again she heard, — form, feature, inflection came back ; lost in thought, and her purchase suspended, she stood like a statue, and worshipped the pansies. Did God charge her with idolatry, or was he not more to her in the pansies than in the sky? What metallic ear, or resonant plate, or resolution of sound into motion, is so marvellous as this phonography of the soul? The surprise in the phonograph is that pitch and tone can be printed in and reverberate from so small a space, like the Lord's Prayer on a gold dollar. But how much finer is the entry in and recovery from the human brain! The old accents, gracious or peevish, the upward or downward slides of the voice, in what fac-similes sharper than coins from the mint, come back through all the confusions of scores of years! This rejoinder of brain and nerve is more delicately accurate than the invisible tracery of the phonograph needle. It shames all lace-work in its transcript on this bone-protected cerebral inner curve, and in these living molecules which physiologists number by millions, as if there were one to store every single impression and pack it so close! The merchant's blotting-book to copy letters is not, to a comma, so correct. What magazines of knowledge, beyond treasuries of nations and exchequers of kings, are contained somehow within these arched walls we call our pericranium; in the head of a scholar and even a numskull, — for a fool has more wit and information in his gray lobes and the minor receiving ganglia than could be engraven on Egyptian obelisks or dinted into the layers of the globe. There is no understood or calculable length of time to which, on the revolving cylinder of tin-foil, like a bonded warehouse, the soft, imperceptible marks that imprison syllables will not keep and cry out. Though the thin sheet were transferred to another instrument a thousand miles away, they will return like a resurrection from the dead. But finer-woven yet in the human organism is a film, with all our declarations and promises under lock and key, however long it be before the bolted wards be sprung. Is this film, too, transferable from our present embodiment so smooth and round? As the cranked cylinder turns, we feel the membrane of sensibility quiver and the needle of moral feeling prick, as though a live metaphor were in the revolution and recitation of the senseless tool. How surely in the sphere of our own being we carry the heaven and hell we so superstitiously locate and map out in space! What a mocking-bird is in our heart! "Those were his very words," said a young woman of what had been

spoken by a tempting man. Must they not come back
to him, as with the unpaid bill of a bad debt in their
hand? And if they touch on " the fear of something
after death," shall it be a ghost-story to frighten children with? Let the vital phonograph answer as it
shall work! " To know my deed, 't were best not know
myself," says Macbeth in the play. But our deed is
web and woof of our self. It is more than any flight
of fancy, though it were Homer's or Shakspeare's. It
makes our personal identity; and the shuttle is our will.
We are an incarnate responsive liturgy for ourselves, and
from our own lips will come the collect or the curse.

Telegram is the lightning's message. What is the
Bible but a body of phonograms? In it are cruel laws
and barbarous edicts, bulls, or bulletins of fanatical
tribes and savage men. But there are other proclama-
tions, precious beyond negations of unbelief or encycli-
cals of popes, and so matching the wants and dumb
predictions of our nature, that only from the breath of
God could they be blown. Modulated by a living instrument, they became audible to instruct and console
millions of mankind.

There is a background of our being and a foreground.
The background is God and the foreground is heaven.
But we know in order that we may do. If a thought
be the ancestor, an act is the heir. Knowledge is but
clothing and armor for the will. It is building-material
for character, like timber for our house or ship. Of the
great questions, *Whence, How, Whither, Wherefore,* and
What, the positivist affirms we can deal but with the
last. But ideas on the other four must throw light by
which alone the fifth can be clearly shown; else his

knowledge is only skin-deep. A dog with his bone and kennel knows *what is what;* and what is human life more than a kennel and a bone, if confined to the sensible facts? We understand superficially, but we are moral to the core. How much less we are hurt by ignorance of nature than by a misunderstanding of each other or of ourselves! In delicate conditions of health or of nervous apprehension, how a sentiment has power of life and death a thousand times oftener than the sheriff executes doom! The fable of the basilisk, with its fatal glance, is a sober truth. We live on a justice of which no law on the statute-book is sponsor. We commit crimes of which no jury can convict. We exercise a goodness which it would be insult to pay with any paradise. It is its own reward. In a lively French play an interlocutor satirizes that *woman*, as he calls her, with the scales in her hand on the top of the court-house; saying, he observes *there is nothing in them.* The weights of equity in this perpetual counterbalance of existence will be nowhere if not in our deeds, which are born of our choice.

The experimenter with telegraph, telephone, or phonograph can elect what he will make the pen or mouth of his implement speak. Into the little opening, no larger than a lady's ear, he may spout an oration, reel off rhymes, hum a tune, or wind a horn. But his arbitrary decision ends with that. The undulations carry the message. It is an infinitesimal parcel, tied up and compacted in the airy bubbles or balloons. The vessel or vesicle goes undisturbed though a thunderbolt strike the building or an earthquake rock the ground; and, a century after, a touch at the handle would return the vocal letter-missive. Nothing could hinder, short of a violence that should destroy the impression or the machine. But the mental imprint no such interference can annul. You determine, at the telegraph office, your communication. Halloo after the lightning, will your cry fetch the order back? You can only add the arrow of another despatch! So the voluntary passes over into the involuntary in our breast. Let us come into the elective state, and get out of the gusty latitudes, the Cape Horn and Bay of Biscay of capricious inclination and selfish passion! The region of choice is safe; for no man ever chose to be a drunkard or profligate. He was swept into villany by desire he had lost power to control. They choose well who are able to choose at all.

There is necessity for us. We admire a quality in man or woman as we do the landscape. It is involuntary, but, O Lord, if it be wrong, please kill me at once, for it is necessary in my own nature so long as I live. It rids me of all that is low in myself, as we pray the "angels ever bright and fair" to take us, in our oratorio song. The navigator, long buffeted by the storm and by shifting squally weather, is glad to get into the trade-wind. Right permanent direction of our appetites and longings is the trade-wind of the mind. Still must the pilot hold his tiller; and we must be electors in the endless sessions and questions that are put to vote in our own breast. That record is the only one we must for ever read. We say of a person, he is a man of one book. This inward bible is for us all. How the preacher mistakes, to say our acts are irrevocable, when in the endless revoking all compensation or retribution consists!

Science deals with the universe only in one aspect or part. The president of a scientific association sums up its scope in " the registration of facts or phenomena under uniform laws." But there is a manifold experience not reckonable as phenomenon or fact. It is a state, perhaps an ecstasy or exaltation of mind. Scientific men would bring whatever is or transpires under the head of material for scientific estimate and report. But there are operations of human nature too vast and elusive to be so published or surveyed. There are revelations, visions, and extraordinary communions with God. Doubtless there may be a philosophy of the soul in all its conditions and acts. But it is no science, properly and technically so called. Only by being overstrained can the word *science* be applied. It is a not unhappy doom for some persons to consider and study the passions by which they are moved. Such an observer Goethe was, who could not rest till he had printed his transport in Werther, Wilhelm Meister, or Faust. No one ever felt or knew love more deeply than he. His information was accurate and his tidings sincere. He may not have come by his knowledge honestly always. But, after Shakspeare's women, his are best, and he offers some varieties beyond the English dramatist's survey, doing more justice to certain forms of lowly maiden life. But how he would scoff at any scientist's imputation that he had sounded all the depths of this ocean of human feeling with his deep-sea line! Dear companionship bids knowledge stand aside, wait as a servant, look on apart, and own it cannot fathom or comprehend the blessed intercourse. Darwin, making out his theory, tells us what in his own infants he has observed; but his evolution could no more exhibit all that was in them than Newton's gravitation can spread before us the contents of the stars. Science knows not commencement. Only procedure it surveys. The puzzle by which it is perpetually balked is the origin of life. Science is finite in its aim; and life is infinite in its relations, in the least mite that stirs. Semitic genius gives us the sentence, immortal and sublime : "In the beginning God made the heavens and the earth." It is an unscientific statement, which no school or academy can accept. Every literary author confesses the inadequacy of his pen to the vital secret, which an atom manifests and which all creation is. "Why leave the Christ out of your list of Representative Men?" I asked my friend. "Because," he answered, "it takes too much strength of constitution to put him in." We may miscall our inspirations and emotions *occurrences*, if we will ; but no clerk can take account of their stock. They range immensely beyond the student's eye, as the shifting scenes and live tablets of the city transcend the watchman's beat. No explorer has sailed up these streams to the fountain-head, and no coast-surveyor by triangulation has measured these shores. Whoever loves navigates, like Columbus, into latitudes and longitudes before unknown ; and whoever imagines transcends. When toward my headland the Atlantic dips its bowl, I have other and more interesting occupation with it than to weigh its tons of tide. I lose the beauty if I set myself to analyzing the beams of the day. When what astronomers call the Milky Way, but which is rather to the eye the thinnest veil of gauze ever woven, hangs athwart the face of the southern sky, it is curious to learn or remember it is made of worlds round and solid like the earth and sun; but I would not know, if I could, how many they are or how big. Like Moses, I see the skirt of God's garment; and, like Kepler and Linnæus, beholding the same laws above and below, I mark *him passing by;* and I exchange the arithmetic that would reduce the spectacle to bushel and yardstick, for a prophecy and a song. When I note the little beach-birds hopping so safely in the billows' edge, I think of One who makes them so fearless and at home, without whom the sparrow neither falls nor flies; and I have to try hard not to hate those men who are after them with their murderous guns! As, lately, the declining sun shone under the ragged line of the retiring storm, some sea-birds rose over the sea, half flying and half floating on the breeze, that still briskly stirred. How their buoyancy occupied the sky! Animated bits, as of pure white paper scattered from some hand that could throw them so far, with idle freedom and the luxury of motion, they wavered up and down. They stretched landwards, or sought the offing anon. They revelled in the wind which, with effortless pinion, they beat. It seemed to me as if the firmament was stretched and the gale blew for them alone. It was unscientific, but was it wrong, when my gazing fancy turned them into images of human life and love? These images have their atmosphere, which they, with other plumage, strike in their flight. Their pinions lift them toward the heavens for a while, on that gale which mortality is. But the wind is more than the wing, and when that is folded, will still spring up. Shall not they be fledged again? The soul is a migratory bird: it has another atmosphere, and can well afford, at its moulting season, to let the feathers drop it is sustained by in time ; not doubting it shall have new outfit and find softer climes, and continue to soar.

In the wide pæan for science I would join, were it not loud enough without my voice. The orchestral conductor discovers at once and summons to its duty the too faint instrument in his band; compared with the thirst for knowledge, would not our leader decide that the spirit of a just charity is feeble in our time? History, at least, grows more tolerant. How it rehabilitates persons long disreputable and under the ban! We are thinking not so ill as we did of Roman emperors and Romish popes. The verdict depends not alone on the information of the censor, but on his disposition and point of view. Ernest Renan, as large and liberal as he is scholarly and exact, comes to rescue the reputation even of the Empress Faustina, wife of Marcus Aurelius, from the cloud of disgrace that has covered it, without moving, for many an age ; and her figure now forms, under his pen, not as a traitress and adulteress, but only with free manners as well as splendid charms ; one whom the solemn synod of graybeard courtiers, that the irreproachable Emperor had gathered about him, misjudged, while the handsome Queen always kept his own honor as well as had his heart. The very ignominy burnt into a man or woman may become a glory and encaustic painting of their worth. The prints of the nails in the hands and feet of Jesus were *stigmata* once ; but the stigmas have become points of love and admiration for the world. His very country, France, qualifies Renan not to be harsh on what was gay and unrestrained, and possibly innocent, at Rome. He gives at least, as the old royal shade sits to him, the benefit of the doubt; and observing how merciless moral decisions are rendered by puritanic notions in our day, one inclines to take part with the antiquarian student, not more generous than he is deep and keen. Since the daughter of Herodias danced off John the Baptist's head, all dancing has been, with some, an unpardonable sin, which David's performance before the ark fails to bless; and I have known an excellent Doctor of Divinity to scowl on the young girl that came back to his house rather late from the ball. Let us have mercy! Guns are rifled to whirl without bias the bullet true to its aim. Could we so rifle our minds, the process were of more worth!

The chief science were equity to those whose course or opinion is against our own. It does not come with emancipation from superstitious creeds. None fling harder words at their opponents, or at each other when they disagree, than those from whom every lending of tradition has been cast away. Robert Browning gives to Bishop Blougram the best of the argument with the sceptic; and it is not certain that, if the dissenter's view be larger, his virtue is more safe. Luther's wife inquires of her husband why the family prayers, under his brave protest, are losing warmth. Mr. Lecky finds that, in taking off the strain of a fanatical faith, some risk is run. May we be so rational in our speculation as to lose the earnestness of our life? Renan, discoursing of the degradation of language, says an everlasting balancing appears to be the law of human things. We must have either nobility for a small number, he declares, or vulgarity for all. But a conclusion so sad must be incorrect. As the entire level of continents has been lifted above the sea, so the tribes that inhabit them are raised. There is small danger that the mass of men will be scientific to excess! But humanity becomes deformity in such as are scientific alone.

Centralization is better than secession in the state, and specialization disintegrates if it do not serve generalization. Mountains and seas cannot become private property. Nothing grand in nature can be marked off. It is churlish for the proprietor to warn back, with his dog or man or bolted gate, the human race from Niagara, Mount Washington, or the Atlantic shore; and there is no appropriation or private interpretation of truth. The towns on the coast insist on retaining the old beaches and ocean-walks; and that is no precious possession or invention in which the whole humanity is not concerned. What a degraded menial is the lightning if it carry only a sharp bargain or bloody threat! If the wires be not busy with worthy errands, how useless is their stretch and how idle is the nimble Ariel they can command! The fatalist Turk, whose tropic clime has never been reflected in any sunny face of his own, and whose crescent has become a waning moon, as he curses with immobility the population he rules and the soil he tills, " means but that he is lazy when he says that Allah is great!" As an abstraction, without application, how impertinent it is to speak of loving the truth! Is it an affection like Zerah Colburn's for the multiplication-table? It is barren if it would stop even in Isaac Newton's contemplation of the stars! Can it hover over a collection of manuscripts, coins, or fossil remains?

What would it signify to fill the Patent Office with discoveries of no profit to mankind? Science must be
touched with feeling to be welcome; yet we must not
doubt a benefit in all we find out, and an object in
whatever mankind pursues. My atheistic friend, gazing at the piles of theology in the British Library, des-
cants to the showman on such a monument of waste.
But, as the bees have not misspent their day at their
yellow masonry, though the time come when no more
honey is held in their wax, and as the coral-insects do not
throw away themselves and their time, as they mortar
together, under the sea, the solid banks that shall look
white and ruddy as they at last shore up the world,
and edge the continents with cities of men, so all faithful study, of things human or divine, shall be a stay
for civilization and some time see the light, even if
afterward, under the roll of centuries, it crumble and
disappear. The mind is instinctively wistful concerning itself, and would know its origin and end. While
it drinks at whatever spring its curiosity may find to
slake its thirst, who is this that, in the name of freedom, would drug the cup? There is no opiate that can
put intellect to sleep.

Science should be equivalent to knowledge. But the
explosion of a heap of biblical assumptions or misin-
terpretations has aggravated and sped materialism,
which is the drift of this generation, to limit knowledge
to the information which the senses import into the
mind. There is a knowledge of things, or rather only
a little knowledge about any thing. But there is, too,
a knowledge of ideas which are not things, a knowledge
of beauty which is but a spirit expressed, and a knowl-

edge of persons who are not things ; and in comparison with this knowledge, all that comes by weight and measure, and can be circumscribed in any definite time and space, is shallow and of little worth. Do I not know my friend, for whom I have no formula? The faculty for spiritual and personal knowledge is compound, like the instrument with its apparatus in an observatory ; but its result is simple, and not ephemeral, like all the statements of physical science. We know Justice, but never saw her scales ; she is known by that conscience in us which is her even beam. We know love not by an observation, but an unsought impression, and by that answer in our own breast but for which another's affection would be like the Indian Standing Bear's speech without an interpreter. Paul writes about "knowing the love of Christ." Was it Christ's love for the disciple, or the disciple's for him? It was both ; for the love was bigger than the Master or follower, as the love betwixt any two is bigger than we and all mankind, and uses us and every one for its own ends. We know by certain tests how much pressure or strain our building materials will bear in an iron girder, steel span, or granite arch. We know the endurance of our companion as well, but may have no calculation of its strength and reach. If it be a divine property, the gravitation of the globe cannot crush it or the roll of years tire it out. Jesus knew God, as any saint may, with transcendent knowledge.

But how know aught of the future, in the way religious people pretend? "Do you know any thing about it?" asked the sick man, as an orthodox saint talked to him about heaven. Does not the scientist know that

an Alpine glacier will, though imperceptibly, slip down
the mountain gorge ; that the boat or log in the rapids
of Niagara will be swept over the brink ; that a particular plant or tree, and no other, will come of this or
that seed ; and, by the law of heredity, a certain sort of
parent will propagate children of his or her own kind?
Is not all this knowledge not only of the present, but
of what is to come?   I know that he who drinks and
drabs is going to hell, and that he who joyfully gives
his life for others is going to heaven, as much as I
know that the congregation on the steps is coming in,
or the boy, with his books and slate under his arm, is
going to school.   Things follow their tendencies ; what
do we all know better than that?   The prophet and his
prophecy are possible and true by virtue of this law
and fact.   But heaven is not a matter of chronology, or
bit of territory, beyond the tomb, staked out.   It is a
state of mind with a mortgage on paradise which eternity alone can pay.   The athlete knows he can leap
over a ditch ; and a completely developed soul knows
it can jump across the yawning chasm of the grave,
though it drop its garment by the way.   Business men
proceed on the principle that causes produce effects ;
and if matter originated mind, or the impersonal
brought forth personality, it would be in violation of
the law that from the lower the higher cannot come.
Stories of bodily resurrection are invented for such as
cannot know their immortality in the lift and rapture
of their powers.   When Raphael makes the figures of
Jesus, Moses, and Elias float as if a wind blew their raiment up, we credit the transfiguration, because we all
have seasons of inward ascension, in which we know

we are like balloons struggling at their last cords, held back from glory but for a time. If we have such religious knowledge that heaven and hell are but harvestings of a crop which in wet or drought, cold or heat, can never fail, then where, in what school, public or private or parochial, and under whatever auspices of Church or State, should it not be taught? By what right do reading, writing, and arithmetic, which are but the bare language of knowledge, take precedence or prior importance to knowledge itself? Can we get out of the atmosphere, or go where we shall have no need of light and water and ground, or where the attractions of nature are not obeyed? Even there we could not escape God, or be rid of the hold of his law.

V.

ART.

THE human mind has long refused the pre-eminent claim of art in its " court of common pleas," and estops it still, through a superstition as to the sacredness, above all transformations by industry, of the crude matter of the globe. Thus, in the name of religion, is aggravated among us that materialism of which artists from Europe complain. But that avarice of gain, which is half our worship, ends in a rude shock when, with the keen logic of Mammon, our clerks pilfer bonds from the precious little trunks so tempting to their hands, and when we ourselves municipally illustrate the swindling we reprobate, as we " set a thief to catch a thief," compound with felony, and bait our trap for a criminal with a crime. Art, in its noble sense and with its superior joy, has use to lure us away from mean delights ; for we do not seem, with all our churches, to be made honest by religion alone. Sorely we need, and heartily should hail, that truer interpretation of nature which presents the world but as a block for us to shape, as a father throws a bit of wood to a boy for him to cut out his whistle or boat. The Menai Straits bridge, the Mont Cenis tunnel, the New York wharves on the North and East rivers, the pontooning of the deep with a thousand steamers, and the driving of locomotive trains to mountain-tops, are not an accretion, excrescence, or parasite-growth, but an increase and extension of the world, like the chasing and incrustation from which some precious substance gets half its worth. The broken flower-pot in a poor man's window has a sentimental value which the loam could not compare with before it revolved on the potter's wheel; and the plant itself, produced from many crossings, is a work of art, as also is the enormous horse, of Dutch breed, in a London dray.

Is not man himself a cultivated animal? Nothing is left of all that was in Noah's ark; and the ark is no more behind a Cunarder or Baltimore clipper than all its biped or quadruped contents lag after the living forms of to-day. Piety consists not in letting Nature have the upper hand, but in getting the weather-gauge of her; and when one carries his respect for her so far as to say we speak of *weeds* only because we know not their uses, his worship takes a low flight. Man's vocation is to exalt the earth-maker's work in degrees without end, as from a tree we get timber, from the timber staves, from the staves a powder-cask, from the powder-cask a painted jar. Is not the Arch of Titus at Rome worth more than its tons avoirdupois of stone or square rood of ground, as the history of Judæa nestles in its engravings and hangs on its walls, while the procession of the golden candlestick lights up its interior space? Not in the rough planet, but its *tidings*, are we concerned; and as emotion stirs the preacher or painter, words and colors are thrown up like waves of the sea. Magnitude is nothing; spirit is all. There are great heads on medals which are very small. The pleasure from a large landscape or a little picture, said our Hunt, is the same.

Has conscience any place in art? When Corot said, about his own picture, "Now I must make some *air* among the branches for the birds to fly through," was it not a *just* intent? When caught with his comrades in a storm, he said, "Let us go in-doors and paint, then we can make what *weather* we please," was there no moral sense for improving the time? The truth of history, as well as the requisitions of art, suffers not the tragic in its pictured drama to be quite left out among its shows of delight. "Crown of Thorns," "Calvary," "Descent from the Cross," and "Entombment," as well as "Annunciation," "Conception," and "Resurrection," must have place. "Laocoön" and the "Greek Slave" the chisel must give us, with the "Mercury" and "Apollo." Beethoven, in music, must add an iron string to Mozart's soft and silken chords. My friend objects to Goethe's "Faust" as a painful book, and to Browning's "Paracelsus" as a wolfish plot; but the poets had to write their veracious tales.

One modern people seems especially chosen to minister to our hunger and thirst for art. A national genius for it belongs to the French alone. "In the bellowing of battle," says the Roman historian, "the laws are dumb." But, despite war and cholera, wasted vineyards and inundated streams, how these modern Gauls, descendants of the old Romans, will play and paint! If the Asiatic plague comes, they set it as an actor on the stage. Gay and beautiful France, we, as in compassion for a butterfly folk, call their land. But their thin booth stands solid as Cyclopean architecture, or like a Coliseum in every town. The sketchers from their studios swarm to the crisis of every scene. They make bee-lines to Cordillera ranges, to Chinese famines, volcanic eruptions, and dead popes. The *Illustration*, a newspaper in Paris, will have our civil war and the last royal progress in India on its luminous page, and relate all contemporary annals with a photographer's report and an etcher's tool. Prussian troops may bombard their city, and they will show in sun-pictures of rent walls what the cannons do. During the German siege Parisian scientists made their calculations, scholars carried on their peaceful discussions, and within the military parallels artists chalked out their quite different lines, while soldiers bravely manned and defended the walls; and the light-hearted, wonderful people, that keep their footing in an earthquake and make merry with death, when the conflict ceases and the fine is imposed, step politely forth, and in their two hands of industry and economy bring to their astonished foe the indemnity which was their cruel tax, and which German improvidence fails to turn into expected wealth. Not from vineyard and silk-factory, or trade and commerce alone, but from the beauty-loving skill to turn cheap material to attractive uses, and from the pictures that convert values into enormous multiplicands, their resources come, making for them as for all a benediction of art. Frugal to consume and copious to produce what civilization must have of a finer food; with a profusion on their sunny soil of that light which must *flood* the canvas, as Thomas Couture said, they have for work each day of the year. How complete is the explanation, in their Briarean dexterity, of their amazing thrift! What a mistake if they do not put their future glory in bloodless conquests alone! As a manufacturer, mu-

sician, comedian, entertainer, child or set of children,
born democrat, — leaving behind her armed head, and
struggling into a republic at last, — France will unlearn
strife, and become, as nature means, a garden and conservatory where all other tribes shall go to school.

Man's permanent necessity is art. An acre of ground
will support a family; but there is a mute craving which
corn and wheat cannot satisfy and no science can
appease, albeit in our day the imaginative appetite is
the last to open its mouth. What volumes of meaning a
creative artist will condense on a single cloth or wooden
page! How many words of history are supplied, or,
like bank-notes, cancelled, in Turner's "Slave-Ship"!
That laboring bark, tossed in the trough of the sea, was
our American ship of state. Our confused politics were
those swirling waves, and our retribution was in that
yawning deep. The picture is criticised as abnormal;
but, unnatural or supernatural, why should not that
painted heaving main be contrary to nature, as our
evil system or any English slavery was? So all sorts
of monstrous and impossible fishes swarm in the watery chasm to devour. The miraculous billows will
not swallow even the iron fetters, but vomit them back
among the foaming crests, and make the cruel links cry
from the ocean, like Abel's blood from the ground.
What bottom have the wasteful caverns to allow such
dreadful offences to sink? At what port of safety
can a vessel arrive so "rigged with curses and built in
the eclipse"? Is not the cargo too heavy for any craft?
Shall not birds of prey peck at the carcase, for which
fierce jaws open below? What but doom on iniquity
would the artist depict? Yet in his fancy it is no eter-

nal thing, but as limited as it is dire. The tempest, horrid phantom, a fugitive in fright, — as in a moment, shall blow away. Through a rift in the black and blood-stained clouds shoots the steady shaft of light, to scatter, like a proclaimed emancipation, the dark. Its gleam shall edge the horizon and fill the sky. The clearing shall be a Christian redemption, not a Greek fate. We have lightened the ship by throwing over the chains and not the slave, who helps to work her and his passage now.

Such pictures as Turner's show that when England flowers in literature or art, though she blossom not all over like France, it is yet with expansion more splendid and tough. But she has scarce such a cluster of artists as Millet, Corot, and Couture with his classic heads, part of whose picture of the "Volunteers of 1792" has come to us to illustrate the strength more than the finish of his style. We see at once in the two figures that *home* is behind and the battle before. They are not conscripts, but willing offerings. What in reality they have left struggles with what in imagination they go to, in their mind. One of them, drooping, has flung his arms about the other for support, and the second, as he sustains his comrade, lifts his own eyes to heaven, because, said the artist, "poor fellow, he knows not where else to look." Perhaps in no modern picture does a natural situation more suggest the ideal than in Mr. Couture's "Day-Dreams," in which a boy, having laid his books in a strapped bundle on the bench, in a room open to the light, follows with rapt vision the bubbles he is blowing into the air. What breadth of prospect, height of hope, lustre of good cheer, vista of accomplishment, and immortality for his plans, appear in the sport so familiar to childhood, in which time is annihilated, and stints of study are suspended and forgot! No kitten playing with its tail was ever more happily occupied or utterly lost; nor could unity be more perfectly combined with variety in any scene. It is a masterpiece in the French style and Italian too; for, as one of her historians has said, Gaul is the real though cisalpine Rome, an Italy transferred, and the old blood preserved yet refined, purged somewhat of that greed for aggrandizement which was so over-strained by the subtle Corsican, who, as Victor Hugo says, with his wars *wearied God.* France will fulfil her better destiny if she beware of artifice while cultivating art. Scarce a French novel or play but introduces and justifies deceit; and this signifies a civilization without root or depth of earth. "Great bloomers, but not hardy," said one of certain plausibly untruthful persons; and some communities are social plants of this agreeable and unpromising type.

For the masters in *music* we must cross the Rhine; although the present writer dares not attempt to pay his own debt to this art, for all its refreshment and peace, lying so deep as it does in the universal mind. The whole air is one capacity for *airs,* Lydian or Tyntæan; the atmosphere is a potential concord and latent symphony and slumbering hymn of praise, which every voice or viol, pipe or string, throat of bird, insect, or man, is but the means to arouse. Even when it is pro-voked to harshness and tortured into dissonance, dis-tance, as if it were an atmospheric repentance, eliminates discord, and softens, without rendering inaudible, the roughest notes.   In what sweetness come back the echoes of a braying horn among the hills!   It is said the Covenanters' rude songs in the Scotch Highlands became melodies indescribably winsome to travellers' ears afar.   Historic philosophers are wont to call musical nations weak politically, citing Italy and Germany as cases in point.   Is it in spite, or at all in consequence of a musical spring in the mind, that Germany, twenty years ago feeble as so many scattered sticks, has become the strongly bound fagot in Æsop's fable, and the so long oppressed and derided Italy a free kingdom, reacting on the papal sway?   No religious or civil accusation will hold against art, of whatsoever sort.   Any art, like any nature, may be turned to a sensual purpose, but only by abuse.   If Shakspeare tell us all art is but nature, we will answer all nature is but art; and from the Fashioner of the world, in his own example, comes the summons of all our forgetive faculties to a serious though cheerful end.   My friend, the music-teacher, hates to hear people say of a concert how they *enjoyed* it!   His music is his religion, as to Jean Paul Richter a solemn strain suggested what he had never experienced nor should behold, a blessedness almost painful because too vast for hope.   What a span from the guttural trumpet or high note of the tenor drum and scream of the fife stirring up the fray, to the slow and soothing dirge that bears the dead soldier to his rest, and from anthems of worship to the twanging strings that lead on the lively dance!   How consoling, at the funeral, is a choir!   That is never quite sad which we can sing about.   Love sings, faith sings, and sorrow sings as it is converted into joy.

Without his chorister in the tabernacle, how poorly the revivalist would fare, ill suited to a song as some of the dark old dogmas are! What a river of God, full of water, runs in the fugues of Sebastian Bach! How celestial harmonies must have spilled over on Beethoven's inner ear! What a lark at heaven's gate was Mozart, and how the oratorios of Haydn and Handel and Mendelssohn seem to continue some chorus of angels on high! Paradise would not be believed in but for our snatches of their notes. Columbus knew the neighborhood of a continent by the floating weeds and a fragrance in the air; what we catch of a diviner color and odor "beyond the reaches of our souls" is proof that we coast the edges of another world. Amid doctrinal wrangles comes the all-reconciling psalm. I can sing Trinitarian doxologies in Orthodox companies, — all but the *words!* A good voice is of no sect, but mediator of all; and the dull sermon or more tedious prayer, in many a village-church, is sanctified or atoned for by the fresh voices in the organ-loft, while the solemn pipes, by whose resonance they are surmounted and led, seem to furnish vernacular language and a mother-tongue to the reverent soul.

Hearing supplements vision; for while the eye is a rolling and too often unfixed and restless orb, the ear is an aperture and open door. Let us not only chant or play faithfully what is set down in the score, but modulate the inflections of our daily speech till there shall be but cordial invitation and gracious welcome, with no yelling in the house, and children's voices be trained into tune. Some intonations instinct with tenderness strike more kindly and stay longer in the bosom's audience-chamber than any *tremolo* or *sostenuto* of Braham or Malibran. Not Webster's clarion or Everett's violin or Kemble's flute-note resounds in my ear like the unconsciously intoned affection of some young maiden or man, half ashamed or unawares.

But from any art can the dark and dreadful side of life be left out? The thunder intrudes in the " Pastoral Symphony," and in the Last Supper Judas darkens the door. The *unspeakable Turk* challenges yet for his crooked cimeter a needful task. · What a gap in nature would be made by the instant extinction of violent passions or the sudden removal of wild beasts ! It would be like the rise and retreat of that huge *bore* into which submarine earthquakes urge the waves, and would compel immediate alteration of every constitution and human law. How to arrange or govern or understand we should no longer know. Charity let us have. If we would be able to describe, we must not judge, save that the Lord means something in all he makes ; nor denounce qualities that differ from ours, like some besotted fashionist that roars against Mohammedan or Mongolian costume. What are all our notions but the dress of our minds?

There is a prejudice of fanatics that art is a cold business and the artist a cold man as he bends so calmly and unexcitedly to his patient task. " Goethe," says some sentimental critic, " was a piece of ice," and Shakspeare surveys the unfolding of dire situations with what a passionless eye ! But is it a virtue to cultivate tears? " Genius burns, but does not weep." Is the actor or author heartless and indifferent because he keeps his temper, as he keeps a fire, under control?

In the chemic arts flames are used of an intensity superior to that which consumes a building or cracks the marble and melts the iron in the conflagration of a town ; but naphtha and blow-pipe and nitro-glycerine and bottled lightning are held to service. They are the only sort of unemancipated slaves. But we are mastered by a careless candle, or an overset kerosene-lamp, or a spark that escapes from a tinder-box or match. If we would know what caloric is, we go to the blacksmith and white-smith, not to a flustered cook or burnt child. If we would understand intellectual heat, we run not after the blazing straw or bonfire of some short-lived romance, but to the anvils where scholars and poets forge their enduring thoughts. Are Æschylus and Dante pitiless because they will not spoil with cheap fortunes the dignity of their characters and the consistency of their plots? They would lose nature in losing poise. A blaze is dissipation of warmth. Poets are tide-waiters upon God. Like becalmed vessels, they look for a breeze. We must be slow that we may be swift. Many persons are impatient of the tardy evolution of humanity, and accuse Providence of being indifferent and cold. Does God indeed see and hear, that the thunder of his wrath at iniquity delays to strike? But his eye and ear include all, sinner and saint; and his interpreters are like himself.

The most ardent of men in my memory was a Methodist preacher, who was an artist too. A transcendent enthusiast, considering his topics like red-hot spikes which another could not hold, yet no kindling on the hearth and no northern aurora or crinkling flash in the cloud ever described the line of beauty more truly than

the sallies of his speech, which was not from his mouth
alone, but in every motion and feature of his frame and
face. One day, without rising from his seat at the table,
this consummate performer, who never had any training for the stage, described to the company a spinning
dervish. Into the character he was himself transformed ; and we, who looked and listened, were transported to the East, or rather the strange Oriental figure
was imported into the room. In what amazing gesture
and gyration the forms of a Christian piety were for the
moment lost or laid aside as so much frippery from a
wardrobe, while the sense of the infinite in another religion was shown ! We beheld as in a mirror the wild
prophet of the desert, as though on those farther than
California sand-lots, or rising through the floor. But
Arab or Yankee, it mattered not which to this clerical
performer's versatile skill. In a certain political cam-
paign one of our Eastern men was so assured of his
party's success that he engaged to trundle a barrel of
apples on a wheelbarrow some thirty miles to Boston
in case of its defeat ; and he actually both incurred and
himself executed the penalty, on losing his singular bet.
The Bethel preacher, to whose histrionic ability I refer,
was not absent when that singular freight came along
the street ; and more than a score of years has not
dimmed the vividness of his account at the time. The
lively expectation of the grotesque figure about to
come had lined with spectators the long and crooked
route. " Young men and maidens, old men and children," crowded the squares, planted themselves at the
corners of every avenue, hung on the fences, peered over
the brick walls, and thrust their heads out of the win-

dows, each face aglow with the humor of the occasion. The city wore, or *was*, one universal smile. Its population had melted into sympathy for once. It had become an expectant theatre. At last " a little man with oakum whiskers" pushed his wheel, tugging at the bent handles, through the throng. From the amusing situation came a fellowship whose ties no solemn sermon could weave; and the novel communion administered was pictured in tone and gesture, such as might be envied by Kean or Garrick or any star on the stage, by our transcendent mime. In this great actor, in or out of the desk, was no *mimicry* or painstaking imitation of the signs of feeling, as the critics questioned whether Rachel did not display. The elder Booth was no more " to the manner born," nor touched perfection closer in every detail. At the festival of an order of believers not his own, being invited to speak, he told of his visit to Virginia, where he was born, — his great wish being to see " Little Johnny," with whom he had played as a boy. Much he inquired and long he hunted for his mate, but in vain. " Little Johnny" no one seemed to know. Still he urged his pursuit, inquired of all the folks, entered into particulars about the family and the early circumstances of his own connection with it, till finally " Little Johnny" was actually brought in — not the brisk, rosy lad he remembered, but an aged, gray-haired, stooping, and trembling veteran — to stand by his side; and he found he himself was no longer a boy. How the dramatic representation filled the hall, and how the thousand persons in it gazed all together while they heard! The Unitarian president with his supporting dignitaries had disappeared in the spectators and the spectacle. He, the sole actor, that strode as if alone on the platform, was the entire troupe he depicted, — old man, "Little Johnny," and himself. Had the wall behind, like that of Belshazzar's palace, blazed into letters of fate under a miraculous hand, the sight could not have been more real to the eye.

The exhaustion that followed on such exhibitions as I but faintly hint was demonstration how the soul may be exercised by what is called fiction more profoundly than by any fact. Anton Rubinstein told me his life was habitual torture, with only gleaming intervals of joy ; so overwrought was he by the double genius to compose and perform, till he was ready to accuse the heavens of injustice because they would not tell him which of the two to do. If the artist be cold, it is because he shivers at the awful shapes that beckon in his vision to be introduced on earth. So only is Balzac, George Eliot, or George Sand cool. They are not like glass that lets through a sunbeam, or the plate that takes the impression of a photograph, or the telescope that reports a star. These revealers are consubstantial with the revelation they make. But they, the revealers, must not be swept away. How could they measure what they were mastered by? They must wrestle, like Jacob, until dawn, and not be thrown, though their "thigh be out of joint"! The poet Horace says we must weep first if we would make others weep. But we must not be dissolved, drowned in, or choked by our tears. If the preachers cry, and do not articulate, we have a baby at home who can do that! The dramatist may pity the victim as he conducts him to doom, but he cannot stop to have compassion on himself. He may

despise the villain he cannot afford to destroy. Said a
certain actor in a whisper to one that supported him in
the play, "I am *feeling* too much to perform my part."
To perform is always, and to give way or give up is
never, the business in hand, be our calling or profession
to set forth a scene, assist at a tragedy in real life, warn
or persuade, console or heal. The surgeon can have
only a surgical smile or tear. If the artist seem icy,
it is because he is disinterested; and his "frost," in
Milton's phrase, "performs the effect of fire." Ary
Scheffer sketches Dante's scene in the "Inferno," where
Dante and Virgil together look on the whirl of retribution in which, as in a rolling cloud, Francesca di Rimini
with her lover is involved. How calm and unmoved as
marble statues the poets appear, standing motionless
to see the judgment of God! Deep thought stills us,
as Michael Angelo's figure called the "Thinker" shows.
Equally quiet are we under intense feeling. Words-
worth had "thoughts too deep for tears."

The arts, like the old muses or furies, are sisters,
yet they cannot be transformed into each other. When
a lady requested Mendelssohn to put certain poetic
lines into a musical score, he refused, not because tones
are less definite, but, as he said, more so than words.
That all the arts, including nature, the divine and everlasting one, have a common root, is evident from the
fact that we speak of a *beautiful* picture, voice, speech,
manner, essay, scene, or expression, not doubting the
equal appropriateness of the term to all these things,
though they cannot be converted into each other like
electricity, magnetism, light, and heat.

The objection of piety to art only accuses piety, if

piety honor that Bible which tells of Hiram and Tubal
with their brass vessels and Paul at his tent-making,
which preaches the beauty of holiness, and is itself of
all our performance only the programme. The artisan,
more than the artist proper, wins both our reward and
our respect. The latter among us is poor to a proverb, in more than one sense, of reputation as well as
pocket. Painter or sculptor, what an unnecessary person he is, dealing at best in a luxury, not a necessity of
life! The maiden that makes a pretty face an excuse
for sloth and expensive dress of silks and rings is
called, with some irony, the ornament of the family;
and the supreme artist that embalms and immortalizes
what is best of nature and man, in color and form, canvas and stone, has in general society less standing and
acceptance than the great banker, railway-builder,
manufacturer, or engineer. As the Japanese put the
milkman above the merchant, so in this country the
name of the successful stock-speculator is blown farther
from the trumpet of fame than that of the picture-maker,
whom we patronize or dispense with as we please.
How few have heard of Stuart the portrait-painter,
compared with the millions that know about Stewart the
millionnaire! Washington Allston or Cornelius Vander-
bilt, — which in our cities and in our history passes for
the greater name? Against the common disparaging
judgment let me show the bearing of art on the character and welfare of the community.

It is, first, a consolation and joy in our eager, toiling,
bargain-driving, hurried, nerve-wearing, and insanity-
producing American life. What a pregnant sketch
of an influence to soothe and make glad we have

to this point in the Acts of the Apostles! A born cripple is laid daily at the " Gate of the Temple called Beautiful." As in reading we hurry on to the miracle of healing reported as done by Peter, we forget to ask why and for what purpose every morning the lame man was carried to that spot. For the same reason, was it not, that the unfortunate appeal to us in the market and at the corner of the street, because he would be there in the current and concourse of the population, particularly that throng among which would be the greatest number of such as might be inclined to charity. But what lame man, blind man, or beggar of any sort, would take his station, on a week-day or any day, on the granite or marble steps of a New York or Boston sanctuary? He would find nobody there stopping to help him or even to hear his tale. He would be quite out of the stream of passers-by. Why was he in it near Solomon's Porch at Jerusalem? Because the Jews frequented their house of praise, their place of prayer, and it was a meeting-house indeed; because they worshipped God with a joint homage which many so-called Christians, that despise and class them with heathens, regularly omit; because there was more love of beauty and fondness for art, the minister of beauty, among those Hebrews whom we turn the cold shoulder to and fancy we have left so far behind, than among us of the Yankee breed; because Judæa inherited a love and taste for what charms the eye and soothes the soul, and because, too, the spirit of Greece had got into Judæa; because they had time to pause and peacefully survey the glory of the edifice, as they were entering, and were not, in that better age

of Israel, bitten with this our American tarantula of
the greed of gain, which, like an evil humor, or skin
disease once contracted, itches and torments its victim
to his dying day, and leaves his safe or chest to the
beaks and claws of his heirs; because that one gate
called Beautiful, made of the Corinthian brass, which,
delicately wrought, had a price and dignity, the historian
tells us, superior to gold, drew the majority of the quiet
procession to the sacred shrine; and because, moreover, the poor man with his congenital defect found not
only a convenience and sustenance in the alms which
he solicited, but also a solace for his disability and pain,
as he whiled away the time in gazing at those pillars in
their proportions and polish so handsome and grateful
to the eye.

Have we no deeper than a bodily deficiency or malady, to be likewise supplied or assuaged by beauty of
art in that *pictorial* allurement, which is more effectual
than any arch or lintel or carved column to make us
forget our want or distress? When we see a man limping along the street with a crutch or wooden leg, we
pity him for his misfortune, we grudge the accident —
some fall or blow, coupling of the cars or bullet in the
wars — that maimed his living member or clove it swiftly
away. Is there in us no cause, from an undeveloped or
mutilated mind, for sorer lament, and calling for a
more benignant cure, from such a gracious influence as
divine beauty in art? If we pass over a noble scene,
natural or represented by the brush, and disparage the
exquisite portraiture as of no account; if we discourage
art-culture in the community as of no ethical or spiritual worth, — our mental constitution is lacking, if not

sick. What are the satisfactions and consolations of such as care not for that beauty in which God has wrapped the world, in order that his children might know his essence, and both admire and copy his work? Heavy and costly dinners, to eat and drink and smoke, to perfume and adorn the person, to drive and clothe and sail?

But not only or mainly to assuage trouble or substitute higher pleasure, not only as an opiate or antidote, not only as contemplative but also as creative, does art claim our regard. Thousands looked at " the Beautiful Gate of the Temple ; " but one designed and made it, and had in it the chief honor and benefit. Somehow we should all be artists after God, whose art is all we are and see. Something we should all design and make for others' advantage and delight and the unfolding of our own powers. The constructive and creative faculty is more or less in us all ; else why have we this hand ? Are its uses exhausted in putting on our clothes, carrying food to our mouth, grasping another hand, bearing arms in war-time, or being doubled up into a fist, — this wonderful hand, which from the world's foundation and crude substance makes its own tools, directs the most delicate instruments of science, and rules the heaviest machines? It signifies the inmost soul with a gesture, and it also sows and reaps, hoists the rope and holds the helm, receives the new-born babe and lays out the dead, and should not itself be cold and still before it has left for others' welfare some memorial in the world. The eye is a nobler sense than touch, but the eye is an idler without the executive hand.

But, one says, I cannot do any thing in the way of

art. I cannot paint, or model, or mould, or build, or contrive a chest of drawers, or even drive a nail. I have no hand to lend or give! Sometimes, from obstructed circulation, the hand or foot is, as we say, asleep while the rest of the body is wide awake. If we do not a stroke or stitch of work, our hand, in all that makes the virtue and glory of it, is asleep all the time. Many a hand is unused because the owner has got ahead and is forehanded, and can leave to his less prosperous fellows what he considers lower pursuits. But, as not a soul is born without this double-handed provision, industrial education is a just claimant that has its perfect triumph but postponed to a better age. Meantime, leaving aside manual accomplishment in all its low or lofty range, there is a want of meaning, an awkward, ugly deformity, a clumsy managing, or else a beautiful art, in every human hand. If our senses be exercised spiritually, we discern in every man or woman whether they have a hand of bounty and service, or one close and cruel and mean. Fair or unfair handling is the tale composed by all these fingers, and writ on every palm. To do is more than to know.

But what, in its peculiar, proud, and pictorial sense, is the use of art? What but a poor, half-successful attempt to *imitate* nature is it at best? Why care for this small fragment and petty mimicry of a landscape framed and hung on the wall, when we have the whole glorious and vast *original* out of doors? If we think it a mere copy or fac-simile or repetition of nature, we misunderstand art. The artist is a soul, an observing, sensitive, selecting intelligence, reproducing what charms him in another form, diverse from and substantially adding to the natural scene. Topography or photography is not art. With the same imagination and feeling we rejoice in both nature and art. But in a picture are always three elements, — nature, art, and the artist, or the way he is touched by what he sees. As much as a tent pitched, or as the old patriarch himself, adds to the wilderness, or a procession to the street, or a great gathering in every city, East or West, to the now peaceful march through the land of the hero of our civil war, so much genius, which is sensibility and effort combined, adds to the situation it descries, conceives, and portrays. It celebrates the theme it paints. It chooses from nature. It tells us what is admirable and lovely, in its admiration and love. It emphasizes and calls us to notice that which stirs its own adoration and delight. As the Fourth of July differs from another day, though the same earth be underfoot and the same heaven overhead, so does a canvas from the wide waste of things. Though purged of all egotism or individualism, there is a strong personality in every genuine production of the chisel or the brush. We peruse with interest the *lives* of great men. But we shall find the biography and autobiography of Michael Angelo, not in any words written concerning him, not even in his own, so much as in the awful and beautiful ceiling of the Sistine Chapel; in his figure of Moses and the " Creation of Adam ; " in the " Thinker," so called ; in his sublime portraitures of the " Separation of Light from Darkness," and of " Night and Day," that bring us face to face with the Creator of the world. No doubt will remain how he thought and felt and wrought. Is not that all there is of any man? Does the heaven on earth of the French

Corot's landscapes not let you into his heart? Is any question left of Millet's humanity, after you have seen what his pencil tells of French peasant life?

True art is not a trifling, superficial, and inconsiderable adjunct to the leisure of our life, — an entertainment for which we are to give a compliment, as we bow to a stranger and pass by. If roads and ships and telegraphs and tunnels through the hills are its grosser demonstrations, appreciated by all, the picture and statue are to what is immortal in us how much more precious and fine! If I must, for my instruction, learn dead languages and turn over the leaves of Gibbon and Hume, I shall not overlook art's tongues and narratives alive. By my fatigue, as I retire, I know I have been exercised and taught as much in the galleries as in the books. Our art is imperfect, as it has many a step forward to take, and to make the good and beautiful more largely its theme, leaving the evil or painful, as in dying or dead men or game, which is so ephemeral, proportionally out. But such a subject as that "Good Samaritan," on the Public Garden, with his ether for mortal anguish, and as that just-inaugurated "Emancipation Group," on the Square yonder, must not only affect but refine and exalt the common mind, as a sort of silent and incessant sermon and exhortation to mercy. I met an unshaved, coarsely dressed, and not very lately washed fellow-citizen, who had stopped to gaze with me at the Abraham Lincoln, in bronze, meeting with his downcast eye the upward glance of the unfettered slave. "I have no fault to find with that," he said; "and, sure as you are alive, it will do good." It had to him!

Art is the jubilee of nature; and an art-museum is

the place of permanent sessions where it is held, being itself a monumental, ever-increasing dividend of charity from many a merchant's cargo, tradesman's sales, professional man's salary, and scholar's fee, to set up a new gospel for the poor, two days every week, "without money and without price," and to open a bible of beauty, vying with that of truth, to call men from debasing pleasures of lazy hours to the indulgence of appetites that do not injure but exalt.

VI.

LOVE.

THE tragedy of life is that a feeling promising to be eternal should so quickly pass. The Spanish Lola Montes represents a gentleman, uneasy under the sting of a new affection, saying to himself as a consolation derived from former experience, "It will not last." The new German philosophy tells us, love is but the species wishing to continue and laying hold of the individuals as its instruments, cheating them with illusory expectations of happiness the flesh cannot yield ; while our American poet tells us that the fairy which the virgin maid seems to be is lost in the "gentle wife," that the man must surrender his beloved at her faintest surmise of joy in another person, and that the pain which has no balm is when love loses the companionship of thought which he calls "the muse." Science, going down meantime to the lowest unions of insect, bird, and beast, finds in offspring the lovers' bond, — how transient with the animal, but more lasting with man ! Into the midst of many fond hopes, defeated and broken vows, and mutual relations tolerated with ill-disguised disgust, the outward alliance checkmated with inward repulse, stalks the spectre of a sexual independence, or free love, maintained on principle and carried out in practice, to transform into assumed virtue what our fathers and our

Scriptures pronounce a vice. Let us ask how love once felt may be confirmed.

First, by service. We love what we labor for, though but a tree we plant or a wall we build. How dear the invalid for whom we care, the ailing partner or the crippled child! What we give binds us, not what we receive. How fast must be God's tie with all his creatures! When in the simple story we read that " having loved his own," Jesus " loved them unto the end," do we reflect out of what need to minister to their ignorance and to bear with their infirmities his interest arose? Had it lived on the returns, how soon it must have starved! Well does *helpmate* denote the closest link. Redoubled attention must come to the rescue when the first flush of transport fades and the youthful joy ebbs : and they will fix a better color and fill any void. Love exists for those between whom is no boundary. Such persons commune indeed, while the Lord's Supper is but the service of communion. The bliss comes of being delivered from loneliness or feeling lonesome in the world ; and as love consists in a blended existence, no solitude is possible while it endures, and it is literally true that death has no power to part. How perpetuate this fusion in which, like those rivers whose individuality is scarce traceable while their currents mix, husband and wife are one? By waiting on each other with that perpetual aid which taking each other by the arm and breaking bread together express. A woman for whom I spoke the marriage-vows after a year sought a divorce. " Did you love the man when you were first joined with him?" I asked. " Indeed, I did," was the reply. How but by gradually abated service, turning to neglect, were caresses at last exchanged for blows?

But beneath this handiwork of service lies justice, which we think due to the household as a unit and from without, heedless of its dearer import between the members, and which we reckon in dollars and cents while we overlook its deeper score of motives on the tables of the heart. No unfairness of an opponent strikes so hard, pierces so sore, and refuses so long to be healed as that of the one most familiar, whose head is on our breast. We can defend ourselves against a foe; but they whom inveterate fondness has made part of ourselves are too close for us either to ward or answer the stroke. I fear not the criticism of the newspaper, but that of the heart, and the censorship by my side of such as know me outweighs all other blame. Even good-humored banter, that questions the purity of our designs, - should be sparing from the lips we daily kiss. Equity is scant enough in the world, whose politics, business, and religion are but diverse modes of war; and perfect honor is so rare that we scarce need to have the disparagement pursue us to our fireside and board, like a billow that only diminishes its volume as it rolls to dash its serpentine folds in venomous fury on the shore; while no delight is more exquisite to young and old than to have our dispositions and aims rightly and generously esteemed. The ship, after offing, needs repairs in port. Would you still mutually love, rectify at home the beam, biassed by gusts on the open sea of life.

Trust is, moreover, needful, that this manna of love may keep; trust being justice raised to the highest power, and holding more of the heart than such faith as has intellectual propositions for its base. If justice appreciates what another has done or meant in the past, trust confides present and future to his hands and cannot conceive of his ever doing or intending ill. It sells him its whole estate and takes no security. Mortgage implies liability to die, and love trusts because it ignores death. There is such a thrill of pleasure, exceeding that which any fondness can impart, in our friend's rest and repose in our righteous purpose toward him ; and it so puts us on our honor, which is dearer than any *person* can be to the soul, that we cannot help thinking in his children's trust in him God himself must be blest. But just in the same proportion distrust is offence and woe. It is a spy ; and we alienate those whom we watch by our emissaries dogging their steps, opening their letters, or searching their drawers with our hands, or cross-questioning them as to whom they saw, what they said, or whither they went and came ! A jealous glance, a suspicious eye upon us, is the dagger whose thrust kills love. Peering observation is a fetter in the air, heavier than the iron chain for a slave ; and though *slave* be sometimes a lover's name, no man or woman is permanently inclined to barter liberty for the love which distrust kills. Affection may wish to live despite insult, and in a grand sense it may survive treachery ; but the peculiar tenderness of a personal intimacy cannot defend itself against and survive continual stabs of doubt, which is heart-murder and puts to actual death. A great deal of such slaying is not reckoned as a crime on any criminal code. When one expires we would always know the cause ; but the disease is often too obscure for any inquest to ascertain. O man or woman, tormentor with your daily envious questions and peevish pricks of the one you swore to cherish as your own flesh, this sensitive object

for which your tongue is a lash and your eye a sword,
this living target of your wrath and scorn, will draw the
last breath some time, and then you will have nothing to
expend your temper on, or brace yourself against when
you are nervous! Your hungry passions will lose their
habitual food. You will have — how often I have seen
it! — a great funeral; and the flowers laboriously
wrought by some hired florist, expert for obsequies,
will excite much admiring remark. But I, who know
something of your history, shall have my attention
drawn rather to the interwoven crosses and the broken
harp-strings than to the wreaths or crowns! In the
mournful hush, or while rises the solemn prayer, the
inward witness is plain with you, and in its silence it
says, As to the real malady in this case, the doctor in
his statement has made a mistake! It was deeper
than fever or cancer, consumption or paralytic stroke!
Your unkindness made the decease premature; your
sharp tongue was the needle that stitched every thread
in that shroud; your anger drove every nail in that
coffin; your exactions robbed that poor corse of half
its rightful years, and put a full moiety of the misery
into all the days of strength and motion with you it
had. With many of us it has not come to that yet.
Let us prevent such noiseless sentence, which is the
verdict of God! Be not undertakers in your own
houses for your own kith and kin. The sexton is
sometimes a sham, and does but the external and
ceremonial part. By those that seem to lament the
departure the burial is made! We do not think of
this when our envy to our fellows makes things hard
and rough. We file on their nerves, and it does not

11

enter our mind that we are going to file them utterly
away. Nevertheless are we all in each other's hands
to thrive or to pine, and as we bless or curse to
lengthen or shorten the mortal career. We think by
animadversions to correct our companions' faults. But
distrust never created an atom of virtue since the foundation of the world, while those we associate with tend
to the nobility which we manifest and expect, as planets
gravitate to the sun. The saddest sign in the shop-
door is that familiar placard, " No Trust." Over our
threshold be it never inscribed! It means no peace,
harmony, or continuing love.

But still, furthermore, love must be kept by that sincerity which dispenses with all necessity for inquisition, and
is the ground of trust. Sure as the sleuth-hound scents
the beast, its natural enemy, in the hole however hid,
so every human covert invites scrutiny, the stricter the
more the burrower is near by. But sincerity must not
be overstrained or misunderstood. It consists in my
freely communicating to you whatever facts, being my
property, are by our mutual relations made also yours ;
not in admitting into others' secrets in my possession
your intrusive probe. You must not define my sincerity
by your hankering curiosity. No two, owning each
other, are absolute owners. We are held in a responsibility of manifold ties. Not to ask or wish to know
what belongs to a third party who, should we divulge
it, would be betrayed, is truer in friendship than that
insisting to have every circumstance disclosed which is
as false as any other form of selfish hate. Interrogation is meanness, and the grandeur of character is
abstinence from inquiry. Forbearance to examine into

what your partner withholds is the measure of your
affectional worth. We must confess, truth is in our
community the missing link. Sympathy is a drug,
and may become a poison if given in an overdose.
Forgiveness we carry to excess, till the divine attribute
becomes a human vice. Capital crimes have sunk from
two hundred to two, — murder and treason ; and " we
give the traitor an office and pardon the murderer out."
Humanity, ever-growing, a modern virtue and not ancient even in name, is the crown and glory of our time ;
and the French Leroux, were he alive on earth, would
see that his solidarity has come. But verity is, even
for the shrine of compassion, a sacrifice too dear.
Were one child to starve to death within its borders,
the United States would be ashamed. But should we
dare to poll the nation for a majority on the question
whether to lie rather than tell what we think our interlocutor should not claim. What big liars in pulpit and
press and parlor and court! When your child tells a
lie, says one, confess to it you have told a hundred!
Certainly less on pity and commiseration than on candor should preaching now lay its stress. But when you
complain that your friend has not been frank with you,
reflect whether your indiscreet query have not forced his
closeness, as the clam and oyster, at the touch of your
stick, shut their valves. Generosity opens the shell,
and love is the mother of that truth which becomes
in turn her body-guard and defence.

In fine, love is maintained not by uxorious doting,
but by respect. Is the woman fond of expression and
demonstration, not forgiving coldness, as George Eliot
says, even when it is the mask of love? No token is

more precious to her than the respect which is the premise of her personality. She resents being treated as a tool or a thing. No soft humility can satisfy her with being absorbed by the man. Let neither obliterate nor cancel, but bestow each the other ever afresh! God's judgment-seat is in every breast, and we should be formidable to each other as well as dear, never taking for granted that our chosen and devoted *second* self will be sympathizer and sharer with us in any sin, but recognizing the added conscience to make of our several souls no support in evil but a compound battery against wrong, and to find in our mate the other wing for our spiritual ascent.

But in this list of conditions I must add that, after all, love is its own warrant, and is a self-preserver. When genuine, it scarce needs any foreign stay. Like some rich merchant, insuring his own ventures and taking out no policy for his ships, it is free from care, invents the aid, improvises and affords the solace and protection it needs. It keeps itself and keeps us with it, and predicts immortality while it blesses time; for in its height and purity it can have no idea of extinction in its object or in itself. If *it* died, God would! He is it.

Love supplies its own fuel, lights its own fire, and is self-feeding like the sun. Does that flaming ball need a return from the planet that it may burn and shine still? I am conscious of a sentiment alike independent of the objects by which it is occasioned, but not created or caused. So, as Shakspeare says, 't is " far from accident." It needs not even to be known to the person on whom it is fixed; and if, when tendered, it be not reciprocated, it will not be withdrawn. It has, once arising, a character of necessity to abide, not living on favor of any sort from woman or man ; for God is always left, though the human creature be ungrateful as a gulf or cold as stone. Wives are with some multiplied, and mistresses forsaken, and the youth or maiden once so gracious is, without a twinge, seen in another's arms ; but Dante's Beatrice or Michael Angelo's Vittoria Colonna, to all who know the secret and are worthy to be initiated to degrees conferred by no college or lodge, stands for a sentiment immortal as the soul which it thrills. Why, after long absence of many years, should a woman on her death-bed feel her heart glow for one with whom she has had, and can hope for, no terms in this or any world but of cordial respect? Because there are emotions, sensual souls and unbelievers in virtue are strangers to, which outlast all opinions and calculations, and justify Balzac's definition that love is " a transfer of the *me* into another, without whom we cannot live." Therefore the heart, which disease eats into, only widens its room for the dear image that shall be carried away from the consuming of its mortal chambers, as we save the pictures from a burning house. Let me, in passing, mention some particular traits.

First, love gives no account of itself. It acknowledges no higher court. It obeys the summons to no tribunal of reason or conscience, far less of social custom or human law, as above itself. Doubtless, it is reasonable and right. There are expressions in this world to which it may lay no claim. In the living web which we call society, it will tear no thread. It guards every real relation, for it weaves it, and unravels not its own work.

The soul of honor is its offspring, and naught dishonorable can it do.

Secondly, it is not a wish or an appetite. Were it not an absolute principle, it might be an infinite desire. But it craves nothing for itself. It is not recipiency, but communication. Self-love is the cistern, but *it* is the spring. It emanates, whatever else may absorb. Hence its longevity is in its original activity. What is in the passive voice may pass away, and that alone is eternal whose cause of motion is in itself. Therefore, it is not enough to be loved, even by God; our title is not perfect unless we love Him.

Thirdly, it consists not in, nor subsists upon, any expression, kiss, caress, or embrace. It depends not on giving or taking of signs. It is for ever conscious of inability to tell itself, or be told by those it possesses, as Deity cannot be expended or wholly manifest in any words or works. It chooses demonstrations which do not exhaust, but react and deepen. If it ebb in expression, it is like the ebbing of the sea for a speedy flood, only washing some other shore till the tide shall turn.

Fourthly, its peculiar delight is not in the pleasure, but in the self-forgetful life of its exercise. It is not the pride one may have in being dear to another, but the balm to wounds that bleed in every breast. Unless it heal, it cannot be whole. The sacred oil flowed down Aaron's beard to the hem of his garment; but no ointment for priest or king, and no alabaster-box for the Master's feet, ever bore the health and joy of its conscious trickling through the bosom, and, like some subtle element we pour to search into slight crevices, finding out every sore place in our heart. Did Jesus have sore

places in his heart, which even the woman, who was a
sinner, knew how to discover and soothe? Was he,
who came to save the lost, by a lost sinner saved from
pain himself? Surely so only can the situation be explained! What cared he for the precious paste or liquid
on his limbs? Was it a smooth feeling on his skin by
which he was moved? Did the woman's fingers touch
the tired feet with a relief no spikenard could bring?
And was the washing of her tears which, whatever her
fault, were holy water such as no cathedral-basin ever
held, a cleansing for him whom the church declares to
have had no share in Adam's fall? The woman's feeling was to him more than her weeping, or the costly
fragrance of her gift, or soft clasp of hands with which
it was bestowed. Is there any refreshment like that of
being loved? Is there any inn for the weary, wayfaring,
and footsore traveller like that it opens? That woman knew there was a famishing which even Simon's
board could not stay! Woman's love is more disinterested than man's. Is not her very sin a self-sacrifice?
Therefore the Christ's sentence on it was so mild! Man
is the aggressor. He solicits, and the woman yields.
Solomon, as an expert, renders his judgment that the
strange woman is a " deep ditch." He had often been in
it, but the deepest and the last ditch was himself! The
woman withholds nothing when she has given her heart.
Is she lost when she deliberates? Woe to the man, here
and beyond the grave, who forces the weaker vessel to
struggle with the more strong! Rather than that this
crime lie at my door, or have the groans of one deceived
sister disturb my slumbers, or her blood cleave to the
skirts of my garments, let any other transgression named

in the decalogue arise to stare me in the face at the judg-
ment-day! O tempter. of the helpless, whose self-denial
hides your blame, all the courtesy with which through
slow and constant pressure you mislead is but veneered
villany, the polish of the weapon with which you destroy.
Despising your seductive arts, I denounce you on earth
and summon you to answer at the final bar. Your voice
may be eloquent at the forum or in the sacred desk.
You may add perjury to lust, and meanness to both;
but the ring of false oaths will sink to a whisper when
the time for equivocation and forswearing has gone by.
I would not, as the Lord did not, excuse the feebler sex
from the iniquity they partake, but only plead that the
other party has in it the lion's share.

Love as a sentiment has no limits. It is more than
sleep for "hurt minds." Lazarus stays not in his
tomb when he hears its voice. It is the chief virtue
and great atonement for sin. "Her sins are forgiven,
for she loved much," is the boldest sentence in the Bible,
which we scarce dare read, and which it must have
taken the Pharisee's breath away to hear. Love is the
source of purity. What were air and water as puri-
fiers without fire! The sun cleanses as well as creates;
and if love contract a stain, it will yet *wash* like cloth
of gold.

Lastly, love has no designs on its object. It has no
designs at all. It exists for and in itself; and those it
possesses exist for it. It is its own end, and the beginning and end of the creation. Therefore we cannot
get round or beyond to master or measure it; but it
masters and measures us, and swears us to fidelity and
sanctity, passing all social engagements and altar-vows,

administering an oath to bless and never hurt what is
in its bond. As mayor of the city of God, it embodies
every statute against what is injurious or unjust. The
mountain-torrent is stronger a million-fold than man's
hand, yet how his touch guides it in channels of beauty
and use! Duty makes of love not an overwhelming
freshet, but a fertilizing stream. Very humble and familiar are the tasks which our affections set. Rarely
they call us to what is counted sublime; of ten thousand ragged bits, they make the fair temple and the easy ,
path. By no seer has heaven been revealed. By no
straining eye can it be discerned. They only will
reach it, who by self-denial make a stepping-stone of
the earth.

Love is truth! It has no licentious secrets, but a
lawful privacy, all intrusion on which is profane. As
the bird hides her nest amongst the leaves of the
thicket, not for deceit but to be true to her nature and
her offspring, and would be false to herself and to her
Author, if with foolish candor she exposed the delicate
beauty of her eggs to every prowling eye or careless
tread of the passing foot, so no frankness could impart
to vulgar curiosity the truth of responsive breasts. Of
all eavesdroppers and overhearers he is basest who
lurks, walks softly on tiptoe, and puts his eye and ear
to the key-hole to catch the gentle confession or surprise the ingenuous blush. There are scenes in which
kith and kin have no part to act, and from which churls
and tattlers should be whipped. But all privilege of
mutual converse apart has a solemnity which no gay
throng is overshadowed by. If it be perverted, a
heavier responsibility is attached. But there is a love

which avoids collisions and clears all obstacles, as a
bird threads, without touching, the boughs in the wood.
So interior and ideal is it, that not even by the wandering of the eye on its object can it be caught. It is
a simple sentiment, but not therefore less lasting or
strong. A sentiment or idea, in David Hume's, as
in all sceptical or materialistic philosophy, is but the
ghost and remnant of a sensation. But were sensations
in nature the real powers, which in thoughts only dwin-
dle and in feelings are diluted and reduced, then beasts
were mightier than men! Vulgar people have maintained that on sexual appetite rests the commonwealth.
On the attraction betwixt man and woman society is
based; but its refined is greater than its gross force,
and its weight is like the gravitation of the globe.
That is the most ardent and enduring love wherein is
no aim at pleasure or posterity, but which survives all
earthly contingencies and knows it can be out of the
body and in any other or heavenly form. The hen ruf-
fling for her chickens at the hawk, and the walrus
making herself a target for her young against the
hunter's spear, disprove the selfish theory, as much as
do men fighting for their homes, and mothers sacrificing themselves for their offspring every day. Whoever
loves would yield every drop of blood for the beloved,
and would not take in pay for the affection a single
tear. This fact, not any temple, tower, or snow-
capped hill, is the glory of the world. My friend, I
love you not for your favor or aught you can give for
my delectation, but for the very nature or quality that
you are! Nay, if you hate or despise me, I should
love you still, and you cannot repel the sentiment; for,

as Goethe says, " if I love you, what is that to you?"
Electricity travels by a sure iron path, over land or
under sea; but my heart knows a cable never broken,
a wire that is in order and always works! Away with
the notion that fondness is indispensable to nourish
regard! Feeling may be in inverse ratio to demonstration. How often, in this mystery of mutual communication, people are moved by what we suppress and
withhold! I love my country, but cannot embrace it
with my arms, although sometimes a returning king has
saluted, by lying down on its soil, or a poet, like Byron,
sent it the farewell of a song. Christians love their
Lord, though they cannot touch, and only in imagination embrace, his image. It is a lower greeting when
crucifix or picture is handled or kissed by some devotee.
It is no vanity for a worshipper to love his God, though
he cannot locate or metaphysically define him or prove
the personality he adores.

Is sensation the sun and is sentiment the pale moon
in the firmament of the soul? There are affections in-
expressible because intense! There are exercises and
emotions animal men know nothing of, to which their
coarser movement is a smoky and smouldering fire.
Love cannot, in its highest flight on earth, quite get rid
of the outward form. But it has learned that our
body is the temple of the Holy Ghost, and that " holiness becometh thy house, O Lord, for ever; " and it
worships God less in dedicated courts or the sanctuary
of the sky than in the human frame, which it exalts
and sublimes. In Michael Angelo's forms of saint,
sibyl, and seer we seem to behold all that human creatures can be or do or say. What need of the long his-

tory or drama on the stage? Thomas Couture calls the brush the best of pens.

Pure love is peace. If it long for its object, God comes and says: "Am I not enough? Art not content with me, in all this order and beauty without, and the witnessing spirit within?" But neither the divine nor the human can be loved as an abstraction. We must shape it as alive and conscious to our thought, as a harmony to the inward eye and ear. There is an external and an internal perception. Not those who accurately distinguish diverse shades, and are farthest from being color-blind, are certain to dress with most taste. A performer may know the musical chords to perfection, and not play with expression or be able to compose a piece. A rhetorician is not apt to be eloquent, and I knew a complete anatomist in marble who could carve no beautiful work. How profound is the discernment of beauty! It is so deep it knows all is well; and its transport is in no one fading shape, but in the universe. There is a restless sort of genius to which nothing is settled, and which would tear up the very platform on which it stands. But perceptive love adores God in the creation he has made, and thinks it the best he could do up to date; and it fixes on his creature for no half-hour of desperate joy, but with look of continual bliss and eternal hope. For love has no limits. There is naught it will not do or endure. All it is or has it gives. Nothing can it withhold. With itself every thing goes. It is Godhead in mortal dress; for what is God but infinite communication and perpetual gift? The lover's mistake and the tragedy of time is to take or covet the outward before the inward is won or bestows itself.

To illustrate what I cannot define, let me draw a portrait, real and ideal too. I see a young girl who exchanges with her lover glances and the clasp of hands, when suddenly, in my vision, he faints on the journey and vanishes away. The object is gone, but the sentiment remains. They who look on and pass by say she need not sacrifice to it her youth, the bloom and beauty of her days! Some other companionship will be as acceptable and become even more dear. The sweets of domestic life for her are still in store, and her children, to a long line, shall yet rise up and call their mother blessed. But not so; her wordless oath she keeps till death. She cherishes the image of the bridegroom unespoused. She reserves her wedding-garment till her arrival among those whom the Revelation pictures as clad all in white; and no household happiness, where the morning salutations of a faithful partnership never fail, and little ones run gayly about in their guileless sport, can know how rare is her visionary bliss. It is called romantic, a mirage of fancy, a mere memory and a dream. But when the gray-haired woman herself at last departs, does she not, a maiden still, find the long-lost mate? Yes, if God's promise holds, his creatures will keep tryst. This ecstasy of imagination and of ideal love proves that naught is so real and solid on earth as the gleam and glamour of hope. As the train I had taken passage in rolled on toward the city station, which was yet miles afar, a little boy pointed out of the window to the State House dome, and said to his father, "That shiny place is where I want to go!" It was but the glimmer of myriad sunbeams from the State House dome, as they shifted and danced, that was in his eye. Yet it was more substantial than all the architecture of the stony street that should so soon entrance his gaze. Our distant view is an annunciation of the heaven that can but continue its own ever-prospective bliss. The little girl gathered up the yellow straw from the floor of the car rattling on the highway, and smiled to mark its golden color, more intense as the open window poured in the bright rays. What gold will ever charm her so much? Cheap seem the elements of our daily life. But in the light of those affections that come from the heaven to which they reach back, what a transfiguration the coarsest circumstances take! We all, like Peter and James and John, have with Jesus gone up into the Mount.

Love finds its dignity in its depth. First, it is in our thought, next in the look, afterward in the voice, and last in the touch or hand; and a perfect contentment in absence attends the sentiment in its higher degrees. Its growing intensity dispenses with bodily presence, and makes it strike with electric speed through earth and time. It is what Jesus called the "coming like lightning of the Son of Man;" and it can find what it cares for in heaven as well. There are faces which we can see clearly without the aid of light! How they beam upon us through the spaces and the years, and light up midnight for us as we lie on our bed, though they mayhap vanished long ago away! If perchance any one near by frown or speak roughly, we cannot hear the harshness or see the scowl for the charm and melody unsuspected by revilers, whose voices fill the air. There is sound philosophy in the language by which *being put to the question* denoted instruments of torture in the Inquisition ; and a certain mode of interrogation signifies still the chief penalty and pain. But we want no explanations or apologies from those whom we hold dear, and by none are we held dear who insist on them from us. Kind treatment we would have for what is sore in our body or mind ; but, O friend, leave to a wholesome and healing neglect even the wounds you have yourself poured balm into and bound up ! Inquire not too much into your bosom-companion's griefs, nor compel him to tell all the tale of his life. Much and all will be told to those that do not ask ; and you shall have the secrets into which you do not pry.

What a wonder is wrought in such communication ! We want for food or stimulant no turning of water into wine or multiplied fishes and loaves of bread, nor care we to cast out any demons but those of jealousy and doubt. Then I know that the tenure of my being cannot slip, when I can perceive no difference between my feeling for another and another's feeling for me ; for the mighty cause of blessedness like this is not a power that leaves a miracle half done.

More than moral, even immortal, is our love. We promise it to the child that will do right. But true love has no such condition in God or man. " If you are naughty, I shall not love you," said the nurse. " I shall love you whether you are naughty or not," replied the little boy. Which had the divinity? I love a certain nature or being ; the love does not depend on the person's behavior. I will not threaten, for I could not succeed to withdraw it, were he or she evil to others or unfaithful to myself. His or her goodness and purity shall touch my heart to finer issues, but never dam the genial current up, because no morality is so deep as its spring. It seems indeed, when we love one, there never was a time when we did not know and feel the love. It is Plato's pre-existent soul. The maiden asks the man why he loves her, for she wonders and cannot tell; but he marvels no less, and cannot tell wherefore or how, or whence or whither, only that he loves. Either can affirm the positive *what* which neither can fathom; but, like one that gazes on some wrinkling bottomless tarn in the woods, only survey the surface of the solemn fact. Love is the vent toward the individual of the whole heart of mankind and of God. But how lover and beloved are transformed by their mutual sentiment, all can note. Verily, what it cannot make beautiful must be an awkward form and ugly face! How it moulds and tints the features, and is that power that prophesies in the Revelation, "Behold, I make all things new"! It is regeneration and religion, and the vastness of the feeling can never be quite given to or received by the human object, but escapes in thanks to the infinite receptacle and source. "I thank God for your kindness" is a Mohammedan phrase. Let woman judge of man by this test. If he does not worship the Giver in the gift, and enshrine that living boon in the sanctity of devotion and prayer; if, irreverently rushing, he invades her sphere, or by a word or sign desecrates the shrine before which he should tremble with awe even in his hope and joy, — then he is a pretender, who will possess only to desert and betray.

How marvellous the feeling, possession with which

makes one little face eclipse the sun and moon! The artist's nimbus of glory around any saintly countenance shall fade away; but the dear features we have once loved will hold their fast color. The cow and the sheep, that nibble and chew all day long in the field, shall lose their appetite and their pasture too; but the taste shall abide, of which disinterested affection is both the feeder and the food. There is a house in us which it inhabits, and both builds and keeps from all false fondness clear and clean. It is that prophet an apostle spoke of, to which the spirits are subject. For it heaven is not too large, nor eternity too long.

If any Cato of virtue, who never felt that flame which spires into the line of beauty, object to the height even above the moral sense which it attains, let the censor remember that God is love, and not conscience, which implies a sense of sin; and what monsters conscientious angels would be! But, though righteousness can never mount to love, love must descend in righteousness, which is the eternal law for God and angels and men. The question is but of cause and consequence, the fountain and the stream.

VII.

LIFE.

LIFE cannot proceed in society or the world without death. Birth and death are like two guide-boards at the crossings of country roads leading to the same city, and we read one direction on the cradle and the grave. The doctrine, so curiously traced and clearly expounded by Darwin, in regard to the structure of plants and animals, that there is a principle of selection and variation to transform species so that the fittest will survive, was anticipated in its spiritual meaning thousands of years ago. It is the commonplace of Christianity that a man must be born again, and that the willing loss is the saving of one's life. What is birth but death to a former state of the babe that shivers as it comes, winking at the candle or the sun, into a world to which the womb is a prison? Out of the world of the senses into that of thought and love and worship it will in due time be brought forth. What the earth is to it at first will then seem a narrower jail than ever can one's mother's breast. Life out of death is the law of nature which I would unfold.

Even in the mineral kingdom its commencement or prediction appears. Something in the primeval rock from immemorial time struggled up toward life. A rude beginning of organization is in granite and gneiss and mica and slate. The huge strata of the globe attempt and undertake to blossom. Their flowers are gems, — diamond and ruby, sapphire and emerald, amethyst and pearl. Why are these called precious stones, but that they express the ascent of matter towards man, on whose hand they shall sparkle and in whose diadem they shall shine? The diamond means truth, the ruby love, the pearl purity, the sapphire faith, and the amethyst hope. In cold and senseless things the Lord has begun to knit living ties of affection and honor, and to weave his creatures and children together. What is the jewel but the mineral dying to itself, — that is, to those first properties of size, coarseness, opacity, and a peculiar specific gravity that made it mineral, — and putting on the color, weight, density, temperature, and transparency into which out of the vast, almost formless layers it is born again, and becomes a gem and regeneration of the clod. A German philosopher, Zöllner, thinks that in crystallization there may be sensibility. It is at least affectation of life.

In the vegetable, but more marked, is this statute of death as the condition of life. The seed dies in the ground to live more gloriously above it. The bark dies on every plant and tree, that the life it protects and encloses may expand and flourish. Some species of trees continue this process of dying to live again and more abundantly as long as they stand in the dusky wood. The pine-tree drops year after year its decayed branches so as to keep its trunk straight and round and tapering, and lift its evergreen top more aloft into the skies, with what a musical murmuring in the wind for its voice, a song at once of triumph and a sigh over the grave!

These are outward figures and prophecies of the fact that in the animal and human kingdom, too, death is the condition of life. Even in the beast is illustration of the invariable rule. It is common, especially for theologians, to say the animal races make no progress. But of either races or individuals the saying is not true. Why should *an old fox* be the title we apply to a man as sly as is sometimes the governor of a State, if the old fox had not carried cunning a little farther than the young one? When a dog picked up the purse containing nearly a thousand dollars which a man had dropped, and trotted swiftly after to turn round ahead, and courteously present it to the owner, who afterwards rewarded him with a silver collar, was it not a cultivated and intelligent generosity which no puppy of a month could have displayed? The lower tribes are raised by converse with man. Lions and tigers, wild cats and leopards, die somewhat to their native ferocity. They moderate, and under a kindly keeper's hand, with some evident effort hush their roar or scream or growl.

But in humanity proper is the crowning demonstration of death as the condition of life. That verily is a barren and melancholy history for anybody which is not one long register of the decline and extinction of rudimental tastes and appetites, as childhood goes on to youth and manhood succeeds to both, and all leave so far behind infancy for dear life sucking at its mother's breast. How the boy that longed for a sled, a pony, a fishing-rod, and a gun as the joys and grandeurs of being, and could not do, he thought, without them, himself now a grave and gray-headed judge, preacher, manufacturer, or trader, looks back on them all as toys, by his fancy for which he is in recollection surprised and amused! O mother, with your children at your knee, what care you for the doll which is such a pleasure and pastime or serious concern to your little girl? Some of us men remember when we did not pass by the window of a candy-shop with a very rapid foot! I bear in mind a confectioner's store, where the stage stopped half-way on a journey to Boston fifty years ago, as so punctually the driver drew up his team at the inn hard by. The Italian who kept it, Dominic Peduzzi, must long since have had some heavenly recompense for his fair dealing in earthly sweets. How we smile now that we ever wanted to beat in the race or bear the college honors off! Channing was a famous wrestler. What at last would he throw but error and sin! How dead we all who have grown old have become to what were once the keenest delights and liveliest pursuits! We could no longer stay in our earliest dispositions than in our frocks and long clothes. Dead and buried, how much and how many, how far away and long ago! But not sad or deplorable is the burial or death. It is the condition of resurrection. Not a few of our notions, some of our political opinions and religious creeds, have died, not to leave a vacuum and void, but to make room for better views. In vain you tell me I do not preach precisely the tenets of forty years ago. Why should I? They have perished; I have interred them: some of my books and pamphlets are perhaps their tombs. No doubt the loving and inspiring sentiments by which they were animated survive; but the particular form and construction have passed like dis-

solving views, crumbling frames, and withering leaves.
When my Orthodox friend quoted the admonition of
John Robinson, the Pilgrim minister, to his Leyden flock,
that "more truth yet would break out of God's Holy
Word," I replied there would be also from God more
word, to which the rejoinder was, "Men in these days
can be illuminated, but not inspired," as if God were
dead, or dumb, or had abdicated like some earthly monarch, Bonaparte or Charles V., and was never going to
speak to his children on earth again, being in fact in
certain prophets and apostles embalmed, and in bound
volumes embargoed and locked up! But we do not
worship a great *Deaf-mute* or defunct Deity. We say
with Jesus, "He is not the God of the dead, but of the
living." We wait for his bidding, and hear his com-
forting voice.

Affections for persons as well as things sometimes
die, as die they must, if they are affections founded
upon selfish or superficial considerations. To the funeral of love no officiating minister is called. At its
grave no prayer is offered aloud. No sexton's spade
can be bespoken or employed on that inner ground
where the sepulture is made. Two spots in once mutually throbbing breasts are required for one affection to
be laid away to eternal rest. It is a ceremony private,
secret, unspeakably dreadful while it lasts. But how
can a carnal, shallow, and egotistic regard last, however
eager it may be and warm! It is death-struck in its
conception, and diseased in all its duration; not a true
birth, but an abortion of the soul. Do not cry your
eyes out, or bleed your heart to death, when one who
has sought you from interested and collateral aims, be it

man or woman, in fine like a traitor, deserts when his ambition or her vanity and conceit can no longer be served. Drop the acquaintance, when your power no longer is permitted to go along with your hearty good-will. Good-by, and God bless you, I say to such as by their own changed feeling and purpose in street or hall, church or house, make all the coolness and distance there is betwixt them and me. But this social death is condition and preparation for the heart's better life. The regard even for a truly beloved one that never faltered may indeed have a sort of death from which it rises and ascends to be glorified. Perhaps it was a face, a voice, a manner, a graceful carriage, even a fine ribbon or well-fitting robe, we in our greener judgment loved. How can an enduring affection be so produced? The chronology of it must be short. But if our sentiment penetrate to a quality in the dear one's nature, to a charm of temper, and to fineness of feeling which is ardor too, to a divinity of aspiration in which we find our poor fragment of God's image in another bosom complete, then our love shall outlive the stars. Perhaps out of the sepulchre of an at first indiscriminating propensity the holy and indefeasible passion rose. So wondrous are the transformations! There is, as our poet tells us, " the initial, the demonic, and the celestial love."

What a man shall take in exchange for his life, through which alone any thing can be enjoyed or felt, seems a question too absurd to be asked. Who would sell the least part of life, any bodily sense, member, or faculty, an eye, ear, hand, or foot, for a sum of money? A man of princely fortune, afflicted with gout in his feet, was inquired of what he would take for his splendid turnout of a carriage drawn by a beautiful span of horses, and his answer was, "The poorest pair of legs in State Street." I meet a man who is dim-eyed, hard of hearing, or limps as he walks. Would I accept his infirmity with his millions at the bank? Yet if by life we mean the vital power from this curiously connected spirit and flesh, how freely, every day, it is parted with and must be given for some object, grand or mean! The sun is reeling off our thread with his ceaseless motion, and the stars are the fatal sisters, which the Greeks personified, to spin and cut this mortal yarn. If ours be twenty or seventy turnings of the wheel, what shall we do with the existence which with all these earthly events they weave? Our poet pictures himself as gathering some cheap trifles or herbs out of all this fruit and treasure offered by the passing days, and as their troop retires, observing too late their scorn on his folly. What was our horror while the highest bidder had men and women in our land! But as the abolition of the lottery by law has not stopped gambling in business or in saloons, in upper-chambers and underground dens, so the auction-block for flesh and blood still stands despite the emancipation of slaves. It is not long since a young woman of great personal attractions and no fondness for low pleasure said to me she had thought of selling herself for a subsistence instead of depending on charitable aid. Not only houses and ships are sold in open market, and foreign bills payable at sight by the merchants, and wheat and cotton from the West and South, and oil, iron, silver, and gold from Lake Superior, Pennsylvania wells, and California mines; but votes are purchased

by all parties on principle and without a blush. News-
papers buy *views* not held by the writers by whom they
are expressed, just as legal arguments are bought from
arguers who know the unsoundness of what they say
in court. Is it more wrong for the witness to render
false testimony than for the lawyer to make what he
knows to be the worse appear the better reason in
his plea? There is a perjury of intellect as well as of
fact; and the counsellor is forsworn who would give to
any representation with judge or jury a weight it has
not in reason and his own mind, — a thing which it is
said neither Daniel Webster nor Abraham Lincoln could
do, everybody presently perceiving, by their faintness
and faltering, when those great advocates had no confidence in their own case. A conviction, any more than an
affection, cannot be sold, only a pretension to the faith
or love which does not exist; and hypocrisy so weakens
the hypocrite that in the end it never pays. It cannot
have, in private converse or public discourse, the power
that comes from real persuasion alone. Truly eloquent
falsehood or insincerity cannot be. Candor is the
thing to succeed! The late famous editor of the London Times, Mr. Delane, owed, it is said, his remarkable strength at his post largely to one of his rules,
which was never to employ any contributors to maintain positions in his columns which they did not
privately hold themselves. The Times was not consistent, as the *times* are not from which it took its
name. As English policy varied, so the paper would
veer. It was a paper kite; it was a weathercock.
It would say with Camille Desmoulins, "It is not
the vane that has shifted, but the wind!" Yet the

particular writer for this indicator and plaything of public opinion must have his whole heart and soul, nevertheless, in the particular piece he brought; and that is a matter of policy and thrift for the "Thunderer," as that British sheet is called, although it looks sometimes rather like the painted ball you amuse yourself to throw for your trained terrier to catch, than a bolt from the skies. But we cannot credit most persons or organs with being hearty and without inward scruple in what they loudly and unscrupulously say for the public. They have sold their tongues and pens to some political party, business affair, or religious sect. Our soul, however, we cannot sell; only its mask. Faust did not sell his soul to the devil, as Goethe writes, nor Galileo his to the Pope: for though the former made a bargain, the mighty remorseful soul in him could not carry it out; and though the latter recanted in words his discovery of the earth's revolution, he swore all the time under his breath, "Yet indeed it does move!" All that can be purchased of us is to play a part in which is no cordiality or truth. This is as near to perdition as we can come, and it is near enough! How ashamed we are, with a mortification the mercenary author does not seem to feel, at the regular leader in type of some daily sheet devoted to the rotten cause! "What is sold in the shambles eat, asking no questions for conscience' sake," didst thou say, O Paul, not reflecting how much would so be sold beside animal food? But if there are base things there are noble ones, too, in this great, many-colored booth of the globe, to be purchased with life. Nothing of a moral concern can be so small but existence has been

economically laid down for it on the counter like a note
of hand or bit of coin from the purse.   Long life is at a
rate too dear if secured with the least sacrifice of truth
or honor, be it the last subscription to a refuted creed,
or ancient pinch of incense the first Christians would
not throw on Jupiter's shrine.

But can we exchange life for release from pain?
Have we a right to procure deliverance from personal
distress of mind, body, or estate by ending our own
sublunary stay?   By no religion, philosophy, or verdict
of the world's conscience, has this inquiry ever been
solved.   Even its discussion must be prudent not to
hurt the public health.   Yet by the frequency of suicide how some consideration of it is irresistibly urged !
I would propose no dogma, but ask consideration and
compassion for those who are thus dead.   The self-
murderer's body was once flung out of city-walls to be
buried shamefully and obscurely at some crossing of
country-roads ; and by our horror of his act, every one
in imagination flings an additional stone at his ignominious cairn, if we cannot forget where he lies !·
But the motives, no less than the circumstances, of the
ghastly deed differ so widely that a uniform judgment
on those who deal the fatal blow is alike unjust and
absurd.   We may admire in one case what in another
we denounce.   When the Hebrew Saul and the Roman
Brutus, unable to survive defeat, fall on their own
swords ; when the Greek Zeno, at a great age, rather
than be a helpless cripple, lets the blood from his veins ;
when Judas the traitor hangs himself to " go to his
own place," neither history nor Scripture condemns, and
at other tribunals the judges will not agree.   When

the persecuted Elijah under the juniper-tree requests
the Lord to take away his life, and the sore-afflicted
Job, though he will not curse God, levels a malediction
on the day of his birth, and hunts about for his own
grave, their piety is brought under no final attaint.
When the violated Lucretia stabs herself, and with the
bloody knife in her hand summons and leads the state,
with all its munitions and arms, to expel the Tarquins,
she wins an honor of which by no Jesuitical casuistry
she can be robbed.   What reader of " Ivanhoe" would
not have had Scott's Rebecca leap from the battlements
of Front de Bœuf's castle, had the insolent and sensual
Templar drawn nearer by an inch ; or for whose tomb,
now, would the whitest marble of the quarry be so soon
sought as for whoever of our own kith and kin should
in like emergency take the same step, were it the forlorn and only escape?

Whether such a step would be justified on account
of physical anguish, nervous prostration, and utter despair, we may differ and doubt.   But we must inquire
how and by whose fault such a hopeless and dismal
condition has been produced.   For not seldom murder
instead of suicide were the fitter term !   As induced electricity is potent in its own way, so we are responsible
for whatever actions proceed from the state into which
we bring others' minds.   The stroke terminating earthly
existence, which we call voluntary in him by whom it is
dealt on himself, has been, in fact, how often delivered
like a bullet at long range from some other hand !
Were the tables of vital statistics amended, we should
know how many, who in all the wars of the world have
rushed into the path of the cannon-ball, were driven

forth by intolerable relations and from unhappy homes. Death is Misery's recruiting-sergeant; and Rip Van Winkle expelled from the threshold is a mere theatrical example of many banishments in real life. As cruel landholders evict impoverished tenants, many a lord and lady have exiled their mates heart-broken to find no refuge but the grave. Abandoned wretches, indeed, that have not secured that other retreat of an appeal to the One that knows and cares! Religion is reference to him; and it is a salvation on the earth, be there or not any ascension for us into the skies. Let us beware of forcing our companions nearer or faster than they must go to the edge of that precipice over which we must all disappear. Make not others weary of living, whatever you do with your own life. Let not our own be such a trial to them in theirs that, in a fancy which is not foreboding, they shall behold us defunct, and actually cast the horoscope of our own decease! Parents may use so harshly with their children the power they possess, and husbands may pinch their wives so closely in the means which they niggardly dole out, that in the demise of these misers and tyrants will be the only bounty and tolerance they so unintentionally bestow. If the man himself be less coveted, cared for, or thought of than his estate, and the chief rejoicing in him by inmates of his household is that they may be his providential survivors and heirs, then his being is no blessing, but such a ban that it would seem he, like Iscariot in the Master's sentence, had better never have been born.

Life is the largest of words in the elevations and profundities of meaning it spans. But in the common, carnal sense what is it worth? It is as cheap as any

counter of wood or bone with which we play a game.
Only by what we win with it are we really touched.
Christians find their example in Jesus the Christ; and
how early and prematurely, in strict consequence of his
own behavior, he was cut off ! On scarce more than
one of his thirty years is our interest fixed. How did
he contrive to crowd causes of influence so many and
mighty on his countrymen and mankind into a dozen
passing months? Wherefore the immortal pregnancy
in his few fleeting words, brief sufferings, and scattered
though gracious works? Answer to such points as we
may, on his own declaration, to his own will or to his
choice of his Father's, we must refer the shortness of
a career whose term might have been doubled on a plan
of conduct different from his actual design. For he
solemnly avers to his followers that he is the author of
his own death. He affirms that no man taketh his life
away from him, but he layeth it down of himself; and
moreover that he had power, or in a better translation
an express commission, from God to lay it down and
take it again. So he waves away the swords he had
ordered perhaps for his disciples' protection, certainly
not for his own defence. How did he finish his life by
his own act and decree? He used the passions of the
people, the outcries of the mob in Jerusalem, the fanaticism of the Pharisees, the imputed outrage from him
on Cæsar's authority, and the mockeries of Pilate, Peter's cowardly denial, and Judas's treacherous kiss, as
well as the official swords and staves in the garden
and at the cross, borne to Calvary on his own road-weary
back, for the weapons with which to pierce and drain
his own breast. "He died as the fool dieth," said an

officer of the law respecting the martyr Lovejoy, who fell in Alton, Illinois, thirty years ago, defending against the pro-slavery rioters his own printing-press. No unbeliever has ever ventured to characterize the crucifixion so! If that were foolish, what was ever wise? Unbelief has stood with a holy fear before that spectacle, at which it is said the heavens were veiled; and we tremble in every heart-string when we ask what this capitulator and destroyer of his own existence gained by his great surrender. We speak of men assailed by assassins or in the battle-field's dreadful fray as determining to sell their life dear. Did the crucifiers know how high they bid? Who shall calculate the spiritual dividend from that sublime abnegation by our Lord of mortal delight? It seems almost an extravagance of God that by the door of that single exit so much should be allowed to enter the world! Did that Son of his, as he · chose to date his own term here below, himself comprehend the results of new life and light and joy and hope? Did he understand that the real angels to visit and issue from his tomb were not to be the ones clad in shining garments, but worthier principles and purer affections in the world for all time to come? Of traders in their own life, selfish or disinterested, do we speak? Here was a merchant that transacted with death on a vast scale! He was verily on that exchange of which he made a figure for all men. All your bonds and per cents and funds are but zero to that! He was no cheated or incompetent dealer with the last enemy of us all. He died how willingly! He decided emphatically to die. But he permitted not death to get any advantage of him, not a jot. With that grisly phantom he insisted on fair and honest terms. To that foe, which we picture now with a scythe, again with a dart or hour-glass, and anon as a skeleton in a shadowy dance, he gave only his fading fleshly frame, over both which and its destroyer the undying soul in triumph arose.

In the gospel story he is reported as saying to his followers that he was a shepherd laying down his life for the sheep; and "greater love hath no man than this, that a man lay down his life for his friends." And Paul, his chief apostle and continuer of his work, adds that, though scarce for a righteous man would one die, and yet for a good man some would even dare to die, "God had commended his love to us in that, while we were yet sinners, Christ died for us." To give our life as God does the rising light for others, be they good or evil, just or unjust, is indeed the pitch beyond which no virtue or goodness can go. But to give it in labors, offerings, and privations every day is a consecration as real and lofty as though we were to drown in trying to save from the flood, or burn in effort to deliver from the suffocating fire and smoke, or face the devouring sword for our fellows, or mount the gallows, or lay our head on the block for any cause of freedom or truth.

"What will you take for it?" is the question every day. What will I take for my life? It is a cipher to which value is given only by the numeral that stands before. I will take knowledge, friendship, integrity, love. I will take a good conscience, be satisfied, and call it *quits*. I will starve rather than cheat, and die sooner than default and betray my bonds. If my life be wretched, I will not throw it up and away like an

empty sponge. But I will not sit on the bench, and
sentence those who do. Whether one's life should be
relinquished or another's ended for any such cause,
science and religion may some time pronounce. But
when a man has forfeited his life by a capital crime, or
is a monster unfit to live, let there be in future some
kinder quietus than the hangman's cord and noose or
headsman's axe. Let our life be devotion to duty,
which is transcendent and everlasting life.

But there are occasions that cheapen life, and in similar situations how diverse it is! Crowding to the table
on a canal-boat or ocean-steamer, elbowing each other
to get a nearer look at the ashes and smoking walls
after a conflagration, forming into procession in the
street to honor a benefactor or celebrate a great event,
rushing into battle for their homes or to conquer in
Afghanistan, thronging to the theatre, concert-room, or
church, human creatures are a species which it defies us
to classify or span. How often one may say of himself, What am I but a blowing wind or running stream,
able to decide not the native volume of my power, but
only something of the direction in which I shall blow or
run? Said the American youth, My life is ignominy if
I keep it back when union and liberty are at stake, and
the black flag of bondage is upreared and threatens
to flaunt its inhuman folds all over the land. Into
the sea of bloody atonement I empty my veins. Human nature is depraved, says the old creed. Nay, it is
more holy and sublime than the sun and the stars,
when wives and mothers, loving maidens and sisters
and young daughters, grudge not what in manhood is
manifold dear to them, but gird on it the armor, weave

the silken colors, put flowers into the muzzles of the guns, and bid God-speed away from their sight all that is precious to it on earth, when the fray is for freedom, and when the nation is brought to bay by those same bloodhounds that pursued the fugitive negro. But lo! in the lapse of years a generation is already on the stage that know nothing of the civil war. From their cradle, ere it was rocked, the cloud charged with such thunderbolts had rolled. Yet patriotic or religious duty has not changed. Why, O preacher, emphasize so the fact that Jesus gave his life? Was it more than he and we all ought? Is it not demoralizing rather than helpful to present the single case as such a rarity and miracle of goodness? When I love any one, what so easy as either on any sudden occasion or all the time to give my life? We love and honor the Master for doing what is but an example and encouragement quite natural and not prodigious. Are we saved by his merits as so many indulgences for past, though not, as the Rome which Luther resisted construed them, for future sins? He had no merits. He but returned what he had received. What he had under God derived from humanity he restored. As blossom or fruit on the bough renders back in fragrance and food the juices it has sucked from the soil, so alone did the Saviour of the world yield from the genealogical tree on which he grew. He was lifted by successive throes of this same old human heart to the mountain-top of the race; and the fertilizing streams therefrom, of which his soul was the spring, as they originated from, so they are the property of mankind, as much as the Jordan and the Amazon belong to the earth out of whose distilled ocean-waters their fountains were formed. However rich prophet, apostle, and redeemer may be, they are but as kings bound to spend on the people the treasury which the people have filled. No exchequer of virtue in the most highly gifted but is due to all the rest. We are just only when we feel that of any grace or talent with which we may shine not a farthing is our own.

But if humanity be our root, was not the divinity that of Christ? Divinity whence or where? In outward space and handiwork of earth and sky, in the laws of nature we imagine broken or behold fulfilled? Not so, but in that human soul which is more than all without. At the breast of divinity in humanity that wondrous child was nursed to become the same person, whether we call him Son of man or Son of God. Beyond all beside, he has indeed broken the general level of history with his Hebrew height. He is a mountain unmeasured, a tower not of Babel, whose top reaches heaven, and a life we have never been able yet to transcend. "He represents nobody but himself," said one of a vainglorious sage. But there are representative men. Many have been called Charles, there was but one Charlemagne. Some men take possession, like spirits, of their neighborhood, country, or kind. Napoleon's army was his arm. All the Buddhists grow out of one Buddh; Mohammed mohammedizes the East. New England was once Webster, and South Carolina was Calhoun. Every universal or local celebrity illustrates the law. But, on the same principle, what possession in the best of earth's population for some thousands of years Jesus Christ has taken of the human soul, so that they and he, as far as his influence goes, are one!

Is it ill to merge individualities so? I answer, Every noble mind will value most in itself not its peculiarity, but the quality it shares; for this sharing, as it makes wealth in the joint-stock corporation and the business firm, makes also society and the commonwealth. Our individual distinctions are no better than savage ornaments and war-paint. I can respect your proud social hedge to keep others out no more than I do Standing Bear's necklace of bears' claws. Our selfishness, our separation, our insulated and isolated condition, is our sin and woe. If the overleaping by Jesus of the bounds of his historic personality to occupy the world's consciousness so widely and long be mythical, then he is a myth. But the myth is more alive than ever his flesh was; and if we try to put him back into the strait-jacket of a thirty years' bodily form, and reduce him to the dimensions of his manger, his cross, and his tomb, our criticism is at fault. Jesus was the apparition of a year; but Christ cannot be dated or dispossessed. Christianity is not a dogma, but a life and growth. Not liberty of thought, but its misnomer and pale negation, is it to say that the Christian life in the current era is an antiquated phrase with an obsolete sense. For our religion is like the California mine that opens richer the more it is wrought. Valor is virtue, said the Roman people, and still says the Latin tongue. But the strength of the sword-arm in battle has its limit in quantity and an ever-stricter measure of worth. The new style of morals as well as of the calendar, which our Master brought, puts meekness and lowliness for pride

and wrath. We may talk of its going out of fashion
when it shall not only have been generally adopted as
a habit, but a better garb shall have been devised!
Meantime, while none are haughtier, more ambitious,
quicker to quarrel, and loosen their tongue into more
unmeasured terms of opprobrium on dissenters and
foes, than those by whom this old gospel is assailed,
we shall guess it is a retrograde and no forward movement which they propose. Jesus " made himself of no
reputation." Does his critic seek notice? Is he greedy
of praise and ready to bespeak eulogists of his own
work? Verily, he is beneath his subject, and disappointment will be his doom. For the trumpet of fame
is not an instrument that, like some orchestral band of
performers, can be hired! Men may procure some horn
of notoriety for their ambition to blow for a day; but,
as only a real honor can fill the ear or be music to the
heart of mankind, there must be a ground of the
world's respect for that Jewish teacher who expired,
yet by whom all his censors will be survived, and who
will be dethroned and displaced only and surely when
some wiser instructor and worthier soul shall undermine his humility, outcompass his humanity, and over-
top his prayer, beating all his dimensions of light and
grace. We learn from him that life is not a tale that is
told, as Solomon might say, or even a song of degrees,
as one or another of David's psalms is called, but an
element capable of endless refinement, and defying all
graduation of space and time.

We are not so many units. There is a human soul,
which is the source and sum of individual men. We are
not its creators, but derivatives. It is the only media-

tor between God and us.   Poets, prophets, and redeem-
ers are its blossoms ; and when we say it has had no
better flowering than in Christ, we mean no prodigy,
but the rare unfolding of a seed in us all.   If we speak
of our ideal, we do not intend that any flesh can hold
a perfect pattern of beauty, goodness, or truth, any
more than one building can be the shape of all architectural grandeur and grace.   The Greek beauty appeared
in the Parthenon, German worship reared the cathedral
at Cologne, and the traveller observes that the obliquity
of the Chinese edifice repeats that of the Chinese face.
Our character reproduces our thought ; but our thought
is harder to trace to its original springs than for past
ages of exploration has been the river Nile.   Surely
Christianity is one of its undried and unexhausted lakes
of supply, and Egypt back of Palestine, in the dawn of
history, is a main confluent stream.

Life cannot be defined, and only by figures described.   It is a boon, a trial, a tragedy, a battle, a
stream, the wind.   The man who, waking " with conscious awe," once more " rejoices to be ; " the sailor-boy
that " whistles to the morning-star ; " the bobolink that
flies and sings at once ; the bee that navigates its burly
form with a buzz, which seems a far-off echo of the
bull's murmuring in the field ; and the cock on the fence
greeting the universe and saying good-day to God, —
have a common life, which in the broken-legged horse
seems so worthless to him and his owner that he can
only be shot.   Yet the hopeless lunatic, beating the
bars of his cage, is in a worse condition ; and the committees for insane asylums question if for some of the
patients life is a blessing that ought to be prolonged.

But the reformer, who suggests the abbreviation of any misery by anodynes, though of a man caught in the couplings of the cars, and begging to be put out of pain, is like the scout of an army who discharges his piece and retreats, although he knows the whole army must come up at last. Napoleon cured a mania for suicide among his soldiers in their cold sentry-boxes by exposing the dead bodies; and a wholesome shame at this *disgrace* of death, as the Italians call it, should make us, even when forlorn, content and patient with life, as most of this eating and drinking mortal set verily are. We make too much of our afflictions and of all we call evil. If it be a bad world and a bad race, it is a bad God! In trouble we must help each other out, like comrades amid the snows of the mountain-wolds. Leaning over the gunwale of the ship, from whose seams the tropic sun boiled out the pitch, and by whose side through the blue water floated the brown moss of the middle latitudes, which is softer than lace, I might in my nervous despair have slipped, but for the affection that held me back. Paul said, in the struggles of his mind with his lot, that he died every day, as we do in sleep every night, and yet cannot tell what slumber is. Our surveying instruments, as it approaches, drop from our hands unawares, and we cannot take them up quickly enough to observe what it is to awake! The present writer has died four times, having been overlaid in infancy, drowned in youth, run over by a train of cars in manhood, and struck by lightning in age. But, for all this experience, he knows no better what it is to die.

Nor do we understand what time is. To Newton

among his problems, or Webster musing on the Marshfield shore, it is one thing, and quite another to President Washington when he reproves Hamilton for making him wait ten minutes. I should now be old as Methuselah, had every day been as long to me as that well-remembered one when the doctor, threescore years ago, wrapped his bandanna handkerchief around his forceps to extract my tooth; and I should be a sort of ephemeron had all my life passed as rapidly as have some of its pleasant hours, when the clock seemed striking all the time, so swift is joy!

While there is any position for us left we shall live. No thing can be spared, and no person. Should an atom crumble, the universe would fall into the hole! An effete moon or lost pleiad were a small ruin compared to an annihilated mind. Our vast hopes and plans savor of immortality. "I should like," said a child, "to be very rich." "What for?" asked the mother. "To pay the national debt," the little one replied. "I want to see this thing through," said Josiah Quincy, as our civil conflict roared around him in his old age. The triumph of justice and truth is in our instinctive faith; but how long must we live for that? Cœur de Lion, in the tournament at Ashby, or at the siege of Front de Bœuf's castle, we feel must prevail. Freedom knows that bondage, as they wrestle together, must be under and go down; and a man with a moral inspiration is persuaded he shall overcome his foe. Does the soul so measure itself with death? Yes, in its very dawn! When a king dies he lies in state. Egypt gave him a pyramid for his tomb. When a pope dies, art goes to sketch every detail of the situation

of the defunct vicar of God. When our martyr-president dies, his body, with a procession of forty million
mourners, is borne through the land. But God loves
a babe as well as he does any one of them ; and while we
pray to him over the cold clay, does he not pray to us,
entreating us to hope and trust? It is a bitter cup we
have to drink ; but only a *cup* can be bitter, and the
fountain is sweet. " Whom God deceives," says Goethe,
" is well deceived ;" but that life should not be an illusion
concerns the honor of God ! " My bereavement," said
a mother over her dead child, " must be right, else he
could not have withstood my prayers !" Will he raise
false expectations? " Do you believe men are immortal?" Abraham Lincoln was once asked. " All or none,"
he replied. It is not any peculiarity of our *selves*, which
when separate are always small, from which our title
can be derived, but the common property of our race.

VIII.

BUSINESS.

WHEN, apart or together, men spend strength of head or hand for some definite result, they work. If capital or credit be added, overplus of gain or accumulation contemplated, and permanence in one occupation maintained, they do business. If the element of risk, which is always involved, enter largely, the business is speculative. It becomes gambling if they make rash ventures, snatch at chance prizes, take unfair advantages, aim at sudden or premature success, and trust to luck. Business is so far a lottery in modern life as to make it our main concern to observe those business principles which reach wider than any nationality, form of government, or religion. The Exchange runs beyond any British drum-beat around the world. In every city what important characters are the banker and broker, to loan money, compare and dispose of property, and watch that thermometer of the stock-board, more restless than that of spirit or quicksilver in the glass tube! The rise and fall in worth of any regular species of possession is determined by causes so extended and subtle as to try the sagacity of the wisest mind. A foreseer of the fluctuation might make a million dollars every week. The kings of railways, mills, or foreign merchandise are limited monarchs, and liable to

be deposed. There are more business failures than political overthrows, defeats in court, or disappointments
in love. Daniel Webster, than whom no man better
understood the legal aspects of property, declared there
is no such science as political economy ; and an actuary
of one of our greatest institutions for the care of riches,
himself an eminent lawyer for fifty years, said he did
not pretend to any comprehension of finance. How
many otherwise intelligent men have been confused
by discussions of the silver-bill, resumption of specie-
payment, issue of greenbacks as legal-tender, till all
moral standards about money are thrown down, and we
are content to conclude that of a national debt only the
interest is secure in England, France, and the United
States. The private conscience is corrupted by public
repudiation, and by the example set by a nation of
a partly counterfeit coin, which the individual forger
only adulterates a few grains more. Pecuniary right or
wrong is made the accident of legislation, and a color is
given by government to every unrighteous theory and
extravagant scheme. As the hungry wayfarer plucks
another man's fruit rather than starve, a people in peril
will insist on owning and owing every thing, on being
debtor and creditor in one, and forcing all the riches of
the community to rotate to one spot at its own will,
rather than give up the ghost! But the medicine of
the constitution becomes poison when used as its daily
bread ; and if we have warped our rules in battle, let
us straighten them in peace.

For business has no peculiarity properly exempting
it from ethical rules applicable to domestic, civil, or ecclesiastical affairs. It is alike amenable to the law of

truth, never in its favor to be repealed. The ship-owner
who told the insurer not to make out the bespoken policy
because his vessel had been heard from, he having
learned she was lost and knowing the policy would be
pressed upon him, as it immediately was, sacrificed his
veracity to his case. The importer, eager to sell dam-
aged copperas to his customer who hoped the dealer
had not heard of a rise in the article abroad, bit the
neighbor who was trying to bite him, and both played
each other false. The dealer who hides defects and
heightens the virtues in his goods, and goes then to
church to glorify the truth in a doxology or collect of
prayer, worships mammon and makes an idol of God.
If I chant or cheapen wares of my own or another's,
what odds does it make whether they be roads and
blocks of building or sour fruit on an apple-stand?
What signifies the size of your operation when an unfair purpose renders it small just in proportion as it is
large? You may handle Erie or Hudson or Pennsylvania Central or New York and Hartford; but if you
do it in disguise, let me stand in the shoes of the poor
woman who puts the biggest oranges on top, or turns
the rotten peach inside, or is tempted to count eleven
for twelve, rather than in the seven-leagued boots you
play the highwayman and freebooter in, as you travel,
and hurry to ruin others, and damn yourself! A man
is a swindler who offers a mortgage on real estate that
does not exist. What shall we say of the atrocity of
selling bonds to pay for building the railway which is
made the basis, when it is but begun and runs to com-
pletion only in the scheming brain, while the stacks of
linen paper in handsome print are shuffled and dealt like

packs of cards, and held under lock and key in trunks
and safety-vaults, as if any robber would touch them,
knowing what they are and that no hand will ever be
tired cutting off with scissors their promising coupons?
Treasurers and bank-presidents, who confound in their
transactions their official capacity with their personal
wants, and trade on the funds in their hands or use the
credit of the corporation to prevent or break their fall,
do in their guilty selves accuse of a dishonored and degraded condition the community in which they can hold
up their heads. We have come to that state in which
it is held by some judges a cruelty and an outrage when
a thief is imprisoned or a defalcator pursued; but not
from the emptied pockets do the loud apologies and
sentimental pleas for swindling proceed! In the first
and least departure from candor all enormity of evil
has its germ. He who says business is business and
religion is religion, to advocate their divorce, really
says business is fraud, just as one says all is fair in politics; and he who says there is no friendship in trade
makes trade a worse hell than Calvin ever consigned
heretics to, and blasphemes God's decree that all true
trade is friendship, and no bargain should be made in
which both parties are not better off. If in certain circumstances, as is alleged, a man must cheat or starve,
then let us have the starvation; for one instance of integrity so sublime would outweigh the effect of millions
in the Indian famine. Starvers, as once were beggars,
would become an order in the church, their martyrdom
grander than that of the stake or the cross. There is
plenty of amiability; but our heart-strings are limp, re-
laxed from rectitude. They need to be wound up by

conscience, and toned and tuned to humane conduct.
We do not want any confessors of the old stamp or new
professors of poverty, but saints on 'Change and suf-
ferers for convictions that are better than any creed.
When an English Lord forsook the liberal party and
called their notions cant, Earl Russell answered, "There
is no cant so bad as the re-cant of patriotism." It is
a poor dress of righteousness that will not stand any
moral climate, but has to be put off and laid aside to
suit custom and fashion in particular latitudes. It is
not the wedding-garment, opening heaven to the guest.

Yet who expects absolute verity on both sides in a
bargain? Of the cunning that gave them the advantage how many will boast! They got that furniture or
picture from the distressed owner or ignorant dealer for
such a pitiful price, concealing their knowledge and joy
under cold indifference, and a mask of unwinking eyes,
and pretending their purchase was naught: mean and
forsworn hypocrites that they are, instead of the noble masters of knowledge for which they would pass!
"Let him find out for himself; 'tis not my business to
tell him the age of my horse, texture of my stuff, lien
on my land, or goodness of my note of hand!" So by
successive touches the sharper, who is own cousin to
the trickster, whets his tool. "What do you pretend
to ask?" is thought a respectful question, as if you had
a price you expected to come down from, and there
were a false bottom in every contract, when God fixes
the principle of barter in the fact that something each
has is worth more to the other, and the only equity is
to find out how much. Hucksters' Row, to which I was
sent as a boy, in the town where I lived, to fetch pur-

chases home, is a long street and runs through all the cities of the world! Not only mendacity, but waste of talent and time is in all the subterfuges and demands of this bantering and chaffering style; and the great Judge will call us to account for the loss of life and faculty in this deceitful crying up and crying down, which puts a useless or devilish diligence for productive industry, and in the competitions of the great auction which business becomes, stirs so much ill-blood, and substitutes for strife with guns and fists but a new war of words.

Religion is the recognition in every negotiation of the third party, the unseen witness and silent member in the firm, that makes his record and prepares his award of destiny after the measures of earthly right and wrong. Said an old lawyer, "I never knew one sharp who was not apt to be unfair; taking the advantage in that border-land of felony, where the legal is not seldom the immoral way." But merchant-princes, like Job, become rich not by trickery, but by large views, original plans, and humane desires to unite in mutual benefit the ends of the earth, while commonly but a small success is got by shoving and keeping others out, like that of the California photographer who, having taken an impression of a cataract, cut down the splendid trees beside it which were part of the picture he would monopolize for his own sale. He alone can greatly prosper who makes others thrive with him, not as a destroyer but creator of natural wealth by human art, opening treasure from the bowels of the earth and turning the rivers into laborers without fatigue, the Penobscot as a sawyer, the Merrimack as a weaver, the

Nashua as a knitter, and Niagara as a spinner that could move all the wheels in the world as a water-power. " *That* is not business," said a generous trader, when he saw one running to and fro betwixt rival aspirants for a bit of real estate, and spurring them to bid and bet while he refused to fix any price. Business is or may be not only true, just, and humane, but poetic, imagination being the eye to see values of certain kinds. Let me relate a case that has occurred a hundred times. A man bought a promontory of rock jutting into the sea, and cut in two by a valley of barren blowing sand. All the neighbors declared he would come out of his purchase only with a broken skin, and the experts from State Street keenest in affairs commiserated his mistake, and feared he would never be whole. But while five hundred millions of railway bonds were stopping payment in the land, the sea-washed crags stood, and drew those who loved Nature for something more than the grass and potatoes she could bring forth, even for the eternal magnificence of her ideal charms. There is a market for beauty, and sublimity has its worth and can be quoted, while beyond all price, though so many an acute operator despise the article and cannot for his life tell what it means. But the old billows roll on their sounding way, and the shores abide, and the planted woods grow, as one balloon after another of speculation bursts and throws the aeronaut limping to the ground, while the buyer of brambles and stones ceases to be considered as a fool, is credited with having a long head though with no skill, but a simple love of scenery; and the character of fancy property shifts from his beaches and rocks to the factories and iron roads. Even a man's theology may rise with his house-lots. What in his thoughts had been branded as moonshine may become sober reality, as Shakspeare tells us the moonlight sleeps upon a bank, and the useful planet we so profanely use as a type of hollowness lays her steady lustre on the solid ground. Heresy is condoned by business sagacity.

Business is religion in this, that its enterprises, to stand and last, must with a prudent judgment conform to all the laws of the mind and the world. Whence the crash of ruin and the long prostration from which it takes so many years to get up? Violated conditions of progress and of permanent possession show the cause. With over-sanguine hope the present borrows of the future and then has to wait, unable to pay the debt. In enforced inactivity it lies long in jail! Anticipating freight and passengers that do not exist and will not for a score of years be raised and born, our stations rot and our rails rust in the rain. Manufactured cloths, which nobody is begotten to wear, lie piled up on the shelf till the hum of the spindles is checked by their weight. The responsibility is not on the waste of war alone, nor on wrong legislation, nor on the hard times with whose name we cover our sins, but on avaricious property, on the love of money transgressing the law of real increase, and ending in bubbles of nominal value that like whirlwinds or waterspouts break in ruin. Capital, depraved by greed, like Æsop's dog, grasps at the shadow and drops the substance in the stream, while signs of value fall below their mark as representing power to purchase actual good, like half-emptied

14

.

vessels, or ponds that dry up in the summer heat; and labor looks on jealous of the wit that, like a black art, multiplies the signs in the hands of their possessors, labor's dollar being still heavy and hard to lift, till strikes like thunderbolts assail the showy fabric of prosperity, and the spectre of communism throws petroleum in Paris and in Pittsburg blocks the trains. Nor is the organ of destructiveness in the human brain stirred by any intent of capital to oppress labor, so much as by the rupture of sympathy and separation of the capitalist and laborer into separate classes, so that, under all our fine republican and democratic names, society is cut in twain, and the community ceases to exist. The employer knows not how his servant lives, or what he thinks; Christianity becomes a form in the cathedral, and for human fellowship we have ministries for the poor.

Universal suffrage, unless enlightened, fails to cure the disease. No man is born free; and no two, though twin, are equal or alike. What a trail of heritage and bond of necessity are peculiar to every child! "Glittering generalities" be they, or "blazing ubiquities," that we launched as lightnings at political tyranny a century ago, with a just claim that all should stand equal before the law, yet the whole truth of nature cannot be contained in French maxims or a Jeffersonian phrase. By divine decree one man will occupy more room than another with his body or soul. The kings that know and *can*, and the nobles best to rule, are not titular, with thrones for seats and crowns for hats, any more than the queen-bee is such in a hive or the bellwether of the flock. He that has the eloquence sways the audience, and he that is born to command, Cortes

or Cromwell, leads the troop. In the senate of gods
is Jupiter, and Webster in that of men. We must
have leading, if there be any ducal power, to attend on
the ballot; and the millennium will not come simply
because women vote, as they ought, like men. Is the
clown injured and downtrod because the inventor has
his patent and the author his copyright? Does not the
honor of genius and stimulus to discovery bless both
low and high? O friend, insisting thou art good as
anybody, blazon thy duties and reserve thy rights if
thou wilt not be bad! Jesus and Judas merit not the
same weight in Church or State. The insurgent motto
is not true, that he is born well who is born at all; for,
says the Master, the betrayer had better not have been
born. Until we learn how much we have to do with
right or wrong birth, and that God no more makes a
human creature than a plant outright, using the dust as
his dough, this dreadful span of beauty with deformity
for the world's team will last, and degenerate offspring
through the whole race of idiots ranging into monsters will come unwelcome on the earth. Apply the
doctrine of evolution handsomely as you will to the
beast, horse, cow, dog, and hen for a better breed, yet it
will not signify to save us from our self-created hells of
jails and asylums for the ingrained wicked and insane.
I believe in God, but that he puts men into their own and
each other's hands. After all our clamor for independence, with its·echo of guns and crackers to split our
ears on the Fourth of July, how would it do to adopt the
engraving on the old German shield, and *serve* a little, instead of being so free? For what but to be forty
millions of servants have we liberated four millions of

slaves? All men are born to further one another and
to deny themselves for that grander self of a living
truth and love which they should worship, and in
which they are one.

This is business, the only sort in which we should be
engaged; and this alone is the joy which no fine fortune or fair site in nature can confer, though all the
waves clap their hands to you, and the trees wave their
branches and rustle their leaves. If you have no poise
or projection of power, time shall be the old man of the
mountain on your neck. I will not go to heaven unless
there be some errands for me there! Let whoso under-
takes in this land to abolish mountain and vale in favor
of the level and the swamp beware! Voters are led;
and it is well that among so-called independent characters nine out of ten lack-wits should be in leading-
strings. Find my conductor, and I will follow. Apollo,
not Marsyas, shall teach me poetry and song; Milton
shall dictate my politics, not Salmasius or Charles I.;
and the wise man or the village-Washington for any
measure of improvement shall put a town-meeting to
shame. In that same primary assembly, which is our
boast, our tyranny lies. The highway-robber long ago
dropped visor and holster; but what a smooth citizen or
blustering demagogue, in this ever-shifting masquerade
which we call life, he has become! We are committed to
the ballot in every hand, like a fleet to the gale. But as
many a cannon's weight is rolled across the deck of the
careening frigate to the other side, so our ship of State
must be kept from foundering through our counterbalance of indiscriminate civil privilege by conservative tons of knowledge, religious principle, culture in

art, and mutual respect. "You should have been born in St. Petersburg a half-century ago," it was said to one who doubted the genius of the populace for finance. But we are not driven to choose betwixt despots and the rabble rout. If it is the intelligence, not the ignorance we represent, wisdom will be at the helm; and business is one half of legislation and of the judicial court. Let us follow the light of reason more than of the ecclesiastical indoctrination which scatters that light into party-colors, even as the stained windows of the temple, with the blue, red, and green they so impiously strain the sun into, render it impossible for dim eyes to read the Prayer-book or the Bible, turn the stone shrine into a sepulchre, and make corpses of the men and women, all from shutting out the natural day. A holy worshipper in his own house said, "When the sun reaches the spire yonder across the street, it throws a shadow into my room!" Was darkness on the inside of a building intended as the final issue when the first altar was reared? Better go back to the time of outward offering, to Abel's sacrifice or Cain's on the broad earth and under the open sky, than paint the glass of the sanctuary, or for spiritualist revelations lower the gas and shut the blinds. Ghosts in the churchyard may love the twilight, but so does not God. To him is no darkness; and Adam fled into the thicket when he would not feel his presence or own his voice because he had disobeyed his word.

But business is religious, because religion is justice betwixt men as well as prayer to God; and justice beyond arithmetical calculation includes a sympathetic imagination in either party to a contract, to take the other's point of view, and so obey that Golden Rule which in our Gold Room we daily break, till the fine gold loses its value, and becomes dim. Every metal whose handling is immoral becomes worthless in itself. There can be no equity of procedure or of intent till the dealer look out of the customer's eyes as well as his own; and no worship at Mount Gerizim or at Jerusalem is loftier than such a look. Was it higher in Jesus to kneel the whole night than to gaze at himself out of his crucifiers' eyes, so as to understand their ignorance, and pray for pardon to their sin? It is a large view when we can behold ourselves as we are beheld in our doings by all whom we meet; and poverty, which is intrinsically no better than riches, is not the necessary result of that survey. Extent of vision is a main condition commonly of being rich; and by selfish stickling for little advantages over our neighbor, how small our horizon becomes! There were rich men for James the Apostle to rail at. But the opulent are not always sinners, nor the destitute always saints. Love enlarges power, and we are debilitated and impoverished by hate. But how meagre does absorption in gain, albeit immense, make the man! When we see him, a silver bar seems to run for a stricture across his forehead and to press on his eyes, whose lids contract to let out only that twinkle of light which suits his sordid aim. When, in his sickness, incompetency, or age, the tide of affairs ebbs away, how helpless and wretched he is left! What miserable millionnaires, not knowing what to do with themselves, we have seen! I remember one, with his jaundiced face and thin gray hair at fourscore braided over his head, who complained, when he could

no longer do business, that life had lost its savor and
become stale.   He was a brief appendix to his vast
accumulation.   He had cultivated no love for nature or
art, he cared not for society, and there was in him no
relish for books.   Communion with matter had driven
spirit out.   Yet mammon became a " dull god " to worship when the pile no longer grew.   His mind, instead
of being full like his purse, by dint of long pumping
out of that vital air, which devotion or any generous
affection is, could only suggest the exhausted receiver,
which we cannot contemplate in the curious experiment
without a sort of pain.   Mental and moral vacuum, a
soul like the old chaotic earth without form and void,
what an upshot of a life, and what an account-book, if
there be any last assizes, to carry to the bar !

Business denotes our activity in every form.   Every
mechanical, professional, official, or literary person is
busy, — artist and engineer, ruler and subject, alike.
What is money but *means*, sustenance in peace or sin-
ews of war, the corner-stone without which the pillars
of the commonwealth tremble and there is nothing to
uphold, and synagogue and synod must come to the
ground?   Wealth, like fire, is a good servant, but a bad
master ; and it takes a hero to collar and force it to
its use.   It is written of Morton, the great Indiana
war-governor, that before he was a United States Senator, when a hostile legislature adjourned without ap-
propriating money with which to carry on the State
government, he borrowed two millions of dollars on his
personal assurance, kept the civil machinery in motion,
and paid promptly the interest of the debt ; and when
the thunder-clouds from North and South met, he sent

two hundred thousand soldiers into the field. Money as the guard of law, the maul against secession, and sword of execution on slavery, as well as new under-pinning and prop of liberty, is no root of evil when for such ends it is loved and used. The draft on its treas-ury which such a patriot and philanthropist makes shall be honored at a bank that never breaks. No spectacle is more noble than when a State for righteousness fol-lows a man, as Indiana did Morton, and Massachusetts did Andrew, and California did King. Then the soul sits sceptred, and we learn the meaning of the text, that "the meek shall inherit the earth," which is but a causeway to heaven.

For business, in the sense of what one can be in or out of, is incidental. It is irreligious if made the end or even the means of wealth instead of the test of worth, and but one in our chest of character-building tools. The play is for the soul; and all the outward plans and exchangeable results are but like the figures on the board betwixt the youth and Satan, in the allegorical game of chess. Saith the Spirit, no man has his price, and no woman can be bought or sold. No virtue is in pawn. We sometimes see a face in whose expression is disdain of fortune, like an eagle's scorn of the ground, and which no bribe would dare approach. It is not culture, but nature. When the poor sailor was offered a reward for saving a man from drowning at the risk of his own life, what moved him to say that a Marblehead boy will not do such a thing for money, but the feeling that any pay, though it were paradise, taints the nobility of our deed? Between the venal and the unpurchasable runs the line and yawns the unpassable gulf. No assumption and make the selfish and self-sacrificing to be peers without overthrowing the judgment-seat. The doctrine of animal descent includes, among many lessons, this, that one man no more than one beast matches another, and that human neighbors or fellow-creatures and fellow-citizens may be no more alike than a sloth is to a beaver, a caterpillar to a silk-worm, or a potato-bug to a bee. Jesus classifies, and predicts classification for ever, into goats and sheep, vipers and doves. The human form or animal life can, no more than the vegetable, identify the individuals by whom it is worn, or prove them more than plants to be excellent alike. The deadly nightshade, apple-peru, or poisonous ivy is not as good and fair as the lily, balm of Gilead, and rose. We may all have equal right, but not right to equal room. The career is open to talent, said Napoleon, and the chief talent is virtue. Business is its principal sphere, in which, however, all iniquity watches its chance.

To have some business in the world, and to mind one's own, is our dignity and only reason for being. With what grace that Englishwoman who recited Shakspeare in our ears, being called out at the end of her readings, said, "I cannot make a speech, it is not in my book." To find and follow where the finger of nature points is the sum of education; and into what more than orchestral harmony, under that conductor, all earthly occupations would come! Nature is the grace of God in the world and the soul, and naught is unnatural but folly and sin.

But affairs are still what a turbulent sea! One man holds the key to release his brother's estate; and,

though it has cost him but little, he will sell it how
dear! Another man no treasure can tempt to a cruel
use of strength, or to alter one word he has said.
"You lose five hundred dollars by your dainty and
delicate notions of propriety," one was told. "I should
have lost more than that by being less honorable to my
rival," he replied. To save bodily life, men on a wreck
have offered all they possessed ; and to save themselves,
men have left wife or child to perish as they swam from
the sinking ship. What means our contempt for such
abandonment of others and preservation of self, but
consciousness of a principle which no flood can drown,
which, out of every deserted corse going as lead to the
bottom or afloat helpless on the wave, will get safe to
shore, and call the recreant to account! Immortality
is a moral necessity. Eternity is not too long for illustration of the truth that our business in time is self-
denial for each other's sake.

The fact that our business sins are so in excess of all
other transgressions shows that acquisitiveness is the
propensity most overstrained. Everybody speculates.
Men on fixed salaries, clerks in banks and mills, are
tempted by the ventures into which their employers
plunge, to use for their own ventures their employers'
means. These little figures in the columns can so
easily be counted up wrong, and these notes and papers
that represent value are so light and readily shifted,
and houses and lands, ships and goods, factories and
roads, in this printed form, can be so quickly put in
one's pocket and carried so far away, and the time
may be so long before the exchange or misreckoning is
found out, that by facile opportunity all but the abso-

lutely upright are seduced to take a hand in the vast
stake played for on the table of chance, as if gambling
were not outlawed, so that protection of property is the
unsolved question of the day. Who shall guard its
guards? An immense evil in all worldly values, under
the spur of this eager pursuit, is their uncertain rate.
It would seem that a quite honest dollar cannot be
found; and those who tamper with the currency, and
would make its volume like any book with as many
pages as are wanted from the printing-press, plead the
fluctuation of gold; metal or parchment, greenback or
consol, is but a representative whose reality does not
exist! Pyrrhonism has left the schools and gone upon
'Change. Hence the melancholy waste of faculty on
the universal and insoluble problem of the worth of
things. Every species of stock rises and sinks. There
is no bottom and no top. The bulls push and the
bears pull! What an amount of strength, that might
be employed in production, is wasted in calculation of
sums that have continually to be done over again, and
never come out altogether right! Arithmetical accounts, books of double entry and geometric surveys,
before such exhausting tasks, are vain to help; and
what thousands are demoralized in this laborious idle-
ness, and turned into busy drones! No wonder that
many, grinding thus like millstones without a grist,
become crazed, and some Napoleon of commerce, for
whom his millions have proved too much, from the long
puzzle of the market goes with a turned head to count
imaginary money in a mad-house. Man, as merchant
only, "walketh in a vain show." My friend, in the
press of affairs heaping up wealth which appears

only in shares on the corporations' books, calls a barren cliff by the sea fancy property. But his is fanciful and the cliff real: for there is somewhat permanent and unchangeable in the beauty where the soul takes its daily bath, — in the horizon whose exquisite line of the meeting land and sea and wood-girdled hill does not waver; in the sky from whose inverted cup, as a horn of plenty to heart and imagination, daily blessings come; and even in the charming phenomenon of the tide, so punctual although never at rest; and in the perpetual and pervading glory, out of which life even as a shadow is cast, — while the possessions on which you can *realize* are more unsubstantial and cloudy than any vapor that floats overhead through the air.

Abject poverty is a curse and a provocation to crime. But unbounded personal appropriation of the signs and symbols of wealth is the very lunacy of conceit. Riches are good for what we can do with them; but if we do nothing but invest and reinvest, using them with no generous design for others' benefit, but only as so much seed-corn and so many nest-eggs to produce more, we impoverish our fellows and might as well be poor ourselves. The miser is a pauper, his counting-room a poor-house; and the worst sort of beggary will be the end and upshot of his destitution of love. None at last need charity so much as do they by whom it has never been shown! This keen scent for gain leaves little conscience. The sharp man will be a sharper, and how near to being dishonest is he who is close! Road and bank presidents, with enterprises outside their office, are tempted to divert corporate or public funds, in their hands or at their command, to their private risks. The accommodator and the accommodated, the lender and the borrower, are one man ! It is a dangerous position ; and thoughtful business men are beginning to ask if directors are not biassed, and whether a president is more safe for being a Crœsus of large and manifold concerns.

Moderation is the lesson taught from all this enforced commercial stagnation. Intemperate undertakings strengthen no more than liquors that make drunk. How hard in this country we have worked to get poor ! Business-mania is that sort of fever on whose heat debility attends ; and we should have been richer to-day had we thought less of riches. Jehu, driving the chariot, is upset. How slowly and leisurely the car off the track is pried back ! Ten years it takes for our business-train to get in motion again. The correction and cure for the business man is to have something beside his affairs to take up his thought. When one has so much to do that he cannot attend to important matters or fulfil friendly relations outside the bargains he shoves and is pushed into a corner and impounded by, he is not doing his business well, and we need not be surprised if he fail. Only by a decent culture of all the faculties can the mind's balance be preserved ; and by its inward poise will outward footing be kept. One may as easily lop a bodily member and not go one-sided or lame, as starve his intellect and depopulate his imagination, yet have good judgment remain ; and any warping or neglect of the moral sense will but aggravate the mischief. Other things being equal, we may trust the banker who loves the fine art that is above his finance, cherishes some exquisite taste and follows some branch of pure knowledge, rather than the one who, having only room for scales in his brain, will surely also have scales on his eyes. To prevent the creeping of cataract over the spiritual vision, we must not look out for worldly advantage till our gaze becomes a dazing stare, but practise ourselves to behold truth in all her forms. To our vocation let us add an avocation if we would keep sane.

Some great affection for God or his creatures is needful too. Atrophy of the heart has been at the bottom of how much earthly niggardliness! Let love be a hoard and hive for others, not ourselves, and we shall be spendthrifts in no sense, but economists in all, and, in Charles Lamb's expression, keep poverty at a sublimer distance than if we had the exchequer of a king. Our Senator Sumner said he had never dipped his hand into the United States treasury, yet who held him poor? Truly there is a fortune that has no wheel!

Business is God's grace to man, with all its errors and enormities on its head. If science be the ruling queen, business is the modern king. Its activities are worth more than its gains, as that good merchant saw who only wished for his children as much happiness in spending as his had been in earning his estate. It is time to have done with decrying riches and success. Professors of poverty exist no longer in the Catholic Church, nor can the beggars of the Middle Ages again become a political force. There is no virtue in being shoeless, or not having where to lay one's head. Doubtless there are God's poor; but he has his rich, too, who are just as good and perhaps more strong for his service. The apostle James, launching his thunders against rich men, missed his Master's point, who bade his disciples not lay up treasure *for themselves.* Disinterested acquisition of knowledge or wealth is the summit of character. Unhappy man who gathers and broods over his selfish store! He is outranked in merit by the hen scratching for her young, by the swallow bearing a worm to the eaves of the barn for her nestling, and by the grub and beetle rolling up a provision, though in a ball of dung, for their offspring. The solitary and loveless human creature whom I saw pick up ordure on the highway in a pail, while he had in the bank thousands of dollars too sacred to touch, is the type of all the misers who, with clean hands and a decent demeanor, do dirtier things. These are but exceptions. Most business men are too intent on great results to stoop to the tricks of trade. From a million spokes turning, and myriad hoofs striking the ground, some dust will fall, and some fire fly. But the immense operation is benign, to educate powers to surpass all issues of worldly profit and loss ; and the contributions by business men of material aid for every want of society, need of the Church, or emergency of the State have been so timely and large that the preacher who denounces money-making as profane and the bawling lecturer who scores bond-holders as the laborer's foes, were their words potential, would but tear down the posts on which their pulpit and platform are reared. What matters, O radical, whom you hate, if you hate? God is not poor, but abundant in means ; and the opulent are as akin to him in nature, while more like in condition, than the destitute. If the reformer and ostensible friend of the forsaken have enmity in his heart, it will reach the class he favors as well as that he resists. If the Irishman wishes to crowd and trample on the African or Chinaman, that has a lower place and a harder struggle than himself, as the house-slave used to visit the field-slave with his contempt, with what face can he pretend to be a philanthropist, while he cares only for his own clan? In the eyes of those he flatters he is cloven-footed, and makes a travelling show of himself, yet is useful to run into the ground the arguments of the demagogue, who in politics is more cunning than he. He is the same rogue and blusterer as the one in broadcloth, only he is by his coarser speech more exposed.

Business is sanctified by a motive for private welfare and for the public good; and the pecuniary thus goes along as a fast friend with the moral capital of the human race. All the winnings, having whatever representation on earth, will be consumed or swept away; but the principles developed by ephemeral transactions will abide.

The merchant is a man in whom prudence is combined with enterprise for a forecast, to whose fruits he is entitled as much as a candidate at the patent-office with his invention, or an author to a reward for his book; and he is to dispose of these fruits at his will. In charity the merit is cheerful giving, and the importunate philanthropist, who will take our dollar in any other fashion, is the last robber on the highway! In this world it is a race of wits. As in the yacht-squadron, all do not get prizes, nor are the prizes all equal, nor have the crowd a right to wrest away any that is fairly won. God makes men to differ in faculty and fortune, and neither their bodies nor their minds can be made alike. A mob has never yet reigned; and the serpent of communism, more threatening than the one Eve talked with in Eden, now rearing its crest, would bring not plenty, but poverty, to everybody with its universal mob law.

But the true merchant will be forbearing as well as just, and consider it a libel on his business to say that the uttermost farthing must be exacted and the last of the forty stripes fall. Commerce is a high school, a college better than Oxford or Cambridge, to educate conscience. But equity has a higher law than legality, and a larger measure than our dues in dollars and cents; and he who spurns or rejoices to outstrip his halting or timid competitors, nor will ever lend a hand but to take advantage when they slip, though he be square with every statute a lawyer could quote, plunders and does not earn. There is an admission fatal to the dignity, and even right to exist, of any calling in the assertion that it offers for any virtue of kindness or mercy no soil to thrive in.

Once more, the merchant that does not worship God, like the undevout astronomer, is mad; for how can he fail to own a preordaining in his sphere as well as in the orbit of the earth or any circuit of the skies? Is it by chance that these great cities stand on the Hudson and Mersey and Seine and Thames, and that they are fed from fertile countries with corn and wheat and whatever the ground can produce? Are not the paths of steamships and the iron tracks of cars prescribed by providential power no less than the river-courses and the tides? The atheistic lecturer declares he sees no agent but

15

man. Has the human creature done all on the globe?
No more than he made the planet itself. The streams
flow from mountain-chains, and the currents of events
and affairs have their springs in other heights of a superhuman wisdom. We see it in the curious suiting of
climate to culture and of material to manufacture, of the
wood and quarry to become both pavement and house,
of the mine to be transformed into the mint, and in all
the flying of supply to want as to a magnet. Man has
done this no more than he has thrown up the Alle-
ghanies for a continent's backbone, or scooped the Gulf,
and shaped the Golden Gate for ports. A ledger should
be a good liturgy read aright, and a bank-book correctly
kept is a collect for the day. From accounts settled
now the final one gets its name; and the temple so
long miscalled for Mammon belongs to God. Already
some church vestries are less sacred than some counting-
rooms. To pick a priest for myself I should not seek
the Confessional · more readily than the Exchange.
Church and clergy must learn to appreciate this great
outside communion of uprightness and honor, whose
members may not be dependent on clerical ministra-
tions or punctual at dedicated shrines, but whose hearts
have been cleansed by tests more searching than a
watery baptism, and nourished and stimulated through
a broad intercourse with humanity and by a better than
sacramental bread and wine. Surely from an unseen
spirit-world must come the motive by which earthly
dealings can be so raised. But not in a wood or marble sanctuary alone is the door by which the impulse
comes or window through which the truth shines; and
many a religious minister will own the incentives de-

rived to his own fidelity from the conduct of not a few of those whom he was sent to save. Merchant-princes may be also merchant-priests, if they have, too, an affection for their home which will never postpone it to the saloon or club-room, make it an appendage to the wharf or office, or permit it to degenerate into a lodging-house or inn, when it should be the altar for all the prosperity from the toiling hand and sweating brow. Piety toward heaven will tend the domestic shrine. As the sun gravitates to the planets it draws, so God bends toward us while we lean on him.

The Persian proverb says, the buyer should be left ignorant of nothing about the article which the seller knows. But trade is a training for both parties of wit as well as honor. The day cannot be spent in explanations, but the bargain made ; and while sly concealment is fraud, judges alone should be purchasers, and fools sent to shops will make mistakes. "Look out!" say the English, and "Take care!" say the French drivers, as they meet and pass on the highway. In affairs or affections we must have our hands steady and our eyes open and clear. No bounty in this world is allotted to the blind. But let the kindness match the keenness of the glance.

IX.

BEASTS.

THAT all life is connected, and species no absolute distinction, only a convenient term, there is both physical and metaphysical proof; but no evidence that ascent more than descent is its law. By no line of demarcation can man and beast be cut apart; and our sympathy, inextinguishable for what is below us, — for the cattle on the hills, the domestic dog and cat, the hen and her brood, the wild tenants of the desert and wood, quadrupeds that excel us in strength or swiftness, and birds that mock us with their superior flight, — is a virtue less of volition than in our blood, and like the natural affection for kith and kin. By what resemblances of persons, not alone with each other, but with the horse, tiger, or fox, we are struck, the relations being in temper as well as looks! Any boundary, clear through, in vain we try to fix. The beasts have no language, we say, meaning our arbitrary signs; for the crows, rooks, and bees not only have natural language with each other, but understand ours in part. They have some apprehension of words. I was told of a dog who knew not what " bone " was in English, but instantly understood it in French. Most dogs will come from out of sight at the call of their name. The communication with each other of the ravens and the ants, of the wedged flock of wild geese, of emigrant swallows, or of the bobolinks is too close for us to discern, and only by our ignorance is it disesteemed. Shall we part ourselves, by our affections, from the beasts? A learned work of a French naturalist has just been tracing human love to its origin in the least and lowest tribes; and the analogies are so curious and minute that our finer seems to open from their coarser sensibility, as the flower is but a blossoming stem of grass, the skull a transformed vertebra, and the fruit a metamorphosed leaf.

Driven from structural claims to exclusiveness, our pride takes its stand at last on ideas, of which it says the beasts have none, as they cannot contemplate nature or turn a reflective eye on themselves, however they may be possessed of certain notions or views. A cow seems to have no aspirations; content with chewing her cud, she surveys the universe with what a blank gaze! But notice a young girl reading a page of some book she has taken from the library. The clock ticks hard by, but with one swing of the pendulum in a hundred glances of her eye, by motions inconceivably rapid, scorning all count, she gathers up the sense of how many letters, syllables, and words! Is matter directing matter in the velocity of that transparent visual ball? Is mud refined both perceiver and perceived? Is it a far-off cousin of the monkey that at last reads and spells? I look off from some headland, and see the sun set not only in the sky but on a thousand points of rock along the ocean-shore, while the reverberating surge that shakes the range of cliff on the offing is comminuted into babbling ripples at that elbow of sea and bay and creek whence my observation is made. But who shall analyze or describe the sensation that rolls in upon me with the diminishing swell of the wave? I only know that the billow, doing what no philosophy can, sweeps away my doubt. Infidelity is impossible in the mood to which I am raised. In the ecstasy of my joy no God is too great to believe in and no heaven is too high for my hope. If the Maker walked in Eden of old, it was no better paradise than mine; and I say to all the godless as Bonaparte on board ship, pointing to the stars, said to the ingenious atheists deriding superstition at his side, " Gentlemen, who made all that?" Do such emotions visit any animal's brain? Is there any thread between these processes of my mind and those of the highest beast, or is every one of my ideas for it a missing link? We can, for answer, but commend to both the evolutionists and the special creationists the old doctrine that the persons must neither be confounded nor the substance divided, as reaching far beyond the trinity to the manifold sum of being, of which we and all that lives are a part so essential that without every thing beside nothing could exist, but the loosening of an atom would ruin the whole.

Beyond thought prayer is prescribed as the highest exercise of our nature. But some of the animals are reverent, as, long before "Vestiges of Creation" appeared, Lord Bacon noted that man is the dog's god. Is it but blank wonder, no adoration, he feels? Our life is wonder no less, and he who goes deepest is astonished most at the world he is in and at himself. I gazed from the top of one in a colony of vast boulders that in some past geologic age had arrived in ships of ice tossed by wave and torrent from the hills. The vessels, melting in milder airs, discharged their enormous freight of stone, and forests grew up, girdling their various bulk. On the disintegrating top of one huge mass, weighing thousands of tons and bedded deep in the earth, several fir-trees rose into the sky. Underneath another, lifted from the bare ledge where it had paused in the old drift by a smaller fragment of triangular shape, I could trace plainly the scratches, showing that it was from the northwest this tremendous fleet had left its mountain-port for a still harbor to stay in, who can tell for how many years? Miles away shone the ocean, retreating from its former domain. The birds, those little optimists, responded to each other with their songs; the sparrow and thrush, to shame all the pessimists in the world, flew above the splintered peaks among the waving boughs, that murmured in the solemn choir to their manifold chant; while the caw of the crow spoke of solitude and the lapse of time, his voice seeming that of chanticleer on the minor key. With all that science could explain or my faculties comprehend, blind amazement, more conscious and profound than that of any beast, was the sentiment in which I was lost. How immense appeared the unseen Worker's plan! With what care these huge piles had been lowered or raised! How big the planet looks when from any height we get the least imagination of its spread and curve! Yet it is but one of the least of the shot fired into the firmament, so full of those blazing cannon-balls of suns and fixed stars. I stand and marvel at the presumption of any man's attempt to solve the thing I contemplate, in his scheme. I am the beast's brother in my surprise; and the steed I drive is no more startled at his first sight and sound of a locomotive, bicycle, military procession,

or billow breaking on the beach, than am I at each successive scene of the creative acts in God's unfinished
play.   The village church yonder, whose spire I see
through the trees, rests on a bit of the ledge sloping
down from my post of vantage, and the preacher within
its walls can guide me so little in my quest he might
better be dumb.   Like the lower creatures, who do not
pretend to fathom the problem or be masters of the
situation, let me too be mute.   .

Philosophy at its last intrenchment would put the
difference betwixt man and beast in the inability of the
latter to classify itself in the universe.   If it could say
I am an ox, an insect, or a pig, it would be such no
longer, but a man!   Is it not, however, venturesome
to say there is in no animal a dim personal sense?
Some philosophers regard self-consciousness as an inferior state of the human mind, the *ego* as a fleeting
phenomenon predicable neither of God nor of the perfectly unfolded man.   Not adopting their speculation, I
yet note in animals some degree of the self-conscious
mood.   I am as sure of my horse as I am of any independent member of my household, that he will do this
and will not do that, will balk at an over-heavy load, as
the llama and camel refuse to rise when the burden is too
great, and will stop at the foot of a steep hill whose
difficulty his eye takes in.   He knows the way back
over the road better than I do, and chooses the right
turn when my ignorance makes me slacken the rein.
He so well remembers and is so grateful for my consideration and kind attention that he will kiss me and lick
my hand when he feels affectionate, will neigh at my
approach when he is indifferent to another person, and

will not suffer himself to be handled by an ostler that
does not treat him well. He learns courage from experience, and scorn of dangers or ugly objects which he
once feared, as we acquire like knowledge. He looks
as earnestly at me as does any companion. In short,
he aspires to be the man who in the great evolution
came with him from a common root. If he do not say
"I," as with self-complacency and so much vainglory I
do, he thinks it all the same, atoning for the less vividness
by the greater modesty of the self-assertion he makes.

But, says the theologian, will you make the beasts that
perish immortal, to encroach on our privilege and gainsay a canonical book? If it be difficult to conceive how
any beast should be immortal, the way of such a fact is
equally hard to imagine for the man, so much of what
he now calls himself must be changed and dropped, left
in dust behind while he draws his real self out of his
present case and environment, in which it is so smothered
and choked. By inward unfolding we become conscious
how much of ourselves we could spare and yet our spirit
or essence not be lost. How then can we justify our
hasty conclusion, excluding aught that can escape from
other animal frames than our own? How can we fail to
observe it in the soaring lark, the fish leaping out of water,
the thoroughbred race-horse erecting his head like a man,
the eye of a hound seeking his master's, the giraffe's
beautiful neck lengthened, — some naturalists have said
in its efforts to crop fruit on the branches at first beyond
its reach, and however taking ages to perfect its form,
signifying an upreaching relish for nobler food? Immortality has its seed not in any outward revelation
or bodily resurrection, but in the sense of limits be-

yond which we yearn to expand. Is there no such
longing in natures lower than our own? We have heard
of a horse swelling in every vein and trembling in
every limb when first put into harness, as a wild African
resents subjection to slavery. Doubtless many a creature feels that we deprive it of liberty. There must be
a heaven for the soul to mount in because the soul is a
mounting thing; and out of that heaven by the sky itself
we seem to be shut. The firmament is a cattle-pound,
the starry orbits do not give us scope, the Milky Way is
a veil we want to tear off, and all the elements are a mob
pursuing us for our life. Like a racer scorning the ground
with his heels, we spurn the earthly confinements that
would cramp us and would make the planets the floor
of our abode. We find that the fixed stars, those uncounted larger suns, are some of them variable, and wax
in splendor and pour out increasing heat, as if to enjoin
elevation and growing ardor upon us. But the scale of
ascension being so immense, who shall say that the seraphim are not as many courses above us as we above the
reptile and the worm?

But no such rising through the chain of being by a law,
and no endless personal continuance or everlasting individuality, but the moral sense prompting to right as
such for its own dignity and charm, is our nature's climax; and can we pretend there is any conscience in the
beast? Undoubtedly there are manifest rudiments of
it in many a case. No man ever shows more evident
mortification and shame than does a setter or colly who
has signally failed of his duty with the game or the
flock. No man is more cast down than a mastiff under
reproach. Who is more lowly than the coach-dog or

spaniel when ordered on occasion not to attend you on
your walk or drive, but to go home, and understanding
so well what is meant by your look or word or pointed
whip?

Will it be said, in fine, that not simple moral feeling,
but disinterestedness or self-sacrifice marks the great
gulf which no animal can pass over to reach the man?
The cow and goat, so patiently yielding to us their milk,
and complaining but for a moment when the offspring
it was meant for is taken to the butcher's knife; the
bees, trained to make honey for their keeper, and light-
ing in harmless swarms upon him as if they had not a
sting in all their throng; and the Newfoundland or St.
Bernard breed of dogs, saving the life of the traveller
cast in the snow or drowning in the flood, — shame one
half of the selfish humanity to which we belong. It is
hard to love a sharper, swindler, or seducer because he
belongs to our race and has an upright form, as we do
the dumb, faithful, sympathetic partner of our joys and
woes, who does not covet our wealth, or corrupt our
virtue, or envy our luxuries, or plot against our life.

Certainly there is a spiritual sublimity in some men
to which no creature ever appears to attain, it being
God manifest in the human breast. A man who never
shuts his own eye before the most formidable testimony,
nor lets another see for him; a man who thinks for himself, and endangers all other men in their low customs,
their institutions, or their ease; a man with might
enough to supplant one religion for a better, and substitute worship in place of superstition, as Jesus disestab-
lished Judaism; a man like John Brown, single-handed,
assailing slavery behind its million bayonets and more

than million whips, feeling that his soul is more than a
match for it, as David trusted his sling against Goliath's
weaver's beam ; a man who does not reckon weapons or
material of war when convinced of the justice of his
cause, for which he is alike willing to live or to die, and
knows that by all the myrmidons of bad usages it can
never be slain, — is an animal of a peculiar sort, whose
graduation out of the trilobite has not been demonstrated,
but whose physical beginning at the meanest base of
organic life cannot be disproved. Who shall tell by
how many and fine steps in its long journey life rises
from the ground to the pinnacle of the temple which
God builds?

But from the nature and destiny of the animal let us
go to its use. First, it makes a picture of the world,
which else were but architecture, a rotunda with stained
walls instead of the animated and moving scene we behold. In what a desert of land and sea and sky, without these creatures, we should live ! But the earth is
made sociable by their diverse kinds almost as much
as by our own. In temples their manifold figures are
carved, and by their forms many a canvas is lighted
up. It is because they are so essential or substantial in
nature that we cannot spare them in art. Should they
all suddenly disappear, how lonely and forlorn we should
be, with such companions and auxiliaries lost, that daily
draw our observation and give our imagination delight !
We are enchanted not only by the largest of them, but
by the least. The pismire building ever anew its pyramids, older than those in Egypt, and dragging the grains
of sand, its blocks, as a tug tows vessels on the stream ;
the bee buzzing, with a voice which is the last echo of the

lowing in the pasture, as it tacks from flower to flower, passing at once if it find but little honey, and hovering and thrusting deep its little spoon if there be much, and on occasion slitting at the bottom the bag of nectar that could not otherwise be reached, shaming the human skill that might well be defied to gather from such minute jars the perfect sweet; the chamois, a living snow-flake and moving spot of beauty on some alpine crag; the snake, charming us, if it do not the birds, with the spiral slide that takes us across all the tramplings of the globe to the garden of Eden, and makes the convoluted line, which no arithmetic can reduce, the type of eternity; the dog, partner, aid, and solace to Indian and white man, savage and civilized, to the ends of the earth, and lavishing on his master perhaps the best and only constant love, defending his property, obeying his orders, and guarding his door; the cat, with its clean and dainty habit and contented purr, a consolation in the house, presenting the kittens, whose play with their own tails is the endless amusement of every child, while sometimes this feline diminuendo of the tiger is a labyrinth of beauty in the marks on its skin, and always the impersonation of grace in its gait, to stir the envy of any actor on the stage; all the herds on the hills, and flocks in the meadows or the folds, with calves and foals and lambs; the barnyard fowl, with chickens and ducklings and goslings, which the baby, feeling their soft resemblance to itself, wants to catch; the sow, with her satisfied sleepy grunt, as her snowy litter are stretched by her side, creep over her back, or suck at her teats,— what a canvas! Into the wilder specimens, of squirrel and rabbit and mole and woodchuck and mink, the domestic varieties shade away, and from African wastes and Indian jungles and Asiatic or Alaskan seas the lion and sea-lion, elephant and sea-horse, zebra and ape, and a hundred sorts beside, must be brought in countless caravans through the world for young and old to visit, cosset, and admire.

Without the panorama of beasts what should we do? How desolate our dwelling and impoverished our fancy would become! Were they instantly extinct, how empty our premises and dismal our walks! The zoological is as needful as any other garden; and, preserved in death, the creatures make the best part of every museum and conservatory. It is not strange Agassiz thought the animal kingdom indispensable in heaven, it could be so ill spared on earth. Were it exterminated, we should long and pine for its meanest and most annoying specimens, could we have no other portions of it back. We should be sorry we had driven out the wolf and catamount and bear! It would please us to hear the wasp warn us with his microscopic bassoon, and the mosquito wind his little horn, and the serpent hiss from its fangs, and the grasshopper light on our gown or sleeve, and the locust voice, on his trumpet, the sultry heat.

Why do we so hold to the beasts, and what is the reason of their spell? They are our relations! It is the tie of blood we feel, — a kindred which, if science did not establish, we could not disown. There is, moreover, a moral interest. The beast is the mirror of the man. In its features, as in a glass, he sees his face. His own qualities, magnified or reduced, return to him from

these inferior shapes ; and if so represented that they run
into extremes, yet he is instructed and pleased, as con-
vex and concave reflectors, even by exaggeration or con-
traction, give us a lesson on the proportions of the face.
How blind and stupid must man be not to discover in
himself the fox, wolf, viper, bear, as Herod was Rey-
nard to Jesus, and the Pharisees were full of slyness and
venom, while both the innocent lamb and the lordly lion
of Judah were emblems of the Christ ! How easily we
distribute the lineaments of our acquaintances among
the four-footed tribes ! "You have made your sitter,"
one said to the artist, " look like a fox." " That is what
he is," the painter replied. Surely no creature creeping,
as with pain, from one green limb to another in the
thicket, to pause and devour its prey, is more truly the
sloth than is many a man, while no claws in the pan-
ther are sharper than some women's to scratch. I have
known a whole town to be no better than a dog in the
manger, not enjoying, nor allowing the ox to enjoy, the
hay. It said to its citizens, " We will not use a certain
territory for one purpose, and you shall not use it for
another. It shall be neither road nor landscape, neither field nor pond." From the gravel-heap in the yard
my older cow regularly hooked her younger sister down.
What is the pulpit but just such a gravel-heap to the
occupant who would confine it to the amount of orthodoxy harvested by his sect or concrete in his brain?

We should thank the beasts for their rhetorical contributions to strengthen and enrich our vernacular tongue.
Said Burke, in the famous trial of Hâstings, " We did
not say he was a lion or tiger ; we said he was a weasel
and a fox." The English orator wished to confine the

culprit for characterization to the baser and deny to him the grander properties of the inferior tribes. It is a poor style of writing or of speech in which meadows do not bloom, and wings fly over, and feet career. It is what we call abstract, that is, dead. The livelier manner of expression will remind hearer or reader of all that stirs and breathes.

In the picture-gallery what a masterpiece every creature may become; and what a clod would be the globe, what a blank the air, and what a drench the sea, but for what lives and plays, cleaves and glides, burrows and mines, paddles and oars its way! Birds were the first navigators, and insects the original, augers. There were nests in banks before men dug with spades, and half our implements are copies of living tools that wrought before

"Adam delved or Eva span."

Let us consider the lessons the animals give. We are told that civilization has its measure in our distance from the beast, as the forehead advances and the jaw retreats. But the high facial angle covers much contrivance of sin. "Work the beast out of your composition," the moralist enjoins. Softly, and not so fast! Much soul of goodness is in these humble forms, would we "observingly distil it out." How temperate and pure nature is in the unpampered brute, that needs take from no Father Mathew the pledge! The swallow cleaning its bill on the bough, the plover washing in the seaside pool, the duck preening its feathers and shaking the cleansing drops from its sides, the cow licking its mate in the pasture or the calf in the stall, the gull and eagle loving the ventilation through every pinion and organ in their lofty flight, make suggestions to those ignorant of the bath, clad untidily, lounging on sofas, or stifling in dens. In some respects it were worse for them to be men than for us to be brutes!

> " He calls it reason, hence his power's increased
> To be far beastlier than any beast,"

says Mephistopheles of the man. To work like a beaver, or be busy as a bee, is the praise of but part of our species! The spider was the first weaver, before the knitting-needle was invented, the spinning-wheel hummed, or shuttles were driven by steam; and man inherited or imitated the constructiveness some of whose operations in his far-away cousins still challenge his own skill. The unfledged chick in his white round tower is in prison. But he secretes a mallet in his bill, and, knocking to find the weakest part of his stony shell, he breaks jail, makes his way out, and soon drops the no longer useful tool, which, like a diamond glass-cutter, he had applied. Was the first performance of that little feat the origin of all the blasting and tunnelling and bridge-building that have altered the face of the world? How was that faculty in immemorial cycles accumulated which is knowledge to-day in a solid form? To know how to do a thing is more than a speculation how it has been or should be done; and by this rule how superior to much of our science is the knowledge of beasts! The Texas ant lays out its garden beds, plants the seed, and gathers the crop; and if some shower drives through its sandy roof to wet the precious store, takes it out to dry in the sun, that it may not rot and spoil. This is good agriculture, and a fine example to all cultivators and husbandmen; and I cannot help the fancy that the progenitors of the little creature had among them some daring Columbus who first discovered the arable properties of the soil, and that in all our harvesting in field or prairie we follow in his wake! We talk proudly of our brains. O phrenologist, in this vivacious proletary of the ant, all skin and legs, show me the lobes that account for his works and wars, and of that system of bondage which I cannot extol him for setting as an example before us! Not all mimicry and mockery of a blind instinct, as we call it, is this industry, but rather the beginning whose rare strokes we pursue. The animals are ethical teachers, to whom many a man might go to school. "Let dogs delight to bark and bite;" but, O Isaac Watts, in how much else they delight far more, — in watchfulness, loyalty, grateful attachment, faithful service, and in guarding for their owner the provisions for lack of which they starve, till their self-denial is our envy and despair! Cats, it is said, love not persons, but places. Would that some men loved home, rather than the saloon or club-room, as much! If there be night-walkers among the feline tribes, it is not apparent why we should follow the poorest patterns in lower races any more than in our own. With what patience, too, the beasts suffer! My horse whinnies to salute his comrade coming home; but, when wounded and bleeding, makes not a whimper or moan. Not having our language, he may think it of no use to complain. If that be an intellectual defect, it is also a moral advantage which our dumb fellows have. I note in some animals a natural piety, too. The house-

dog's deferential look, dropping of his tail, curling of
his body, is his sincere liturgy, never repeated mechan-
ically and without sense. My friend, after long absence
abroad, forgot his dog; but the dog remembered him,
and ran on the other side of the way, as his old master
went from the city to his country-home, and waited for
leave to come across, — a politeness far beneath which
how much of our human courtesy falls, in the street or
the car! We might even learn to be thankful from the
beasts. Dr. Warwick in England relates that a pike in
a pond having bruised its head against a tenter-hook in a
post, he treated it surgically, and healed the wound; and
after that the fish would fondly follow him up and down
in all its movements, and feed from his hands, although
to other persons it continued shy. A traveller whose
dog resisted his starting one morning on his journey by
persistent barking at his horse's head, feared the dog
was mad, and shot at and wounded it; but on going back,
found it bleeding and dying by a bag of treasure he had
carelessly left under a tree where he stopped over night.
The beast's virtue is nature's irony on our vice. There
is no end to the learning animals furnish, to the stints
they set, and to the benefits they impart. They are our
purveyors and commissariat. They provide food, clothing, and decoration. How we ransack nature for their
spoils for our board and our back! I have seen a green
beetle in a lady's ear-ring. Would the lady have crushed
the live beetle as worthless and having no rights to her
respect? The hat, cloak, shoe, shirt, hair-settee, house-
rug, door-mat, or feathered ornament in some bonnet or
cap, has cost a creature's life. How much the horse has
done for humanity, for our delight or profit in riding

and driving, hauling of merchandise and material, and
bearing swiftly the message and messenger of life and
death! Are whip and spur, an overload and lathered
sides, the return and requital? With all our ships and
railways, how could we get along without him? During the horse-disease, when every stable was a hospital,
and no carriage could be got, we learned what the horse
usually does for us even in the burial of the dead, as
he draws the living procession and the clay in the
hearse. As a young woman reproached a gentleman
who took her in his chaise for going slow, he replied,
"You must go then with somebody else, as I use no
whip!" Mounting a hill, we involuntary stoop to get
a purchase on our muscles, and ease the ascent. Un-
check your horse in the same situation; he too has a
back!

Our duty to the beasts is the last point. They are
part of the scale of being; we are on its upper rounds.
As their organism and ours are on the same plan, so they
have hints and rudiments of our faculties and feelings.
In their so-called blind instincts they are argus-eyed,
and in some of their manipulations they have Briareus-
hands, for calculation, construction, engineering, div-
ing, and soaring, for hypæthral and submarine work.
They have love, memory, regret, repentance, grief, of
which, after his long watch at the sick-bed, the dog
will sometimes go to die on the grave, which I am not
sorry to see his marble image sometimes surmount. Our
selfish fickleness and inconstancy is by how few of them
and how seldom shown! Some men and women may be
infatuated with a pet creature to the neglect of more
important ties. But the beast's fate is rather apt to be

in a cruel handling or supercilious scorn. If, however, we be vain, unkind, sly, treacherous, malign, some of the animals lay us under obligation as respects philosophy, in affording us names, — the vulture, coon, wild-cat, or wolf, the headstrong bison, and, in his sudden spring, the crafty bear. The ruminating animals inculcate reflection, and the grazing ones content, as all day long they browse in the pasture and drink only from the brook by the way. I have heard poorer preachers of comfort than the thrush, song-sparrow, and bobolink; and for all his depredations we have never paid the robin in cherries yet. Rather than have the crow exterminated, he shall have part of my corn. I should miss his raven suit, his intonation of distance and solitude, and his noisy consultation with his peers, if he is part of the flock or when he is appointed sentinel on the pine-tree.

For all the advantage we get out of it, with what slaughter we repay the animal world! English travellers have gone to the wild unappropriated territories of the earth with the most improved fire-arms to slay at pleasure the game in every close jungle or lonely reach of waste land, creek or bayou,— the eagle and crocodile for sport; the lion, raccoon, leopard, tiger, seal, otter, fox, mink, and sable for their skins; the elephant for his ivory tusks; and how many a creature for pure wantonness, to see if their fowling-piece would carry so far, and that they may boast of the shot! The African traveller, Cummings, relates that his ball hit the centre of an elephant's forehead, and pierced the skull. Out of the smooth hole oozed the ruddy gore. The creature lifted its trunk slowly, and touched significantly the spot whence its life ebbed away, and then swayed its body to and fro, with an Oriental salaam or sign of worship, and then, as at a tick of the watch, fell dead in its tracks. Were I Mr. Cummings, I should not like to meet that elephant at the judgment! Against the butcher's or fisherman's business I have nothing to say, although eating our fellow-creatures savors of cannibalism since we have discovered the relationship! But shooting or fishing for sport and pastime is barbarism, practised by whatever fine lady in a silk dress, while no spectacle is more revolting than a lout of a boy, for whom his parents have nothing better to do than spend his day hunting some little beach bird from bay to headland with his long and murderous gun. What have the poor creatures done to be so mocked and without mercy assailed? All animal nature is selfish, we are told. But, in order to selfishness, we must have a conscience for comparison, as the ideal term, of which the gross animal nature, however possessed as a rudiment, is relatively devoid. The selfish creature is man! Are the hen and the walrus selfish when defending their offspring against the hawk and the hunter's spear, to which they courageously expose themselves?

I am no doubter about the heavens and all their measureless life and joy. But, as was said of Socrates, that he brought philosophy down from heaven to earth, the same office needs to be done for religion; and the most neglected part of religion concerns our duty to the too little regarded creatures left so entirely at our mercy. The sharpest test of our character is in our treatment of what is in our power, and wholly below us. Our equals can defend themselves, and give and take

as good or bad as they send or get, while there is no
earthly remedy if we refuse or withhold our duty — that
is, what is due — to the mute and helpless life beneath.
Yet it is a law, curious and sublime, of our nature for
all that is high to supply and comfort all that is low.
The weakest thing in the house, the babe, is the
strongest. Its cradle, like the sun, is the blazing centre around which all else revolves. How the mother
hovers over the child that is lame or deformed!
Jesus was God's Son, not by chronological primogeni-
ture, by origin before Abraham or the foundation of
the world, but by preaching to spirits, descending into
hell, seeking and saving the lost. While the calf, foal,
kitten, or callow bird remains young, helpless, and unable to satisfy its own hunger, how the parent tends,
but when it is strong pushes it off to shift for itself!
A certain tenderness to what is a grade under or a step
behind is the touchstone of character, and the disposition to thrust it back is the generation of the Devil.
Sympathy is the grace all-comprehending. The sensitive plant exists to show that flowers have feeling.
When I see some young Nimrod cutting with his whip
at the poppy-heads, which signified the aristocrats to a
certain emperor of Rome, or a girl tearing a rose or a
pink to pieces in her petulant pride, or a gardener at
his trade impaling the just-opened buds with wires, I
think they are hurting live parts of the world. Youthful rudeness will be cruelty when it is ripe! The mal-
treated animals, who must call us to a reckoning at some
future bar, already have some atonement or revenge.
Whence but from our abusing them is this thirst for
brothers' blood which a thousand wars have not slaked?

Had we treated them better, we should have spared each other more. Pity for the feeble and unfortunate be our motto henceforth! It is no task for base men to duck and defer to their superiors, to kings and magistrates, to officials clothed with power, or to those whose wit, genius, and beauty win eminence and applause. What is all this materialization in the circles but a sky-larking after angels, whose shoulders we clap birds' wings to, in sign that they soar, while we are surrounded by substantial shapes of being whose welfare is in our hands? Wherefore is the celestial curtain held so tightly but to notify us that our business is on this side? Too long the host has been divided. Let us halt, and bring up the rear! On our line of march we have halted for the slave, we are halting for the woman, and shall halt for the beast. At last he has his apostles and missionaries and protective societies and legal defences, beginning with the Hebrew statute, not to "muzzle the ox that treadeth out the corn." None can do it if he has the kindly heart that takes pleasure in feeding the animals and, like children at the menagerie, in seeing them fed. Is their fondness for the creatures, caterpillars, and bugs the haunting memory of a pre-existent state; and in all our so often happy intercourse with the beasts do we revert to the ancient womb of our birth? Weary with fashion and ambition, of arts and plots, we find that the beasts are good society! As Walt Whitman says, "They do not make us sick with pretences, apologies, obsequious precedents, and pious airs; nor have they any follies of avaricious possession, respect for persons, or artificial rank." My neighbor's black and white setter is treated

on equal terms by my yellow cur, who has no notion of
inferior rights. What charming simplicity and sobriety
are in the quadrupeds that we do not intoxicate or corrupt! Daniel Webster, coming from wrangling debates
at the Capitol, finds his cattle are better company than
the Senate, and wants them driven up to his door before he dies. William Blake, the English painter, who
satirized the ill-tempered gentleman by painting him
as an enormous flea, would say also of himself, —

> " Am not I a little fly,
> If I live or if I die ? "

Does the fly-catching plant hint the retributions that
lurk below, as well as stoop from above, for such as get
by robbery their support? Justice and generosity to
beasts will win their trust, and bring on that millennium, in which their first impulse will not be to run and
fly and hide in the wall, creep into the hole, or scuttle
away in the water. The keeper of the caravan has
affectionate relations with the anaconda, and puts his
head in the lion's mouth ; and when the elephant to the
sound of music walks so tenderly over his prostrate
frame, everybody weeps. See the expert or natural
charmers to whom the four-footed tribes flock and the
birds fly in clouds around their heads ! Snakes in the
East, at the sound of their master's flute, uncoil from
their wicker cages, and come out to dance while the tune
lasts, and then, like the graceful couples in a ball-room,
glide obediently back each to its own place. How
long shall we wait for the secret of the charm which
shall turn to harmony the whole of life? At least until
we put consideration instead of tyranny for our behav-

ior to these humble pensioners, to whom, as well as to any other members of mankind, a just reckoning must come. Thus far the saints have been too much bent on reaching heaven to manifest themselves as sons of God on earth. Let the revivalist learn that the way of salvation is no scheme or form, no temple-gate or closet-door, but goodness and equity to all by whom with us the boon of existence is shared. We justify our own place on the immense scale of being, by blessing what is next to us. It is a revolving and an ascending scale, in which no creature is for ever confined to one spot, and all creatures are somehow together. The universe is not compartment, but communication. I believe in the cherubim, and would like to call at their dwelling, and sit awhile among their seats. But I do not wish ever to be shut up to angels alone. How tiresome to have only one sort of folk, however garnished with wings and harps and palms and crowns! What the shape may be of the coming life, we cannot tell. The Bible gives us only fancies of what must be, — beyond our conception, various and manifold; the links of life not fewer, its points of progress not blocked, nor its earthly underpinnings torn away. How shall the mother behold the nursling whom death weaned from her breast? With what body shall our beloved come? Shall there be no space under any form for the creatures whose meekness when we strike accuses the irritable lords and ladies that go off like Chinese crackers and Roman candles, a word of insult being the spark of fire?

> " And now beside thee, bleeding lamb,
> I can lie down and sleep,
> Or think on Him who bore thy name,
> Graze after thee and weep."

Such is the disposition to which in the fine hereafter the poet converts the lion, the king of beasts. May it be the mood to which all our roaring fierceness changes now!

The beast is the alphabet of the man and the *a b c* for the child, who finds more pleasure and finer lessons in some playful pup than in its letters or its wooden painted doll, there being betwixt the two little creatures so much kin and common ground. What an astonishing likeness between the horses, that first nip each other in fun, and then bite in earnest, and the men whose jests gradually run into thrusts; and how much worse and more bloody the human behavior often is! Æsop and Lafontaine have not run half the parallels on which animals are made to set us examples and administer reproofs.

Animals are man's memory of his birth and growth. All of them alive, as well as their fossil remains, are links in the development of his frame; and without them there would be no recollection for the human race. When David says, God saw his substance, yet being imperfect, and curiously wrought in the lowest parts of the earth, he anticipated Darwin. Inspired genius in a religious singer penetrated the secret of creation, as Shakspeare, better than any modern physiologist, has described the phenomenon of sleep-walking in Lady Macbeth; and in the King of Denmark's account as a ghost of his mortal poisoning, as in other passages, foreshadows what Harvey afterwards discovered of the circulation of the blood. Let us scorn or look down on nothing; the universe is one stuff! Pull a single thread, and the whole web and woof is stretched to the firmament and outermost circumference of the stars, as it is to the innermost particle of the terrestrial globe. The mouse Burns apostrophizes, disturbed in its nest, quivers with a like nervous apprehension to the man whose dwelling an earthquake shakes or volcano overflows. In a drop of rain the insect finds its waterspout, and in the basin it is unawares launched on its Atlantic sea. Proud men at first wished to distinguish themselves as nobles, then for the whiteness of their skin, and now at last for their human form. But the biped may be a beast, and the quadruped an angel of consolation in unselfish love.

We cannot shut out animal correspondence with man at any point. Is the suspicion of that power we call supernatural limited to us? A monkey, walking up to my friend's porch, and seeing there a small Mexican idol, knocked off its head with his hand. As he retired, the head was restored; but the monkey returning was amazed and awe-struck, stretched out his hand repeatedly, and then drew it back in fear, not daring to touch again the marvellous image he surveyed with as much respect as ever the old idol-worshipper had done. A tall horse, with a wilful temper and good sense, knows how to baffle the ostler-boy by lifting his head above the head-stall, when to the ostler he will lower it at once; and a stinging fly comprehends the advantages it gets from darkness or from your hands' being too much engaged to strike. A two-months' puppy, having a number of friends in the family, will hesitate betwixt their diverse calls, and leap after a particular voice or gesture when it has duly made up its mind. As a mocking-bird will imitate any songster it has heard, and the little child thought the parrot was the first teacher of the human speech it mimics, so what is the beast but a continuation, repetition, and long reverberation of man?

A mark of some beasts, that appears largely in the sagacious elephant as it turns its trunk into an arm to caress or an engine to squirt, and especially, too, in some species of the dog, is the individualizing power by which they mete out a rude justice to reward a friend or punish a foe. What human intelligence is keener than the canine to tell one person from another, and to distinguish between hostile demonstrations and a kind intent? Even the young and untrained creature withdraws his teeth and thrusts his smooth nose into your hand to show his biting was but play; and how his little heart pants to his owner with a grateful love which is discouraged by no check or blow! Does this quick beat in his bosom accompany feeling of a greater warmth? How can he discriminate, better than a bystander, the intent in the finger you lift! He is Fido the faithful, and what a useful guard and servant to fetch and carry he is! The Scotch or Australian colly is a *hand* which the shepherd in the wilderness or on the hills could not tend his flock without. How he races after the stray sheep, seizing deserters by the thick wool, yet careful not to pierce the flesh, roping in the wanderers with his paw and his monitory bark! He is the man extended, and as good for the commander of the fleecy host as for Napoleon was a sentinel or a scout. He is conscious of his importance and constant to his task, albeit with no stipulated pay. Who in danger of drowning or freezing would not have one of the

Alpine or Newfoundland breed in the neighborhood rather than any man? Is the animal savior unaware what is meant by the danger or death from which he redeems? " Beware of dogs," says Paul. " Beware of men," said a wiser than he! The dog must defend us from the man that would break in, and has often been a better protection to a woman than a gun. Yet the custodian is how often unreasonably slain!

Some persons have antipathies to particular beasts, such as the bug, mouse, worm, or snake, which they themselves are in some measure like. In natural constitution we are the creatures exalted and refined. As the gigantic fern softens at last into the moss which we call maiden's hair; as the Saurian monster through natural variability has left not only his fossil in the rock, but his loins and living bones in some delicate quadruped; as savages in a few generations of offspring become saints, and piratical Northmen are converted into Englishmen, time being a missionary more efficacious than all the Board sends out, — so of what rude, remote beginnings is all living beauty the amelioration! Scarce could we conceive what it is to creep or swim or burrow or fly, but that once we did it ourselves! Agassiz said, an angel, resembling a human form, soaring on wings, is nonsense. But we feel the remnants in our shoulders that may sprout again, and capacity for any physical change, though it must be so that all the parts will correspond. All our conversation, at least with the lower creatures, is a going to school to learn about our antecedents and ancestors. We are busy about our genealogical tree; for there is but one tree of life, however many the boughs, and though we know not the future bud. Is the child's peculiar attachment to animals and its endless delight in their ways because it has not travelled so far away from them in its own development as the man? As we see some bit of handiwork grow into proportion after some pattern under the restless needle, and take on its fine hues, we feel that our body is a piece that has been long wrought upon, and is not finished yet; and although we are not blind to the doom to be dissolved of each particular specimen of the human frame, yet we have dim anticipations how the organism could be improved. Every oculist knows there never was a perfect eye. But will such an one never be? The old invalid statesman said the owner of his mortal tenement had refused to make repairs. Was it because of his intent to build a better in its place? What is the grave, or the decay in it, but like the heap of demolition foul and dusty on the street where a new structure is to rise? The ground is worth more than the edifice or any material; and we have a native trust in the architect that the ground-rent, which is our very being, will run on. "Have you finished the lecture you are going to deliver?" a famous speaker was asked. "Never," was his reply. "I have not done with you," is the threat held over one with whom we have an unsettled account. God is not done with us, or we with one another or with ourselves. There is sequel and consequence always. The sinner, like the old thief that drew the oxen backward into his cave, wishes to leave no track to betray his doing. But, as the ancient mud has become stone to tell what creature walked over it, so the mire of our iniquity shall turn to a revealing petrifaction on our path, and testify of our cruelty and abuse, especially to the dumb and unarmed, that could not return our insults, or help and defend themselves. There shall be long echoes from the lash of abuse and the slaughtering gun. Under the shadow of tyrannical sway over the weak and the poor must the author of the book of Genesis have written that man is the lower creation's lord. How much license to crowd these doubly depressed inferiors has been drawn from his words! The time has come to deny ownership so entire and to accuse oppression so severe. Not only a human slave, but whatever breathes, has rights we are bound to respect. "Dead men tell no tales," say the murderers, thinking it best to put witnesses to their crimes out of the way. But at the great assizes will they be absentees, or will God count as murder only that committed against what we call our own kind?

There must be some asylum for the injured beasts, which hospitals for stray dogs predict. Persecuted birds have a notion of escape and refuge. As I sat in a rustic tower, some blue-tailed swallows flew to the trap-door. One entered, evidently in great distress. Others, fearing either to go in or stay out, hovered and stooped on their own bent beaks and fluttering wings, as pictures at once of beauty and despair. Again and again they departed and returned, as if, like the Hebrew Psalmist, these sweet singers too were after some citadel of defence, and seeking an unseen and all-sufficient friend. Later in the day I learned that certain lads had been shooting at the swallows on my ploughed land, who, when remonstrated with, alleged it was gunning for specimens and not for sport, a business and not a pleasure, in which they were engaged. Whereupon a little maiden inquired if the specimens were not intended for their pleasure too! It was a pregnant point to make. There is a gap in the Hebrew catalogue of seers. They give but an occasional hint of that justice to animals, as well as to men, without which no millennium will come on earth or warrant be made out for heaven. To raise what aspires is the duty of angel or mortal, though it were but a worm lifting its head in token of repentance of some ancient sin. Scorn is the original sin; refusal to help is the fall of men, and the waving sword on the wall of Eden is the transgressor's remorse.

It is not strange that we cannot conceive of morality in creatures to whom intelligence is refused, and that they should be ranked not among persons but things, the philosophic notion still being that they are but automatons or animated tools. Rational sense or voluntary expression they have none, —

"For smiles from reason flow, to brutes denied."

The effect of intellect is shown in them as in " this universal frame ; " but we say it is only God who is wise through them, not any skill of their own — as if there were even in us any wisdom but his! Is any beast blindly instinctive alone and not intuitive? The bee, with his bee-line truer than a minie-ball, so that its intersection with a second leads the hunter to the hive in the hollow of a tree ; the beaver, reckoning the force of the stream in his dam ; the squirrel constructing his acorn-store or corn-bin away from the frost and rain ; the bower-bird with her fine coffer-dam and water-works as curious as are made

17

in Lake Michigan or on the Croton River by men ; the
hang-bird and all the feathered tribes, choosing materials
like lumbermen and architects, and suiting to the several
situations their nests ; the many adaptations in the animal
kingdom to the substance brought in, of wood or sand,
and mud or stone, as human builders fit to the bases their
beams, — think we that all these are but actors and acts
in one vast asylum wherein is no mental sight? Then
there is in nature no such thing as an eye ! Instinct is
by what foolish theory set down as imperceptiveness in
an animal when it is the most sagacious faculty in mankind ! It is a talent too, in both alike, by good use entitled to reward. How soon the beasts appreciate our
approval or rebuke ! I have known a motion of the
finger and a warning tone from the lips induce a dog
just weaned to lick instead of bite the hand. Is there
in this no power to contrive, it being fatal to our prerogative to admit aught personal in the beast? What
are these fairy lines stretched outside across your window,
catching minute moisture from the night-fog and turning
the light into such a delicate diamond sparkle as the sun
comes out ! With what stitcher of Honiton lace shall
this weaver, who has retired with his loom, be compared ! The weaver is the shuttle thrown, and out of its
bowels the threads are spun. But where on the street
is the weaver of any stuff so fine? The spider's hands
take her into king's palaces, Solomon tells us. But no
carving of roof or pillar can match the cords with which
the cornice is finished at her touch, for the broom to
sweep away. A little boy, when the housemaid came
to cleanse the porch of cobwebs which he had admired,
remonstrated against the ruthless blows, crying out,

"These are their nests!" We know not how much, in the way of rigging, this spider academy has taught to men, with its computation of forces so exact, to escape from gravitation and anticipate the swaying of the breeze, while by every stay and girder the pressure is distributed as nicely as in any ceiling or bridge, and each little rope tried with the hand bears an astonishing strain before it breaks. All our handiwork is but a cobweb too, which the besom of destruction will level at last! If we must hem in or drive out the insects with all their plans, let us not forget that we are ephemera too, of a little longer date, and let us use some fairness in dividing with them the world and not be behind the Hebrew monarch by despising their pattern or disowning their wit.

What conceit of man in his own glory appears in the chronic wish of his philosophy to make out against other animals a distinction in favor of himself! Only as his own he fancies any divine spark. All else is but scaffolding and preparation, the beasts in all their beauty and variety but a chalking out of the human plan, the announcement and avant-courier of the king! But the true king does not blow his own trumpet In rightly judging and duly caring for his subjects his honor is found. It may be said man seeks an ideal satisfaction in what he rears, and the beast only a supply of animal wants. But there are some creatures among whom our so popular utilitarian philosophy does not appear to prevail, who make subterranean mines and galleries for pure pleasure without search for food or dwelling or gold ; and what but a worse than brutal injustice can doubt that the spinning insects which stretch with such curious ties their gossamer threads in myriad spots have a pleasure

in their task beside what their appetite may secure, **as**
does the fisherman in his creel, the hunter in his trap,
or the warrior in his camp or fort?   If there be any absolute difference of interior frame between us and what
we count below us, no statement of it has appeared.

Could all the observations be gathered up, what a
curious parallel between man and beast might be run !
We cannot deny likeness of temper and disposition, however we arrogate monopoly of mind.   Indeed, we use the
same descriptive phrase for both.   It is our neighbor as
well as his horse that takes the bit in his teeth and must
have his jaws held or broken by the curb of the law ;
and if, instead of wildly rushing, with equal irration-
ality he refuse to go, he too balks on the road, and, like
the obstinate steed, would rather be killed than proceed.
Doubtless there is some cause in either case which
should be explored in order to a cure ; but the resemblance would be comic, if not sad, which gives occasion
for the prophet's exhortation, " Be not as the horse or
the mule," whose pertinency is not less with the lapse
of time.   The sharp distinction which the naturalist
tells us ants make between friends and foes of their own
kind has its instruction bettered among men and women ;
and the moralizing of Jaques on the " poor deer, left
and abandoned of his velvet friends," when he was in
trouble, we find it also how easy to match !

> " Sweep on, you fat and greasy citizens ;
>   'T is just the fashion.   Wherefore do you look
>   Upon that poor and broken bankrupt there ? "

When Jesus bids us ask not our friends and rich neighbors, but the poor and halt and blind to the feast we

make, that we may avoid a recompense, we have a higher strain.

In the good of life shall not our four-footed friends have their share? Does not the common nature we talk of also include them? My little dog, when an alternative is presented to him, one side of which he prefers to the other, and yet is not going to refuse obedience to my command, cants his head reflectively on one side with such curious resemblance to a man's motion in like case, that I cannot question that the inward process is similar, if not the same. Beholding so much likeness of animal with human traits, let us not deny what we do not see, but rather develop what is latent that is best. We shall ourselves not miss paradise by making the humblest creature happy on earth.

If we will give a name to God, the only alternative beside pure abstraction is the concrete term of parentage. He is the Father. So the parental feeling, everywhere infused, is the one sensitive link in which the universe is bound. The lioness whom I saw, in her restless walk through her cage, stop to lick with fierce tongue the young among whom she trampled, and the lion in the Paris Conservatory who, Geoffroy St. Hilaire tells us, stood beside his mate and laid his solemn and tawny paw on her breast, in the sight of him and his friend, the day their whelp died, were but examples of a sentiment which must have begotten what it pervades, and which, shining in the most brutal form, appeals to the highest, and finds in men and angels the reflection of itself.

No materialism is implied in maintaining man's relationship with the beast. The divine inspiration flows, as Theodore Parker said, "into bee and behemoth" as well as into the soul. Each creature receives it according to its measure. But materialism denies that any creature is its receptacle, and will have nothing to do with any one Giver of all. It is the doctrine, not of unity, but of multiplicity; it accredits the elements, but has no faith in spirit; it affirms origins of things, but disowns Origin or Originator. The spiritual philosophy admits physical germs corresponding to archetypes, every person deriving from some one idea, and every animal or plant also having in the great mind an idea of its own.

X.

POLITICS.

ALTHOUGH the Bible have spots, it is no more obsolete than the sun ; and while critics talk of the light having gone out of it, the preachers and people are startled with new applications of ancient texts. What makes daylight of duty for us as well as for the patriarchs is none the worse for being old. So, when the Psalmist warns us against "fellowship with the throne of iniquity that frameth mischief by a law," we seem to be in the District of Columbia, Florida, or Oregon! Legal injustice is the most pernicious and aggravated of all wrong. An injury committed by a private person backed by no statute, but condemned by some specific enactment of Congress or the Legislature, that fits his deed, is small and brief compared with that which an assumed public authority empowers and arms. Examples may be found in laws concerning lotteries, unrestricted sale of intoxicating liquors, the return of fugitive slaves, exclusive privileges, monopolies in trade, penalties disproportioned to crime, and every form of excessive or tyrannical tax. But laws well-meant for the just protection of the community may be so framed, that is, turned and twisted in the executive hand, as to work mischief in the land, as we saw in Louisiana, and now observe in that former part of Massachusetts long ago set off under the name of Maine. It is a curiosity in American politics that in just that territory where the ignorance or illiteracy is the least — the population of Maine being reported the best educated in the common branches in the whole United States — gubernatorial ingenuity should have found errors in spelling among the many petty faults for which it is decided to disfranchise the folks. One who was born and grew up amongst those farmers, teamsters, lumbermen, and fishermen on the Kennebec, Penobscot, and Androscoggin, and along the shore, as well as the Supreme Court whose decision has just so badly broken the gubernatorial chair, may know what plain people they are, rough in speech and manner, and with a grim humor that would have rejoiced Abraham Lincoln's heart, and with not much disposition to be in any way cheated out of their rights. The over-readiness of some even of their clergy in the late crisis to shoulder the old revolutionary musket again, and the harmless but resolute mob in Bangor show what fire the flint of arbitrary imposition may fetch out of their cold constitutional steel, and what a foolish as well as gross offence was committed by the presuming officials who undertook so unrighteously to push them out of the lawful expression of their will. There is a wrath as of kindled shavings on the floor or the crackling of thorns under a pot, and there is an indignation like the sparkling into which the blacksmith provokes the reluctant metal at his forge.

But what has this Northern council-board done more to be reprehended than were the acts of the disreputable Louisiana returning-board, some years since, at the South? These Democrats have but copied after the

Republican pattern, in Shakspeare's phrase, "better-
ing the instruction"! That Southern manipulation of
the ballot-box was an unwarranted liberty and an evil
precedent indeed; and "the bad copy the mistakes of
the good with deplorable rapidity." But on what sort
or system of morality do we justify the imitation of a
crime? Moreover, the cases in some respects are not
parallel. Louisiana was a half-savage region, just
emerging from the barbarism of slavery; and if it
was undeniably an error to count in votes which were
not cast by the freedmen, the cruel suppression which
kept the freedmen from the polls was an offence of still
greater shame. Never in the darkest times of the
Spanish Inquisition or of the despotism of the Czar has
intimidation been carried to a greater extent; and intimidation that prevents the ballot is fraud as real as that
which stuffs the box with tissue-paper votes. Like
blood compared with water it has a darker dye. If the
votes which shot-guns in the South hindered be reckoned, the real voice of Louisiana was expressed in the
announced result, and there was no effectual fraud.
But the voice of Maine was choked outright by its
elected head. In the former case votes that had been
barred out were no doubt improperly counted in. In
the latter case the votes which freemen had thrown were
arbitrarily counted out, till over sixty towns and cities
had their representation as local law-makers and as
factors in the next presidential election absolutely refused. It cannot be expected that people will sit down
quietly under an abuse of technicalities through which
their citizenship is thus destroyed, or be content with a
false balance by which their political weight is cancelled,

and endure a governor's foot in the scales to nullify the will he should express, and turn into ciphers tens of thousands of men. The English Star-Chamber decisions which we shook off a hundred years ago must not be restored among us by plotters who warn their own political friends against the trap of phraseology and informality which they are setting for the other side.

The danger to this country is not from the universal suffrage about which our Jeremiahs and Cassandras have croaked so much, — no, not though it were universal among women as well as men, — but from a perverted construction of the forms of law, to work intents opposite from the purposes for which they were devised. The Apostle Paul was as good a politician as he was theologian when he said, " The letter killeth, but the spirit maketh alive ; " and the unwritten or higher law will in this country, so long as it is true to its fathers and founders, be invoked whenever the written one is framed and fashioned into a weapon against just and equal human claims. We shall ask, What is the use of governors if they are to be more overbearing and truculent than the old kings? Why call that a democracy which is an oligarchy in fact? To the honor and credit of the true democracy of the country, from all its best leaders comes repudiation of the base and villanous conspiracy in Maine. If the Maine executive was but the tool of an intrigue from the Capitol of the nation, and if the key was pitched for the note he was to strike in his place, the tuning-fork was sounded very secretly in his ear, and those who held it dare not appear or show their hand. They that set on the dogs sometimes run away ! Indeed, democracy cannot afford, by fathering

such a crime, to commit suicide. Too much nobility is
left in it for that, and too much honesty is in the
country for aristocracy to be good policy under the
democratic name. What is democracy but popular
government? The *demos* is the mass; and what sort
of rule " by and for and of the people," according to
our famous accepted definition, is it to use every trick
into which the statutory language touching elections
can be tortured to exclude " plain people " from having
in legislative halls the delegates of their choice? It
were a trumpet so constructed as to extinguish the
voice. It were to make the people twist a rope for
their own necks. An uncrossed *t*, an undotted *i*, *ditto*
under a column of figures, the word *scattering* with its
meaning not resolved into all its component parts although the name which has the majority is quite clear,
a vertically instead of horizontally inscribed ballot, the
absence of some single selectman, and the signature of
some *pro tempore* clerk, or any distinguishing mark, —
such are the strands out of which the astute gubernatorial hangman's cord and noose are woven for the good
people's throat! But the good people itself, a little
puzzled to know by what lawyer-like jugglery it has
been converted into a criminal from its honest will, and
angrily rubbing its threatened head, declines to be suspended so. That proposed execution will never take
place. To hoist a State to the gallows requires more
strength than happens to be in the executioner's hand.
They who are of the people have a surmise, vague but
strong, that if anybody in the premises ought to be
hung, it is rather the would-be sheriff and nominal
chief magistrate himself!

It is not likely that any party, old and regular and with a right to be in this country, like the Democratic, would ever have conceived and hatched any thing like this last unspeakable disgrace. Such political vileness was begot of that financial dishonesty which goes by the name of Greenback, in an ill-assorted and baleful union with the Democracy, of which somebody ought to have forbidden the banns. We have had sometimes a coalition, and by it all parties among us have been dishonored more or less by turns. The present dodge is fusion! It is a melting together of parties that have no affinity or real natural bond. Whatever was fair or candid in either it will be found very hard to recover from the melting-pot. It is difficult to restore the stamp and edge and image on a medal that has been once thrown into the fire. It was not silver or gold, but pinchbeck in this case ; and it would not be strange if the furnace of public indignation, with which the usually calm Supreme Court that was appealed to burns so hotly, should gape for all who have been concerned in the flagrant trespass that has flung its lurid light, beyond any calcium blazing, into the remotest borders of our land. For no disrepute visited on a man can match the infamy with which he can brand his own name ; and the real authors of this sin and new American treason will have their characters blackened past washing to all time. No glorious stigmas will theirs be on the cross which they have made for themselves. From dignitaries such as they *the neighbors* will shrink and withhold their hands. Even a president of the United States who has any wise degraded the station he held is sometimes treated with little respect when he has retired to private life. It will be charity to let the lesser luminaries in this base spectacle and ignominious show, leave whatever ill odor it may, go out altogether in the dark when they shall have been dispossessed of the posts in which for a time they unworthily stood.

In a free country, whose citizens are jealous of their reserved rights and easily stirred by injustice to resistance, no transgression can be so great as that malversation or malfeasance in office which moves to rebellion and excites contention. If blood should flow, they would be responsible who have instigated or aided and abetted the civil strife. Men differ congenitally in the acuteness of their moral feeling; and some seem to be so devoid of conscience, in their relations to society and the body politic, that color-blindness is the true figure for their defect of inward sight. But as those who cannot distinguish red from blue or white are not fit for pilots or engineers, so such as are unable to discern betwixt wisdom and cunning, truth and lying, magnanimity and what is mean, ought not to be conductors of the train of our civil affairs or to manage the ship of State. If they attempt to steal a legislature, a commonwealth, or the government of a nation, it is grand and not petty larceny, highway robbery and not ordinary swindling, in which these worst of thieves are engaged; and unless the harpies that prey on the whole people in this continent are pursued till they be exterminated and extinct, our reunion is a fiction, patriotism is plunder, and our political days are numbered, or chaos is at hand to invite the sway of the sword.

For what is the appearance which this swindling operation, not in stocks, but on human beings, presents? A sham legislature, in a State House whose members call themselves representatives, but who do not represent the State, and as a body were never elected by it, but have by tricksters been construed to stand for it, as a doll stands for a baby because by certain artificial springs it moves its limbs and makes a disagreeable noise. When a minority installs itself over a majority in this country we have a tyranny as real and oppressive as though we had taken back the English Parliament and King George to rule us, and all honest parties and decent men should join to put it down. A native of the abused State and an American citizen — which by his business and profession or by any forfeiture one has not ceased to be, though he is a Christian minister — may see and denounce in such a transaction the most alarming menace to all religion and civilization in our land. It is a broad usurpation and wholesale cheat. It is that forgery on a commonwealth which, committed on a small scale for a few dollars, sends a man to jail.

But does not a clergyman go out of his way to meddle with politics under any circumstances, however grave? So it was said when we protested against the extension of slave territory, petitioned for its restriction, expressed disapproval of a Fugitive Slave bill, or ventured even to pray for the slave. The Almighty was brought under the political ban! But without such demonstrations of religious feeling in the cause of humanity, this country would not have been free. As one nation it would to-day not be at all; and now, when once more the forms of law which were made to protect are used to strangle and destroy, as if the cord of an Alpine guide were converted into an executioner's rope, it is time for the pulpit to interfere again.

What party, any more than the whole people, can profit by villany of this style? A party, the Greenback, which is but for a moment, does not deserve to be called. A local democracy is involved with it for the time. But from that real, large democracy, which must be always a potent if not the prevailing principle in our institutions, it is as alien as the Lords are from the Commons or an empire from the republic; and if by any thing, then by wicked combining of this sort the man on horseback, who is predicted as our ruler for life, would be hurried up. It is the Greenback notion of making irredeemable paper a legal tender in payment of our debts, which, pooling its issues with a false and temporary democracy, is with such logical propriety consummated in the high-handed and rapacious seizure of a State, to try in vain to command its treasury and all its goods. It no more truly represents the State than do the rags which it would pass for money till they rot, represent any value of silver or gold.

But for all these theoretic and consequent practical assumptions a remedy will be furnished by the numerical and moral reserved power of the people, a residue and remainder which no perverters of trust can long succeed in neutralizing and affronting.

Meantime some benefit will result if we learn from the vexatious experience how some of our political moralists have misplaced their fears in thinking universal suffrage to be the rock on which we might be wrecked, when for our vessel the reef of peril is on just the opposite shore of a partial suffrage, for which the universal one is on occasion so iniquitously exchanged. With the people that framed our Constitution public honesty is better guarded and our destiny is more secure than with any refined or learned or wealthy class. Voters too may learn that they cannot be careless any more.

The root of trouble, the ground of jeopardy, and the occasion of reasonable terror, is the vicious habit we have in our philosophy contracted, of dividing the whole man or mind into distinct functions, which, like the water-tight compartments of a boat or the fire-proof chambers of a building, have no communication with each other, — a plan as bad for the soul and the community as it is good for the building or the boat. We say, politics is politics, business is business, a bargain is a bargain, and religion is religion. Do you wish to trade, there is the exchange, the market, the brokers' board, the bank, and the gold room! Would you worship, there is the chapel, vestry, and church, and Sunday for the service to begin and end, and your religion to be finished up on the spot! Do you want to vote, choose your list of candidates, whom for any whim or reason, selfish or generous, you have a right to support! You can leave your reverence in the cathedral aisles and your honesty in the shop when you carry your bit of paper for your clique to the ward-room in a school or engine house! But all this dissection of yourself, be it said, is unholy and profane. Your integrity should be in the convention as well as at the counter, and your religion in the caucus as well as in the pew. That love of man or love of country is baseless which rests not on the love of God; and it is because we neither love nor fear him as we ought that we have fallen into this spiritual calamity, and that our chief passion is no longer, as with the fathers, patriotic, but partisan. The love of party more and more, in many quarters, carries the day over love of country ; and patriotism, among such as conduct the nefarious transactions to which I have referred, is a lost virtue, even as antiquarians inform us there are lost arts.

The inducement to party extravagance and unprincipled deceit is in the immense patronage of eighty thousand offices, which the general government has to bestow. While this tremendous and manifold lure shall be held out to the hand of the incoming administration to dispense to its mercenaries, during the term it shall hold the reins, the diverse salaries and fat jobs to as many hungry clamoring mouths, so long the wide-spread corruption will hold on. Civil reform means that the various posts and appointments which the supreme officer controls shall be given to subordinate officials, not as rewards of partisan zeal and as victors' spoils, but for merit and fitness and while good behavior shall last ; and that our elected chief magistrate shall no longer consider it as his main prerogative to turn out all former incumbents of a different stripe of opinion from his own, and then feed the pap of the exchequer to famished aspirants of his set, as a municipal officer ladles out soup to the poor. An impartial equity of civil appointment would be, not partisanship, but patriotism, for which may we, by a good Providence, be inspired and prepared ! Meanwhile such a process as we saw going on in Maine was a dismal, lamentable, and wickedly contemptible setback to any worthy tendency and noble hope. Therefore should it and its operators and apologists by all good men be reproved.

.Let us be no partisans in politics or religion. One party must for the time prevail. But while we would have the best party go in, let us be glad to have the other strong; for every successful party should be a watched trustee, and such doings as we have seen in Florida, Louisiana, Oregon, and Maine show that no party can be trusted out of custody of the people, which is too great, and, notwithstanding all the telegraphs and railroads, moves too slowly, more like a raft than a clipper, to commit all together any atrocity, as it is too honest to countenance crime.

We cannot, however, yield to the natural course of things. Evolution in nature is order. In society it is not salvation, but drift. In governmental administration it is foundering unless duty be at the helm.

Seeing how all parties with long possession of power grow corrupt, let us not wish any party easily, invariably, or by a large majority, in this country ever to prevail. Let it be displaced by some other whenever it is guilty of fraud, or confines the distribution of loaves and fishes to itself. Perpetual vigilance is the price not only of liberty but of purity in public affairs; and if one political side in the use of enormous patronage becomes exclusive, the other side ought to have its turn, till there be better behavior of both. But both must abide the unswerving divine law; and if either wish to slip out of that yoke it but proves its own sin. If politics have nothing to do with religion, if the town-house shall ever be divorced from the meeting-house, the ballot-box insulated from the pulpit, the vote parted from the prayer, Sunday separated from the week, and the community disown its God, then the State will be doomed. Every politi-

cal question is a moral one, every case in court involves
principle, as every sick-bed is the scene of the physician's fidelity or malpractice ; and although any professional man leaves his province if he meddle with details
which he does not understand, it is his sphere to expound the moral law.

When Christ would unite Jew and Greek, how we
stick in the bark and cling to the letter of his meaning,
and do not perceive that what he would intend now is
a cordial understanding between existing peoples, such
as England and America, Austria and Italy, Germany
and France, of Russia in the East with the United
States in the West, every kindred and people and tribe
and tongue being embraced in the horoscope he cast, —
in a prophecy how far from fulfilment yet, while the
Californian hates the Chinaman, and the Irishman the
negro, and the Hibernian the British, and Peru Chili,
and the Prussian the Gaul.

The old Bible anticipates our supposed psychologic
discovery, and always treats nations as persons, moral
and responsible. They are such as truly as are individuals. What a mob of confused and contradictory
inclinations the individual commonly is, there being
few of us that ought not to have the riot-act read
to ourselves ! Our particular natures are no more at-
tuned to that pure and free personality which is the true
state of a human soul than were Israel and Egypt,
Tyre and Sidon, Nineveh and Edom, Babylon and
Capernaum, whom seer or Saviour personified and apos-
trophized, admonished, and summoned to the judgment-
seat. The diverse characters and conflicting qualities
of different realms are shown as clearly as are the dis-

positions to virtue or vice of any of the personages in
any one of their borders or at any era of the world.
Is not Great Britain proud and France vainglorious,
Austria haughty, Russia bearish, Prussia brutal and
rough, Turkey cruel, the Spaniard an aristocrat, the
Jew jealous and money-making, the Italian lazy and
vagabond, the American restless and rebellious, and
the South American disorderly and with his neighbor
always at strife? Putting good traits on the opposite
side of the balance-sheet, need we say which one of
these is polite and which dignified, which is reverent
or enterprising, which lives on its memory and which
in its hope? Is the spirit obsolete and gone out of that
Christian faith which has purposed from the first to
overcome the grudging and envy between hostile races,
and make this footstool of the planet, with the conver-
sational lightning's aid, a friendly meeting-house? So
long as we nurse or allow any prejudice in our breast
against color or kind of the human species, and would
drive the Indian to the Rocky Mountains, or push back
the Mongolian into the sea, or give to the African but
the sharp alternative of exodus to a strange ungenial
clime, or oppression at the muzzle of the shot-gun, crowding and cheating and disfranchising him at home, so long
and so far we contravene the genius of a religion which
will never be antiquated or useless till the growl of anger and the roar of war have died away, and till those
standing armies are disbanded which are the canine
cutting teeth of nations, and kingdoms and republics
shall become a brotherly band.

Politics is the art, in public or private, of getting along
together, — the agreement of individuals with the com-

munity which they create and are created by, as well as concert among those live aggregates we call countries, between which the continents are shared. Independence becomes a faulty individualism when we fail to contribute and gladly to make ourselves a whole burnt-offering· to the commonweal. The old doctrine that we part with a portion of our personal freedom and right in order to become a community is not only erroneous, but the very opposite of the truth. Men are free and have their full rights in communities alone. Is the savage free? Has the hermit all his rights? Is the recluse ever the greatest of men, or is he a monster whose peculiarity lies in the mutilation of his body and mind? In proportion as we cut the threads of that network of universal sympathy which is the circulation of the human frame, we become not giants but dwarfs, overgrown only in selfishness, and undersized in the joy of our nature as in the generosity of our traits. Accordance with all with whom we live, by concession and sacrifice of every thing but honor and truth, is the common law, beyond all that passes with barristers by that name. When Charles Sumner delivered his oration on peace as " the true grandeur of nations," that great lawyer, Jeremiah Mason, said he should as soon think of getting up a society against thunder and lightning as against war. But we have learned that man can modify the climate by art, and by love and justice he will prevent or moderate civil storms. There are individualists, that is, self-seekers against the general good, on a large as well as a little scale ; and the bigger the dimensions the heavier the curse. When the Polish Counts would all be sovereigns, Poland ceased to be. An American explained his incuriosity to see the Queen by saying, "All are sovereigns in the United States." So much the worse were it for the United States! But when Victoria refuses to invite or speak to Robert Peel and William Gladstone because of their conscientious political course, she oversteps her princely prerogative, and becomes an individualist rather than the organ and representative of the realm. The Pope is but a huge individualist in attempting to bind the world by his encyclical, syllabus, or bull. The Orthodox divine is an ecclesiastical individualist when he preaches total depravity for all but his set of saints; for the human race is not a sinner, and never fell! In both the Liberal and the Orthodox church, laying the stress on personal instead of universal salvation was individualism, and in principle a selfishness of the most tremendous sort. But its main haunt was the Calvinistic desk. When Dr. Lyman Beecher was dying he wished one to read to him the passage about Paul's good fight and ready crown. But when the reader of the verse went on, "and not to me only," the sturdy and polemic veteran bade him stop. He was not concerned about other people's crowns, but only his own. Contend we must on the way to that victory which is a righteous peace; as Jesus did with the "small cords," which James Walker said he would not have used at the end of his ministry, while John Weiss thought nothing in the gospel more authentic than the hissing of that lash. The difference between a conservative and a reformatory mind was never more happily displayed.

But no disinterested historian can doubt the part which that name and power, influence or leaven, we call the Christ has played in persuading the segments of our humanity that they belong to the whole being from which they come. So much the Divinity can do by a man! George Augustus Sala, the English traveller and reporter, seeing in Italy a statue of Napoleon, remarks that he alone of the moderns can bear to be put in the nude and classic style of art; for how ridiculous, he says, to represent Lord Brougham or the Duke of Wellington so! Jesus, who is in such contrast of character with any man of this world, needs no Jewish costume, nor more than a setting for the splendor of his excellence in the circumstances of his time. There is nothing accidental or superficial in his sway or in its hold on a future age; for his ideal, while working like leaven, and claiming the elements for its growth like a seed, is still but as a transforming atom in this vast lump of our nature, or like a green sapling in the wood. The thorough-paced critic is blind often in this case to the distinction between the individual and the type. In the great Master whom the Church embodies and owns for its head we have a Godhood and a manhood too; and it is no longer the details of his biography, or even sentences of his speech, that signify so much as the living pattern he has grown into for the conscious soul. If made a finality, he were a fetich. But, as a bit of divine beauty modelled in clay, there is beside naught worthier of the Supreme Artist; and if the reverent feeling for him be characterized as idolatry, let us scrutinize the proper application of that term. In our time the chief idol is not the Christ who is an ideal, but it is matter and the material world. The idolater is the mere scientist; he is not the devotee. As a native reverence cannot be extinguished in the human breast, if it be fixed on nothing in the way of person, it will be fastened on something in the way of law, or in the shape which law grossly takes in earthly stuff; and if we idolize aught, is the size of our idol the important point? Be it small, uncouth, and grotesque as an Egyptian image, or big as a firmament, the superstition in adoring it is all the same. Stock and stone, or planet and sun, one beast, a bug, beetle, crawling reptile, or the whole animal kingdom, protoplasm or finished universe, is to the principle indifferent, if on any thing outward our homage be set. Any worship of Jesus, that historic man and morsel of our race, is idolatry, but of a nobler sort than the worship of fossil remains or of the Milky Way. But the worship of Deity in him and in all men is the loftiest exercise of the mind; and the turning of our attention to the union and reunion out of all strife of the jarring human elements to own and obey the Father is the politics of that city of God which is some time to show its foundations on earth as in heaven. It is no wonder or dishonor that all the millions who have gazed on the cross should revere the temper out of which the blood there trickled down! Atonement is what it meant.

The reconciler and reconciliation must include also in one the Church and State. There are corruptions in both. But in the dismal game of iniquity the latter so commonly wins that the scheme eagerly urged of turning the former into it so as to have nothing left but the State is hostility and treason to mankind. Because particular local churches have shown a bias irrational or inhumane, there is no reason to denounce and destroy the Church, or confound it with the political machine, with whose uses to keep the peace and protect industry we cannot dispense, any more than is the profligacy in the members of some families cause for abolishing the home. Society is a double-flowering plant, and the inner row of its petals is the Church. The time for the State to decease may come when we have risen above our quarrelling, and our utilitarian plane. But the Church, even in heaven, will never disappear. The radical censor while he assails ecclesiastical abuses is in place; but in attacking the Church he runs against the bosses of the Almighty, or kicks against the pricks. Society, when it shall be perfected, may reabsorb into itself every political or ecclesiastical form which it has in its imperfection put forth. But it would stab a vital part and commit suicide could it rend apart even the organic Church to-day. That we must not cut that thread of tradition which we at the moment of our little earthly span compose is now taught with equal emphasis by the scientist and ecclesiastic; and when infidel or atheist levels his organ of destructiveness and the battery of his brain against all religious institutions, we rejoice to look around, and see that in spite of the repeated discharge not only Liberalism, but Orthodoxy, Episcopacy, and Romanism still stand to make of his cannon a popgun, whose execution has only the measure of a little noise or smoke.

Besides, to the demand for secularizing the State we must reply by an inquiry what secularity is. It is the course of things and the train of affairs. Literally, it is the following, personal or of principle, which gets established in time. It is the logic of events. It is human conduct as the sequel and consequence of human thought. The import of the Latin *sæculum* is scarce expressed in the English *age*. What, then, in the line of progress has been the human connection, like a coupling of the cars? Surely it has been no discarding of the gods. The cycle of dispensation was created through Christ, says the writer to the Hebrews. Irreligion would throw us from the track which from the earliest times has been pursued. It would be disintegration and no reconstruction. It would, especially in this land, not deepen and propel, but dam or divert, the social stream ; for it were a special impiety to the fathers, who made fear of God the beginning and the basis of our State. By what strange and insane reversal of sense has secularity come to mean organized unbelief? To be fair and just to all our citizens, and to govern by equal laws, it seems there must be no religious atmosphere in our schools, prayers in our legislatures or judicial courts, chaplains in army or navy, oath or affirmation, in Heaven's ear, of witness in the box or of prisoner at the bar! Law-maker, high officer, or judge, if he would shun guilt of treason to the republic, must never take the sacred name on his public lips ; nor must we let any convicted criminal in the last extremity appeal for justice or mercy to a higher bench. As, in tyrannical or revolutionary times, when the headsman was ready, the voice of condemned innocence, that would cry at once to the crowd below and to the skies above, has been drowned by the beating of drums and the shouts of the mob, so to all petitions referred to an Omnipotent Arbiter let us be made deaf by the loud, calculated, and utilitarian din! This

would be a secularity of selfishness, of endless contention and bottomless despair, substituted for what
has always existed to console the abandoned and forlorn, namely, that leading by mutual bonds in a religious trust by which men amid this world's dangers have
hung together, like travellers amid Alpine crevasses
to the cord of their guide. What are statesman and
churchman but one and the same man?

In this better civil service, which all religious service issues in or is, there is one more reconciliation of
science with faith. The worst foes are those of our
own household, and science and faith are brethren that
have fallen out by the way. When Samuel Rogers,
the poet, was told respecting certain persons who he
knew were in some trouble together, that they were
" like a band of brothers," he answered that he was
well aware of their disagreements, but had not supposed it was so bad as that! Let us trust that art,
science, political economy, and religion will be a sisterhood, if that gentler name be a more harmonious
one.

Science gazing up or down through its lens cannot
rule out that other " inward eye which is the bliss of
solitude," because what appears to it is too great to be
verified by the test of the understanding. But the theologian must no longer, as true religion never did, tell
us of a six days' creation, of a universal deluge, or of
any miracles that look like juggles with substances
suddenly and unlawfully transformed. Such tales we
marvel at, but do not admire. The food in the corn,
the fish in the sea, and wine in the vineyard feed our
wonder; but the reported prodigious multiplyings and

dislocations, as aught more than pictures, affront our mind ; and our crediting them is the blasphemy of supposing that God would go back on us and on himself, and contradict his own lessons to our eyes. Stories of a resurrection of decomposed bodies, of a blasted fig-tree, or of a Roman coin from the mouth of the first fish that should bite a hook, lack dignity as much as rationality. Science will furnish better figures of power that have the signal advantage we find in all observed truth.

This reconciliation is not equalization of angels or of men. As great trees furnish masts for admirals, so the forest of humanity supplies great men. The hills enrich the plains ; and without heroes the world were hard and dead as an ivory ball. Individuality is the condition of communion. But individualism and communism are ugly and ungracious twins ; and the division of society into mutually misunderstood classes opens intervening morasses, which are the breeding-places of strikes and riots, of feverish excitements and mobs. It is said that in Sable Island the loosened horses draw off into different sets, the lame going one way, and the sound in limb another. But it is not a good example for men ! A better pattern is set by cows in the pasture, that lick each other's faces even across the fences, than by such as lock horns. We are but vagabonds and bandits until we exist to serve our race. Stars in clusters, plants in beds, trees in groves, beasts in herds, and birds in flocks show how we should live and grow ; and when we behold heaven's grace in a great man, let us not straightway excommunicate him because he is better and wiser than we ! To exclude Robertson in

England or Parker in America is a mistake, if indeed
it be a misfortune and a bad sign for the Church when
the saints are outside! For religion cannot be put
into any radical or conservative pigeon-hole. Said
Taylor, the Bethel preacher, "I own part of Boston
Common, and I will never tell which part it is!" It is
the noble universal soul in Jesus by which we are re-·
deemed, and he saves us less by his blood as he sheds
it than as it runs in his veins.. When did he ever make
of civil and religious duty two things? He could do it
no more than Solomon could divide asunder the living
child. He refers us for judgment to that spirit which
has an inlet to every heart. The philosophy of utility
and experience would say, Act on the consent of the
competent and for the greatest good of the greatest
number, — a rule which would stop procedure and block
the way till we should ascertain what is the greatest good
and who are the competent! We must go to "the
Holy Ghost the Comforter;" else we are put upon an
inclined plane or sliding-scale of personalities, — first
Jesus, then the Virgin, next her mother, whose names
are called, whose bones are kept, and whose prayers are
invoked, but whose worship lets us down from all our
reaching up to the Supreme. Let us beware what we
adore! "My name will I not give to another." The
name of God is not in our Constitution. But it is in a
more venerable instrument that has needed no amend-
ments, the Declaration of Independence; and no rose,
lily, eagle, lion, or liberty and union, for a war-cry or in
the blazonry of banners, can so shine or sound! What
our agreement consists in all may feel, but none can
define. It is in a glance; for who can tell how far,

even into heaven, a look may go? It is in a tone; for there are accents of the human voice which the Seraphim must overhear. It is in a smile; for there are smiles that include the universe!

Jesus the Christ is the chosen name, because he that bore it resisted the whole evil tendency that was downward in the gravitation of mankind. What a memory that name means, still pungent and sweet! The cradle takes it to rock the new-born babe with, and the bier catches it in the procession to the tomb. It pierced into the catacombs of the first disciples, and it hangs around uncounted graveyards that hold the once throbbing dust. It is a sign that what in us once aspired shall ascend again, lie low as it may now. It designates nothing carnal but what is latent in our bosom waiting to be awaked.

If politics be the art of getting along together, in ruling a city and composing civil strife, it has, to order and harmonize our faculties, another interior sphere; and there is a wider reach than Paul suspected in his own words when he besought the Corinthians to be reconciled to God. But Bishop Butler raised a new question in charging on nature the same difficulties that exist in revelation; for the moral sense finds it hard to stomach how much that providentially occurs! No moral standard can cover the whole ground, as may be shown in a single flagrant illustration. Dr. Channing, whose religion was a total morality as much as any other man's, has in his most famous paper well arraigned Napoleon for his selfish ambition and many other imperial faults. But Channing does not recognize the import of that piece of nature, that so exceptional and phenomenal man, hewn by circumstances out of the rock of reality, whom we call Bonaparte, — not so much Emperor of France as dominator of the world! There was a *daimonic* as well as voluntary portion of his soul. He had a star, although it was not the one that led to Bethlehem. He was the child of destiny, spoiled child of fortune though he became. He rode for a while in that chariot of the Lord, under whose wheels at last he fell. His ablest critic has not an appreciable fraction of his enormous weight. For this was the one man who could seize the wild horses of anarchy by the rein, who could curb and check revolutionary excess, and say, "Gentlemen, come to order," in that chaos of blood and fire into which a nation was cast. Aught corrupt afterwards in his motives or insincere in his speech Heaven will compensate and men must condemn. But how wrong and narrow wholly to cover and cancel anybody's services with his sins! His sins were indeed grave, but his services were immense, although not even a clerical eulogist, like Abbott, his American admirer and biographer, can persuade us to make a Sunday-school book of the annals of his reign. The statesman he was is shown by his word in the civil code, and the soldier by his hand on the sword. This modern mob-hater and foe of lawlessness, hurling at disorder his deathly dart, was, as much as Attila, at least the scourge of God; and in some dark fashion he too was an angel from the sky. Out of its cloud leaped this thunderbolt of war. Did not this armed head of democracy prepare for the republic of to-day? He was the savior, if alternately the oppressor, of France. This solid and subtle Cor-

sican was a consummate actor, as he made the costly
vase he shivered to pieces on the floor and the hat
he tossed into the corner of the room, in affected passion or actual rage, a language to tell his scorn and
his resolve. "In comparison with my purpose what,"
he asked, "are a million of men?" Battle against old
authority was his mission; his unparalleled magnetism
of his troops was his certificate; and he wanted to meet
Scipio and the other great generals on the other side
of the grave, although he said with a smile, "Such an
assembly might even there occasion some alarm!"
Who will pronounce the verdict for such a man or anticipate the award? Who can deny the use Providence
had for movements of which he was the centre? He
was a strange religionist! Of all tributes to Jesus
Christ his, in conversation with General Bertrand, is
the most striking. Men have never known what to
do with this prodigy of power, and perhaps angels
do not! He cannot quite be subjected to weight and
measure by any yet invented ethical yardsticks or
scales. The size of him is so monstrous, and the
conflict of good and evil in him so dire; his anger
was so dreadful, and he had a winsomeness so complete, that into no crucible for our analysis will he
readily go. Of downright meanness our judgment can
easily dispose. But greatness defies us by being, while
it lasts, simple and one. Charlemagne or the Russian
Peter composing nations, Luther and Sakya Mouni re-
forming faith, and Shakspeare and Goethe setting a
language with gems, before which all in the mine turn
pale, are alike sent of God, and not to be damned for
a defect, more than a gun-ship should be for a knot in

her bulwarks or a California pine for a worm in its
bark. Mohammed was the same man in the closet or
in the field. Did not Jesus for a moment think of re-
sorting to arms? Was not Washington as good as
William Penn? Does Seward the diplomat rank the
warrior Grant? The circumstance does not signify so
much as the aim. In strife or in peace duty is all.

The French historian, Nisard, says Cæsar had charm.
How else explain Napoleon's hold on his men, so great
that when the Pope, being a prisoner in Paris, adjured
the sentinel to let him pass, the answer, with presented
bayonet, was. "If it were the body of our Lord that
would go out here, I should run it through. I have
been in many a bloody battle with my master, and expect to have to go through hell for him yet!" It is
difficult to believe there was no heart in one to whom
his soldiers were so attached! Yet he told Talleyrand,
when friends had deceased, "I have no time to occupy
myself with the dead." This saying makes one remember
another and sacred sentence from which it would almost
seem to have been borrowed. When the excuse of a
father's funeral was offered for not following Jesus, he
replied, "Let the dead bury their dead." "We cannot judge him, he is too great," said Thackeray of
Goethe. We cannot *judge* any one. We cannot apply
the moral law to the whole of the humblest life; and
our inability is not lessened by the immensity of the
scale on which humanity acts. But such cases and
considerations show out of how many still jarring elements the reconciliation, proposed in all just politics,
must be brought to pass. Politics is morality not of
a private person, but of the multitude, as made parts

of each other by an organic law. It is fair dealing of
fellow-men together in complicated ties. It is equity in
the web of relations, and it is the weaving into beauty
of all our bonds. It should be as worthy a title as the
grander one, statesmanship, and it reaches more widely.
Only the base tricks of politicians have given it a bad
name.

The real atonement, which is the object alike of religious revelation and of the civil law, is in the faculties
and desires that so often pull diverse ways in our own
minds; and never man lived more aware than was the
Master of Christians how vast is the work of this reconciliation within. His fine feelings, both in and out
of the Church, have been extolled at the expense of his
understanding, because, in order to be understood, he
was obliged to use the language, with some of its erroneous implications, of his country and his time. There
may have been defects in his theory, or mistakes in his
philosophy, of the universe. Has the sphinx spoken to
us so that we construe the riddle surely aright? His
answers are the best rendered yet; and they show
that the ideas in his head were as lofty as the Divine
love was deep in his heart. But of all traits in his disciples sincerity is the first. John Ruskin says that "the
oath of a thief or street-walker is in the eye of God
as sinless as a hawk's cry or a gnat's murmur, compared with that of the responses in the church-service
of the usurer and adulterer." If by civil or ecclesiastical politics be meant a form, made empty, mechanical,
and hypocritical in order to be catholic and include
all persons, every sacred name is blasphemed and
profaned. The Christian general in command of the

forces in the Pine-tree State, who, being a soldier, did not draw but sheathed the sword, a warrior who was a reconciler, a man of battle who kept the peace, and a hero who stood in the breach between a commonwealth and anarchy, declining to be superseded and relieved of his charge by a pretending chief-magistrate, whose authority had no warrant of constitution and law, is worthy of the highest trust any people could bestow.

XI.

PLAY.

THERE is a mental state in which motion and rest are the same, as an eagle at once floats on and flies through the sky, buoyed up while it ascends. It is absence of obstruction before the presence of unconscious strength. The sport of children is an escape from them of that energy which is painful if confined. When David tells Joab to " play the men" against the Syrians and Ammonites, what does he mean but that men fighting for home and native land may so lay all private will on the altar, and be so kindled with courage from its live coals, that even their dreadful deeds are sportive and inspired. Play is force without effort, as in an engine or fountain. Men work at the grindstone or pump; but the musician plays on an instrument if, while he addresses himself to his performance, all obstacles vanish, and the theme performs itself. Just in proportion as the artist works he is weak, and his exhibition is " a labored affair." Beasts and birds play. It is play for a horse to slip his halter, to run from his stall, and as he capers and careers over the ground to revert from the bondage of his harness to the infancy of his race. The kitten plays with its tail, and its mother with the mouse; and kids and calves have their social gambols and games. In what waltzes or round

dances, making a ballroom of the atmosphere, the summer insects whirl! With what unmistakable courtesy
the swallows, like partners, meet or take their leave!
Even fishes toil and travail little for subsistence. They
have much transport with their fins. In human beings,
while virtue exerts itself, grace plays. What is the
leaping of the fish, in uncontainable exultation, out
of the water but the beginning and figure of the spirit's
soaring into heaven?

We speak of God's works; but the self-representing
Will into which Schopenhauer would reduce the world's
perpetual push must be so successful in accomplishment as to be unconscious of attempt. God wins no
victory, for he has no foe. Do we play with the cue on
the billiard-table? What but easy play is his tossing
of enormous balls in ethereal air?

Play is plenty of resource, be it spent in the smooth
wards of a lock, the endless somersaults with puffs of
pleasure of the porpoises, or of the whales, who throw
in the spouting as an elegance of the profession as they
come to the surface to breathe. These creatures say that
bare subsistence is not enough without a vital overplus
for merriment and fun. It is a play of the wild waves
themselves which the poet sings. In all mechanism the
object is fit movement without rub or noise, as the grass
grows, and the air clasps us, and the waters ebb and
flow. The wood is shaven, the iron and steel filed,
and the strap drawn to suit the grooving in the wheel.
But our art goes to Nature to school. We copy her
centres of motion in the jewelled pivots of a watch, of
the play of whose works we speak; and the soul must
be automatic or self-moved before morality is complete.

Paul's mission was to deliver his countrymen from "the works of the law." Ceremonial law we say in our gloss, yet it was a law into whose obedience their conscience went as much as ours does into the actions and customs that discharge our ethical heat. But grace surpasses all painstaking. It cannot be put aside or abandon itself. "For his bounty it had no winter in it;" and the sons of God are manifest in a goodness that abounds. "Oil is in their vessels with their lamps." Heaven above is not labor, but play. We figure the angels in choirs and with their "chorus on high."

What is love but the heart's play? If you find it hard work to love us, we pray you not to love us at all! It is enough to have a force-pump in the house, but feeling finds its own level, and must be under no restraint. It is the pressure itself! We say ironically of one who is obliged to make much preparation for any occasion that he is "getting up the steam;" but love is eloquence. What but the magnet and steel and needle to the pole are our favorite illustrations of friendship that is real and sincere? Lovers fly to each other's embrace. The benevolent man is nourished by others' needs. If the destitute did not ask, charity would die. Hunger and nakedness and all poverty and ignorance are its field, without which it were smothered in its own excess. A locomotive does not object to the track, and good affections are always in running order. Love is the paying and receiving teller alike in God's bank. In some ministry at large is the benefactor or beneficiary to be congratulated most? As the courser is breathed on the course, so goodness runs and is not weary; and the orthodox doctrine is true, that there is no merit in the best works.

But is not life full of hard tasks, as Harriet Martineau's childish maxim was, — "Duty first and pleasure afterwards"? We may begin with application and proceed to agony; but we end in a composure, which is rapture too. It is like the process of filling a balloon which sways awkwardly and without balance on the ground, not knowing for a time what to do. But it rights itself more and more as the finer element which is to be its stay fills its hungry interior and presses out its silken sides. At length it tugs at and spurns the cords that confine it to the earth, waiting only till they be cut for it to soar, and become part of the airy current on which it is borne. Duty is the wish of the soul raised to the highest power, and rushing to pay what it owes, as the honest man rejoices less in making money than in paying his debts. Nor is it trivial obligations alone that mostly thrill and recreate the mind. A tragedy, "Othello" or "Macbeth," on the stage is still a play. So are dire encounters in real life. When, in Nelson's phrase, England expected every man to do his duty, at Aboukir or Trafalgar, was it not beauty too to every man? When the Federals and Confederates exchanged rations, fruit, or tobacco jocosely across the lines, or when at the gates of Paris a Uhlan and a French soldier smiled on each other, after the deadly thrust and grip, just before they both died, were they not quite aware it was not hatred, but a game? At the playhouse our great President met his doom, but in what a theatre he had been chief character outside! He would have been capable of a good-natured jest at his assassin's expense, like Thomas More when he told the executioner to spare his long beard, as "that at least had committed no treason." John Brown, being dragged in the cart to the gallows, amazes and amuses the driver by light-hearted talk on the fine scenery in whose neighborhood they passed. Of what was this modern Judas Macca-bæus with his Hebrew zeal thinking, as the wheels of the van that held him rattled on? But how joyfully he had acted his part at the difficult post where, by a power that would not be gainsaid, he had been set; while a solace from a horizon more glorious than the Virginia hills beamed on his believing soul, so shortly by the great Manager to be released from its blessed rôle, and refreshed. In him body and mind had constitution-ally a certain noble sway and elastic tread, and he had well and often in his heart's chambers practised and rehearsed what he did such justice to in the eyes of mankind. It was a serious sort of play. It is not the grim Puritan but the good-natured man that is most in earnest. The true hero is less grave than gay. He is Bayard and Sidney rather than John Bal-four of Burley. When on the country-road a sweet fragrance of flowers is wafted from the yard, we feel that generosity with love of beauty, not selfish moiling, lives in the house; and the atmosphere of greatness is always sweet.

Jesus himself was an actor in the same sense. A modern school of theologians speaks of the crucifixion not as a vicarious bloody atonement, but a dramatic ex-hibition of God's horror of sin; and the ancient Docetæ thought Calvary was but a show of suffering. There was no real expiring at Golgotha. The deathless soul enacted the whole scene, and made room for all the *dramatis personæ* in one breast. Christ must have looked out of his murderers' eyes on himself when he based his prayer for their pardon on their ignorance of their deed. He *was* the disciple whom he made a son to his own mother instead of himself ; and he was the mother to whom he knew what it was to give a son. Yet he left not his own station on the nails that held him against the tree. He insisted on tasting the last drop of penal anguish from banded Judæa and Rome. He refused to deaden one pang with the wonted compliment of vinegar and myrrh.

Most scholars and critics now agree that the temptation recorded by the Evangelist was no outward fact arranged by a visible devil with the Lord, but that it transpired in his own bosom, as ambition, appetite, ostentation, spread the lures which he instantly declined to follow, and the snares in which he could not be caught. An imaginative mind of such a poet of God as Christ was would lay out the various careers he might have the option to pursue. But the stones to be made bread, the pinnacle of the temple, and the exceeding high mountain displaying all the glories of the world, were but vision and magnificent dream of real heights and possible degradations, not alone of fancy, but of the intellectual faculty and moral sense, for a picture to hang for ever in the galleries of time !

When the natural elements are at their best, and health is in every dew-drop, and the morning breeze moves gently with the shining of the unclouded sun, then there is a sparkle on the sea. So there is hilarity in the man who is inwardly well. He is like the sentinel I heard pace on a summer night in Santa Cruz, and sing, "All is serene." When the dwelling is in order, the children can play! Our affections will play, if they exist. The bounty is not acceptable which we have to hoist up or hesitate about. As the experts making the best time in the regatta do not spurt at the oar, but with even breath from the rowlocks pull, in their long and almost noiseless sweep, so the race of goodness is not turbulent and fretful, but constant and smooth; and our eulogy on any marvellous feat is that it was done in sport, — there being more where that came from, and plenty to spare! It was after Delilah had robbed Samson of his hair that the Philistines seized and brought him to Gaza, and put out his eyes, and made him sweat and grind. Ability is silent, and debility is loud.

Genius or character has its programme long ago made out in the skies. When a great performer professed he was unhappy, with only moments of bliss and months of torture, from something beside his inspiration his woe must have come! While we do the bidding and run on the errand we are glad, and nothing can be out of joint. Before the breath of God, if it come, I am a projectile like a cannon-ball, which does the execution and does not question the aim. Hence the stamp of necessity in the result. "As well," says Coleridge, "push a brick out of the solid cemented wall as a word out of Shakspeare's line;" and a mortar more firm holds edges finer hewn in every true life. Its most dismal passages are like pits the day is let into, or graves where resurrections have taken place.

There are shadows on the playground, and we may

as well object to the landscape as to the just report of it the artist makes. How can he who is too dainty to listen to the tale endure to survey the actual human scene? If to "purify by pity and terror" be the business of the muse, then by avoiding the process we shall miss the result. We must have the labor and the pain that we may have the play. We would cheerfully make room, though it should take the whole planet, for a patient endurance or an heroic deed. We are in an army; and what is righteousness but not breaking the ranks? As there is a prelude for the orchestra and a rehearsal for the stage, so work must prepare always for play. How the fingers of the pianist fly over the keys, and are no longer aware of the motions and intervals which at first were compassed with such toil and drill! What dexterity in his composition the experienced type-setter displays, and in what artless, charming order the accomplished orator's sentences flow! By steps of equal care and diligence must we mount to the Zion where the singers and players are. As you behold the ocean rolling afar from the summit of the White Hills or the Alps, so the ascent of principles is the condition of spiritual sight. Michael Angelo toiled slowly when he began; but the marble chips flew from his chisel at last.

Fine manners also are a certain play or overplus of the heart, as a feast is more than enough to eat and drink. What but the unfolding of an at first rude and savage deportment once in the Greek language turned the sense of a word from *stranger* to *guest?* Nature is always teaching the lesson of this "touch beyond" and something over. So to every visitor we give our best, withholding it in his favor from the members of our household and from ourselves. We make whoever comes welcome to the largest room, to the most savory morsel, the window of best prospect, the most delightful drive, and complete entertainment every way. Our enjoyment reaches its highest pitch in his. Barbarism formerly was a rough repulse or a bloody assault, as of naked Otaheitans or murderous Malays. It now consists in a stinted hospitality or a cool and scanty salute! From the Divine overflow we get our lesson. God's work everywhere rises or runs into play. The winds whistle and the waves dance. In the Greek poetry the billows have a multitudinous laugh. There is no strain or falling short in any natural supply, but exulting sufficiency, more oxygen than we can breathe, and more water than we need to quench our thirst. The sun is no lantern or hand-lamp, just enabling us to find our way and get about. We cannot use a tithe of his rays, while the Word of the Lord is a lamp to our feet.

Who says that Nature is sad? Only an echo is her minor key! We give her the pitch of the tune. If she sings a dirge, it is her courtesy to our grief, and no sorrow brooding in her own breast. A band of music can make the same instruments gay or doleful. If the refrain in Nature be a moan, it is only that our misfortune or bereavement takes hold of her pipes and strings. She can and would be fair and merry with us in her great picture-gallery and concert-hall! Her charm, in Wordsworth's apostrophe, robs conscience of its sting, —

"Flowers laugh before thee on their beds,
And fragrance in thy footing treads."

Every blossom is her superfluity. With what odors she greets us as we walk in the fields and the woods! The crowded petals of cultivation cannot vie with the single row in the wild rose, so lithe and sweet. Every fruit-tree is a basket of flowers first. How the breeze waves the grass and the grain to nod, and in sham fight brandish their spears! Why has the wheat, beside the kernel, its green and yellow bud and bloom? Wherefore the spindling and the silk tassels of the corn, but for some such reason as we have tents and arbors and awnings and carpets to give our politeness full course? The harvest smiles on us before it feeds. There is a hum and murmur of promise in the air from the growing crops. Whoever noticed the sailing of clouds in the sky and the cloud-shadows over the 'forest-edges and along the mountain-sides, or the scores of diverse crystals in the snow, but felt the Divine solicitude that we might be pleased? Flowering introduces and is essential to fruit. The potato, that lowly esculent, would not thrive for us under ground but that it blossoms above. The surly curmudgeons and conceited wiseacres fall below this ground-apple, as it is called by the French. The landscape laughs at the dignity with which some proud citizen marches by, his eye fixed on a distant planet, and having to gyrate like a telescope to bring into its focus objects so small and near as his fellow-men. What an icy response of far-off recognition he sends to your cordial good-morning and to your half-wasted bow! But fine manners play freely as the rippling folds of a streamer from its staff. You are not polite if you try to be so! Genuine courtesy is the escape of your love in every trifle, like a whiff of the wind, the glitter of the deep or of drops of dew, the aroma that fills the chamber from a hidden source. There are persons whose simple and unconscious ways lay on us a strange spell. The atmosphere of others repels. When I lamented the mendacity of a certain person, the reply was, "It is not the lying that troubles me, for that I can defend myself against; it is the other disagreeable qualities." The manners of some people are a centrifugal force. Every material body exudes its own "airs from heaven or blasts from hell." Personal attraction or revulsion is a mystery and foreordination before the founding of the world.

> "Say when in lapsed ages I knew thee of old;
> And what was the service for which I was sold?"

Happy is it if any two persons can keep their footing together, and be a binary star.

Delicate sensibility is the condition of perfect manners. Edison's apparatus feels the star before it is seen; and a quiver of feeling gauges whatever personality sweeps into our field of view. In naval architecture the safety is in a structure most quick and buoyant to mind the swell of the sea. The Great Eastern is demoralized like a cast horse in the stable, and thrown on her beam-ends. She would not "stoop to conquer," and the waves, whose stoop no quadrant or chart can reckon, hustled her into the trough of the sea; while the little Gloucester dory and the Nautilus skiff from New York cross the Atlantic, defying whirlwind and storm. The deference to each other of persons as they pass, as well as careering ships, is, however, no abject submission, but reference to the centre of all.

We do with ease what we do with our whole heart. That is feeble which just rubs and goes. There must be no wax if the wheel in its box or over its pivot is to be swift. Devotion at its acme rises and leaps and sings as in Miriam with her timbrel at the Red Sea, and in David before the ark, in Madame Guyon whose feet, when the passion of piety is on her, can scarce touch the ground, and in all the levitation and ardor of the saints, which signifies more than gravity and the long or sour face. How the hard prayer, more than the dull sermon, afflicts a congregation, and is like the asses' chewing of thistles, which we are impatient to stop! Only when the Godhead is an element which the minister bears us into, as a horse runs, the bird flies, or a fish swims, can his fellow-worshippers be raised or led. But the public act of prayer is often a difficult scramble in the Congregational order, as it is with the Episcopal a perfunctory form. A liturgy is convenient where the spirit does not move! But it contains not only the mournful confession which the " miserable sinners " make ; it admits no path to heaven but the old ancestral road with all its unmended ruts. If the responses have no life in them, then the decorous phrases of the Common Prayer are shamed by the swarm and hum of the Florida negroes over their pine sanctuary floor.

No instituted religion can furnish all the play we need. Poet, story-teller, artist, and actor are auxiliaries for the unfinished business of the priest ; and there is in their truth to their several callings as much religion as in any ritual he can rehearse. It was a clergyman, rich in culture as broad in love, and de-

voted to the American nation when life and liberty were
the stakes for which with ball and bayonet it played,
who first among us effectually confronted superstitious
prejudice with a masterly defence of the stage. Is the
church sacred and the theatre profane? The pulpit-
curtain in itself is no holier than that which hangs at
the proscenium, and the servant ministering at the altar
may be less pure than the impersonator of any character in Shakspeare or Dumas. We have heard poorer
sermons than from Rip Van Winkle or Lord Dundreary.
I honored Charlotte Cushman and Horace Bushnell
alike, as in their common Master's service they employed all their time and strength. There are no more
sticks in the stock company than in the desk. The
clerical profession has been hurt by nothing more than
by assumptions of superior sanctity or peculiar authority. An *opera* has been called a play worked; and
there is as much working and as little of flying wing
often in the parish incumbent as in the wire-puller that
sets up his travelling booth.

It is sometimes said of persons of wit and humor
that we know not whether they are in earnest or jest.
But if a matter is touching us to the quick, these merry
men may mean to protect us with the turn they give!
As a soft skin covers the nerves, which would suffer if
exposed, so deeper sensibilities find in superficial banter a shield and sheath. Is love always downright and
blunt? Rather it waits and goes round, and gently
breaks or remotely hints any message of pain. Was
not the prophet Nathan a player when he made a fable
of David's sin? Were not all Christ's parables and
miracles plays to represent eternal laws? The square

and bold putting of things which you boast of is no more true to human nature than it is kind; and the annals of philanthropy abound in precious specimens of injustice and hate. Into this internecine strife of reform comes the humane mediator, like the middle-man in Goethe's tale of "Elective Affinities," to parry the edge of the sword; and his fencing is play. So, while war thundered, Abraham Lincoln played.

There is nothing profounder than that play of imagination by which we translate ourself into another, and transmute another into ourself. Yet such realization differs from the histrionic art. The purpose of that art is to reproduce a character in outward appearance, to please spectators with the show. It is enough for the actor if he master the signs and use the language by which the soul of Hamlet or Juliet is put forth as an image is projected on a screen. But by assimilation we become the one we devotedly follow and admire. So we "put on Jesus Christ." The actor can put his mask on or off, but the moral transfiguration lasts. It is the vocation of the actor to entertain by pleasantly filling the hour. We have our pastime of private theatricals and charades. But in the real graft or appropriation of noble traits to the wild olive-tree of our nature we hope for eternal growth. When theological candidates are exhorted, as they get into the pulpit, if they do not feel their subject, nevertheless "to act as if they felt it, in order to carry their congregation," a rule is laid down whose practice would abolish the distinction between the pulpit and the stage, and turn serious pleading with sinners into mimicry and a mock. No orthodoxy but must be demoralized by the following of such advice.

Imagination is so potent that we must regulate if we adopt it as a guide. Physicians confess how much it has to do with the healing of disease. It puts virtue into remedies and applications too slight and neutral properly to have any efficacy of themselves. It invests outward nature with charms not her own. In human nature its influence is more marked. Is it simply a person, or somewhat an imagination of one, that I love, and that another loves in me? Does our affection lie in a mutual astonishment that of what each thinks so little in himself the other thinks so much? If love wax cold with such speculation, let us not do our great Partner the wrong to be forlorn, nor cease to have Nature for our playmate and bride! On her exquisite complexion and shapely form let us still fix our eye! She will restore us to mutual faith.

Truth is positive. It is the essence, not the attribute, of God; and if we construe Christianity as letting it slip, Hindu and Javanese and Tonga ethics will still remain to report, through our linguistic scholars, that "there is nothing without truth." The ingenious writer, Alphonse Karr, says, "God's goodness to the poor appears in the profusion of wayside flowers, which are of the color of the sky." As many are of the color of the sun! "Gray and melancholy waste," in Bryant's phrase, save for the sepulchral design in his poem, does not quite describe the sea, which has many a cheerful chameleon hue. In communion with that beauty which the universe is, I cannot be desolate, however forsaken and betrayed. Chaos is kosmos to the discerning eye. I am glad even among the ragged rocks, split with myriad fine wedges of the frost, eaten into by the toothed waves, and half beaten down to a sandy floor, with long deep clefts strung with boulders as beads, through whose spaces the upper firmament shines. Play on, O elements, and please my posterity as well as ye do me !

How exquisite, too, the live adjustment is ! My shepherd dog, a two months' puppy, plays with the kittens, who play together, each small pussy standing her ground against the big shaggy lout. But he has learned, from many a past encounter of wits and of paws with claws, the relative sharpness of the un-sheathed weapons, as also of the respective teeth, and just how far it is safe in his onset to go. He growls, and pretends to be very fierce, but is quite prudent withal, and does not propose to lay his handsome muz-zle open to the mischance of any sudden and perhaps bloody blow, offered to him so frequently and like a flash. What a duel, as if to match that with a fencing-master, it is ! How the interest of the spectacle comes from the likeness to what they see of those who look, before whom as spectators the little beasts perform, acting themselves, covertly, the part of spectators too ! When in the game temper comes in, and bites and cuffs are exchanged, how the parallels of this resem-blance still hold !

There is a foreign metaphysic, according to which pain is the substance and pleasure but the outside of life, as the popular theology makes sin the kernel and virtue only the hull. But, while the creatures are at play, the interest proceeds from the deeps ; and when they growl and scratch and hook in a barnyard or on a battle-field, they are on the surface more. A thunderstorm is but a passing scream of the electric force; and it is said the lightning-rod draws the perilous stuff from the air above our house in silence, and all the time. Let us put up moral conductors, and not fear the darker clouds.

In proportion as things rub, they do not play; and the object is to overcome the friction at every point. What a loss of power was in the old drag on which heavy weights were hauled over the stony ground! What a gain of tractile force is in the wrought-iron wheels that glide with freight of uncounted tons along the polished steel rails! There is a shock at the least obstacle, as when by the ring-bolt the flapping sail or the wanton steer is brought up. But the wheels will not bite the over-smooth rails; and there must be some friction to get along in human life. Yet to diminish it at every point as much as we may should be our aim, pouring oil on the waves and into the iron boxes and joints; for the spokes kindle which are not lubricated. What meant the anointing of prophets and kings, but to soften the collisions of men's savage passions, cool their rages, and keep their hatreds from flaming out? What were the oil "that ran down Aaron's beard to the skirts of his garments" but a childish display and foolish expenditure, save for this significance in the temple and the realm? Jesus was anointed "Prince of Peace" for what but that he might reconcile the alienated, make friends of foes, and still worse storms than went down, it is said, on the Sea of Galilee at his word? How to get speed with safety, and how to check advance when peril is in the way, is the object of the band and rein and linch-pin and air-brake; and the moral devices of wise precepts and good laws contemplate no other end. Religion itself, as an exercise, will be useless when life becomes perfect as play. The property and office of great men is to promote this consummation, and in their presence how the soul dances and sings!

There is a yearning in the youngest heart for the exercise of sympathy. When I told a little girl of the burning of a litter of common pigs, she said she was " sorry they were not guinea-pigs, that she might pity them more!" Compassion is such a luxury that it is a question if we could be altogether happy were every subject of commiseration removed.

But in the game of life let us observe the rules, be it money, position, place, and repute we play for, or truth, honor, human welfare, and the glory of God. According to our direction, ill blood or blessing shall be the conclusion; and only if the purpose be noble shall the play itself last. It will break up in confusion if it be carried on with selfishness. We must tug not a little to get through! Few are so accomplished as not to need on their work something like the fine emery or grating sand, if not the rasp. The axe ground into sharpness figures the disappointment and opposition which our faculties and affections must be whet by. By what firm yet exquisite touches the polish is put upon gems! God is a jeweller, and "those gems he sets most store by he hath oftenest his hands on," and will put into that crown which is both ours and his. Certain pieces of horn and shell become like glossy mirrors only under contact with the human hand; and there is a pressure on us so strong and sensible that we call it the hand of God! He means all parts of our nature to fit, like a choir to an anthem or the keys of a flute to its ventages and stops. No instrument of thought or feeling in this parlor of the human breast, discourse melodiously as it may, but will get out of order and require attention sometimes. But by no mortal hand can it be altogether restored. The music-master whose skill we require is unseen, yet what creature is so ready as the Creator to serve?

If order be the work, beauty is the play of God. It is not only " its own excuse for being," but we cannot tell how it is. " The beauty of flowering plants," says Mr. Darwin, " is useful in attracting insects to fertilize and perpetuate them." But the manner or reason of its first existence his theory does not explain; and the botanist finds many blossoms, conspicuously beautiful, insects are not drawn to, and which therefore serve no such end; so that the utilitarian philosophy breaks down often at the points of its own chosen application, while it utterly fails to account for beauty in the inorganic world. The insects themselves, in being lured to brilliant forms, share with us in an enjoyment which we do not understand more than they, thus owning a common bond. The domesticated animals know, as well as do our children, what it is to play. The dog has his duties; but he never comes so close to his master as when they play together. By much referring to his superior's gesture and look he becomes partaker of human nature, as by that reference which we call prayer we become partakers of the Divine. Where we can detect her method and follow her uniform step, perhaps Nature may be said to work. But she unfolds, under the gardener's eye, many *sporting* varieties, beyond what he had expected or contrived, and which are peculiarly suited to stir admiration by their tint and shape. So vast and minute, so changeful and surprising, are the charms, which no knowledge can dissect or fathom in all her realms, we feel that the inmost of her Author is revealed in the outmost of her displays, and that our communion together and with him is no solemn task or formal service, but even that play which is the height of our powers, and that pleasure which is joy in the Holy Ghost.

PART II.

PORTRAITS.

PART II.

PORTRAITS.

I.

THE PERSONALITY OF SHAKSPEARE.

THAT French philosopher, Fernand Papillon, the farthest possible from the butterfly signified by his name, in the "Revue de deux Mondes," relates that an Englishman having told his groom to go over the way after his friend Shakspeare, the servant inquired how he should know him in the crowd; and the master replied, "He alone looks like a man; all the rest are animals." Yet, while we worship the poet, we say the man has no character. We question as respects the greatest name in the classic school, if there were any Homer or many singers of the Iliad and Odyssey; and the supreme romantic English bard does not appear in his work, and never had his portrait taken. He effaces himself. With a matchless mind he led, so it is said, an obscure and profane life, and was a mere master of the revels and entertainer at the Blackfriars' Theatre, open to Mahomet's reproach from the gods to the merry-makers, "Think ye we have made the heaven and earth for sport?" Shakspeare was not a genteel, fashionable person, not a great leader, a religious reformer, a military captain, an ecclesiastical officer, or a conventional saint.

But we must not ask one man to be all men, — Goethe to be a politician, or Shakspeare a courtier, Moses an orator, or Luther a general in the field. If the pith of manhood goes into what one does or says, he pays his passage or cumbers not the ground. It is sometimes said of a humorist that we cannot tell when he is serious, as if in aught were more reality than there is in wit. Shakspeare was a dramatist; but "all the world's a stage and the men and women merely players," and the end of the creation may prove to be play rather than work. What is the universe but God's theatre, in which, without jar or grating, every piece of scenery slides? Despite pain and grief and sin and death, the object is that harmony of perfect play which is prophesied in every childish game. In his essence Shakspeare was a player, as Garrick, perhaps his chief impersonator, was never so much himself as when enacting some part. When he was missed at the inn his friends found him in a back-yard, throwing a negro boy, his solitary spectator, into convulsions of laughter, as he mocked the feathery fuss of a turkey-cock. Shakspeare was no notable and forward personage. We imagine him looking shyly at every thing and through everybody. No doubt he, as do all the great, liked obscurity. Fénelon wished to be unknown, Wesley wanted no monument, Moses declined to be an orator, Turner was gruff to bores, Agassiz hated interruption, Hawthorne drew up the ladder into his study, and Jesus hid himself. Emerson, when the callers came, missed his mighty gods. Hunt cared much for Michael Angelo and little for connoisseurs, and Whittier would prefer the good opinion of his neighbors to the fame of Shakspeare! Father Taylor goes alone, and mutters to himself because he says he " likes to talk to a sensible man ; " and to a fine compliment Carlyle says, " Pshaw, I don't believe a word of it! " Webster had fits of silence which it was dangerous to disturb. Charles Lowell so enjoyed his devotions that he would rather have been the author of Isaac Watts's hymns than of Shakspeare's plays. All high character or genius is on condition of heeding the law of incubation on the finer than roc's egg of thought. The soul may have been a bird once, it so loves still to brood ! It is not fond of interviewers and reporters. So, to be obscure and profane, in some sense, was Shakspeare's note of worth.

It was glorious to run from the pursuit of glory ; all the better if Essex and Leicester would not speak save in condescension to the playwright as they passed. He kept low company, as the old scribes and Pharisees said a certain other person did, and as Socrates consorted with disreputable persons earlier still. Even sinners are better society than the self-righteous. Must not one get clear of his own shadow and make himself of no reputation in order that he may see clearly? Benjamin Paul Blood says we learn more as we come to after anæsthesia, than from Fichte or Hegel. But Shakspeare dwelt in the land of surprise, and was coming to all the time. Genius is the child of wonder, and able to envisage all being in its own. It takes a low position and gazes from a covert. The artist does not stare at things or at people, but catches them with half-shut eye at a sidelong look. No stealth is like his! Nothing is worth observing which he does not behold. Our thoughts do not come to the front and present themselves in full dress, but sidle in and startle us with their unexpected salute and sudden good-morning. The thinker is not a bold hunter, but lurks modestly for his game.

We search in vain for any man's personality in his notoriety. We must come at Shakspeare's in his pen, remembering that it is a false distinction which would certify more significance in a deed than in a word. But, as we treat of his representations, the puritanic criticism recurs in another form, that he slights the lowly and flatters the chivalrous and high-born, holding in honor no such characters as some that Goethe chooses, especially of women from common life. We must not ask Shakspeare to be a modern four centuries after his death; but that he was less republican than Goethe would be hard to prove, either from his conduct or his lines. The German, in the little court of Saxe-Weimar, deferred to potentate and prince; while a fine ear detects a false poetic ring in the compliment to Queen Elizabeth, hinting that it did not come from Shakspeare's creative hand.

It is a more serious charge that he was indifferent to moral distinctions, and with impartial pencil drew the sinner and saint. Is God indifferent, with his equal sun and rain over all? Did Shakspeare care for all alike? Would you know what he loved or hated, mark what he makes you love or hate! What was he? What his pages make you wish to be! Do you feel nobler, reading him? He was noble, too. He weighs what his works weigh. How many pulpits would it take for an equivalent? Could we not spare all the churches and cathedrals of England, and sink the sea-girt isle rather than that one book? The little booth he admits us into becomes a world-wide audience-chamber with a solemn desk. The Globe Theatre expands into the dimensions of the globe. What does human nature, not any commentator, think of him? Reverently I say it, he too "draws all men to him," sitting, as our poet has it,

"Lone as the blessed Jew."

That touch of nature which, he says, "makes the whole world kin," he gives; and the enthusiasts for him are on the continent of Europe as much as on his native soil. Pastime does he give? Sober study too, as he condenses the drift of history on his page! He furnishes texts for new treatises in art, history, nature, and natural history, medicine, and law. Says a doctor to me, "Shakspeare guessed before Harvey the circulation of the blood; he described better than any later observer the phenomena of sleep-walking; and he enumerates the offices of sleep with a perfection which the most recent physiologist cannot excel." When he calls it "chief nourisher in life's feast," he states the scientific fact! A volume has been written by a Canada professor to prove that his Caliban is Darwin's missing link. Dickens's Quilp, or Victor Hugo's Quasimodo, is perhaps not quite in nature; but Caliban, an odder creature, is immortal, a species by himself, and cannot be left out.

Had he no moral judgment because he pronounces no sentence from the bench? Be sure that your opinion of Iago, Othello, Shylock, and Richard III. was his.

Plain men from the country, on their first visit to the theatre, want to interfere and choke some of those worthies on the spot and before the time. Did Shakspeare make Timon the misanthrope as weighty in his approval as Alcibiades, or as the Merchant in his scale? He loves all indeed, like the Maker, and condemns only as he describes! ‾Like a detective he photographs the murderer and the thief. "Your portrait," one said to an artist, "is that of a fox." "The sitter is one," he replied. Does Shakspeare rate villain and noble alike, because he paints them with like care? Only as the naturalist so values bat and beetle, fish and scorpion, mastodon and man, because all the skeletons are in his museum, or in his alcoholic bottles creatures fierce and gentle are at peace. Shakspeare was not portrait-painter for Her Majesty, but for the human race. The sun may err, but not his pencil; and you may as well criticise the landscape as his scenes. He keeps himself out; no atom of his individuality intrudes into his pictures. All his lendings and limitations are dropped, like a traveller's cloak in the entry or a snake's skin in the woods. It has been said, Goethe is the more perfect artist and Shakspeare the greater nature. But what is art, if not the power to delineate others and omit one's self?

Who was Shakspeare? But small part of him is in the parish-register or tomb, that tells us he reached his fifty-third year, or states the parentage of what so exceeded that by which it was begotten or born. The physical geography, says Mr. Buckle, largely determines the character of the population; but in this case what has Stratford-upon-Avon to say? Can we find the man we are after in the supposed boyish poacher on his neighbor's estate, in the landholder's prosecution of a debtor for corn, in the lad flinging jests from the turnstile at the passers-by, in the testator's bequest of his second best bed to the wife who may have legally inherited the best, or in the blessing and ban on the gravestone, — as if after he had done with them he really could care for his bones? We know at least what he was not. He was no court-clown, such as kings once kept. Never lived one to whom the world was less a jest! As grotesque as nature, so is he. The Psalmist says, God laughs at certain persons and has them in derision ; and our poet catches from the Divine countenance the trick of that smiling ; but no more than the Arab prophet himself is he exposed to the curse of the Koran on any trifling unfit to the time. For if heaven and earth were not made for sport, no more were those tragedies, with whose characters the muse must have travailed in pain, before they stalked forth on the planetary stage which they will never quit. What a collection and what a preservation it is! This amber holds the fly, and it holds the world. The mortal millions pass. Kings and princes are dead. Their forms are gone, beyond art of Egypt to embalm ; while, out of the realm of imagination and rock of ages, who is this that quarries Hamlet and Lear and Imogen and Desdemona, — ideal shapes to abide beyond any actual, and shadows which no man ever saw in this buckram we wear of flesh and blood, yet of more than human substance to walk over our ashes, to survive our frame, to mock this short-lived set of egoists that we are, and challenge for themselves alike longevity and perpetual youth? Whence such creations? From no buffoonery and no levity of a privileged joker commissioned to supply the boards with mirth, but out of a gravity like that which made the satellites and the sun.

Who was Shakspeare? No materialist at least. The Sadducees can make nothing of him. It were cutting matter very fine to whittle it into all the products his brain swarmed with, and to find room in its convolutions for what has flown out of that hive to hover and hum in all the gardens and over all the field-flowers of the world. You blame this plenipotentiary for being a good fellow? But does the greatest earnestness frown or weep? No, it burns and is benign to bless! Was all the levity with Thackeray and Dickens, and did the seriousness belong but to John Calvin and John Knox?

> "There are more things in heaven and earth
> Than are dreamt of in your philosophy."

This author gets himself quoted more than are those theologic polemics now, even on themes supramundane. The "majesty of buried Denmark" convinces us of a "bourn" beyond, whether travellers return from it or not. The ghosts in the sittings and circles all vanish; Shakspeare's remain. Of what tough material are they made? The witches, withered and wild in their attire on the blasted heath, the fairies, Puck and Oberon with their tricksy ways, like Goethe's *mothers* and Milton's angels, persuade us of other orders of being than go to market, or crowd on 'Change, or dispute in the legislature, or clasp gold crucifixes, or recite from illuminated missals, count beads, and bow with velvet propriety in church.

Who was Shakspeare? A greater architect than Inigo

Jones or Christopher Wren! Nobody has taken up the line between matter and spirit with hand so deft. Wherefore do his delegates from the invisible stand and keep their footing as denizens here below, but for somewhat perdurable in the stuff they, like dreams, are made of? What credit would there be for his association of the seraph and worm, save from a constitutional suspicion that the soaring seraph as well as the grovelling worm exists? Without this substratum of innate belief, the spectres were ludicrous assumptions, blown light as down instead of being cut in some divine cameo, till these ethereal forms, which the hand can pass through, but the eye not close upon, become adamant to the mind. How much literary work perishes as an extinct species, while Shakspeare's is the fittest and survives!

The puritanic conscience cross-questions him on the point of piety, and doubts if he were a religious man; and if, to be a sample of devoutness, one must be morose and sour, with longitude and no latitude of face, then this genial creature and creator cannot meet any ecclesiastical committee with his claims, and with the oval features that had nothing in them lean. But supreme genius is prayer and answer to prayer in Homer, in Dante, in Milton, and Goethe too, who but for a pious experience never could have written the " Confessions of a Beautiful Soul." Irreverent unbelief marks inferior power in Byron, Heine, and Poe. In the light of intuition, and over the gulf of atheistic understanding, Shakspeare springs the arch of faith; and no Greek or English prayer-book affords finer collects than come from the mouths of his interlocutors in the action of many a piece, as it naturally flows. He knew what it

means to " cast thy burden on the Lord," and that
such inspiration is the next act after despair ! For the
poet speaks under influence. He is mastered by the
muse and never its master, although it have conditions
for its gifts. Its stream bursts like an artesian well
after much digging. " The wind bloweth where it listeth ; " but it listeth to blow through some channel of
conscious need, that, like a vacuum of air around a
headland, sucks its current in ! The heavenly or the
possessed man whom we call artist, and who drinks
from God like the saint, cannot explain his ways ;
and, if he could, he would decease and go by default.
The trickster, Cagliostro or any other, can let you into
the secret, show his hand, and tell how he does his
trick ! But study can only build the staging on which
power appears, miraculous and never understanding itself. Perfect art is but preparation for perfect nature
and the breathing-hole of genius, as its lungs and the
sea help the whale to gambol and sport. God works,
but does not labor. His effort is ease, and his accomplishment perpetual play.

Where so much is memorable in an author one fears
to quote. The quoter cites himself ! Do we not judge
of the sort of insect by its flying to a honeysuckle or
seeking tainted food ? But is not Ferdinand's asking
Miranda's name chiefly that he might " set it in his
prayers," and Hamlet's begging Ophelia,

> " Nymph, in thy orisons
> Be all my sins remembered,"

and the usurping king's appeal,

> " Help, angels, make assay !
> Bow, stubborn knees ! and, heart, with strings of steel,
> Be soft as sinews of the new-born babe,"

proof for the poet that his closet had a door?   A
Shakspeare expurgated by a scientist of what he counts
superstition no scientist could read.   The divinity is
not lacking, but lurking in ten thousand lines which
mention not its name.   The elements are our poet's
pigments.   All nature is in solution for his experiments ;
and his handling is more dexterous than that of the
man who does the puzzle of knots and rings.   It is not
ingenuity, but that vitality indispensable in all the arts,
which have this common bond.   How it lures us in the
landscapes of Millet and Corot, and the portraits of
Couture !   The burden of old oppression, the pathos of
meek suffering, the forming cloud of political revolution,
as, in the picture of the " Sower," the poor peasants drive
home from the furrows the sunset team, enter, as we
gaze, into the quick.   The canvas of Corot is saturated
with tender sentiment, and pervaded as with a thin
smoke from human homes, while a certain grandeur in
Couture's motive and execution reminds us of the ancient style.   But Shakspeare was a painter too.   Human nature sat to him, and nature furnished the tints.
The world was his studio, and his values were right.
The physical immensities subserve his spiritual designs.

> " There 's not the smallest orb, which thou behold'st,
>   But in his motion like an angel sings,
>   Still quiring to the young-eyed cherubins."

Could Job or David do better?   Lorenzo tells Stephano
to bring his " music forth into the air," because soft
stillness and the night become its " touches ; " and
straightway the little twangling pipes and chords are
lifted to the spheres, and the stars made the servants

of a serenade. Daybreak ceases to be an event in nature. It is the time for the lover to leave his mistress's window, and for the ghost to flee as it snuffs the morning air. A vegetable shall be an example.

> " And winking Mary-buds begin
> To ope their golden eyes :
> With every thing, that pretty bin,
> My lady sweet, arise ! "

All without is tool or plaything for the poet's purpose. In his exchange the world is converted like paper into coin. Always it is specie payment with him. All nature is the note of hand and the gold-room in his mind. When Duncan, in " Macbeth," says,

> " This castle hath a pleasant seat; the air
> Nimbly and sweetly recommends itself
> Unto our gentle senses,"

do we think it is for the description's sake? What threat of rising tempest could surpass the suggestiveness of this charming frontispiece? As a white cloud in Indian seas hides the terrible thunder and wind, so what sketches of passion, cyclones of ambition, whirls of supernatural visiting, and lightnings of fate lie behind this foreground, so softly shining, lovely, and pure ! In Shakspeare's orrery comet or planet has its place.

But was Shakspeare a moral man? We must judge him by his handling of his instrument, in the same measure as we do David by his harp; and what a tuning-key he holds ! Nature has no more success in her choir, composed of the roar of the sea, ripple on the beach, and wind in the trees, to accompany the birds, than has our poet in making the strong passions and the tender affections to chime. Shylock or Iago strikes some bass drum or bassoon in the orchestra; and were that note missed, the concert would be marred. "This is Beethoven's Gethsemane," said a performer of some strain full of struggle. From Shakspeare's harmony no sin or sorrow can escape. Be the jarring what it may, he persuades us that the world is concord. Could Judas be spared out of the gospel picture? Nothing and no one can be spared. Shakspeare was no ascetic; but who shall say it was not innocent pleasure in which he lived? He was no professor of religion, like loose Queen Mary or cruel Elizabeth, and he enjoyed a quip at strait-laced puritans and long-faced hypocrites; but how he delighted to communicate joy! He teaches us to reserve no good; and in case of heart-bleeding, so to sympathize with our fellow, brother or sister, as not to know from which heart it comes! But no drunkard or debauchee could he have been. When Daniel Webster was charged with being continually in his cups, — as one said, " the ship of State in full career, with a drunkard at the helm," — it was answered, Webster's were not the works of an habitual sot! From what but a constant and immense sobriety could Shakspeare's works, which we call plays, have come? Napoleon allowed himself four hours' sleep. Could *he* the poet have had more, who achieved his stint in scarce above a score of years? Through what big, chaste, well-ordered apartments must the characters from his all-conceiving imagination have trooped!

Who was he? Doubtless a hearty despiser of all pretence. "Dost thou think, because thou art virtuous, there shall be no more cakes and ale?" in "Twelfth Night" says Sir Toby to the Clown, who answers,

" Yes, and ginger shall be hot i' the mouth too." But, if so much may be cited against any principle or policy of prohibition, or the making of abstinence a boast and all indulgence a sin, how Hamlet, on the other hand, brands and scores intemperance when he tells Horatio, " We will teach you to drink deep ere you depart," and says the custom is " honored more in the breach than in the observance " ! To what disgrace and pinching torment, in " The Tempest," come the sottish Trinculo and Stephano? What account in the Bible has more of shame and woe than that of the witty and profligate Falstaff, as King Henry puts him aside with the epithet " vain man " ? When the dissolute courtier expires, fumbling the sheets, babbling of green fields, and crying out, " God, God, God," what draft or revision of the Ten Commandments was ever more solemn since the covers of the Pentateuch were put on? When the guilty Alonzo was supernaturally thrown into dreams which make nature the voice of conscience, when the billows spoke and the winds sang and the thunder " did bass his trespass," then in this scripture of humanity what a halo of beauty, discourse of harmony, and illustration of law !

Indecencies are by Shakspeare expressed; but no one ever told the story of uncleanness more cleanly, with greater simplicity, or with less relish of his own imparted in his style. There is something to skip in the Old Testament, and the preacher must have a washed mouth for some passages in the New. There is in our author naught to tempt or corrupt for whoever surveys fairly the relations in every scene. In Solomon's Proverbs or David's fifty-first penitential Psalm

is purity more awful than in " Measure for Measure," in
the tale of Angelo and Isabel? If life be a masquerade,
here is an unmasker who lets no veil or visor stay ; and
the revealer is no saint in his own esteem, but constructs
a confessional with which no curtained priestly box can
vie. Who can refuse to absolve him on reading the
tender sonnet beginning

"Oh, for my sake do you with Fortune chide ! "

Is nothing known of Shakspeare's character? Behold
in his poetry his personality ! He is but half concealed
in every figure in which he impersonates another, and
he is openly shown in every sonnet where he personates
himself. More subtle, deep, and full-proportioned is
the man in his dramas than in the sonnets, that but
circle around his individuality, like those arrested currents that wear smooth basins in rocky beds among the
hills. This world of his was not made out of nothing,
nor the brick for his building fashioned without straw
and fire and fierce kneading in the furnace, though the
smoke be gone, and not a foul atom left from the chimney that burned its own soot.

Who was Shakspeare? He was not Lord Bacon,
who lacked virtue even more, if possible, than he did
genius for the task which some have imputed as his.
Internal evidence is there in all these benignant gospels
that their writer was a truth-teller at least and in-
comparably just. He was a very un-Romish Catholic,
one comma of whose pen could not by the gold of kingdoms be bribed. Bacon is strong to draw along loaded
wagons of treasure in his Essays ; but where is the
light and lambent flame which in this alchemist's lab-

oratory licks into airy beauty every atom of the work?
Where in the stately and ponderous sage is the melody
which in the bard so sweetens and lifts every lyric and
interluding snatch, as well as in the argument every
sober line? We think that as a musical composer must
have his notes in imagination before he puts down his
score, so Shakspeare's, like Mendelssohn's, must at first
have been "songs without words."

Who was Shakspeare? A genial friend, trusted by
the townsfolk with business in London, and himself a
thriving man. His wares did not indeed come out of
a wretched garret. His muse was not poverty, nor
to misery goes the credit or responsibility for what he
brought to pass. It were unreasonable in Anne Hatha-
way not to be content with her spouse! Was aught
free and easy in his manners? He could be no acid
bigot, not intolerant, uncharitable, self-righteous, or
spiritually proud. He had a humanity, liberality, and
forgiveness Heaven-like and world-wide. Fanaticism
may have its excellence, and good-nature its defect.
But in the balance let me shrink from the first and
incur the last, though at the cost of overlooking some
follies in my fellows or having some weaknesses to pardon in myself, remembering what one said about "the
holier than thou"! What avails purity in one that
stings us with his persistent notional rebuke, and like a
buzzing insect returns to the same spot; in a masculine
or feminine spy whose interrogations keep alive the inquisition, torturing and killing with inquiry; in a human
brier that takes toll of the skin or wool of every creature that may pass? Shakspeare was, and teaches us
to be, none such. When he deprecates being com-
memorated, .

> "Lest the wise world should look into your moan,
> And mock you with me after I am gone,"

we think of some étude of Chopin, some sonata or funeral march of Beethoven; and we enshrine the writer in the recollection he repudiates and abjures. Was he not a serious man who said   •

> " Love is not love
> Which alters when it alteration finds " ?

Was his disinterestedness betrayed?   In the oft-quoted lines,

> "Take, oh, take those lips away,"

the close is commonly omitted,

> " But my kisses bring again,"

which is the most touching and imaginative part. Charles Lamb has an essay on persons one would wish to have seen.   Would not our curiosity spare all the courts in Christendom to meet Shakspeare?   But do we not meet him personally, if not individually?   Individuality is one's distinction from another.   It may be in beast, tree, stone, or in any thing as well as man.   Personality is one's expression of universal spirit and truth. It is a property of the soul.   It is the organ and instrument of the spirit within or above.   Individually, we may part company; personally, we unite.   The personality is not our *selves*, wherein is separateness, but our self; and the self we are to love is in all, as in our own breast.   " I shall be delighted with *me* when it comes." The woman was *personal* who said that!   She adored the Infinite Personality we all share.   As from under the old actor's mask sounded through his voice the sense of the character he would set forth, so all mortal shapes are masks of God. He exists in countless persons, not in three alone. In proportion as the utterance is vast and delicate and pure, the man is great and divine. What a personage is Shakspeare by this rule! Something of whatever we handle will stick to the palm. In California a thief greased his fingers when he came to try the sample of gold dust in the cask at his neighbor's store. "Will a man rob God?" He may as much as he will, and the riches will never decrease. He who steals thus also bestows. How much Shakspeare imparted of the great fund!

It is said, one can write what he does not feel. The poets enchant us with a figure or spectacle of sentiments which they do not partake. It is all imagination! But what is imagination? It is the eye of the soul, with which only "the pure in heart" can see either God or man. It was well said, "Show me the poetry composed by a bad man, and I will show you wherein it is not poetry." On this principle, I think Shakspeare was good, as holy as Saint Augustine, without such grossness in him to overlook.

Who was he? Could any one but a patriot have written as he did, in "King John," concerning

> "That pale, that white-faced shore"?

In "Henry V." the Duke of Exeter says,

> "Never king of England
> Had nobles richer, and more loyal subjects;
> Whose hearts have left their bodies here in England,
> And lie pavilioned in the fields of France."

Of this vision of an army across the Straits and with their tents on the sunny foreign plains, without a bugle

blown, foot on the march, or sail spread, who can calculate the effect on English courage since?   The poet's
service to his country all her consols could not pay.
He was not a poorer patriot for being cosmopolite.   In
the same play the description of York's and Suffolk's
death shows a feeling that neither gushed nor was
ashamed to flow.

So I call Shakspeare not impersonal, but an immense
personality. We think the earth is flat, because we see
not its curve; and we say Shakspeare exists only as an
influence, because we cannot measure his will.   God is
held to be impersonal on the same ground.   What are
all our faculties but as paper or leather visors to trans-
mit the Divine voice?   We must not call such an one a
showman, who is here to please us with his menagerie
of performers, spangled riders, tame monkeys, and wild
beasts ! A little water shut in by a dam turns the wheels
of a tide-mill.   But it was lifted on the shoulders of the
sun and moon.   It takes a greater energy to supply the
motive-power of the soul.   Whence but from a vigor
equal to all heroic deeds could this portrait come?

> "Danger knows full well
> That Cæsar is more dangerous than he.
> We were two lions, littered in one day,
> And I the elder and more terrible."

Can one picture that with which he is in no wise possessed? Yet from this pitch he can come down to
"Audrey," as her lover says, "a poor thing, but mine
own," and fix her in our memory as well as he does the
ruler of Rome.   What is the width of the solar system
to this mental parallax?

A provider of pleasure was Shakspeare, like any other story-teller; but beyond all beside, — Scott, Cervantes, George Eliot, or George Sand, — he was an apostle of verity, a preacher of righteousness, and a son of consolation. What burial-service in all the liturgies of the churches and nations has a musical sadness and solace to compare with the song in "Cymbeline" over the body of Cloten? What "Ode to the Duke of Wellington" shall be laid beside it? Who was Cloten but a foolish boy, though born prince? Yet what king, priest, or pope had such a funeral hymn?

You tell me Shakspeare was not religious! Who ever mused more deeply on the duty and end of man? Had he not "chewed the cud of sweet and bitter fancy"? Of what material did he weave? Handel, Haydn, Mozart, felt not their subjects more.

The sort of man he was? One that had loved, — what particular man or woman matters not, doubtless all women and all men, hating none; and if betrayed or deserted, he could forgive.

> "Say that thou didst forsake me for some fault,
>   And I will comment upon that offence;
> Speak of my lameness, and I straight will halt,
>   Against thy reasons making no defence."

What Æolian harp in the window lamenting one gone out of the door, what "Elegy in a Country Churchyard," what unheard chant of inward grief over the unseen grave where dead hopes lie buried never to rise again, or what obsequies of our own affections, to which we go, could in tender, mournful depth exceed the

> "Blow, blow, thou winter wind!"

But, as though there were naught dismal in the world, no " Amiens " melancholy, no Jaques or Hamlet half mad, how, without recollection of grief or a wrinkle of pain, the same artist can give us the rapture and radiance of first love in Ferdinand and Miranda, —

> " At first sight they have changed eyes."

Who shall try to describe the same thing in other words? Each is conscious only of the sight with which he or she is viewed, and two souls are one in a single look!

" The Tempest" seems the last and loftiest of this mountain-chain, the Himalaya of our literature, and firm in the world as any of its continental backbones. Surely Shakspeare is Prospero.

But go from magic to history; and in the historic plays we have not only the Greeks, the Romans, and the Egyptians presented well, but the English filing out in squadrons, and the head Englishman, with martial blood in his cool and fiery veins, *shaking a spear* as verily his ancestors did! Cæsar and Coriolanus are drawn as justly as the Henries. Egypt is perfect in " Antony and Cleopatra," which for sustained action is the top round, — the sentences a succession of shocks as from a battery, or photographs from a ship rocking on the waves, or portraits taken by a flash.

> " Far along
> From peak to peak, the rattling crags among,
> Leaps the live thunder "

of war, overridden with battling desires of the potentates by whom it is waged. Yet Shakspeare is not in any one of them, so much as he is the magician in his

cell on the enchanted island, or in the soothsayer, the
truth-teller.

> "In Nature's infinite book of secrecy
> A little I have read."

In "Antony and Cleopatra" the start is as of a horse
at full speed, who never slackens his rate, though the
rider holds bridle, till he touches the goal, while we are
all taken *en croupe* on the hot steed.

Who, then, is Shakspeare? Creator and colonizer of
the world with a host of beings more real than any flesh
and blood, and a multiplier of the inhabitants of the
globe. For, while mortals drop like leaves, and vanish
like vapors, and pass as shadows of the night, the planet
has a permanent population. It is made up in part of
actual heroes, founders and fathers, martyrs and saints.
In religion we have Abraham, Moses, and Jesus. In art
we have Michael Angelo, Raphael, and their compeers.
In war we have Alexander and Napoleon, who are not
inclined yet quite to take their leave. In law we have
Solon and Lycurgus. In philosophy we have Plato and
Aristotle. In music we have Beethoven and Mozart.
We have great men that become myths, like Hercules
and Achilles; and good men that cast reflections of a
patriarchal stature across the landscape, like the Pilgrims; and poets, like Homer, Dante, and Shakspeare,
whose classes and types may outlive all individual
forms. What living king, queen, courtier, or statesman could we not better dispense with than with the
portraitures which show us what a mistress, governor,
gentleman, or lady is or ought to be?

The women are equal or equivalent to the men.
"The ever-womanly" drew on Goethe and Shakspeare.

If only a man could write of woman as Shakspeare does, only from love of woman and from woman's love could he write. Such is the condition of manly genius, of which no hater or despiser of woman ever had one spark! Woman's inspiration prompts every best word of a man's pen. These word-pictures of female heads shall hold their colors when the tints of Titian and Murillo are pale on the wall. Who was Shakspeare? A man that did justice to the sex, and waited not for the slowly revolving wheels of reform.

It goes as a proverb, that we know naught of Shakspeare the man. Yet I would wager my life that there was no cruelty in him, but that he was kind to those fellow-creatures whom we libel as dumb and irrational. Let them answer for him, — the lark "that sings at heaven's gate," the crow that "flies in heaven's sweetest air," and the dogs he paints better than Landseer, or the wounded deer that bids the rest of the herd

"Sweep on, ye fat and greasy citizens!"

Was he not a song-bird himself?

"Or sweetest Shakspeare, fancy's child,
Warble his native wood-notes wild."

He was a composition of man, woman, and child. Was it the unprecedented goodness of Jesus to women, not a word from his mouth being ever uttered against one of them, which made Chaucer write,

"Christ was a maid ere he was shapen as a man"?

Surely our poet too entered into their very heart. "A woman does not forgive coldness, even if it be the mask of love," writes George Eliot; and while the authorship of the novels under this title was in doubt.

22

a critic said no man ever could have written that sentence. But when the bad news comes of Antony's marriage, and Cleopatra says,

"Pity me, Charmian, but do not speak to me,"

might not as sharp an objection arise to male authorship?

In fine, this freshest eye that ever looked on the world was of a man who did not disown or dishonor the past.

"All before us lies the way,"

yet we must look back. The great leaders are behind. The doctrines of evolution and survival of the fittest, which it is the glory of our Spencer and Darwin to expound, must have some abatement to be square with the facts. Antiquity never loses its claim. The old mountains are the highest; and the last one thrown up, Monte Nuovo near Naples, has an altitude of but a few hundred feet. Very ancient are the mountain ridges and peaks of human greatness! The traveller, after he has passed, turns to gaze on Mount Washington and Mont Blanc. Mankind is a traveller, and cannot take off its eyes from shapes that dwarf all present illustration of its glories and aims, — those of Socrates and Plato, of the Hindoo Sakya Mouni and the Hebrew Messiah. One of these memorable benefactors is of Anglo-Saxon blood, high up in his stature to any Greek, Roman, or Jewish level, chief intellectual influence of the modern world. Was he a trifler because an inditer and actor of plays? The universe is God's play or his playground! All our work will be play in paradise. We wait but to perfect our powers of thought and love for that. Shakspeare takes up the line between sacred literature and profane. Do the New Testament writers mean to express the inferiority of matter to spírit by their picture of a final conflagration of the world? They surpass not in sublimity Prospero's speech to Ferdinand, —

> " The great globe itself,
> Yea, all which it inherit, shall dissolve ;
> And, like this insubstantial pageant faded,
> Leave not a rack behind : we are such stuff
> As dreams are made on, and our little life
> Is rounded with a sleep."

Did he think that was the end, — he that put into Hamlet's soliloquy the words, " to sleep, perchance to dream," and who wrote,

> " Angels and ministers of grace defend us ! "

and to the priest's objurgation of doom and " ground unsanctified " for Ophelia's burial makes Laertes reply,

> " A ministering angel shall my sister be
> When thou liest howling " ?

The poet knew how to reverse an ecclesiastical decision. What a refuge he affords, in his region of beauty, from the pretence of sectarists to settle questions by other authority than the human mind ! Renan speaks of *les hommes rangés*, the drilled men. Shakspeare is a liberator ; and Milton the Puritan, with his

> " Dear son of memory, great heir of fame,"

is a eulogist of this spiritual renewer, in any one of whose lines is more delight for us than in the most flattering compliment we ever received. He is an auto-biographer. He is as well known as anybody that ever lived. He was a transcendent moralist before transcendentalism was born. But morality with him is a principle, not a rule. Was Desdemona the " liar " she was called by Othello? When the disciples ask Jesus who had sinned, the parents or the blind man, and he answers, " Neither," would not an Orthodox professor have to convict the Master of falsehood, and say, "Both."? By either teacher, the great head of the Church or the humble player in the booth, instinct was alike revered, and by no dogma or wilful standard was it set aside. Principles cannot, like cattle, be put in pound, nor right become a rut. Jesus orders swords, and condemns their use. The Quaker may drop his custom with his coat, when Sumter is under fire. " Nice customs courtesy to great kings ; " and those kings are laws by which all establishments are overridden or undercut. Man is a law to himself. One may honestly call for a world's convention of peace, yet, in peculiar circumstances, long for the gunship Canandaigua to open her guns in Samana Bay, on San Domingo Isle. We must know the whole story before we can be sure whether certain acts or intimacies of human creatures, be they men or women, are right or wrong. Circumstances do not alter cases, for every case is determined from the centre of the soul's point of view. The real person is identical with the real truth. From the serious smiling poet none of this wisdom was hid.

The truth, which Pilate asked for, is to be told at all times, yet it can never be fully told. It is not fact, but a spirit in and over all details. All persons do not have property in a fact. It may be mine or yours, and fitly kept in an iron vault or in the safe of your or my mind. We must be true to persons ; but telling their just secrets is how false ! Judas spoke the truth when he told where Jesus was to be found ; in his veracity he was an informer, a spy, and a traitor, deserving the lowest place in hell, Dante being judge. Of all things, hatred and selfishness are the most untrue. How loving, unselfish, and true Desdemona was in shielding her husband, and exposing herself, — poor, tender buckler ! The exposure was eternal honor for her. So we will not disparage Shakspeare, nor lower her from her niche of fame.

II.

CHANNING, THE PREACHER.

IT will soon be thirty-seven years since the subject of this essay died, or disappeared. But I observe, after longer lapses of time, the figures walk down from their frames in our parlors or in Faneuil Hall for every new crisis of action or thought. The picture on our walls whose beauty sinks into and becomes part of us is a living blessing; how much more the fresh incarnation of a good and great man! My sketch of Channing has a background in my own experience far away. It must be nearly sixty years since, in the town of Freeport, Maine, I heard my father and uncle talking with much animation of a preacher whose voice had been heard somewhere in the neighborhood, and some printed word also from whom had reached their eyes; and the lift and lightening of their faces seemed to the little boy to extend to the landscape and embrace the horizon. To men of the present generation it were hard to conceive of the cloud of a gloomy theology then brooding over New England. The joy of my relatives in their new-found teacher of liberty and love was for me, at seven years of age, nothing less than the removal of a curse. When, of a hot summer afternoon, in the ill-ventilated church women fainted and were borne out, my childish thought was that they had been summoned to the dreadful judgment the minister had just preached. I used to walk and wander alone, repeating for the hundredth time to myself, " God be merciful to me, a sinner," although of what particular sin I had committed I was not aware, only I could imagine no escape from the universal depravity and doom. In the intermission of service, .my father's sister having been the minister's wife, how closely I was kept at her house or our room ! But occasionally being allowed of a Sunday afternoon to go to a rocky height in my father's pasture, and take turns with him looking through a spy-glass after the sails of his vessels expected home from sea, I had a pleasure which prayer or sermon seldom gave. There was annually a trip from the village out among the nearest of the three hundred and sixty-five islands in the Penobscot Bay, which excursion bound the seasons in a beautiful ring whose gems were the sparkling waves. But I remember no delight like that of the new dispensation of religion by the prophet whom I so longed to see. Drawn at length, it may be by that very impulse, in due course to the Divinity School in Cambridge, the Federal Street Church in Boston became straightway a magnet. I listened to the famous Liberal, went to see him in Newport and in Portsmouth, Rhode Island, and on my settlement found but a street between his residence and my own. For the last five years of his life I visited him or received calls from him, walked and talked in his company, discussed with him all the subjects on which he loved to dwell, and now am glad, as in some humble way among the trustees of his reputation, to testify of the traits of his disposition and his mind.

But his bodily feature and bearing must not be passed

by. Channing was insignificant in figure. Short, slender, thin, as I knew him, scarce more than a hundred pounds of flesh clothed and served in him the informing soul. One introduced to him exclaimed in amazement at the slight stature of the mighty preacher, "I thought you were six feet tall." Certainly in the desk he was of a commanding height. But he had to wrap his weak chest in many a covering, when he went out, against the damp and cold, and was very often only able to pace up and down on the sidewalk before his dwelling in the sun, till his slowly moving form became one of the sights in Boston. But he might have said to any one, as Napoleon to the marshal who reached to the Emperor a book from an upper shelf remarking, "I am higher than you, sire," — "Longer, not higher!" His eyes were so communicative that his friends disputed about the color, which was lost in the expression. Where was the hiding of the power of that marvellous voice, — one of the three most eloquent, says Emerson, he has heard; and surely like none beside, having more in it of the violin than the flute, yet with liquid notes such as Wilhelmj or Joiachim can fetch from the strings, and with an habitual rising inflection, rather than cadence, at the end of the sentence, which seemed to raise every hearer to the skies. It melted and resounded, was clear when it whispered, and a clarion when it rang. He told me that with speaking for many years new tones had been developed in his voice. Very peculiar in its charm was his reading of the Scriptures and of the hymns, of which Emerson says again, "He read into them more than I could afterwards find." When on an Easter Sunday the line left his lips,

"Angel, roll the stone away,"

the stone never, in the infinite distance, seemed to cease to roll.

> " Vain are the charms and faint the rays
>   The brightest creatures boast,
> And all their grandeur and their praise
>   Are in *Thy* presence lost."

He threw an insignificance on the first three lines in amazing contrast with the majestic close. He had a theory about public speaking which he expounded for my edification, that it was simply a matter of light and shade in the sentence. But I fancy that only with the particular artist, as with Titian or Tintoretto, the effect could ever come. However sensitive to just expression of his thought, he was more concerned with what he said, and to whom, than how he said it. An unbeliever at his house complaining of Christ's severity to the Pharisees, Channing turned to the passage, and recited the Wo upon Wo, until the unbeliever cried out, " I withdraw my objection if he spoke in that tone!" Indeed in sweet voices was the advent of the new faith. Edward Everett, whose own utterance was such an entrancing spell, said he firmly believed Buckminster's voice the most melodious that ever issued from human lips. Henry Clay's voice was called a band of music; Webster's was a trumpet, Channing's a harp.

But it is the man's interior I would portray; and character, even more than genius, was his mark. He had not so much visions as views. One long fit of contemplation and reflection was his life. His intellect was of the ideal stamp. But one, regarding his thoughts as rather derivative than original, somewhat

cynically called him a " potted Plato." He shared the
Platonism which existed before Plato was born.

Leaving his philosophy, I note in his character, first,
its height. He suggested the zenith. He told me
what a relief always it was for him to look up from the
troubled earth into the unruffled sky. His elevation
was so habitual that going to see him was like mounting an observatory; you must ascend, he could not
come down, and you found him adjusting his instrument,
and caring only that you should look through the long
reflector with himself. As Wordsworth said of Milton,

" His soul was like a star and dwelt apart."

Channing could not turn his eye to you without turning
his head. As on an elevated railway lay his track. People were vexed at having to go up so high to get nothing, as they sometimes said; for, with all the love and
wisdom in him like a climate, there was no flash, no surprising play of wit, little original suggestion, and not
the least condescension to a lower state. Edward T.
Taylor, that prince and playfellow of imagination, of
whom Channing said he knew all about the Platonic
wings, admitted Channing's talents, but denied his education! He was not, like Taylor, a graduate of the
university of the world.

I note, next, Channing's simplicity, of which Fénelon
had not more. Returning from a great dinner, he said
it was an enormous sacrifice to the flesh, but he was
comforted to find how little of it was consumed, and
he spoke as if he had been in a strange land among the
Fijis and got safely back. Taking wine one day at his
medical brother's prescription, he observed that it tasted

as he supposed brandy must, he was so unused to it.
Going out of his entry, he put on a young companion's
hat, and as it went down over his ears, turned and
said, "I did not suppose your head was bigger than
mine." Being invited to preach a New York dedica-
tion-sermon, he declined from lack of sympathy with
the building of fine churches. He needed no cathedral
aids to make his own service impressive. "When he
spoke of the human soul," says Taylor, "I thought I
should have gone over the gallery;" and he added,
"Hear such preaching as that and go to hell after
all?" The flowers in his garden cheered him not for
their own sake, but as prophecies of a better condition
of mankind. The ocean delivered his soul of struggling thoughts, and accompanied with its resonance his
anthems of praise. His quality was not the conscious
and affected simpleness which Matthew Arnold satirizes, but the Homeric simplicity the same essayist com-
mends. Not a smart sentence, rolled under the tongue
and calculated for effect, or intended as wit, can be
quoted from his books. Like Paul, he often said "I;"
but that pronoun was never his object, rarely his subject. always his instrument and means. As he said of
Milton, "he rose without effort or affectation to the
style of an apostle." It was a scriptural style and the
Master's manner. The ponderous Johnsonian method,
prevalent in his time, of approaching as by siege-par-
allels a subject, he broke up with an unprecedented di-
rectness, and, as one said, proposed, like General Grant,
to move immediately on the enemy's works. There
was nothing mystical in his mode. His page is a limpid,
rushing stream. He did not kindle by condensing, nor

as with a compound blow-pipe could he fuse refractory
substances, but by dint of the reality and the repeating
of his convictions won his way; and it takes now a
good deal of him or of his writing to appreciate his
property, as it does a large quantity of the air to get
the blue of the sky. He was devoid of ambition.
Fénelon's wish to be unknown, Wesley's to have no
monument, and the hiding of Moses's tomb, found
echoes in his heart. He scarce looked to see where his
shot struck, brave marksman as he was. A higher
than any personal aim is the lesson of his life. He was
the best of listeners, and not talkative himself. He
that is greedy of an audience has nothing to say! A
lad brought him a book with the publishers' request to
dedicate it to him. He replied at the threshold, "Boy,
take it away!" He asked people in church, if they
could, to suppress their 'cough, conversing, as with
friends, from the desk. He did not read notices of
himself in the public press; and when a dear brother
clergyman had printed a review of his book, he asked
his wife to read to him not the eulogistic but the critical parts. He did not reply to attacks, fearing, he said,
the lowering effect of lingering about his own writ-
ings, and thinking "men were enslaved to none so
much as to themselves." He but wanted, as Edmund
Burke told his electors, to be allowed to go on. An
almost incredible childlikeness is affirmed in some
authentic anecdotes of him. After trying in vain to
make some ladies understand a point he was making,
he relapsed slowly into his chair, saying, "I wish women had more mind!" He erased one word, "very,"
from a letter conveying a compliment to a friend from

others, that his statement might be exactly correct; and he rewrote a second and third time his articles, not to make them more taking, but more true. He said to me, "I hope prosperity will not relax your study; I do not think it has mine."

The sincerity which is the offspring of simplicity was conspicuous in him; and he stated the ground of sincerity as being interested in what one had to say. He did not care to utter aught but what was precious to his own soul, what he *was*, and had lived and loved before he spoke. Many a boisterous speaker, we feel, has no affection in his own heart for the positions he so proudly takes, and would, like a retained lawyer, argue the other side, the next day, with equal zeal. No such loud forensic pleader or platform-pretender was our true divine. He could not bear what was underhand. "Stop!" cried he to one talking scandal of the absent, "or I shall go and tell them every word you say." When one informed him that he had written an anonymous letter to a dealer in intoxicating liquors, Channing answered, "I am sorry so good a man as you should have done that!" This frankness made him never so young and enterprising as at threescore. "Were I to begin life again," said an English statesman, "it would be as an agitator." Theologically the boy Channing was the conservative, so far as he was such at all, and the radical was the man. But the youth had not got through college or finished his college part before, like Tennyson's sailor-boy,

> "He whistled to the morning-star."

He had that sign of all greatness, gravitation to the truth. In this he resembled Webster, Lincoln, Galla-

tin, Marshall, and other great men of state. He as well
as they knew that if the centre be unstable, or the fulcrum slip, the purchase will fail. Channing's passion was
to see how the thing stood. At Naushon, being found
with a cue in his hand at a small billiard-table, playing
all by himself, he said, as if to excuse himself, " I am
trying to find out the principle of this game." But
that was his invariable question, for ivory ball or great
globe. After three persons of his family had tried in
vain to make the toast savory, when he was unwell, he
said, " It is not good, — the perfect is what all our life
we seek after and never attain."   •

But in this image I must trace not only veracity, but
sensibility as well, — a trait which gravity like his might
conceal from some. Tenderness must have its shield ;
and the gentlest persons may pass for cold, while those
who are profuse in offers to such as need no help have
an oily courtesy running like the ointment over Aaron's
beard and to his garments' skirts, and get the credit of
unction and warmth. Real sentiment appears in its unconscious escapes. Channing told me it was the mobility
of feature in Dickens with which he was struck. The
coarse and profane language he hears in his journey,
while yet a youth, " cuts him to the heart." Describ-
ing the effect of a dancing girlish vision on his young
mind, he lays his hand on his wife's arm to say that
only in his fancy the picture lay. Walking with him
around Boston Common, we met a woman remembered
as an admirable teacher and mother, giving two sons,
Charles and James, to the war. After we had traversed
the street, interchanging remarks on various themes, he
paused and said, " What a sweet expression on Mrs.

Lowell's face; it has not gone from me yet!" His emotion was not demonstration, but abstinence from any aim at effect. He had atmosphere, but no airs. He was not absent-minded, but absorbed. He walked the streets with eyes that saw not the shows in the shop-windows. Yet humorous observation, in his early years keen and in later ones subordinated in him, was never quite outgrown. He hits off the schoolmistress like Cruikshank or Hogarth. He made merry over an attorney-general's criticisms on his philanthropy in the martyr Lovejoy's case, and over a certain doctor of divinity's assault on the Transcendentalists, Channing included. At the ordination of Barnard and Gray to the ministry at large, in Boston, all the world had come to hear Channing's charge. Tuckerman preached for an hour and a half. After the services Parkman, the clerical wag of the city, said, " Brother Tuckerman, your sermon was excellent, but undeniably too long. Brother Channing, was n't Brother Tuckerman too long?" " Ha, ha," said Channing, who was not going to be caught in this trap to hurt his friend Tuckerman's feelings, — " ha, ha," with that dry laugh in his throat which was all he could attain, while he knocked together the shoes that held his emaciated feet, " Brother Parkman, *were* you tired? I was tired before Brother Tuckerman began!"

Let me recall, next, Channing's spirituality, with but enough of the mortal in him to hold it down, his ascension being continual, and he himself but anchored below and tugging like a balloon at the last binding cord, yet with no flutter or levity but incomparable weight and moment in his mien as he swayed and ever threatened to rise. Some in their direction go from within

without, others from without within ; and these last never
get in.   The soul must react for experience to become
the master-light.   Channing had found the centre.
With a presence like Washington's he overcame the company and filled the room.   No man more respected other
minds, but his own made a temple wherever he was.
Naught indecent was possible before a sanctity so complete.   When a gross fault had occurred in his social
circle, he repudiated the politic concealments with which
in modern society scandals about distinguished persons
are sometimes covered up.   Materialism would have
been an organic anomaly for him.

Serenity in him was manifest no less, yet with the
swiftness of a courser well-trained.   He observed the
Shakspeare-player's " temperance ; " and my professor
of rhetoric classed him with Robert Hall as an example
of the dignified style.   Boston ought to give to him,
on the score of public merits, a statue, as to Franklin,
Webster, Everett, Sumner, and Mann ; and the bronze
should tell in its outward composure his inward poise
and peace, the same that appeared in Borromeo, St.
Francis of Assisi, Savonarola, Thomas à Kempis, Jacob
Böhme, or Jonathan Edwards, — for it is limited to no
sect, nor, more than one of Raphael's pictures, can be
a subject of dispute.   That assurance, which exceeds all
vicarious insurance, was in his breast.   The moral was
dominant in his mind.   A Christian Cato, if he was
censor it was first in his own soul.   This watchman on
the walls was ever on his good behavior to himself and
on his guard, never threw the reins on the horse's neck,
and did not become quite a joyfully emancipated child,
but kept in his manners some rigidity and restraint,

which was contagious. Yet, though sober, he was not sombre. He was an immense personality and motive-power, perhaps the chief religious momentum of his time, a Miltonic self, not so much a reporter of the spirit as he was the thing reported on and the report. I call him not religious; he was religion, and "righteous overmuch." He was the core of piety, of which we are on the edge! He thinks he is too serious, struggles against his earnest bent, complains of his inaptness for the play of human friendship and converse, tries to be more familiar, but never feels far from his Infinite Friend. Like Christ, he continues in prayer all night or all day.

He had a soldier's courage to challenge injurious dogmas and maintain right of judgment for the private soul; and he affirmed, if he had done aught worthy of remembrance after he should go, it was in his withstanding the imposing of a tyrannical yoke in the name of religion. The stuff of a martyr was in that frail form. As he stood in the arena, so he would have stood at the stake. More hero than poet was he in his make. Subtle correspondences, nature's cipher-despatches, he was not keen to read; nor did he poetically penetrate the inner sense of land and sea, whose outward aspect was to him such joy. Controversy left in him no muddy sediment or malign heat. All dispute was to him a breaking bubble, the froth of the hour.

So the attribute of liberality is pre-eminently his. The Universalists were a very odious and unpopular body in the Church forty years ago. But when they were assailed as holding forth a doctrine licentious and sure to corrupt, he averred how lofty was their idea of the final triumph of good. When the Perfectionists

23

were charged with like lax assumption, he rebated their antagonists for proclaiming the necessity of sin, and accorded with Father Taylor, who, on being asked if he really thought anybody had ever lived as good as Jesus Christ, answered, " Yes, millions," and laughed at some mournful confessor at a Unitarian conference, as busy rolling his dirty beetle-ball of sin. Channing died in the perfectionist faith of the perfectibility and final actual perfection of every human soul. In 1840, charging John S. Dwight, our Boston judge of music, for a min- istry in Northampton, he bids him visit the spot where Edwards brought forth his profound works, and, despite all difference with his opinions, breathe the consecra- tion which his name had spread over the place, and emu- late "his single-hearted devotion of his great powers to the investigation of truth." So to the doctrinal antipodes Channing's charity reached. His eulogy on the good Roman Catholic bishop, Cheverus, was well answered by the tolling of the Catholic bell over the way from the spot where the great Protestant left his handful of clay, with a chiming which they both at once must have heard in heaven. Channing had never taken part in denounc- ing Rome. Does it not announce the millennium when Orthodoxy accepts the Free-thinker as a saint? Moses Stuart, on reading Channing's Memoirs, said, "I did not know what a devoted man he was." If nobody sends us to hell for diversity of opinion now, it is an exemption none did so much as Channing to earn.

Because he said, "I am little of a Unitarian, but willingly bear the name as a title of reproach," some have claimed him as Orthodox, and even fancied a Trinity lurking in his thought. This his nephew and

biographer,. William Henry Channing, denounces as a
calumny; and his only son, Dr. William F. Channing,
declares he departed from Orthodox views more widely
the longer he lived.   He himself explicitly pronounces
that there is "no trace of a Trinity in nature or the
soul," while he discovers also in the Bible only the
Supreme One.   It were as plausible to claim Lyman
Beecher for a Unitarian.   But he was imprisoned in
no Unitarian denomination or sect, but a Liberal and
catholic in the ranks.   When a young man, Mr. Eustis,
afterwards teacher of the Freedmen on the islands off
the Georgia shore, being called to a Unitarian pulpit,
wished to be excused from administering the elements
of bread and wine in what is named the Lord's Supper, and a barrier against his admission was raised on
this account, Channing took the Quaker ground, and
protested against raising a wall of form to block any
faithful ministry out.

He differed with Theodore Parker about the miracles
of Jesus Christ and his place in the creation.   He
thought no system of morals or of abstract ideas could,
as a substitute for the historic religion, have power to
redeem mankind.   Yet he sent his love to Parker, and
exhorted him to "pour out all his heart."   One day,
as I entered his room, I found him reading Hazlitt's
Essays.   He remarked, "Hazlitt has said hard things
of me, and I am taking my revenge by studying his
books."   Hazlitt had ridiculed him for dividing greatness into three orders and putting himself at the head,
in his article on Napoleon, that most famous of his
literary attempts.   Hazlitt, though English, was a
partisan of Bonaparte, Channing's treatment of whom

seemed so harsh as to make the only instance of il-
liberality, or rather narrowness, we might cite; and
Channing himself, in the preface to his works, as if
touched in conscience by the criticism he had launched,
begs the reader to notice the date of that piece.

Let me indicate the claim of Channing's literary work.
Its earnestness all will admit. It had, too, the great
merit of *continuity*. It was a flow, a flight, and a flame.
The stream, the bird, and the sun are its types. It
was lofty, and had a long wind. With some of his literary judgments it were easy to find fault, as, for example, that Milton's "Paradise Lost" is "perhaps the
noblest monument of human genius." Against such a
verdict the shades of Homer and Æschylus and Dante
and Goethe protest! His Election Sermon, as fine a
rapture on the theme of mental liberty as exists in any
tongue, shows in its best state this at once running,
soaring, and burning quality. That on "Partaking the
Divine Nature" is unsurpassed as a strain of transport-
ing piety, while the essay on Fénelon, in its examination of the great Catholic's doctrine of self-denial, is
his best attempt at criticism, and remains sound and
unanswerable to this day.

As a prophet of human nature he must mainly stand.
He early discarded the dogma of total depravity. When
he was a lad his father took him along in the chaise as
he went to hear a famous preacher, who in his sermon
announced eternal doom. It was not thought the child
would take the dreadful burden in, or pay any heed to
what should be said. But he listened, and shrank.
The service over, the father starting on the way back
began to whistle; and on getting home, in apparent un-

concern for all those phials of the Revelation that had been uncorked, searched for the newspaper, and began to read, while the little one said in his heart, " He does not believe what he has heard, and it is not true!" He doubted the Trinity at first, as he rejected it to the last. It may be questioned if he understood its philosophy, its reason for being, or the end at which it aims, namely, to find betwixt the human and divine a bond or common term. God is one, but his unity is not numerical singularity. Father and Son are in each other; and we must not shut up God in his high house of heaven, or with Hebrew narrowness make him a local Lord, only grander than the heathen ones, as in his chariot he thunders and careers through the sky, but domesticate him with his offspring on the earth; and the Trinity is a grand and noble endeavor to fill with a more majestic presence the household niche from which the pagan Penates have been expelled. Possibly, it misses the mark in confining the Incarnation to an individual, one only begotten, when from all eternity of the family of God there can be no count; but it hits the centre in affirming that childhood is no less essential than parentage in the Deity. " I and my Father are one." *He* would fall if I did, as the universe would crumble if punctured at a point. Not only immanent, but identical at the root are God and man; and the Trinity, in recognizing and trying to formulate or state this sameness, avoiding pantheism, is worthy of honor even in its failure or its partial success. Its office is precious also to resist individualism as a form of atheism, and to substitute community or communion, which is truth and good, for the communism which is folly and hate. But the Trinity has peradventure a second defect in leaving out Nature, on which science so well insists; while with science concurs art, or that love of nature which in artist and poet is so much a modern sentiment, having a harbor in every musing mind. I suppose no theologian would meet this objection with the metaphysical plea that nature is but a mirror or mode of mind; and as, on the whole, honors are divided between the two theologic parties in this debate, no denominational color can be suspected in these remarks. Be the measureless and unfathomed scene we are part of created or evolved, no solution of the problem will answer which does not include the panorama, the foreground, and background, as well as the figures in the picture. So must not all Unitarian or Trinitarian schemes give place to the conception of God as one and manifold? In this or in any direction I do not claim for Channing supreme genius or philosophic depth. He lacked talent or temper to speculate. He held hard to ethics, and he stuck close as his skin to his own spiritual frame. His idealism was realism. His affirmations were ruddy, and his negations were never pale. His saintly soul was steeped in reverence and infantile innocence. He stood in awe of God and of his own soul. In no man did conscience tread a loftier stage. One even said of him, "He was kept from the highest goodness by his love of rectitude." His estimate of human nature had a logical tie with his philanthropy. He espoused betimes the cause of the slave. He had condemned the harsh speech of the Abolitionists. But when Samuel J. May inquired of him, "If they speak ill, why do not you speak well?" he meekly answered,

"I ought to have spoken before." When he and Garrison met in amity, it was said, "Mercy and truth are met together; righteousness and peace have kissed each other." There was no doubt a moral quality not only in the impetuosity of some, but in the hesitancy of other good men, at the outbreak of the antislavery strife; and to this honest ethical pause justice has not yet been done. But Channing once in motion was no more considerate and charitable than he was brave. When the City Government of Boston had refused the use of Faneuil Hall to celebrate the martyrdom of the printer Lovejoy, editor of the "Alton Observer," in Illinois, who had fallen defending his press, then, by an appeal to the people which made the streets ring beyond the toll of bells or rattle of the wheels, Channing constrained the municipal authority to recede, and the old Cradle of Liberty rocked again.

My motive is not to recommend a partisan, which, either in politics or religion, Channing never was. Like Milton, he was an Arian in the earlier time; but all moot points of belief, and the idea of Christ's pre-existence among them, lost import with him, and at length, before his engrossment in humane interests, faded away.

The tributes to him come from all quarters now. The German Lutheran, Baron Bunsen, in his well-rounded characterization, calls him "in humanity a Greek, in citizenship a Roman, in Christianity an apostle," adding, "If such a one is not a Christian apostle of the presence of God in man, I know of none." Dean Stanley, lately in this country, requested to be taken to Mount Auburn to see the tomb of Channing. Dom Pedro, Emperor of Brazil, expressed the same wish. Like the bee-lines that meet over the hive, these directions of famous men from diverse latitudes joined at one spot.

In general, I designate Channing not as a naturalist, but rather as a supernaturalist. With Plato and Dr. Edward Beecher, he thought the soul to be older than the body. On miracles, which he never ruled out, he came, however, at last not to lay the stress. He told me he thought the *works* in nature were of more worth. But he relished no flouting of the supernatural aureole around the Master's head, — the halo which that head rays out, and which no science can disperse. Indeed, has not *myth* a place as well as fact; and is not the hand profane that would rend it away? As well blow out the atmosphere as the superhuman. We may drive the angels from the Bible, when we send the witches in "Macbeth" from the blasted heath! A persuasion haunts us of that Infinite Reality, which the rumor of apparitions, on whatever ground accredited or discredited, represents, and which we obstinately believe ought and some time will be true! The *supernatural* is that which, expelled with whatever fork of the understanding, *nature* will return to with inevitable attraction and unappeasable zest. But Channing, with all his faith, could not be irrational; and the vicarious atonement by an infinite sacrifice, which is to many excellent Christians so unspeakably dear, he could not abide, as it offended his moral sense.

Humanity was his crown. He told me how consistent he thought his view of the dignity of human nature was with personal humility. "He loved love," says Balzac of one of his heroes. Channing was a lover of amity and peace, and of Noah Worcester, the apostle of peace. He said of the portraits and busts made of himself, that he cared less for the intellectual expression than that they should beam good-will to his fellow-creatures. The sight or thought of inhumanity he was too tender to bear, and he hoped he might be excused from perusing details of cruelty, the particulars of pain. He said that the slaveholder was very much an abstraction to him, whereupon Garrison asked, "Is he an abstraction to the slave?" He was a prophet of the soul, and judged that the highest nature could not, more than the lowest, leave its appointed track. Such a man as the historian Prescott thought him a sublime and visionary generalizer; but he put his notion with genuine force: it struck a million minds, and is not a spent ball yet. He originated a new way of regarding mankind, although, when he could not manage a special case, he was glad to be helped by the minister-at-large, at the birth of whose work he assisted. Pierpont, the practical reformer, said, "Throw him from his protections into the street, and he would die." But, no more than our chronometer or mirror, could we so cast him out. One of his brethren called him a Jacobin, and he only smiled. He headed a petition for the pardon of Abner Kneeland for blasphemy, which the present writer signed, drawing from a Judge in his congregation the observation, "It is the only mistake our young minister has made." His faith in the soundness of the human root is the prime condition of all faith in the planter, God.

To whom does this pearl of character belong? To no party. Diverse sects would appropriate signal excellence, as the old cities disputed where Homer was born. Dean Stanley puts Christ's wisdom in his refusal to be classified. M. Renan, on being asked, in 1870, if Prussia would be absorbed in Germany, answered that he could not tell, as M. Bismarck had not yet submitted himself to analysis. Swedenborgians have claimed Channing's spirit. He had affinities with Whitefield and Wesley, Anthony Woolman and George Fox. A great soul transcends orders, and is a law to itself. It is more fast in righteousness than an engine to the rails or a planet on its path. We, in this land, have had occasion to see that there is in human nature itself not only freedom, but the higher law. Channing's mind was a pervasive force. He corresponded with Henry Clay, in private, to discover at first hand the facts of human bondage, though the letters that passed have never found their way into print. But a Kentucky planter bound up Channing's public one to Clay with blank leaves, for entries of his own reflections, showing the hold on his heart of perhaps unwelcome truth.

This surpassing power was lodged in a body so invalid that its tenant could scarce endure the grasp of a hand. But Ichabod Nichols said, only on such conditions of sensitiveness and delicacy could a Channing be had. But the tenderness was firmness too. Channing was lofty and lowly, like a branching elm. As a solution is the greatest potency of a drug, so in that humility, which is God's door of entrance to the soul, his dignity was solved. There is something in every thing save our conceit, and of that he was devoid.

He was taken ill in a hotel, in Bennington, Vermont, October 2, 1842. As the vital flame in him burned low, he said, "I have received many messages from the spirit." He had, while he lived, got at people especially, he said, through their voices. His whisper was his last communication. With declining day his countenance sank. Being assisted, he turned to the window at the east. The curtains were drawn back, and the light fell on his face. He gazed over the valleys and wooded hills, and none but God and the spirit knew when his soul passed to that prospect which the horizon could not bound. Taylor, the Bethel-preacher, and his great compeer, described the scene, — the sunset after such a morning glow, the clambering vines dropping their leaves outside, and the loving watchers over what, like a leaf, loosened from the tree of life within, — and, at the close of a sort of vocal requiem, the great Methodist cried or sang, "Walk in the Light." The French Laboulaye, finding one of Channing's books at a stall in Paris, said, "I have discovered a man." Born, April 7, 1780, Channing's centennial commemoration, for his country and race, will come this year.

The fact is easily explained that the image of Channing in the memory of scholars and in the common mind is unsmiling and severe, more of the puritan than the pilgrim type. At the beginning of his ministry his health was broken by overwork, and he never recovered from the nervous wreck. He had to gather the remnants of his strength as fuel to keep the vital spark alive, and nurse and warm himself ever after as best he could. But there was no overplus of high spirits to sparkle or radiate; and his engagement in his themes was too constant and intense to spare a morsel of his

energy for sport. After a brief salutation, the visitor
was taken into the laboratory at once. If he was not interested in the experiments on hand, or was a lion-hunter
ambitious for the acquaintance of a great man, the case
was simply one with which Channing could not affect
any interest and was quite helpless to deal. He was
an observer, and wanted to get others' observations.
He was all the time considering high matters, and could
not understand any one whose object was not, like his,
to seek the truth. How reverentially he waited for
every one's contribution of thought, till in his silence
he seemed freezing cold! Any attempt at merriment
drew from him only a passing wintry smile, like that of
the Arctic regions at a glint of the sun. To no man
was life more serious, duty more solemn, or the call
more urgent to improve the time. It has been said of
the veteran Dr. Ripley, that he was "good at a fire."
Channing was disabled during the last forty years of
his life for any but the most cautious muscular exer-
tion; and the marvel is, not that he was incompetent
to any feat of bodily strength, and afraid of the least
exposure, but that his sobriety of body and mind was
mixed with such good cheer. Morose he never was.
Long after the prime of bodily vigor was passed, he
would, in hours of relaxation, play and wrestle with
his son, and stretch out his arms for the lad, of whom
he made a companion, to run into across the floor, or
tell him stories, that grew toward their climax, with corresponding illustration of characters and figures in the
speech, by drawings with a pencil on a slate, — which
ended usually in a donkey. But intellectual inquiry took
possession of him more and more every day he lived. If

there can be a passion not only for persons but for the
truth, no man that ever breathed burned with it more.
His faculties for study were rare. We respect men
that speak from conviction, as none that listened to
him could doubt that he did. But his immortalizing
peculiarity was less that of the genius than of the saint.
It is the most cheering sign of hope for mankind that,
beyond all ingenuity or depth of argument, consecration
of talent wins their regard. Jonathan Edwards lives
in our honor more by his unworldly temper than by his
essay on the Freedom of the Will; and Channing will be
a name in the calendar and on the canon when all his
works may be forgotten. His thought was a river and
a fountain too; not a canal cut through him, but a running stream. His Missouri arose in his own mind.
Dr. Wayland remarked how he was transformed out of
apparent coldness and reserve when he wrote or spoke.
It was indeed the difference of a cannon-ball in the
armory and in the air. It is our faith that such a projectile can never stop.

III.

BUSHNELL, THE THEOLOGIAN.

AMONG recent American authors Horace Bushnell was one of the foremost in devoting his genius completely to Theology, that queen of the sciences, yet so uncertain in her character and unstable in her reign, and never more than in these days needing some master-mind at her court. All the former schemes have been shaken, but none appears to take their place. The loud demand for a rational religion results in no agreement or generally accepted creed, even among those by whom it is sought. Channing protests against and in some points convicts the old schedule, but he formulates nothing new. Parker's " Theism " was the weakest of his works ; and our modern Liberalism, so called, is so untheologic that it waits for proof that God exists. It disowns the Church, and would divorce it from the State. It denies the foundation of morals in parts of its practice, and in its theory holds it in suspense. Horace Bushnell, a man con-genitally compelled to see all things in the light of rea-son, espoused at the beginning and maintained to the end the cause of the Orthodox faith. It has had no other ex-pounder of equal genius in our time. He was, however, no such severe dialectician as Calvin. While he would be logical, the forms of logic he despised. His method was that of suggestion. He was more a poet than an advocate. No man drew out his discriminations in sharper lines. But in his nature underneath every line of argument was mystical piety for a daily refuge, and no romance charmed him like a book of prayer. He had that charity for his opponents which sprang from an understanding of their positions as well as from the tenderness of his own heart. He knew why and how one could differ from him; and his imagination, alike fine and broad, showed him on what ground had stood any and every scheme of religion that had prevailed in the world. The political formulas, says Carlyle, were swallowed by Mirabeau; and Bushnell declared he could take down all the theological statements with no lack of edification.

But he was a force and factor in our New England religion. Whenever a thinker comes in any sectarian fellowship he brings a crisis, disturbs the communion, and starts a revolution until his ideas are outgrown or absorbed. But Bushnell said of the chief antagonist of his views that he but wished to put him into "an attitude of comprehensive repugnance;" so devoid of personal heat and bitterness his own character and constitution required him to be. Yet he was as keen as he was kind. His eye, while soft and receptive, had the glitter of a spear or of a diamond's edge. It laughed before his lips smiled, and was merry while the other features were still grave, but scintillated and shrewdly penetrated to the point. What shafts of wit and humor he habitually shot! When a doctor of divinity told him that he had been "laying out the Presbyterian doctrine" to the present writer, Bushnell replied, "You mean, I suppose, that you have been putting a shroud on it; for that's what they do when they lay things out!" He hated sanctimonious mimicry. No dogma that had become a stereotyped mechanical recitative was safe from his stroke. He condemned it if it was customary and trite. Every article, to be accepted or pass with him, must be restated and reformed, and have the word of the latest intelligence for its countersign. He was a " son of Agamémnon terrible to purify." He averred that he was not a Calvinist; but said he thought " a Calvinist could be a Christian," which Father Taylor denied, as he inquired how such Calvinists as might be admitted to heaven by an arbitrary decree, irrespective of moral conduct, would like it, should the Master come along and " turn the stick round" with a verdict as absolute as was the first, yet that should lodge them in hell! To this imputed uncertainty of a salvation on principle, purely elective and wholly unearned, Bushnell replied by heartily joining in the Bethel-preacher's well-grounded and very sober fun.

Being utterly sincere, incapable of sophistry, and instantly discarding in his views any unsoundness of which he was aware, how then did he present his case, to save the truth and Orthodoxy too? I can testify on one point at least. The dispute about everlasting punishment, that rends the Congregational body to-day, was easily solved in his mind by the belief that the persistently wicked would not in the future world survive their sin. This opinion is cited from private conversation in the latter years of his life, and may never have been by him publicly preached. Yet my interest in the subject, as in the man, renders impossible any mistake in my recollection of the emphasis with which he affirmed that " every thing looks as if they who are unreclaimed from transgression must go down and go out, and no more be." But this Darwinian doctrine of the survival of the fittest, carried beyond the grave, shocks the consciousness of Christendom, and by no church is it yet received. Only an individual and numerical, not moral or spiritual, immortality is still held. But few think any individual is perishable. No heresy could be more flagrant in any sect than to doubt the everlasting personal continuance alike of the giant in iniquity and of the still-born child. But a crisis is at hand to test the thought, which was not Bushnell's alone. The motive to virtue of an eternal perdition for every particular shareholder in the depravity of the race is slowly and fatally being withdrawn, leaving a vacuum for the conscience which some other and better incentive must fill, if we would not have the motive power fail and the human train stop in all conscious motion to a future destiny. What inducement to well-doing could be so wholesome and strong as to suspend upon faithfulness, instead of an indestructible entity, all our hope of being at all? What expectation of any proper immortality can they have who are not immortal in their thoughts and affections now? In our experience alone is any fact whatsoever sure; and before heaven is in our vision, it must be in our heart. Unfelt as a reality, it cannot be honestly preached as a faith; and so we read of the Son of Man that he was in heaven while he stayed and seemed to be on the earth.

Dr. Bushnell was a Trinitarian. He tried to show that a threefold divinity is not only taught in Scripture, but is credible in itself and conformable to human want.

24

But he held that the substance of Deity is one, and only the manifestation triune. If, however, in the composition of the Trinity the essence be abandoned and the expression kept, it loses not only its importance but its ground. When we come to the showings of Deity, how all number fails, and counting must be given up! Three or three thousand in our arithmetic can never surround or ascend to all the jets from the infinite spring. If not a triad but simple unity be the subsistence of God, no Trinitarian theory touches bottom, or more than resembles a deep-sea line beyond soundings and dangling in the waves. If the Father be the first term, the Son must be not only second but secondary; and how could the first be Father unless he were already the third, that is, the Spirit too, as by Jesus he is called? In all parentage childhood is implied; but childhood is the offspring or procreation, and that which all earthly parentage figures is unbegotten and unborn.

The trouble with Trinitarianism — and it is a difficulty more formidable and threatening every day — is that it leaves Nature out; and Nature will not consent either to be omitted or to remain under the ban. The original curse laid upon her is antiquated long ago. Nature with every step and discovery of science becomes in all systems a factor of greater weight; and the knowledge of Nature is reinforced by that love of Nature, distinctively a modern sentiment, so informing all piety, as well as poetry and music and pictorial art, that whatever speculation may presume to affront and wrestle with it is sure to be discredited, shoved aside, or overthrown. What then has Nature, this last and not untrustworthy witness, to say about God?

But let us not slur the previous question, whether Nature is not in theology a term to be altogether suppressed. Science or the scientific man, it is perhaps correctly said, knows nothing of God. But Nature's meaning is by no scientist ever divined and drawn out. Many things in nature we can scarce conceive that God, save under necessities which our thought cannot fathom, although our faith must accommodate, could directly intend or do. Natural evil, as with a whip of scorpions, drives us back to find the witness of his justice and goodness in our own conscience and heart. Philosophy joins with religion, as witness here. We denounce Calvinism as impious and absurd. But how far pessimism, the last word of German speculation, in its malediction on our Mother Earth suckling us at her breast, has outstripped any indictment by the Genevan divine! To Dr. Bushnell Nature is hardly more than a phantom, the clothing of a god, or the shadow of a man. He never lies down quite content in her maternal lap. The stars are to him but a larger spread of tinsel or shine of gilding; and, in the case of the Christ, he comes near to abolishing human nature too, as he makes nothing to be significant in Jesus but the divinity which he is and reveals. The humanity of the Lord is only appearance and veneer, a frame for the picture or a setting for the gem. Bushnell's most remarkable and elaborate essay is a monograph inscribed with this view. Did he have any mistrust that he was thus dropping out of his beloved Trinity the indispensable equivalent of the second term? In his "Nature and the Supernatural" he does so take up the line betwixt the two that it becomes as hard to distinguish them in his treatment as it is to many persons to part them in fact! But until the boundary is discovered all miracle will be in doubt; and probably he believed in no miracle as a violation of law.

But for such disparagement or counting out Nature has her revenge. She forces upon our author, in all his acute profundity, the rehabilitation of herself. He finds a retroactive effect, as by an *ex post facto* law, of the curse of Adam's sin on living forms of reptile and fish before the first man was fashioned on the earth. The deformity of such a creature, for example, as the flounder was in veritable anticipation of the ugliness of the human fall, as if, to borrow the criticism of another, Nature had misshapen herself with a fit or shudder beforehand at the consequences of Adam's eating, a myriad of ages after, the forbidden fruit.

But this supersubtle reasoner concerning the native corruption of the race, in his discourses on "Christian Nurture," struck at the doctrine of total depravity the heaviest blow it has ever received. He perceived that some idea of human nature must be held. The Liberal theology has dealt with men as individuals, so many souls personally responsible, each one. Orthodoxy has at least grappled with the real problem of the whole body of humanity, or the organic solidarity of the race. Despite the Prophet's rebuke to such as quoted for their own exculpation the proverb, "the fathers *have* eaten sour grapes, and the children's teeth are set on edge." The latest investigations, with no ecclesiastical bias, only confirm heredity as a universal law. But Bushnell insisted on a working of that law not only as degrading, but, through religious inheritance, benign. He held that it is in the Church a hurtful superstition to base

redemption on any sudden conversion, as by a new
birth, children being regenerate in their devout parentage without special prodigy of grace, the need of which
in every case the Congregationalist and Baptist orders
have so vehemently affirmed. His elucidation and courageous reassertion of this so well-taken point after a
long ecclesiastical dulness made the Church ring all its
bells once more! But at the touch of reproach and persecution he did not waver or flinch. His year of controversy on this subject within the borders of his own
brotherhood made the romantic period of his life, and
proved, as in the furnace, the metal of which he was
made. The volume of sermons, which were disserta-
tions on the Church as being a nursery and not a
revival camp or rink, was the most valuable of his publications, for all parties in our New England Christendom of thirty years ago. It called alike Unitarian and
Trinitarian individualism to order. It broke down in
part and for a while the partition-wall between the
two sides in this community. It was a new atonement, and no discussions of any thesis of diverse belief
have had an interest among us so lively or lasting so
long. The pages of Bushnell devoted to them have a
fresh stimulus and generous nutriment still, as of communion bread and wine.

His repeated attempts to rationalize the doctrine of
God's reconcilement to man, or propitiation by vicarious suffering, were masterly pleas for positions hard of
defence, and which he really forsook in undertaking to
maintain, so satisfying neither party in the strife. He
was like a lawyer whose damaging admissions after the
most ingenious argument are ruinous to his client's

case. In his reconstruction nothing of the notion which he was retained to demonstrate was left. Calvinism found in him, indeed, its vanishing point, and Orthodoxy became heterodox by every plain issue it had, according to the Liberals, ever made with reason and the moral sense. "Hast thou appealed unto Cæsar? Unto Cæsar shalt thou go," said Festus to Paul. The Cæsar to whose tribunal every word from Bushnell summoned the popular creed was the ethical reason, and the consequence was that every dogma that was tried at this bar was either altered or given up. This doom on the old body of divinity reminds us of Ariel's song to Ferdinand in " The Tempest,"

> " Full fathom five thy father lies;
>   Of his bones are coral made;
>   Those are pearls that were his eyes;
>   Nothing of him that doth fade
>   But doth suffer a sea-change
>   Into something rich and strange.
>   Sea-nymphs hourly ring his knell:
>   Ding-dong.
>   Hark! now I hear them, — ding-dong, bell."

In Dr. Bushnell's occasional discourses, where he holds in hand no theologic prescription or brief, his genius is most happily displayed. The Phi Beta Kappa oration was perhaps the most perfect of its kind in our day. The sermon on " Barbarism the First Danger," that on " Unconscious Influence," and the " Address on Music " are specimens of original power which in the pulpit of any denomination or in the lyceum are seldom matched. In the now two centuries of puritanic tradition in this land no man has appeared since Jonathan Edwards whose vision of the point in debate went more deeply, or whose vigor was more conspicuous in unfolding its vital contents. We have had famous orators in the Orthodox desk, who could, on occasion, bravely spurn what hampered them like a ball and chain, and dash forward into a larger field of survey. But anon they would retreat to the familiar repetitions and symbolical books of the synagogue to which they belonged! Bushnell held whatever ground he conquered, occupied in force the fortress he won, and was not only a theologian, but a devotee and a divine. From his childhood, through all his boyhood and college-days, he illustrated that descent of sacred influence whose law he set forth. Eunice and Lois no more sent it down to Timothy than it came progenitally to him, so that the main theme of his life was an heirloom in his blood.

The increasing value of Nature in the theological sum is what mainly now we have to take into account. Once matter, or the stuff of Nature, was so evil that God must not soil his hands with it, but intrust to some lower deity, or demiurgus, the creation of the world; and afterwards the whole structure as finished was so hurt by sin, like a tool or machine broken the moment it came into actual use, that it went by default, and was set aside. In the modern sense of an entity or unity, idealized or abstractly conceived, — unless Cicero be an exception to this remark, — Nature did not exist to the ancient mind, sacred or profane. But recently she has arisen, like one with confused senses waking from sleep. Her name nowhere, with our full meaning, is found even in Holy Writ. But now she claims to be the offspring of God. She scorns the possibility of being, in herself or her offspring, totally depraved.

She has shown that she has a constitution whose power
has not been measured, or health ruined, or proportions
gauged. Her frame, at every successive glance of her
children who have learned to call her mother, discloses
new beauty, with a promise to cancel all deformity, and
a harmony to resolve every discordant note. That good
Churchman, John Ruskin, who under the title of art
has written with unmatched eloquence of her grandeur
and charm, recognizes in no part of her fashion the
ancient theological ban. He smites the actual sinner,
whom ancestral apology cannot excuse. He describes
him as, in the English ritual, " concealing the manner
of his sin from men, while confessing the quantity of it
to God."

Nature, once esteemed as nothing but a positive hin-
drance to piety or a minus amount in the mathematics of
our religious means, at present, with every art for her
witness, is vindicating herself from past insult and dis-
inheritance. Her previous nonentity has among scientists become the only entity in perhaps the majority of
modern minds. From cold and empty zero she has
ascended what measureless degrees! There is no limit
to this scale. Such a thing as literal supernature, which
Bushnell identified with spirit, is everywhere dislodged.
By no imagination can it be clearly grasped. What is
pure spirit but an image for absolute spirit supplied by
the wind? It does not in fact exist. The world is
God's habit; but he cannot take off his dress. A naked
Deity he never was! Why should he disrobe who never
lies down to sleep? Without this self-woven atomic garment, tough and vast and many-colored, which he wears
and cannot wear out, he was never seen to go forth;

nor as distinct from it shall we behold him even in heaven. We have, in our little time-span, crept under the border of it on earth. But for that cover we could not have a moment's life and breath; and, though we be stripped of this fleshly raiment when we die, the same old nature or matter must, in some finer style, furnish our ascension robes, if such we are indeed to have. Nature clothes us for our cradle below, and will reclothe us for our journey hence, as a mother does her children, be they infant or grown up. When we converse with a noble soul, a monad like Channing or Bushnell, we feel that, in the language of Paul, it is not to " be unclothed, but clothed upon, that mortality might be swallowed up of life." To what better uses can this outward material, in all its strong and subtile textures, be put, than as the vehicle, or to afford successive vehicles, to a loving and adoring spirit, to a musing and scrutinizing intelligence, and to a resolute and all-projecting will? What finer service in the counsels of the Most High, among grasses and flowers, animal organisms, sublimity in the hills, or graceful shape and changing hue in " the plighted clouds," can it render, than to comfort continuously a thinking and aspiring nature of intrinsic superiority to itself, to guard it against blasts in the dark valley, and repair it from all the wastes of time? Wherefore does it hint an inestimable potency in the lightning or the thunder-crash, and wrap up in molecules an enormous force, but to hint capacity in its delicate drawers for all angelic and immortal demands? When matter is mended into a pen to write words for us on the other side of the sea, or shaped into a tongue to talk our messages into listening ears scores of miles away, and without leaving our chair to communicate our wishes either to a distant town or a neighboring street, does it not justify our cordial apprehension that it is an eternal agent and our appointed servant for ever, still to wait upon us when all space shall be but our sitting-room and what we call time shall be no more? Ofttimes we are shrewdly pinched with it, and in its grip heavily thrown; but a notion stubbornly clings to us that we cannot be vanquished at last, or confounded with any of its wrecks. Not seldom in some warm and pleasing shape it may contrive our destruction, and lure us to the pit. But to glorify us with grace of a resisted temptation or a repented transgression is its real and ultimate design. "No cross, no crown" is a sacred proverb; and when we see crosses wrought into diadems on the heads of kings, the transfiguration of all calamity is symbolized and foreseen.

Materialism or naturalism is not to-day among us here in vain, albeit the apparent dominant and dismal belief of the age. It awaits its transformation, like a worm out of its skinny crib or a body in its unlighted tomb. There must be some collateral intent in the obstinacy with which even the gross dogma of "a resurrection of the body" clings to the confession of the Church. It signifies the inability of our thought to envisage any being, human or divine, without form! If we are to rise, it must be not only with some essence, but with some substance as well. So only does it seem to us that we can escape the prison of the body, and avoid the voracity of the grave. If rising in another form, or, in the grand Scripture-phrase, "the resurrection of the dead," were substituted in cathedral-chancels and in the misnamed Apostles' Creed for "resurrection of the body," these would, without offence to reason, be a furtherance of faith.

We think, accordingly, that in his endeavor to draw a line betwixt nature and the supernatural Dr. Bushnell has no satisfying success. To some of his descriptions does not a remnant of the old contempt for nature adhere? If all of spirit, if the element of prayer and even the action of the human will, be supernatural, as he would represent, what, indeed, that is natural in any worthy sense is left? In the processes of our experimenter's laboratory Nature has, in fact, been incremated or calcined, and only a dead powder of dregs or cinder of ashes remains. She was but a sort of serpent which Aaron's rod has devoured; or as insubstantial as Berkeley makes all that is external to be in his philosophy; or as that magical Prospero, who is Shakspeare, in his speech at the funeral obsequies of matter, pictures and wipes out the world. Rather, is there not some confusion in the masterly statement of our theologian, who is a psalmist too? Idealism or realism as a system we may understand. But the spheres which we confound, we destroy. Perhaps a metaphysic, more hazy than profound, hanging over our author's exposition of this particular subject, may account for the comparatively slight influence of a dissertation perhaps abler, as it is more voluminous, than any other of his single efforts, while less marked than others of them with justness of view and a sturdy common-sense.

But we so respect his extraordinary faculty as to apprehend that what he could not do cannot be done, and that the natural and the supernatural may in no wise be cut apart. As things not conterminous or interfering, they interpenetrate, yet do not mix. Do we predicate the supernatural and the superhuman of God? But God most of all pervades, as he enfolds Nature and humanity too. "The Lord," says the Swedenborgian, "is a man." But he is Nature too. She is the mediator more than any one man can be; and the doom of failure is on all attempts, even the most astute, to cast out her name as evil or as naught in the communion of saints or in the work of redeeming love. She will not evacuate the premises, but will hold on more firmly every day, whatever hypothesis-maker may bid her go. Unresentful of his foolish and puny plan, she continues to supply language for the liberal setting forth of his thought! Her emblems are the fashions of his literary costume. Out of her armory he gathers the weapons which he turns against her breast. From her ample vestry come both the color and pattern of the style he employs for her abuse, as her wardrobe will give, without money or purchase-price, his outfit when he shall quit his present abode in her precincts for any other or higher of her endless and boundless scenes. That she will always be our introduction and introducer to spirit is a noble suspicion we cannot shun. Could we clean her out of her own premises, or be clear of her ourselves, no longer were we ourselves! We cannot pare matter down to spirit, and we cannot merge spirit in matter; but when soul is conceived as separate from form, or the name of spiritualism is bestowed on the circle-manifestations to sheer sense, or the incarnation is limited as a prodigy to a single historic case, we may well call upon materialism, bald and downright, to restore the disturbed balance, and acknowledge our debt to the materialist, who at least holds that something is extant, without which the infinite were lost.

Were miracles possible, in the sense of nullified laws, they must perforce be wrought in the stuff of Nature, and thus keep some of her statutes, whatever others they break, so picking and choosing the marvellous, which the phantoms of dead men in the dusky séance make out of the whole cloth. But God need not depart from his character of lawgiver to be lover too ; and if men be translated or transformed to angels, science can specify no law which would thus be annulled. Reverent waiting, not curiosity, is here in place, and he who begins with inquisitiveness will not end with prayer.

But all the reports that science has made, or ever will render in, must in no wise be considered as identical with or equivalent to Nature herself. Science but traces some part or section of her structural mode, which is but the outside of her method ; and it is incompetent to codify all her laws, to map her operations, or exhaust her contents. Science will be for ever disabled for such tasks, inasmuch as to other than the scientific faculties Nature appeals, and her entire significance can even be apprehended only by the whole soul. Her summons to our understanding is her least and faintest address. She accosts every feeling. She greets and stirs our imagination, she arouses our wonder, and she offers an altar for our prayer ; and the heart dedicated to any object, visible or unseen, is provided by her with countless correspondences and cipher despatches of its sentiment, and has never found her last token of its worship and love. Homer and Shakspeare and Dante and Goethe are more profound interpreters of what she intends and would say than even Newton and Kepler and Humboldt and Laplace ; and we shall go to Words-worth rather than to Huxley now to have her riddle read.

> " Throned on the sun's descending car,
>   What power unseen diffuses far
>   This tenderness of mind ?
>   What genius smiles on yonder flood ?
>   What god, in whispers from the wood,
>   Bids every thought be kind ? "

On one of those spring days when the Lord seems to keep open house, is there not in Nature's liturgy indeed such a collect as this? Does she not chant our ascriptions, repeat our doxologies, and make the real responses in our service of praise? If she be not alive, but only the echo or sounding-board of our affections, yet her reverberation intensifies and prolongs every cry of devotion or compassion, every whisper of trust or lisp of hope from the human breast.

Dr. Bushnell was not insensible to her sustenance and succor for the diverse emotions breathed by the solitary and excommunicated, or by the socially jaded and sorely persecuted, into her ever-hospitable ear. But his theological situation and antecedents restricted him, native singer though he were, to little use of her as a religious instructor and ally. His ratiocination hung as a veil between her and his eyes ; and we may find one defect of the popular creed in general in its scanty draughts on her so precious fund.

In this instance my criticism, however inadequate, of the theologian, must pass instead of any full portraiture of the man. But for delicacy to the living I might

match the gifts and achievements of this Orthodox student with some sketch of scholarly talent and learning on
the Liberal side. I deem it better to let his picture hang
by itself, as that of one who spent his life in profound
reflection on religious themes, going from barefoot digging for exercise in the actual soil to more serious exer-
citation, pen in hand, at his desk; with little society of
his peers, and seldom any companion to cope with on
equal terms, and with still less amusement or recreation
of a very enlivening sort, yet as cheerful and merry as
he was heroic at each sober task, ever busy and preoccupied with some intellectual proposition, or, as he told
me, taking a Park with him to bed, — he having been much
concerned with securing to the city of Hartford, where
he lived and preached, the fine Common that goes by
that name, — and when, toward the last, he was too
weak to walk, wanting, if any one of his household had
been willing to answer his inquiry for that purpose, to
put on his boots and go out with a visitor who had
called.

Dr. Bushnell for friendly fellowship was one of the
most winsome, as in his appearance he was one of the
handsomest of men. Nature had struck out his face,
and never again used the same die. It resembled the
stamp of Channing's countenance, with the same delicacy of feature and deep-cut orbit for the organs of vision, and an equal spiritualization of the traits, till every
line and atom of flesh served for expression. He had
greater vivacity and mobility, and a recurring humor
that had at length almost faded out of the look of
the great Unitarian divine. Both alike were votaries of ideas; and both grew younger and fresher the

longer they lived. I feel often still the glance of Bushnell, so searching and kindly, and am conscious of his
presence and influence in my mind; and I find in his
writing a complementary color of close and cogent argument for Channing's more generalizing method, as well
as his less playful wit. He had also that satisfaction in
consecration to duty, independent of reputation and applause, which marks all the truly great. If the true
author or artist did not find his joy in his business, or if
he had to wait for fair remuneration in order to be happy,
he would lack comfort indeed, were he not even, in the
Apostle's phrase, "of all men most miserable;" for
wealth and honor have but a cursory and cold greeting
for supreme merit on the canvas of the one or on the
page of the other. When Moltke, the matchless Prussian strategist, who fights his battles with pins in the
map before he conquers the enemy in the field, and rehearses struggle and victory, long before the time of conflict, in his capacious brain, was receiving his abundant
dividend from the general glory of the army for a signal
success over the Austrian hosts, he said, "I have a
hatred for all fulsome praise; it completely upsets me
for the whole day." Let not our living benefactors or
their surviving friends lament that for services in peace,
more precious than trophies of war, the unappreciative
general public pays them honor in small declarations or
installs as its favorites inferior men! Flattery is interruption of study and diversion from our affair; and
scarce ever does any vivid eulogy discriminate or come
up to the worth of those deceased, whom any of us
have well known and dearly loved. Their true shrine
is in our breast. They run for sanctuary to a temple

within.   If one person think well of us, we are sheltered
enough ; or, if by none human we be understood, we
refer for judgment to the One who is divine.   " The
secret witness of all-judging Jove" was to the heathen
mind what a Father's approval is to the Christian ; and
no evolution in religion will carry us beyond paganism,
against or without our own will.   " Why," I asked an
old musician, " is not Amati excelled by the last makers
of the violin ? " " Because," he replied, " they do not
consider it a holy mission."   He added that the latest
expert with the bow is a " pygmy to Paganini."   It is
not when we conform to, but leave nature in the world
and our own soul, that we depart from God.   The artificial is the harmful as well as the false in our life, our
manners; and our worship.   " They showed me," said
a pious traveller in Italy, " so many painted Madonnas
and carved crucifixes that I was sick and wanted to see
a cow ; " and verily no idols in color or stone, but the
creatures with whom our existence is shared, will lead
us to the Creator.   We shall be with him while we are
with them in love.

25

IV.

THE GENIUS OF WEISS.

MEN may have a genius for various and even for opposite things, and it is with most persons another name for irregularity, as we find or fancy something erratic or eccentric in the orbit which we have but partly traced. A comet might be a figure for John Weiss. None who knew him but felt that he was possessed or under the influence and control of a rare spirit, to hurry or restrain him, superior to his individual self. So his character is not easy to solve. He was one and contradictory. He was cordial, yet apart. He beamed brightly, yet his hand was scarce worth taking, the grasp was so cool and slight. He was unconventional and seemed inconsistent. He had at times a womanish petulance, yet was without any will of his own. He was intense in his aim, yet so jocose as to pass for a trifler. He was an original thinker and a mime. Men recover from the habit of drinking or smoking, but never from that of wit; and he relieved his seriousness, like Abraham Lincoln, with many a jest. He did not succeed in proportion to his powers, but he was in his subtle influence a success. He was a live antinomy and antithesis. Did he appear saucy, he was devout. Underneath his waggery was awe. Anti-supernatural in faith, yet how supernatural and preternatural he was in fact! How he opposed spiritualism, yet what a medium he was, as if this modern Jew had descended from those old Hebrews that dealt with familiar spirits! But after one trial on the nerves of others which frightened the spectators and the operator himself still more, he did not dare to put forth his power again. He felt like a child who, touching a spring, has drawn a deluge and set all the mill-wheels turning. He resisted the animal magnetism he possessed, which yet stole into and produced in part the peculiar electric attraction of his public and private speech. He was mysterious, and the wire of some telluric current ended in his brain. He was telegraphic. One day, miles away from his residence, where he was at the time, he saw out of sight a powder-train laid to an arsenal; and the explosion duly took place! At another time and in another house he was fearfully excited at beholding that some catastrophe was befalling in a far-off town, in which that very hour there was a calamitous death by burning, indeed. Swedenborg conversed with angels, and saw with spiritual eye a distant city, Stockholm, in flames. Of the same divine madness Weiss had some touch.

His second sight, however, was unreal sometimes. On occasion of a famous regatta between English and American oarsmen, on the Thames, he being at the Isles of Shoals, it had been arranged that the captain of the English steamer should announce from the Portsmouth shore the result, by a single rocket if the victory lay with Oxford, but followed after a short interval by a second if Cambridge prevailed. One rocket arose, and was clearly descried by the assembled crowd; and after the concerted pause part of the company, with Mr. Weiss, affirmed that they discerned its fellow cleave the sky. Five minutes later, the process was repeated on the main shore ; and again Mr. Weiss observed, with many of his companions, the repeated ascent, which from all the rest of the company was concealed. It turned out that there was actually but one rocket in either case. The additional fiery discharge was of course in the brain, kindled with patriotic anticipation of triumph for our side. But to the perception he would have taken his oath in court. Indeed, that a vision occurred, physiology is now in a position to maintain ; but it was recurrent cerebral vision without any corresponding object in the air. How far science may go thus to explain so-called miraculous visions present or past, I leave for scientists to say. But no science can determine that all second sight is illusory, or that in it the greatest of realities may not be revealed. Mr. Weiss had, too, that singular faculty of being impressed with the character of a writer whose letter he held in his hand.

But he never exchanged his soul for the world. An atheist to some, an infidel as construed by the popular church, he yet was, like Spinoza, "drunk with God." He resembled his ancestral David, in that from the Infinite Presence he could not flee. His piety was heredity. But how half-ashamed to own he was pious at all! He said he so rejoiced in the phrase "still to be" in the old hymn, when he awoke in the morning, that he had a mind to have family prayers! Such humor to a superficial judgment might pass for irreverence. But there was in it a godly fear which he would feel mortified, as though he must be a Pharisee, to profess. Yet whoso reads his books will find them pervaded in and between the lines with the spirit that animated his heart, illumined his face, intoned his voice, and bowed in secret his knees.

The chime of opposites which the man was, appears in his style. How negative and yet how positive in statement this most unassuming yet earnest of creatures was! Light and airy as if, with Mr. Home's levitation, he were going up straightway, yet how levity was absent and gravity present in every gesture of his hand and in each stroke of his pen! How wrought like iron was every period, and how girt for toil, as at the forge, he stood! His paragraphs are shaped too curiously, and hammered overmuch. The main stream of his thought catches, and eddies, and returns in circles without end, when it might seem better, propelled with his abundant enthusiasm, forthright and swiftly to proceed. But this craftsman, with Hebrew, Spanish, French, Italian, and German blood mingling in his veins, was as sturdy as he was quick. To every stint he put ten thousand patient strokes. To get every notion and illustration somehow into the pattern, he wove the cloth heavy and thick. Like George Eliot and Balzac, from his faithful and exact design he could leave nothing out. With all its vital and vivacious quality, the dress was cumbrous and impeding, and, like many a wrap on one's person, hindered a run. He cannot be read at a glance, or his sense gathered if a word be skipped. There is no want of lucidness or unity, but failure rather of broad stretch, long flight, and thorough light, although he holds with unrelenting clutch to his theme; and sweet and solid is the kernel, however hard to crack may be the shell.

The answer to any charge of lightness in his deportment is the incessant severity of his task; as one said, quoting his favorite Browning,

> " I judge his childishness the true relapse
> To boyhood of a man, who has worked lately
> And presently will work, so meantime plays;
> Whence more than ever I believe in him."

Surely he was no ascetic. Puritanic abstinence from good things he even despised; and if hilarity in him ever became an error, and ran into excess, then, to cite again,

> " When the dead man is praised on his journey,
>   Bear, bear him along,
> With his few faults shut up like dead flowrets :
>   .   .   .   .   The land is left none such
> As he on the bier."

He composed well, and was himself a rare composition. He desired no good time which he did not want everybody else to have. Innocent and infantine at heart, he never posed for greatness, or imposed on anybody. With a touch of the Phidian Jove in his features, he was playfellow for a child. Dispute personally he would not. He surrendered in the battle of words at once. He did not assert himself enough. Had he, among the debaters, stood more to his guns, he would patently have been the greater man he latently was. But he dropped the controversy. He would not pick up the challenger's glove. He was even comic over all the bravado and defiant assault. He filled the room with his atmosphere and his thought, but not with any grand, overcoming personality in the way of combat or defence. He would say, " It is no matter and what is the use?" With a glance or motion he would penetrate and show off the situation, so that the initiated would understand it and

him in it, and then with a slight smile or merry laugh
he would retire. He had matchless faculty, with a wink,
a gesture, a scarce perceptible change of his countenance, or a turn of the head, to indicate what in the
matter in hand was ludicrous and absurd ; and for him
this was an all-sufficient and satisfactory reply. He
fought no wordy duel, and accepted no cartel. It were
painful to him anywise to contend ; so he withdrew.
If quarrel were proposed, he was not there, he ab-
sented himself. Like a missing second or contestant, he
did not appear on the ground. Indeed, he never made
an appointment, however others might, in his behalf, for
the fight. How he differed from those who lift the horn
or insert the probe at every possible point ! His spirit
had a fairy-like gift of travelling far away from his
body. He was like the benignant and imaginative
Rufus Choate in this respect. When personal accusation was to be met or an angry antagonist repelled, he
was not on the spot ! Gracious stillness and absentee-
ism worthy of all praise, like the silence and distance
of that preoccupied Lord and Master, who, when before
Pilate he was accused of many things, answered nothing, practising good economy in the household of faith
and the kingdom of God !

He was jealous of the prodigious in all sacred narratives. The anti-miraculous temper may be religious.
Yet perhaps the man instructed in law should be tender
to that taste for marvels which he may remember in himself, as for those curious volutes and finials in architectural pillars which add nothing to the temple's strength.
Some of the boasted and registered prodigies to thoughtful persons not only sink into insignificance but become

an offence. None of them can be more than the momentary spark from the Lord's chariot-wheels as they thunder on their orderly track. A wilful leaving or breaking up of the line would but puzzle the mind, and incline it to feel as if it were being played fast and loose with by the superior force, with which, so taunted, it could have no more to do. God cannot have opposite and inconsistent ways of accomplishing the same thing. Let us argue the question of monsters or sports of nature calmly, but not suppose them essential to the creative plan, or that, existing or non-existing, they can for our destiny turn one hair white or black.

The best supernature and disclosure of Deity is that class of intellect to which Mr. Weiss belongs. The ability so marked in him to crowd all the meaning of a topic into one flaming word and flashing bolt is more divine than any trick with matter, however authentic and allowed; while the slight which Jesus himself was sometimes disposed to put upon the marvellous, with his uniform subordination of it to the moral, shows how little it would in another have availed with him.

The real miracle is the soul itself realizing its possibilities in any mood or act. By supreme attention, or by dint of steady observation, the human figure becomes a statue and the face a stupid stare; and this person of whom I speak could transport himself out of obvious relations till his absorption made him appear indifferent and hard. He had but refined himself, or by a strange energy, doing with him what it would, had been lifted out of all visible ties; and if summoned to a concern in affairs or persons that ought of right to interest him most, he would in these trances declare he had of them no knowl-

edge, not the least! Let not the holy professor or prac-
titioner of every-day proprieties harshly judge this state.
Whoever has experienced will understand the preoccupation that so dismisses interruption. Did not the great
apostle conceive a condition in which distinctions vanished, and there was no longer any barbarian, Scythian,
male or female, bond or free? May not one venture to
say that in his own case husband, parent, priest, citizen, sometimes fall away, and he tempts for a while that
Northwest passage of the soul to some circumpolar sea,
which he shall traverse at last, and find himself in circumstances of that fresh posture to all that is old or new
which he so vividly anticipates now? It was in no low
or selfish pleasure that Mr. Weiss was thus rapt. Give
him his study-table, his book, and his pen, with no
noise in the entry, and not even the children to disturb
him, yet with whom he would sit on the floor for a car-
nival of sugar-plums by and by, and he was content
with his celestial situation and angelic frame. What
was most affecting at his obsequies was the occupation
by so many sitters of that very spot so habitually trans-
figured to him with the blessed work to which he clung
while it lifted him like a cross. It was as quiet and
still as when he sat there alone. But all the more
for the company there seemed a disappearance, an absence, ascension, or vacancy of space and void in the
heart, which he was but getting ready to fill with a life
intenser and a beauty more satisfying. Then, as the
eye turned to the remote casket containing the form of
one whose peculiar traits could so easily persuade us of
the truth of the old figure of men as but pilgrims here
below, such a veritable stranger and sojourner as he was,

how strongly stirred the feeling of the reverence with
which we should think and speak, on the arrival at such
a way-station of those whom we ignorantly call the dead,
especially when so extraordinary has been the manifestation which has so suddenly and utterly ceased. Lo!
the speechless figure never lay on the bed in slumber so
profound as now on the bier. It can no longer explain
to us why it has spoken or acted in past time thus and
so. Did it never defend itself with recriminations?
It will make no rejoinder at last! Was there some
tragedy in its life? Without voice it begs you to reflect
how happy in God's boon of being it was nevertheless.
Had sphere and scope suited to its powers never been
afforded by the contingencies of this sublunary lot? It
entreats the bystander to remember, notwithstanding,
how content and grateful, as for overplus of good, it
was, and how seldom and slightly it complained. Had
it seen its inferiors exalted to stations above itself?
It beseeches you to consider that at their privilege or
prosperity it never had a tooth of envy to gnaw. Had
it, by bodily infirmity, or by social disappointment in
any of its own supporters, been continually shifted into
a succession of diverse posts? It bids you bear in mind
how pleased as a child, while it remained in any of them,
it was with the kindness and the opportunity brought.
Did any project fail to put it in desk or on platform
where, for its acknowledged talents, the proper audience
for the permanent influence would meet? Our own recollection assures us that no feeling of wrong, sense of
others' deficiency, or baffled ambition of its own ever
took away its courage or quenched its good cheer. Was
it suspected of discarding the fundamentals of religious

faith? It was too much diverted with the magnificent spectacle of the world, and marvelled too much at the providential plan, as it was too busy on the clew of that method of God which threads the labyrinth of things, to be troubled with excommunication of the major or minor sort. So we will not even say,

> " Let them rave ;
> Thou art quiet in thy grave : "

for, before thy dust went thither, thou hadst the "central peace subsisting at the heart of endless agitation," and didst hoist for us on this mortal sea one more signal for sight of land.

This man was the prey of his mind, engrossed and consumed with his thought. His blood was so determined to his head that he seemed to imagine that an idea could save the world! But we cannot plant a church in the soil of abstractions, or grow a religion on the culture of the brain. On those in whom the plate was prepared, what a photograph he impressed! His soft finger found the way in hundreds of souls to that secret place where he touched the waiting spring, unfolded to them what they were or were meant to be, and reconstructed or regenerated their nature while he made an era in their life and consoled their inmost grief. But he was so semi-detached from human existence in its ordinary forms that his language, which in his early efforts was simple, became at last multiplex and hard to spell, and he lost the power to appreciate those traditions on which common folk must largely feed. There is precious import in a cerebral flash. But the cathedral on the corner, which we gaze at every day, holds of a long

past, and a future too ; and what light can strain through
the colored, cobwebbed, and unwashed windows from antiquated tales is of more worth to the worshippers within
than the dark denials from the sensuous understanding
in all their heap. Men must have nourishment; and
even if it be mixed with gravel and dirt, it serves them
better than the piled husks of speculation that have
ceased to hold corn.

Intelligence, in which the whole nature acts, is fair as
the morning, and promising as a reaper in the field.
But the pure intellect may be a selfish cormorant devouring the heart! In the most disinterested devotion
to fine processes of argument, that reach in practice
no end, we may become inconsiderate of our fellow-
creatures and nearest friends or kin. An involuntary
and tremendous selfishness threatens the thinker, though
it be a Channing or Edwards, on whom the spirit of generalization lays its grasp, as Balzac in one of his most
powerful tales, "The Search after the Absolute," portrays a man sacrificing his family, wife and child, to his
insatiable alchemistic pursuits. Beware of indulgence
of ideality as well as sense! It has, too, its excess.
Mr. Weiss would sink in whatever diving-bell or rise in
whatever balloon would help him to survey more widely
or dredge more deeply, spending hours of bliss in gazing or solitary groping by himself. Then, rising to
breathe after the prolonged watch or endeavor, his soul
would stretch itself, basking like a lazzarone in the sun.
His nature, as we nestle close to it, seems one instinctively born for joy, yet consciously defrauded by
grief, and singing as in a far land the child Mignon's
song, "What have they done to thee?"

More simple, uncalculating enjoyment of nature man never had. Peering through creation, all became such · wonder to him that no particular wonder was left. What would it signify to such a man if he saw all the miracles in the Bible performed before his eyes? They would melt like snow-flakes, and mingle as drops in the boundless amazing sea. Ezra the Prophet sat down "astonied" for a time at a particular thing. But as the great marvel of the universe is unveiled, all special ones are swallowed up and disappear. The absurdity of prodigious stories was to Mr. Weiss at once so transparent and gross that he could scarce patiently abide their being told. But we must not forget the office of fable as well as fact, nor the distinction between the artless gospel-narrative before science had dawned and the coarse literal construction now put upon it in the face and eyes of scientific truth. I will not tear the leaf that keeps the picture of the marriage-feast in Cana of Galilee, more than I would syringe with vitriol Paul Veronese's painting of ruddy wine on his canvas of the scene. Hunting with his keen scent on the trail of the Divine footsteps in the creation, his brain humming and singing with the snatches of the rhythm he might catch, Mr. Weiss lost at length part of the cipher of communication with his fellow-men. He was, with manner and feature and tone, the key to his own works.

> " The silent organ loudest chants
> The master's requiem."

Now that the key is gone, much of the sense to most readers will be hard to unlock, or to those who know not the wards slow will be the opening of the safe. But treasure is in every secret drawer, as truly as in Shakspeare's sonnets and Browning's plays. Great is the writing, but greater was the man.

.Mr. Weiss was handled by a power higher than his own, and conscious in his measure of the wing that bore up Milton and the check Socrates felt. The mighty sweep of the English bard or the awful alighting of the Greek sage may not be repeated. But the lowest pitch or faintest flutter in another spirit proves it akin to them, and fledged in the same nest whence came the singer that

"With no middle flight intends to soar,"

and the teacher who brought down wisdom from heaven to earth. If not a genius, he is possessed with genius who is habitually aware that he is a messenger and errand-bearer in the employ of some *daimon*, as the ancients called it, or the Holy Ghost, according to the new dispensation, and is by the unaccountable potency arrested or spurred; and the person of whom I write conspicuously exhibited either sign.

An artist in colors or words hazards a little his strokes, and lets his thoughts run. He trusts his memory, restrains calculation, hopes for inspiration, keeps his will back, and thus sometimes compasses a felicity beyond elaborate accomplishment. So I let the present portraiture mainly do itself. A flawless character does not exist. Fault is found with Jesus. The reason we cannot describe God is in his perfection. As without background, light, and shade, there can be no picture, so defects or dark places in my theme show off great qualities, without feeling which I would not treat it at all.

If I am perplexed with the variety of traits, I find an advantage in their transparency. Mr. Weiss had no concealments. If there were secrets in his, as there should be in every breast, he had no shameful ones. What he was he appeared to be. He lay open as the day. He wore no official disguise. He wished to make no impression of goodness. He made no reference to his conscience, or to the motives by which he was ruled. Such was his hatred of pretence that he doubtless showed his worst side. But he was an earnest man. Have some been troubled by his temperament, so like a rustling, changeable silk, or an opal flashing with many hues? He was as steady as a drill-sergeant at his post. He would sit and not stir from breakfast to dinner in his study, till his feet were numb and cold, while his head was a globe of light, and he would have to stamp back the circulation of the blood before he could stand and walk. So long and perfect as eternity had been his spiritual joy. He did not like criticism, which yet he patiently bore. But he loved truth, being, as one who had plain dealing from him said, " the sincerest person that ever lived." He would not endure misrepresentation in private, or the altering of any article of his for the public. Should I, contrary to Cromwell's dictate to an artist, paint his complexion with favor he had not, he would appear to me with that loudest of rebukes, an inward one.

He was a very particular man. In large things or little, of the domestic reckoning and procedure, he must have every thing exactly so, and not otherwise. Into this idea he, the most unwilful of men, put his will with irresistible pressure, even in his weakest and sickest hours. If fifty-five drops of medicine were to be taken, he would not have it fifty-four. The order in every scrap of his papers was precise. Yet his nature was

Gothic and manifold. He was not built on a simple plan, like a hall with one ceiling and room ; but rounds within rounds, or height above height, like those Edinburgh houses, seven stories tall.

He believed that all could be discovered. He had no agnostic despair of knowledge. Any tether of our intelligence, or any pillars of Hercules to limit explorers, he did not allow. He never took in sail. Spurning limits of human authority, and vehemently repudiating and ridding himself of ecclesiastical yokes, he would not be confined to any new sect. He revolted from the pioneers when verbal rules were stated or external objects proposed. Perhaps he was not practical enough. Certainly out of any party traces he incontinently slipped. He believed in and gave himself to free thought as an element, and was its organ, but not organizer. He was not belligerent to fight its battles, save frankly on the field of ideas with imagined foes, himself a friend, in fact, to either host armed for the fray. If there were a battery in his brain, it was not commonly loaded, and never masked, but kept mostly useless, like the cannon I saw on the open shore at Teneriffe, marked *inutiles.* He was no coward, yet he would rather run than contend in the war of words ; and, instead of firing back when he had been shot at, he would with a slight shrug say, " I see I have been misunderstood." He knew his superiority, but was too lowly for it to be possible for him to condescend.

It has been said that he grew morose and sorrowful in his later years. This is a mistake. There was no sunset in his face. There were straits of fortune, but no degradation of mind. His style, like that of Carlyle after the essay on Burns, and of Browning in the earlier "Sordello," and later poems, such as "The Ring and the Book," in becoming more compact became less clear. Perhaps the condensed meaning did not always atone for the less melodious strain. But the man was never heated or sour at sixty more than at thirty years of age. Neither a born nor a trained soldier, he avoided conflict, unless some crisis woke him up. He was but too glad to be excused from any fray. Rather than maintain his own rights, he would give them up. He made no push for victory, but threw himself on the knotty questions, more tough than any cords in the prestidigitator's box, which no man has yet been deft or strong enough to untie ; and of his scholarly learning, as of his ready wit, there was no end.

We are sure to find something against the man who differs from us. His character will be at fault if his opinion is. If he be a heretic, we shall account him a foe. All his opposition is bitterness, of course, and he is as preposterous as he is far off ! So the radical will be but a destroyer's other name. Meantime, the conservative, an innocent lamb in his protest, and making the freethinker the scapegoat of all sin, suspects no gall in his own composition, but heaps epithets and multiplies implications on the dissenter's head. "Who should have a scorn like the Christian's?" said Channing ; but must we not learn who the Christian is?

In this man a wondrous equanimity steadied an unmatched sensibility. This magnetic needle, jarred as it might be, ever trembled back to the pole. His failures were in his constitution or preoccupation, not from unfair bias or wrong intent. For much defect there is

26

apology enough in a feeble frame. A fine genius overwrought by hard study or spiritual impulse is not seldom
of an invalid organism, the needful protection of which
may nurse, in such men as both Weiss and Channing
were, a certain self-regard. Both physically undertoned
for forty years, Channing's mind did not play, but what
rollicking and excessive liberty everybody had with Mr.
Weiss! Channing considered every thing, and Weiss
was quite inconsiderate of much it is best not to waive!
Both had to be cared for, and to care for themselves, in
order to keep the cerebral processes, so unlike, yet in
either so delicate, in working trim. Channing was
abstemious, and for blameless enjoyment Weiss had a
laughing and indulgent eye. If Channing stands as the
colossus at the harbor of Rhodes, Weiss is a sphinx or
Memnon's statue in Egyptian sands; and his light and
music did not wane, but waxed, in the later years. Examination of his public discourses and recollection of club
debates or of private interviews prove in him a constant
growth. As the rose-color increases in windows exposed to the sun, so his sensuous fancy deepened; yet
his purity was evident to those who knew him best,
although he was no simulator, like Fielding's " philosopher Square." He never wronged the human brothers
or sisters whom he drew with a strange force, though
without purpose. Joyous in earthly things, none made
more the impression of one ready to rise above them.
There was, indeed, a singular suggestion of ascending in
his look and attitude; and this, in the last photographs
taken of him, was emphasized by lines of pain in the
features. It was a look of " touch and go," as if his
body were filled with ether, and he were only held to

the ground. Native in his temper. to another than the New England climate and soil, he is difficult of comprehension by our puritanic thought.

Things could no doubt be told of all the good in their early days by which their veritable image would be marred. But by a divine law of neglect these little things drop from their images in the human heart. The great man always becomes in time a myth, a vast and splendid ideal. He is taken up into the blood of humanity. He is incarnate in his kind. He is swept and projected in the orbit of history as an unquenchable star. Spies for faults have fancied they found that even such a man as Channing, "who holds," says Laboulaye, "the future of Protestantism," was selfish, penurious, and proud. He did not like to be discomposed! But shall we listen to the poor jealousy that exaggerates foibles and misunderstands the details it picks up, which for all who knew the person pass away before the glory of his thought? Hanging in the same hall of memory a likeness of Weiss, I claim for *that* the generous judgment which is fair.

Mr. Weiss's peculiarity was a hatred of falsehood. In the high places of the pulpit it is not prudent to attack popular errors. All that a well-remembered preacher in this vicinity could say was, that he was " mighty careful to tell no lies." The orator with his wind-chest carries all before him. But let no admired discourser imagine that the excited throng at his temple or tabernacle proves him on the line of advance for mankind! When there was a multitude Jesus took his leave. Goethe in the same sense describes the traveller that goes aside from the crowd. But how the old superstitions and delightful shows still succeed! As Lord Bacon says, " men prefer to the diamond the deeper-colored gems." Why is the ecclesiastic so irritated by the question which a scientist puts, but that it reaches a sore spot, as the physician's finger touches the weak vertebra in his patient's back? O my brother of the clerical cloth, in your displeasure under inquiry I find the uneasiness of your own doubt. But who can measure the boon of loyalty to the inmost persuasions of the breast? Our convictions put us under oath. Such writers as Mr. Weiss are called theorizers. But nothing is so important as correct theories. What mischief from incorrect ones! The irreligious communist throws petroleum and overthrows monuments in France, and in America tears down stations and interrupts trains. The Nihilist in Russia murders the noble, as if assassination could be freedom's womb. The individualist everywhere confounds his own selfishness with universal love, and would promote humanity by inhuman means, imitating the oppressor he would put down. But slavery is not abolished while injustice exists from high or low. The deceived and cheated freedman finds himself in Egypt still, and a new exodus for his only hope.

Mr. Weiss was broadly humane, and veracity most of all I note in him. After Goethe, whom he loved to translate, was over eighty years of age, one of the gentler sex, being also advanced in life, sends him a message to say his fidelity alone saved her from dishonor in a mutual affection of their youth. Such frankness is the test of honor. Truthfulness is a moral trait, and no pure intellect can cover the whole of human life. We do ourselves an ill turn in converting heart into brain.

It is as hardening a process as hepatizing of the lungs. It is transmuting gold into baser metal. The man is more than his performance, and we shall not carry prayer-book or Bible to heaven. What a power in the death that suddenly takes our nearest friend as far from our reach as Adam or Moses! The man I speak of, with all his demonstrations of power, could pass out of himself into another, and be for the time like the creature taking the color of the leaf it is on, becoming Browning or Shakspeare, the English or Greek dramatist, of whom he so well discoursed. Swept by the wind of that mighty planet, Parker, he put on for a while his style of pungent and forthright speech, with the phalanx of facts in battle array. But that intellectual influence passed, and with a subtilty of logic and fancy wholly out of Parker's compass or beat, he became as ingenious and parenthetical as the Apostle Paul. Like Paul, he had such raptures that he can scarce be more conscious of his immortality in heaven than he was at times on the earth. I do not present him as an image of perfection. Perhaps he did not even think it important or intended for any one to be without speck! Had he been a cunning pretender, like some men and clergymen, he might have passed for a saint. But to him the assumption of holiness was so odious that he bordered on scorn for conventional righteousness, and took up the Lord's apologies for such as love had led into sin. Yet by his mercy, like the Master's, the moral quality was only emphasized, and never slurred or blurred. The histrionic actor of virtue he would laugh at; but Christ's not shunning the disrepute of keeping low company he admired, and he indulged in merry-makings which no

true descendant of the Puritans can be expected to
abide. But whatever spots were on or suspected in
him, his substantial excellence is- as blazing as the sun.
His affections were like those of Montaigne, who said
he was blunt and faint to such as he most truly belonged to. You could not tell, by any oath or profession
on his part, how much he cared for you, though you were
brother of his very mind and heart. His *regard* would
be literally in his look, in his manner, or in some humorous epithet on meeting his friend. But he loved
as intensely as he thought, as Bonaparte said of his
feeling that it had the measure of his mind. There are
but two things, loving and being loved, and the chief
pleasure of the last to a noble soul is in the lover's own
delight.

Mr. Weiss was often like the man up in a balloon who
cannot give us a cup of cold water down below. Raphael and Ary Scheffer, in their pictures of the transfig-
ured or consolatory Christ, represent figures that flock
for healing and help, and yet must wait wistfully underneath with eager gaze and outstretched hand. Elevation is purchased at a dear price in exchange for open
sympathy; for we do not credit the interest that is hid.
But Mr. Weiss was nothing, if not true. He said naught
which had to be explained away. Who has not known
the brilliant man in politics and the fine woman of society, by their accommodation and compromise of principle, to contract a blindness which no asylum can shel-
ter or operator cure? Put cunning for conscience in the
desk and the school, and we have an education leaving the spiritual eye unopened, like that of the fish in
the Mammoth Cave. But if unsealing the vision or

widening the horizon be a greater benefit than bread to the hungry or clothing to the naked, how many have had a benefactor in the friend of whom I speak!

Mr. Weiss was a discerner of spirits. He could appraise character, admire the hero, and yet see his defects. In the courageous Parker, who converted him to philanthropy, he noted the combative and doughty self not quite absorbed in his cause ; in Webster, a complete dignity, but not on the highest plane ; in the humane and heroic Sumner, a slight pedantry, so that the majestic American crisis could not make him pass by Greece and Rome, or forget his own name; in Seward, the politic prophet ; in Lincoln, the true seer ; and in John Brown, a simple utter earnestness.

Doubtless he took the wrong side of the question sometimes, or argued it with bad taste. He turned the wine into water, as he ridiculed the turning of water into wine. He dramatized sometimes as a performer when perfect simplicity would have been more in place. He rushed asphyxiated, so he said, from the room when, in wartime at a conference, prayer was proposed instead of action in the field ! He was alternately angel and imp, yet not of mischief, there being no cruelty in him, but only roguish sport. His real and manifold nature could be suppressed by no official proprieties. Dainty, dreamy, and luxurious in his imagination, that parochial visiting, which is half of the minister's duty, was to him an unwelcome and dragging routine, by his neglect of which his usefulness and acceptableness in some situations were stayed. To the tiresome many, with all their petty crosses and cares, he preferred the society of the like-minded and the congenial few. He indulged his preference, and paid the price. Perhaps he was not patient enough with the slow intellectual progress of mankind. "He dug his carrots in August," and wished to reap prematurely from the seed-sowing of truth. He was vexed with the tardy settlement of the national strife ; and although not soldierly as Parker was, yet, like him, he foreshadowed the sword. He was credited with self-assurance in some quarters, and I have heard the term *flippant* applied to his style. But there was an infinite tenderness and a tremulous timidity under his audacity; and I doubt not that his early and faithful preaching on temperance and against slavery cost him many an inward struggle, as well as favor with men whose friendship it pained him to lose. When I add that his nervous system, at once so mighty and so weak, and ever threatening to give way, braced itself with whatever joviality was at hand, I have told every thing against him that I know.

Humor in him was essential and inwrought. When, after a nearly twelve-month prostration by disease, it was necessary for him to have a nurse, he looked her curiously over when she was introduced into the room, then begged a moment's private interview with his faithful and unweariable wife, and with a twinkle bright and wet in his eye, said to her, "You have added a new terror to death!"

He was deeply religious, even while by his smiles, like the eddies that dimple the unfathomed tarn, his pious emotions were hid. His early tender feeling for Jesus never ceased, although his view of the Christ's Messiahship, kingship, and mediatorship widely changed. But Jesus never became to him a mere man. There is no mere man!

Every thing substantial, save the absolute substance, has its shadows. They are cast even by sublime virtues and transcendent gifts. But the measure of merit, as the poet Burns hints, is in what we resist as well as in what we do ; and how incomparable a trait is an irreproachable sanctity in those who, like Mr. Weiss, fascinate and allure ! He was exposed to misconstruction by the playfulness on which he put no check. He could not walk the streets like a doctor of divinity. Instead of wearing a minister's garb, he did not know or care what he had on. As he had no pride of dress, so he did not disguise his thoughts with any false trick. He towered amid our overshadowing pulpit-reputations without taking pains. In intellectual probity he was never surpassed. Happy if those of more note and noise really articulate the spirit in those syllables and sentences which are the trite coinage of the common air !

Not because Mr. Weiss was less but more religious, he discarded the ecclesiasticism that puts for worship a show, for faith superstition, for the wondering sentiment a blank surprise, and some proxy or substitute of sense for God, Christ, or heaven. That, with a portentous temperament and a handwriting like fine sword-thrusts, he could have such geniality in strife, can be accounted for perhaps by early shocks which made it impossible for him to copy others' rage, and by his own keen perception that whoever gets angry gives up the game. The Spartans shamed their children out of intemperance by showing their helots drunk ; and to a sensitive soul one pattern is warning enough against the worse intoxication of wrath, sometimes seen in those who abstain from wine.

The man whom I celebrate did not, in his logic, his rhetoric, or ideas, spare the antagonist side. But, as he would give his last dollar to some poor German at the door, and have nothing left to pay his passage in the car, I think he has reached the gate, as he has taken the journey, which requires no ticket or entrance-fee. Undeceived by loud pretensions, and making light of this world's pomp and personal dignity, he was only half liked by such as had "reverence large," and he displayed little of that sociable talent which makes the minister popular with his flock. But his nature was music; and the great symphonies pleased him as echoes of the harmony of the spheres. Somewhat of Beethoven was in him, and he has gone where he hears the discords no more. He argued for "personal continuance," and was one of its best proofs. There must be more fuel for such a flame! It is more than that on which it is fed. Immortality is no fact of chronology, but that state of mind which implies the other side of the grave. Faith is its own foundation. The soul is not at rest on the earth, as the bird is not as easy in the branches or on the ground as on its perch of air. That constituency of an intellectual and spiritual brotherhood and sisterhood by which he is mourned and whose fancies he refined so exquisitely, while he raised their ideas of God and nature to the utmost pitch, will find in his own so extraordinary traits the demonstration of his hope and their own. Bright as was his intelligence, it was but the lustre of a loving soul, as the flashes of day proceed from the heat and body of the sun. For he too was "a burning and a shining light."

The personal appearance of Mr. Weiss was as remark-

able as his mind. Soft lines of manly beauty enclosed
his olive-colored Oriental features, and his fluent, half-
feminine form. His figure, in middle life, was so thin
and sepulchral that one said he seemed to have ridden
from Mount Auburn into Boston, to preach and then
return; and Theodore Parker, observing his extraordinary delicacy and death-like look, pronounced him a
doomed man, little thinking that his friend would be his
biographer, and survive himself by nearly a score of
years. Yet, nearing his sixty-first birthday, his temples
edged with white, he made no impression of age, but
surprised us as with an unfading spring. Still, like a
fountain, boiled and bubbled the kindly mirth, which
severe and repeated attacks of disease could not check.
His constitutional quality of strangely blended tenderness and strength issued in the singularity of his voice,
which, in its ordinary level tones and easy inflections,
had a mellowness that no woman's utterance could exceed, and among men was beyond compare, yet as,
in passages of great excitement, it rose and stooped,
was touched with the sibyl's frenzy, and burst into a
prophet's scream. As thunder is followed by rain, his
fulgurations ended in tears. His fancy was a kaleido-
scope or painter's palette, where not a pigment was
wanting, and sometimes the colors got mixed and confused. The sublime bordered in his style on the funny,
and the pathetic joined the grotesque. He could be
majestic or tricksy, Prospero or Puck, and not seldom
Ariel too. He relished clown and buffoon as well as
king or courtier in the play. He enacted others, and
was a seer himself. As well blame a mocking-bird for
its changeful notes, or a flamingo for the flashing of its

crimson wings, or the natural sky for its heat-lightning after stormy claps, as this finer alterativeness in human shape. But one thing, his courage, never shifted or flinched. When Sumter is fired at, or bondage grasps new soil, even the stupid feel the shock, and start to their feet. But men sleep on when insidious superstition would buy up free thought, and moor worship to preposterous traditions and discredited forms. This slumber none was more brave than Mr. Weiss to disturb. He would fain rend the veil of the Bible mythology wholly off.

But this radical was to the last the Christian which he would have smiled away any summons to him to claim or confess to be! Of the earthly form of our friend naught is left. But something remains. Love is unquenchable by all the waters that flow through the dark valley and shadow of death. Cord and wheel and pitcher and bowl break and dissolve. But that in a man which is composed of no one or all of these things abides and lives. We will not repine at death. Without it is no progress on a higher plane. The thought would tire us of living for ever in these carnal swathings and first swaddling-clothes.

V.

GARRISON, THE REFORMER.

IT is hard to certify the real author of any benefit, invention, or revolution. Did Columbus, or Americus Vespuccius, or some Northman or Norwegian, or an emigrant tribe from the East, first discover the Western World? Into whose field of view did the new planet first swim? By whom was etherization found out? Did Newton and Darwin make their own discoveries, or does the credit belong to predecessors who put them on the track? Who was Jesus but the fulfiller of Jewish prophecy, a man who got his hints from its antecedents, a flower or century-plant of which Providence dropped obscurely the seed? Was slavery abolished by Abraham Lincoln, by William Lloyd Garrison, by Clarkson and Wilberforce, or by John Brown? By no one of them or all, we are now told, but by the early martyrs in this country of the Methodist Church. There is more than one who cries in the wilderness, who explores the desert or pioneers in the woods. No Alexander Selkirk but comes, as he treads the sandy shore, upon other tracks besides his own. The human race is old, and sends more than one scout in every direction; and if one man cries out " Land " a little sooner than the rest of the sailors in the vessel, it is only because he is by chance at the mast-head. Mankind has a total movement, as all its members are but one body; but its common-sense singles out and settles down upon the particular persons who, as it wins one after another position, gave the word " Forward, march ! " and Garrison will be in history the " Liberator," even as so his newspaper was called.

When we consider what a moral way-station was reached on this continent, inaccessible as by the almost unanimous voice it had been declared, and that what the young man predicted the old man Garrison saw, — that an infamy unparalleled became for him universal fame ; that having been hated and hunted during most of his life, he died in the uncontradicted love and honor of his nation and the human race, and in the odor of sanctity, like a catholic saint, — old Simeon's willingness to depart in peace because a child had been born seems trifling to this man's reason for joy in the discharge of his mission, and to the sublime attitude in which great events placed him at his mortal end.

Herein lay his greatness, that, ironclad warrior as he had been for more than a score of years, it was not necessary to his happiness to continue to fight. They surely had noble and honorable motives who would keep up the antislavery organization after the slaves were freed, in order to defend and protect those wards of philanthropy who in their first tottering steps were still so exposed. But was it not also grand in the leader to wish to ground arms and dissolve when the object was attained, as it was generous to insist on sharing the laurels of the victory, for which he would not have waged war, with the President who had signed the proclamation he was so soon to seal with his blood?

It was just no less; for when the bullet pierced Lincoln's brain, slavery did not in its aim mistake the foe! He had said he would save the nation without destroying slavery, if he could. But he would not let slavery destroy the nation, by whose destruction he knew a common ruin would involve both black and white. The glory of any man is in his unselfish design; and by an equal devotion both of these men were marked. The people smiled with humor and gazed with admiration at the abolitionists who, banded in the early struggle so closely together against the monstrous iniquity they assailed, did not in the later stages of the conflict spare each other in any difference of view. But all the rest of them were singularly indisposed to bring into question the one at their head! There was no mutiny with the captain among the troops. They knew his truth! No one in the ranks more vehemently than he denounced what was proslavery in the Constitution and administration of the land. The terrible phrases, the sharp catchwords, the mottoes on the banner, or proverbs in the mouth, came mostly from his lips and pen. It was as difficult for him as for anybody else that ever fought for a cause to believe in the entire honesty of such as did not in judgment or action agree with him. Yet he did not wish them to be branded or stained. It was not hatred of the sinners so much as horror at the sin that moved him to his task; and his disinterestedness had at least the reward of a tender consideration for himself in all his intercourse with his associates, whatever dissension might arise. In the long course of human controversy nothing is more affecting than the gentleness shown to Garrison by those co-laborers in their conflicts of policy, as they came like Paul and Barnabas, to the parting of the ways. They behaved better than did Barnabas and Paul! This mildness for him, as with a spiritual father, will be remembered especially in one still living, whose name will shine, when his form may vanish, with the name of Garrison as does the blended lustre of a binary star.

After the storm what a charm we feel in the beauty of the serene sky, as it bends over land and sea under the reflection of the sun, that seems to have its setting not only in the horizon, but in every rock and wave and leaf on the tree! The brightness of such a living calm was, during the latter years, in Garrison's face. He wore a strange and sublime look of satisfaction and of completed desire. Other things, indeed, after the great emancipation filled his time and interested his mind, — temperance, woman's rights, a fair chance in our politics for the negroes, and justice to the Chinese. But the work he had done was so vast that every thing else appeared but as an afterpiece, the consequence of the peculiar deliverance, and the ingathering of the fruit that follows the shaking of the boughs. No one, however, could notice any slackening in his activity or cooling of his zeal. Whatever measure of legislation or of associated enterprise he might espouse or oppose, he showed the same independence of opinion and procedure, and that superiority to human fear or favor which was in his original grain.

In the idea held of Garrison among most intelligent and good men forty years ago, he was but a town-crier and bell-ringer disturbing quiet people with his noise; or a new sort of Peter the Hermit provoking an impracticable and profitless crusade, acrid in his own temper and charging baseness on the millions who would not adopt his means. But the fact that his enterprise was never forlorn or hopeless in his own mind proves that he had a faith, beyond that of his censors, in mankind! He felt it was impossible that when they perceived their sins they should not renounce them. That he was bitter against the crime of slavery was not the ugliness but the beauty of the man. Is not the physician disqualified and guilty of malpractice who cannot, on occasion, prescribe pills of wormwood and draughts of gall? Garrison's bitterness was to Garrison no more than is the pungency in the seed that gives the delicious flavor to the berry and fruit. "Purge me with hyssop," cries David, "and I shall be clean;" and our reformer showed himself skilful in his selection and application of the needful and virtuous herbs! The sweet voice and sunny face and benign temper, that made the music and light and air of his dwelling, and were to wife and children a perpetual charm, were not thrown off like an outside garment in order that he might be an east-wind to opponents and a public scold. He was a genial, generous, and honorable foe to men in their bad customs; but he hated no man, North or South. Those from either section who met him delighted in his presence and in his talk; and among the sympathizers in his aim he was the most gracious and merry of the band, which he at first, according to the Master's example, wanted to be of the number of twelve. In one of the earliest assemblies of the faithful, on premises which had formerly served for a barn, he congratulated the company that they had got footing at last " on a stable foundation; " and after some who were present, to whom the prospect seemed gloomy, had spoken in a melancholy strain, he surprised his male and female disciples with the quotation of a familiar poetical quatrain : —

" Oh, come on some cold rainy day,
    When the birds cannot show a dry feather ;
  Bring your sighs and your tears, Granny Gray ;
    Let us all be unhappy together ! "

But misery was no visitor in his house or heart. In his convictions he was tranquil, and in his affections he was fervent and even gay. An earnest man, saying of prevalent dispositions and actions what he thinks, is quite unconscious of the severity which his language imports to the listening ears. He is concerned only with delivering his message, to bear testimony and tell the truth. To describe the situation, not to stigmatize any particular individuals who are involved in making it, is his intent. But the prophet must roll off his burden on whomsoever it may roll ; and Garrison was another Micah to rebuke our unmeaning sacrifices and hypocritical forms.

Mr. Garrison was of a nature so peaceful that he was a non-resistant by profession, yet he was such a respecter of others' freedom of thought and behavior that he would put no obstacle of paternal authority against his son's decision to enlist for the civil war, which, strangely enough, this hater of all violence or of appeals to arms did more than any other man, unintentionally, to provoke. In his philosophy we may think him wrong. He assumed that non-resistance is a principle, when it is but a way, and only one among many, — a Christian precept, precious as enjoining a spirit of forbearance, but not intended or acceptable as an invariable rule. It cannot be held as a principle, as it is but a mode of action, or rather non-action; and a principle will prescribe, according to circumstances, diverse and even opposite ways in which to act. Non-resistance is passivity; but we must act. Truth is a principle, righteousness is a principle, and love is a principle; but whether these, one or all, shall dictate defence of ourselves and our cause, or submission without a blow, depends on the case in hand, the prospect of success, the born soldier's inspiration of courage, and the providence of God. To yield up a State to insurgents against its lawful voters' will without a stroke, if its government be pushed to that pass, were political treason and desertion of a divinely allotted post. Temperance is a principle; but total abstinence is a method, which individuals may practise, or laws attempt to enforce. To denounce as unprincipled any persons who decline to use and urge this method is falsehood and slander combined, until the proof is made out of poison in every drop of wine for the sick and fainting by the way, and for the communicant at the Lord's table, although the evil of strong drink is so dreadful that it seems natural, if not excusable, for the sake of human safety, to confound a temporary measure with a divine law. Yet none more than the zealous reformer should remember that the principle of temperance applies properly to every passion of our nature, motion of our hand, and word on our tongue.

But if by temperance we mean, be the wind with others high or low, to pursue the even tenor of one's way, a more sober man than Garrison never lived. His course was that of a planet, which can be predicted to the end. Nothing could be more barren or strong than

his style. Justice being his point, and infallible rectitude his line, he succeeded by dint of continuance and
repetition. After many a stroke of a hammer at the
same place on a ledge, or on the trunnion of a cannon,
stone and iron give way. A succession of sounds in a
chamber, if they be not usual and monotonous, like the
sighing of the wind or the ticking of a clock, will arouse
one from the heaviest sleep. What we incessantly
and importunately and rightly pray for, be it the consolation of sorrow, improvement of character, or kingdom of God, will surely come! The abolition of slavery
was Garrison's aim and cry, and the unwritten, never
omitted, punctually recited liturgy of his soul. He not
only persisted; he was perseverance incarnate, and he
was equity, too. He wanted, in a friend's house, to
pay for a pane of glass which he had chanced to break.
"A just weight and balance is the Lord's," and was
Garrison's. He awoke the nation at last, called down
Heaven's decree by stress of his petition, and broke the
fetters of the slave by his tremendous claim. Beyond
good sense, a grasp of moral ideas and of historical
details, his intellect was not richly endowed. Compared with some of his own comrades, he had a meagre
mind. His merit was ordinary as a poet or occasional
bard. He was not as eloquent as some of his compeers,
yet his voice, more than theirs, was loaded with a
power as of fate. He was not Aaron persuading the
people, but Moses with his laws; and on the tables,
not of rock, but of men's hearts, he got them finally
engraved. He took by long siege, and overthrew our
old feudal castle of bondage, our bastile of oppression,
by no ingenious search and manifold trial of its vulnera-

ble points, but by one catapult at the nailed and knotty gates. It was a greater triumph than that at Vicksburg. He was omnipotent for that supreme blow, was raised up for that purpose as much as the Isaiah or Amos he loved to quote were for their Hebrew mission, and in comparison he was good for nothing else. He was the oxygen in our air, and embodied the conscience of the land.

In other directions his faculty was commonplace. When he became a musical critic the public was amused. A friend, walking with him through a picture-gallery, was surprised at the judgments he pronounced. But when he voiced the right on any question touching the condition of the downtrodden, the treatment of women, or the duty of purity and self-control, it was an old trumpet of the Lord, or as the roar of the lion of the tribe of Judah, that we heard. What a true refrain, sublime tautology, or unalterable parallelism in a Hebrew psalm, his utterance was! "These chains must be rent or taken off, selah!" was the burden and tune of resonance from an iron string.

His irresistible demand was of equal rights for all of either sex. But while such characters as his are needed and appear, equality of individual constitution and influence cannot exist, any more than the sea could be emptied into a pond, or the Himalayas smoothed to the level of Asia, or the lightnings of the sky reduced to a spark on the hearth. He was the hydrostatic paradox reduced to actual practice in civil and social affairs, holding the ocean in check with a drop; one columnar man in the other side of the scale against and resisting the drift and subsidence of the race. He was original

in this ethical weight.   He did not owe his preponder-
ance to any other hero or foreseer, but proclaimed an
authentic gospel from his own breast.   Had he borrowed, he could not have launched his bolts of fire!
The bow of Ulysses could be bent by none of the selfish suitors, and only by Ulysses himself.

But Garrison was no less a religious than a moral
man, a Christian though not a church-goer, a regular
communicant in a sense as deep as was ever carried by
any bread and wine.   When that honest and almost
unequalled preacher, George Putnam, who said "he
became an abolitionist when the Lord did," remarked
to Garrison, then his neighbor, that he did not see
him at meeting, the reply was, "I go to hear myself
preach sometimes!"   That grand duality, by reason of
which a man is in his own bosom speaker and audience
too, nobody knew better than he.   To such a listener
and overhearer of God in the mind's temple and court,
Jesus himself is not lord and master, but friend, — the
title which, with his first disciples, he craved; and but
for such genuine inspiration at first hand, like a fresh
wind out of the sky, in our own time, Christianity
preached on whatever other and outward authority
could not continue to be received.   On what those who
would drill us in forms and creeds construe as its denial
it depends for its existence in fact!   How could we
believe in

> " Siloa's brook,
> That flowed fast by the oracles of God,"

but for those other brooks "that make the meadows
green" in our daily paths?   We rejoice in whoever
revives our faith that "the Lord reigneth," — as Garri-

son, in his perhaps most favorite citation, ever fondly declared, — even as we do that electricity is not worn out, or the northwest breeze dead, or the sun's lamp spent. Astronomers tell us that the luminary which makes for us the day will at last have consumed its wick, and burnt up from the vessels all its oil. But we should not credit any consumption at the remotest period of the moral sense; and such men as Garrison, by being its organs, are mightier than their reputed intellectual superiors, constraining the giants of debate, Webster and Clay and Calhoun, as well as those of imperial will like Jackson, to stay their hands, hush their utterance, and lower their eyes. After seasons during which fair dealing seems to have disappeared from the earth, this lustre of righteousness, like a star out of its occultation, in such an aspect and figure as that of Garrison returns.

He was not, indeed, the abolisher of slavery by himself alone. The poor negro boy, to the question in the Catechism, put by his teacher, replied, "The Lord made me, but Massa Linkum make me free!" Garrison gave to Lincoln the ample award for his word and deed, while for the blessed consummation, sharing his own meed of honor with the humblest instrument, he would have all men, with him, praise the Most High. Well did the Church, which, however he forsook its assemblies, folded him alive, also take him dead to her arms, saying, "I, through my priesthood, and not you, my son, have been the prodigal; and my aisles shall ring with your praises, although your soul may not ask my prayers."

Garrison was not the only agent; solitary he could

never have prevailed. There would have been too much of his monotonous strain to be borne; and his anti-constitutional doctrine was an error that might have gone to injurious excess but for other influences as essential as his to one and the same end. Those who recoiled from the terrible phantom of disunion and the bloody issue of civil war, from the Red Sea that stretched out on the way to freedom, have encountered much reproach at the hands of such as rushed ahead. All respect is due to him who, in the immense move-ment, was to the fore and at the van, having touched bottom of the truth in this thing. Yet social and na-tional sins are diseases too, to be cured by expectant medicine or by prudent surgery, not lopped off at a stroke of the knife. To stop the iniquity with aboli-tion, immediate and unconditional, was a necessary, no less than a righteous cry. But in this world no great change can be immediate and unconditional. Those who waited, who pondered the problem and sought the wisest way, were servants as loyal and as useful as any who proceeded in haste to the end desired. How many a heart will cry out even now, Would to God that the object might have been won at less cost than "a drop of blood from the sword for every drop of blood from the lash"! in our martyr-President's phrase. If an earlier crisis had destroyed the nation for either black or white, or for them both, the issue would have been made too soon. In the backwardness of thousands of excellent men and women was a quality in the sight of Him, who is not in a hurry, as fine and pleasing as in any cordial and headlong push to deliver the wronged, if how to redeem them effectually were indeed what the hesitants proposed. Dr. Channing, who, once in motion, was as much resolved as were those who started earlier to go on, has been reviled as a temporizer, a time-server, and a coward·in the cause. But no curse can rest on that pure and noble name! It will be more likely to return to the ears of those from whose lips it comes. Channing, as has been said by one who was an abolitionist from the outset, surrendered for his convictions more than Garrison ever had to give up! He was a beloved man and a famous minister, drawing crowds when he spoke, prosperous in his worldly fortunes, and an idol in the desk. When he came out on the antislavery side he was avoided, denounced, and looked at askance; and some of his old friends would not speak to him in the street. For a nature sensitive, like his, was not this a price to pay which should save him from the charge of venality now?

Slavery was abolished by no man, but by all men, — by the Divine behest and by the United States. The cars of progress were coupled for that design; and the brakemen at the wheels, as well as the engineers of the train, did their part. Slavery was abolished as a war-measure and at a stroke of the pen. But the sudden abolition of it, in time of peace and without preparation, would have been a shock perhaps too severe for the social system to bear. The philanthropist who looks at the surface, and would overthrow at once any external ill, would do more harm than good, could he instantaneously have his way. The introduction of universal woman-suffrage on the moment, like an eruption through the ocean-bed, would lift, on the sea of human affairs, one of those prodigious and engulfing billows which could be weathered by no pilot of the ship of State. It will come, if at all, slowly, when it is wanted by women, and can be adjusted to our civil affairs, as a new continent of the globe rises by the gentle and normal pressure of the central force; the holy clamor for it, peradventure, hastening the time by stirring the political deeps.

Mr. Garrison had in this reform an interest second only to that which was the chief mission of his life. He made, on one or another branch of it, solemn and moving speeches in England and at home. The grounds and conclusions of some by whom it is opposed are the grossest affront offered in this age to the human conscience and to common-sense. The premises must be wrong which lead to such doctrines as are still proclaimed. We are told that fear is a shame to a man, but not to a woman; that the virtue of chastity is more important in the woman, inasmuch as she guards the succession of property and name, than in the man; that to impose the same penalties for vice on a man as on a woman would be without the same necessity, and a far greater hardship to him than to her; that a breach of chastity must not be visited with equal condemnation on a man as on a woman; that different values are to be assigned to the same virtue in men and women; and that a man can retrieve lost honor, and a woman cannot. What masculine villain could ask greater license for his iniquities than all this? It is *carte blanche* for transgression in entries of the blackest dye. It is *magna charta* for all the profligacy of the stronger sex that has stained the annals of the

world. What but a worldly policy is the frankly confessed reason for this double standard and division of
virtues betwixt the two sides of humanity, in a distribution which not a sentence from either volume of Holy
Writ can be quoted to justify? A spotless womanhood
in an incorruptible wife must, it is said, secure to
offspring their legitimate family-title! Shall the man
be allowed to have other children of his blood with
other names or with none? Is the escutcheon then
without a blot? Is a cleanly constitution certified,
as a divine bill of health, for the generation to come,
when only one of the parents is clean? Does Christ or
apostle wink at fornication or adultery in either one of
them more than in the other? Does not the old commandment, equally with the new, make honor and holiness alike binding on him who begets as on her who
bears? The plea of the wolf that the lamb, drinking
on the stream below, muddied the water above, is the
only piece of literature with which to characterize so
monstrous a view, on which all honest men and women
should unite in a common oath to have no mercy to
palliate or forgive. Purity, we are informed, is the
virtue for a woman, and truth for a man. Sorely, indeed, he needs veracity in his business; but should she
be less candid in her representations and affairs? She
must be above suspicion in her sexual relations; but is
it of less consequence that grave mistrust of his goings
and comings, if his inclination be questionable, should
dog his steps? All the brethren and sisters that deserve these dear appellations, old as the world, will
unanimously say, No! Man and woman, made together in that image of God which else would be in

either incomplete, must be, like him, both holy alike. Any opinion by which this judgment is contravened is neither intuitive nor inspired. It is a verdict of expediency, from past cycles of error and sin. Its basis is calculation of utility; and even as. such the sum will be found incorrect, and never be proved before God and the instincts of the human soul.

In every way Mr. Garrison was of the future, not of the past. He was a millennial man; and a right relation between man and woman is a larger project, and has its accomplishment farther away, than the emancipation everywhere of the blacks. We feel that the first step of progress has not been taken so long as it is denied that moral excellence of any sort is not common to, or independent of sex; that to be immaculate is more important in our wife, daughter, or sister, than in her mate, who can recover with any credit from derelictions which her reputation cannot survive, because she stands guard over the descent of his! From expediency and a title to earthly goods virtue itself, then, is derived. Purity is based on property; and any other virtue on the same utilitarian principle is of more or less consequence according to circumstances. We had supposed that virtue of every sort was a dictate of conscience, an inspiration of God, and an instinct of the soul; that it was a jewel, and not a bit of paste; that it was not itself, like Nebuchadnezzar's image, a composition, but a constitution, according to which all other things should be created and composed. Behold, it is naught but a pudding-stone of the mind! Then there is no adamant in nature; the grace of God is a mosaic, and his spirit a figure of speech. The elements are our parents, and we have no father beside; and this making all human worth out of selfish calculation is supposed to be a panoply of argument which no critical objection can pierce. Who can find a joint in the armor? is the question put; to which we answer, It gapes, and is open to the spear at every point! It was said of Achilles that he was vulnerable only in his heel; and nothing but the lower extremities of a man seem to be left when he is exempt from any duty which is imposed on a woman, for no reason but because a base custom which men have instituted so bids! The present writer was once adjured by a bridegroom not to require any more in the marriage vows of the bride than of him. But to make the Providence that establishes human society the author of a requisition so unfair carries profanity to the extreme.

That male purity is as momentous, at least, as female, is hinted by the old Scripture-proverb that it was the eating of sour grapes by the " fathers " that had set the children's teeth on edge, and by a modern one concerning the equal fitness of the same condiment to the masculine and feminine of a certain species of domesticated fowl, whose literal terms are too coarse to cite. No Indian squaw or Otaheitan savage would say that aught else is fair. Not to be re-born, but born and begot aright, is the sum of all reform. When we have a true human generation, all the aid societies and philanthropic associations and assemblies for charity may disband and dissolve. Therefore let us take a stronger than Father Mathew's pledge to stand by, and inaugurate whatsoever will promote that coming of a true human race into the world, which any license for either party to the marriage-contract will prevent. It is reported by travellers that when Russian husbands take liberties Russian wives do the same; and a spreading libertinism, which may, in its corrupting sway among the higher classes, go far to account for Nihilism, is the mournful and menacing result. When Napoleon the Great was about to lead his army into the field, he sometimes swore them to be faithful to their country, to their general, and to their flag; and to each adjuration they answered, "We swear," with a murmur that overspread the earth and filled the sky. Let all who would befriend the tie betwixt woman and man join in a like conjuration that, in the mutual engagement, neither party shall be false. Man and woman are made together in the image of God. She is half thereof; and without her womanhood it would be a broken image in all mankind. Moreover, in this image there is a common circulation of virtue through all its parts and forms. No beauty of disposition or grace of character, charm of temper or courage of will, can be confined to either side. Whatsoever is pure and lovely must make in human shape the whole circuit of divinity to have its true potency, as electricity must traverse the wires to and fro before a connection is made and the message sped.

To estimate a virtue by its supposed politico-economical consequences is to make all virtue a compromise. But are there not some virtues that belong less to a woman and more to a man, such as courage and enterprise, as we read that a man once "was famous according as he had lifted up the axe on the thick trees," and as he has always fought in war? Is not fear "a shame in him and not in woman"? I answer, for her to be fearless is not to be unsexed. Bravery in battle or against the elements is, however, a half-physical quality. There are primary and secondary virtues, as there are primary and secondary properties of matter. But truth, honesty, and purity are to vigor and pluck, to contention and resistance, what extension and weight are to color and form; and the moral primaries become and adorn either sex alike. To the plea that man has the stronger appetite to justify him, the reply is, that he should feel all the more bound not to throw the reins on its neck, and needs to be especially restrained and warned; and that moral obligation should not be for him a looser curb, nor apology a thicker palliation cast over his than his companion's fault. To let loose a wayward propensity on principle is worse and more dangerous than a system of polygamy, as among the Mormons, or than Solomon's concubinage in old Jewish times. It would insulate the woman, deprive her of any proper mate, and tempt her, as in France, to take in such manner as she might choose her revenge. But the chief evil of a social philosophy, which gives the least excuse, or opens to any excess a crack of the door, is that it makes virtue an accident or arrangement, not a law. There is thus no commandment in life, but all is a game; and the conduct of every individual is at the hazard of his inclination as on the cast of a die. There would thus be a taint at the source of human behavior, a rot in the thread of every relation, and many a Cain, whom no Bible could take notice of, a vagrant and tramp on the earth.

The historic sense, so indispensable to a historian, becomes tyrannical and false when it puts the eyes in the back of the head, and would stereotype the future on the pattern of the past. However sage in this world's wisdom such a posture may be, it is not the attitude of any hero, reformer, martyr, or saint. It is, indeed, the look and gesture which make what we call conservatism. It is the aspect of despairing and timorous men, who talk of our institutions as a failure, a broken promise, or a forlorn hope. Bright prospect it has none.

Transcendent genius none will claim for Mr. Garrison, yet in ideas was his strength. The missiles discharged in the field can seldom be fired again; but principles are a miraculous ammunition, more mighty the oftener it may be used. Like a boomerang, every weapon with which we justly assail iniquity returns to our hand. Garrison was mistaken for a heated zealot when he was a tranquil marksman. He was the granite hill, against which the raging elements broke to flow down in a fertilizing stream. He was the storm-centre rather than the storm. He was the Spartan bearing his message, though he fell dead at the goal. He belonged .as to a Roman or Macedonian phalanx, which pierced the hostile array like an arrow or wedge. So few were these soldiers of humanity at first that they had, when attacked, to form in hollow square to bear the brunt, being so vastly outnumbered by their foes; and Garrison was as cool as a cannoneer serving his hot and smoky gun. Rather, he was an element of hostility to wrong, and no more than an element of nature to be blamed. As well attempt to delay an earthquake, and put off the deluge, as postpone his onset and charge! The rods with which the proslavery folk sought to protect their dwelling were melted by the lightning which they would avert. God took the controversy up into the whirlwind, as he did the old quarrel with Job! The human issue was a resultant of forces, and not the contribution of any one man. We are at the old Pharisee-business of sepulchre-building now, concealing our shame that we treated the live prophets so ill.

Garrison was a believer in both the end and the means. Explaining to a young man the use of the printing-press, as he handled the lever, he said, "This is the mightiest of things, and with it we hope to abolish slavery in the land." He exposed the trespasser, and never hushed the truth. He put his light on a table, and not under a bushel. Shall I say he was a "starter" of the car of rectitude? Amid what a crowding and confusion his keen whistle was always heard! He was a lonely and a primary man. If he calculated the value of the Union, he never did that of the liberty it was formed to defend. Only one of a million names is engraved on the tablet of fame too deep to be effaced; and his is the millionth name! No political ultimatum is so final as that call for freedom which in a new exodus is more complete to-day. "I never knew," said one, "what was meant by Christ's washing of his disciples' feet till the fugitive African came for me to wash his!" One genuine spring of human love bears refreshment far and wide, as a runnel of living water supplies a town; and Garrison was a fountain. His advance resembled a marching with banners. As a paper that flutters and rustles in the street startles a timid horse, so the "Liberator" alarmed every traveller on the highways. A rope was around his neck in Boston. Where is it now? What a relic it would be, like the holy coat of Tréves, or the bones of martyrs, or a piece of the true cross! By the descendants of the very men that plied and cast it about his neck like a lasso for a wild beast, it would be converted now for an ornament and a charm. He wrote on his dungeon wall the reason of his incarceration. On earth and in heaven he has come out into the light.

Mr. Garrison was a born independent, an incarnate resolution, a man that could go by himself and stand alone; and he was compressed into resisting and resistless power by the right of his cause and the exigency of the case. He did not court any backing, and was indifferent to applause. He stood apart from his peers in his belief in spiritualism and its so-called manifestations; and when I told him that Paul, who never saw the Lord save in spiritual vision, was the chief apostle, and that Thomas, who wanted to put his fingers into the print of the nails, and thrust his hand into the Master's side, was never heard of again, he astonished me by replying that Thomas was worth all the rest of the disciples put together! When an invitation was sent to him to assist in raising the flag at Fort Sumter after the war, he received it with not a sign of exultation but an impassive face. He was as unmoved by the compliment or the glory as a frigate by a shining ripple on her sides. The exigency had been so great and grave that he had lost in it himself.

VI.

HUNT, THE ARTIST.

ART among us is still a sort of wanderer or lost child. But there seems to be occasionally born in this land of the Puritans one who is not puritanic, but rather like the offspring of parents whom some mischance has exiled from their own native climate and soil, yet who comes to remind us that there is such a thing as beauty alike in that nature and art which have both in New England lain so long under a religious curse, and whose spirit the theory and practice of our modern materialism would again, like the old theology, suppress or kill, by making nature the cause in all creation instead of the ever-proceeding effect.

The artist is a silent preacher to whom those material elements which the scientist explores for their own sake, and for the laws they illustrate, have but the intrinsic worth of what they express by proportion and color of the charm and meaning of this world, being but one of the bullets shot from the muzzle of the sun, to undergo during the geologic ages such a subduing process that one might say its Author is an artist, with Nature in his immense studio for a pupil and help. For how the gigantic primeval fauna and flora have been refined! There could have been no rose or lily, more than a Socrates or a Jesus, at the start. But among the atoms a God is at work, because nature is a handi-work of Deity ; and nature and art are thus convertible terms. Science falsely assumes in nature a depth, sci-entifically reached, below what any art can sound. The senses and the understanding, the faculties which Sci-ence employs, deal only with the outside of things. Meantime, she rehearses in secret with her Author all the parts she is to perform. She is for ever veiled. No mortal has lifted her curtain, or been admitted to the little green-room where for the open stage she lays her plots. Thus, while the scientist may regard the artist as but the decorator of her scenery, maker of her cos-tume, and provider of the theatrical properties, the artist holds that the beauty which plays over her sur-face is but an outlet of the essence at her core. Her charms are not like trinkets or bracelets, worn on the arms and neck, but expressions through the counte-nance of uncontainable goodness and immortal grace ; and her interpreter is not the ornamenter but the repre-sentative of her designs. He brings us into close com-munion, nearer to her than does any statement of her facts and laws, in which she is but like a tree in winter stripped of verdure, or a skeleton without the mobile, ruddy, and breathing flesh. Her volume is a picture-book, whose text would be dry and in a foreign tongue without the illustrations. While there are in the world no livelier quarrels than among the scientific and philo-sophic schools, and such a materialist as Haeckel flings vile epithets at Agassiz and Virchow, to prove that he at least has not reached the truth, which is a spirit of justice and love, let us therefore be thankful for a refuge from the strife of tongues in that pavilion of beauty, so many of whose chambers art unlocks.

Let me not disparage the benefit of Science. She takes us forward as in a foot-journey. Then we get into the chariot of Art, to be carried on our endless way, which has so many stations and no goal. I love the philosophers, and but smile to see how none of their explanations suffice! I love their disciples of all schools, and marvel only at those who are led captive by any one man! "Great is Allah, and Mohammed is his prophet," exclaims the Turkish devotee in the Orient. "Great is Nature, and Spencer and Darwin are her prophets," is the outcry of their votaries in the transatlantic West. Greater still are Plato, and Aristotle, and Hegel, and Immanuel Kant, with his morals above expediency, and a conscience beyond those utilitarian calculations which are like a merchant's ledger of profit and loss. But the singers, Shakspeare and Homer, with the painters, Velasquez and Rembrandt, have a stature of equal height. Says that candid master, Darwin, "There is a natural *selection* by which the fittest survive." So, then, there is a will in Nature, beside the mighty original push. She seems to have an alternative and a choice. Beside the gradual incline of her procedure up or down, there are nodes and crises in her movement, little leaps and starts, as when the mushroom breaks through the crust of the ground, or the bourgeon of a plant splits its horny bark with pressure soft as a baby's skin, teaching us how beyond all hammering a constant gentleness will succeed.

The artist's business is to copy Nature, and to "better her instruction" in choosing from her what he likes, as it is said Turner selected what pleased him, and left the rest, being not a Chinese imitator, but a bard with the brush, dipping it in his palette instead of a pen in ink. He was the English Shakspeare; and the canvas was his book, the "Slave-Ship" his tragedy of "Macbeth," and the "Building of Carthage" his "Midsummer Night's Dream."

Some men and women have their brains packed so full of facts or data and laws that there is little room left for music or picture or prayer. But understanding does not, so well as imagination, even *understand* the world. Our American poet can make an image of the "chambered nautilus," but what investigator can detect the primordial germ behind the first curl of its shell? Truth to the intellect is but the shadow of beauty, and beauty is the face of truth. There are many facts that will not fit the system-maker's theory of the world as developed or evolved. But the values of form and color are essentially unalterable. The line of beauty is one, and it suits the soul. Therefore it is written that "out of Zion, the perfection of beauty, God hath shined."

William Morris Hunt, like Horatio Greenough, was a born artist; and, when a boy, began to make pictures on the margins of the leaves of books, and to model figures, as Greenough did, in whatever fit material came to hand, — the promise of the sculptor in him being at first most marked. Whence and wherefore in any one is such irrepressible disposition to reproduce, but as part of the image and inclining of Him who does not analyze and dissect, but for ever puts things together, and himself moulds and paints the world? Surely he has no finer work than in the artist he fashions and sends; and seldom is seen a rarer pattern of

flesh than the one of whom I speak. Such and so
faultless were his form, face, eye, poise, gesture, and
shape of the hand, which was the unconscious attendant of a melodious and eloquent voice, that in any company he would be at once singled out by an observer.
There is a fine portrait of him as a young man with
brown hair and tawny beard, which, in later years long,
waving, and soft as silk, made part of the picture he
was as he walked the street. His disposition was so
genial and benign, as well as communicative of original
imaginations and thoughts, that there was no more popular member in the class in his college-days. A singular
delicacy informed his nervous system and whole frame,
which had much of the woman in it, as has been the
case with many eminent men. Quick to see and to stir,
curious to gaze at and spell out this panorama of things
and persons which the never-resting creation is, he
could scarce have been made a philologist, a metaphy-
sician, or a student of antiquarian lore. Wonderful in
his descriptions of what he observed, and instructive
in conversation, he had sailed, and was always sailing,
round the world in a different way from Captain Cook,
and got all his rich learning not from literature but
from life. He was not only a poet on canvas, as he
might have been on the page, but a Chrysostom, or
talker with the golden mouth. The fine and sensitive
thread with which his mortal garment was sewed together, while it qualified him for his calling, was also,
as it must be in any man, his exposure to pain. Discord is greatest and most extreme on the strings or in
the pipes of the musical instrument that is most com-
plex and perfect, and it is only "*sweet* bells" that can

be " jangled out of tune." If he suffered on account of a constitution exceptionally tender to respond to a breath and quiver at a touch, he but shared the lot of all with like organism, as George Sand says the composer Chopin was wounded by a fold in a rose-leaf and would tremble at a shadow that passed.

It is a question always how to fix any one artist's place among others of his own country or time. The general verdict is likely to be that, while Allston and Stuart and Copley may have excelled Hunt as colorists and painters of single figures, as Allston soared above all his fellows in this land into the heaven of invention, religious sentiment, and a divine calm, so that his pictures show at once what the man loved and where he delighted to abide, yet that Hunt has greater variety, and measures a wider breadth of both nature and humanity in his style. Certainly he belongs to the school which is both modern and French; and he was successively in one and another part of the school-room, first with the more classic and ideal Couture, afterwards with Millet, at once so romantic and humane.

They are gone. How the painters of late have died; and France in her Millet, Corot, and Couture has lost more precious possessions than in her beloved Alsace and Lorraine! Hunt, too, has departed to the majority, and rejoined his peers, leaving his earthly comrades and scholars to mourn. What is his place in the earthly ranks? If a man by an unerring law goes into, and may be discovered by his work, be it with the chisel or brush or pen, how well we must think of Hunt! Not a coarse conception or indecent stroke does aught that ever stood on his easel present; and if any inquire what manner of person this was, all that he produced, without a contradictory vote, answers that goodness and purity, modesty and humility, truth and sincerity, dwelt in his soul. Did he not indeed husband his powers, economize his opportunities, guard with temperance his strength, and improve his time? Were there any, the faintest, testimony to the contrary, it would be from a false witness; for what he has done, so great, various, and manifold in quantity and quality too, comes in proof, which no trivial evidence could rebut, what a hard-working and devoted man he was, getting out of himself for his fellow-creatures' behoof all the music in him that his Creator designed. If he stopped by the wayside, it was but for a moment's play; if he plucked a flower, it was while he was tilling the ground; if he slept, it was beside that "poppy which grows among the corn." His drummer-boy drummed him to his task; his stone-cutter, lifting his hand to his brow to wipe away the sweat, was the painter himself at sorer toil than with any iron pick. Doubtless the "Boy with the Violin" was in literal verity the master in art also, in his leisure hours; and the "Hurdy-Gurdy" was not only from, but had been in, his hand! Had he not laughed and sported sometimes, he could not have labored as he did, and been the most prolific of all in his vocation who have lived in our midst. So, in the solemn phrase of our funeral service, let "his works follow him," and he will have a noble fame on earth and the joy of his Lord in heaven.

In my incompetence of judgment I must leave his professional merit to the verdict of experts, although I have often noticed how much unfairness and animosity

in his decisions an art-critic for the press may display.
"William," said one who knew him best, "had a delicacy of sentiment which even among women is found in
but one of a thousand;" and how his refinement appears in his sketches, in color or charcoal, of the New
England meadows, or of the Florida woods and creeks!
Pond and pasture, river and harbor, sea and shore, —
against which the Atlantic crowds in storm or laps
softly in calm, — what better than Egyptian embalming
they all get from his hand! How lively and fresh, as
he touches it, is every scene! Said John Weiss, "I
did not see the picture in nature, as we walked together,
till it was shown by him." From the port of Gloucester to the Falls of Niagara his pencil goes with the
same power and ease. What boy that ever drove
home the cows over the hill but will thrill with a memory, perhaps fifty years old, in looking at a certain one
of his pastels! Landscape, portrait, and allegory, he
is at home for them all. If before some girlish likeness, or scene on the Charles River, from his pencil,
we are tempted to say he is distinguished by a handling delicate and nice, let us look at the rush of the
water in the rapids above Goat Island, or at the incarnation of law in Chief Justice Shaw!

Mr. Hunt caught by instant sympathy the manner
of his own first or last teacher. How large and ready
was his appropriation and assimilation of every quality,
no grandeur or subtile trick of the business being hid
from his infallible glance! But he worked through all
masters to himself, and exhibited at the close an individuality as pronounced as theirs, to become a master
himself. Never were the pupils of any other man a

more docile and enthusiastic band. He enkindled them, while he taught, as Agassiz did his scientific class. He reserved his own supreme admiration. for Michael Angelo ; and well I remember, at my table, when Mr. Coquerel, of Paris, made some critical exception, which was not to Mr. Hunt's taste, how he trembled and grew white in his seat with artistic wrath, as he declared respecting Angelo's figure of Eve, that he " never could understand how that man could have created the woman from whom he had himself descended ! " Aspiration and ascension, as well as keen inspection, were habitually Mr. Hunt's mental state.   He said, " I am going to treat that subject better than it was ever handled before, — I know I shall not, but I believe I shall."   So Rubinstein said, " I. tell my pupils, if they do not expect to excel Beethoven they must not compose at all."   " In every trial the painter makes," said Mr. Hunt, " there comes a moment of despair ; " and " the artist's affair is to get out of the worst scrapes on his canvas a man ever got into."   He affirmed that his endeavor was to set forth " what no man ever saw, — the soul."   He loved what was alive and beaming more than he did any decay, however picturesque.   Hearing Titiens sing, he said, " The rest of us are raisins, but she is a grape.". His favor was impartial for all that is fair.   When one was reported as liking a willow, but not an oak-tree, he replied, " One that professes to like an oak and not a willow does not like the oak, but is only bullied by it."   He was such a discerner and active explorer of nature that, if he were found with a book reading by the fire, it was known something was the matter with him, and that he must feel unwell ; and during actual illness, his journey being postponed, he showed still the matchless cunning of his fingers as he wrote on a bit of paper characters so minute that only with a microscope could they be read.

Charlotte Cushman said of players, and painters too, that " the moral point is not what takes their eye." But he had a strong sense of what is just in behavior as well as in art, and said he would not send his pictures to a particular exhibition which was ungenerously managed; he " would rather let the flies sit upon them ! " When a lady informed him one morning, " I shall not keep my appointment to sit, I am too yellow to-day," he observed, " The question is not whether she is yellow, but whether I am ! " He meant it should be considered by the sitter whether the artist might be in the mood to paint; and he thought that egoism in the lady had prevailed rather than equity, or *altruism*, as it would be called in the philosophy of our time. He satirized all straining for effect by saying, " A man cannot be smarter than he is ! "

No shrinking maiden had, more than Mr. Hunt, that sensibility which is crossed by deformity, as it is pleased with all that is harmonious, while yet no man was ever braver to bear the anguish he incurred by any jar or dissonance, in the silence of his own breast. He never complained of disappointment or of unkindly treatment, in his vocation or otherwise, to the outside world. Scarcely a lisp concerning his share in the common troubles of mortal life reached the ears even of his intimate friends. He behaved like the Spartan youth who concealed under his cloak the fox that tore at his breast. With the humor that is proper to all genius he

would set out actions and characters with the liveliest
hues, in his speech as with his brush, using perhaps
extravagant expletives, or, when sorely tempted, as innocently as Sterne's Uncle Toby, a round oath; but of
malignity, or desire to give pain to another, his gentle
bosom held not a jot. He would give by turns a piece
of his heart or mind, but there was no poison in his
disposition.

The talk about the artistic temperament may refer
to what is aside from physiological truth. Artists are
of all sorts, sanguine, bilious, and nervous. Some have
the French and Italian mobility, and others the Dutch
phlegm. Genius includes the reserved Englishman and
the stalwart Norwegian in its class. Yet something
peculiarly tender and impressionable must be in the
imagination of all artists alike. They are children, not
adults. They live in the present. They have no past
tense. Like a photographic plate, they catch an object.
Like a turtle from the brook, or a gay summer insect,
they love and take to the sun, and bask or move in it as
their element with more than the pleasure of common
men. Their intellectual instruments have, if not a
frailer construction, yet a more polished edge, like the
tools that must be wiped from moisture of a breath
before they are laid away, or the lenses that have to
be adjusted, and the metres we hang carefully up.
In consideration of their precious benefactions they
should have some liberal indulgence of their tastes
and allowance of their atmosphere; even if, as one
hints, to prevent interruption by such as do not understand, they write "Whim" over their door. There is
domestic and social evidence that even such colossal

men as Milton, Dante, and Goethe possessed their characteristic faculty on condition of an extraordinary susceptibility, which was not always under their own control, so that getting along with them may have sometimes been no easy task. The side of the gifted mortal which worshippers see in his splendid displays and lucid intervals of power, he may not keep uppermost always in debate or habitually at home. The wife of a famous preacher of a former generation is said to have remarked somewhat bitterly on the difference of her husband to his admiring congregation and privately to herself! It is a law of nature that the highest tide should be followed by the lowest; and there is a refluence unavoidable in whatever mind in its occasional efforts may transcend the ordinary mortal capacity or lot, although there cannot for genius be any abrogation of the moral law. But, as we glory in its rising, let us be patient if the flats appear when it subsides! The rare variety it constitutes of our common humanity should be entreated gently. Let us handle it, to change the figure, like a quadrant or a mirror, and not toss it into a corner like a rusty shovel or hoe! .

But few of the inspired ones less need any apology than Mr. Hunt. The present witness knows too well how generously lavish of his attention and time he was, even for those who had little claim; how he would run with his smiling face and mellow voice to one that stood and knocked at his studio-door; with what long-suffering he bore intrusion on his work, and in what a heaping measure or an outpouring flood he gave counsel to those in need. Yet he did not, more than others, relish being bluntly controverted. To oppose him was like thwarting a child. He was a fountain, and it was best to let him flow! Else he would be choked or confused, and one would incontinently miss the riches on the stream of a monologue like that of Coleridge, on themes assuredly not the same.

Genius is a name for transcendent ability constitutionally or providentially determined to a particular line; and it was plain that Mr. Hunt might have been a musician, or an actor, or in any profession an eloquent speaker, had such direction been laid out for him by circumstances. He was a poet, with pigments for his vocabulary of words. He could tell a story equally well with the crayon or the tongue. He could admirably dramatize, either as a vivid narrator or as a portrayer in dumb figures of the living scene for which he cared. His " Prodigal Son," though not literally faithful to the particulars of the Scripture tale, affects us as that does. His " Jewess" is as good as Scott's Rebecca, or as that earlier one that stood by the well. He was at heart a Provençal singer, a wandering minstrel or troubadour, or he could not have drawn the shapes that hint them so to the life. He had in him something of Don Quixote or Miss Brontë's Paul Emanuel. But the spirit of rest, no less than of roving, was his; otherwise he could not have brought back, in such peace from his journeys, " The Mill-Pond at North Easton," or the slow current and slender bayous of the river St. Johns; and *he* must have known every outward or inward meaning of a cloud who drew the brooding of the tempest on Cape Ann.

The last was the most fruitful and in part one of the happiest years of Mr. Hunt's art-life. Apparently in

perfect health, and with great joy, Niagara had from
him, in several large pictures, justice such as the cataract
never received before ! Then came the most important
of all his commissions, which but for the persuasions
of one very near to him he would have declined. It
was to decorate with allegorical situations the Albany
State House walls. Once resolved, however, he entered
on an enterprise so serious with peculiar zeal. That he
proved his adequacy for a sort of undertaking to which
he was so unaccustomed is a signal demonstration how
superior he was alike in execution and in inventive design.
If others in his line among us have been as eminent as
he in portraiture or in sketches from nature, or have
evinced more conspicuously any special excellence as
distinguished from his, no American artist can vie with
him in mural adornment on so large a scale, while
his performance in every way entitled him to scout, as
he often did, the notion that the age of painting has
gone, and that art for the future in any of its branches
is to be contemplated as in a gradual decay. He was
loyal to the ancients ; but he held stoutly that the moderns had appointments and topics of equal moment of
their own, and were not to be arrested or put out of
countenance by the oldest and grandest works.

Yet how he honored the elders, and sat at their feet,
and believed in their spiritual descent and ascent, and
traced their intellectual kith and kin ! Titian in heaven,
he thought, might say to Allston, " You had something
of what I had ; " and Allston would answer, " But you
had so much, basketsful and basketsful ; " and Titian
would reply, " Yet you did so much with what you
had ! "* Hunt's own best touch is not always on his

canvas of largest size. He knew that great work, in order that any result may be great, can and must go into the space of inches and hair-breadths, yet also that it lies not in hair-lines that are to be made visible with a lens, but in the concentration of the artist's intent.

Though Mr. Hunt had a specialty, he was not a specialist in his talent, but a great intelligence applied to art. He understood the pictorial distances, but also the social perspective as well. Having listened to a paper which almost deified a person recently deceased, he remarked on the bad taste of flattering a man " who was just dead and might be behind the door!" When a severe judgment had been pronounced, he said, "There is room in this world for sinners as well as saints."

Declining to make a positive engagement, he excused himself with the plea, " I lie so, in such cases, when I say I will come !" There was in his frankness an innate lowly reserve, which no praise or fame could overcome. His sympathy was narrowed to no class, but ready for the humblest and as wide as the world. He was fond of just appreciation, and indignant at captious and ignorant criticism ; and when one said, " What a pity it is he could not have received alive the ample meed of present approval for what he did !" one of his pupils answered that " he knew it the minute he was dead." Indeed, the applause of his last work at Niagara and Albany seemed to be filling the cup which was to run over, not only from his achievement, but in his firm and happy health. After that came the fatal ebb, in which day by day his strength and joy ran out. He had proposed to refuse for the time all further commissions, and when summer came, to go to Europe for recreation and rest. But he was drawn into new labors, which his ardor and good-nature tempted him to assume; and erelong the consequences appeared in a nervous prostration such as he had never felt before. Vital virtue had gone and was swiftly going out of him. Vacillation of purpose in such a toiler was a sure symptom of constitutional decline. Unnaturally keen apprehension of what he might be liable to, as of poison in the wall-paper and the colored rug, or of dust down the chimney and through the cracks of the floor, to increase the difficulty of his breathing, indicated a weakening in his thought, which had usually been as robust as it was fine. He gained flesh for a while, and lost power. The difference of temperature depressed him when he came from the " Isles of Shoals " to the main-land, even for an hour. His friends offered to take him to the mountains for a fortnight to recruit; and he quietly asked them, " And then, after that?" One day, as a black cloud with sheets of driving rain had overspread the island where he was, he had disappeared. It had been well known by those nearest to him that inability to work and discouraging failure of his wonted vigor, when he made any attempt, had been the drop most bitter to his taste. What takes place psychologically in such a case in the " article of death," who shall say? The flame burns low in the lamp of life, the wick is crusted, only a little blue jet of fire is left, which clings obstinately and long, when by the smallest agitation of the air — is it a puff of wind or the man's own breath? — it is in a moment quenched. The increments of inward disorder are too fine for the medical eye. Of the sufferer's interior condition in this case none but such as have felt, like the present writer, the utter nervous misery can be entitled to speak ; and *they* will speak with tenderness, a word of blame being impossible from their lips, knowing as they do that any providential or divinely permitted escape, when the flesh is a slow and hopeless conflagration of pain, is like rescue from a burning house or the instinctive shrinking from a cauterizing surgical tool. God takes the responsibility for every step of what is indeed abnormal or insane. Let man abstain in it from censure of his fellow-man. The lake is readily ruffled by reason of the very quality that makes it the spotless mirror of the sky. If we are made up of sentiment, how quick we are to resent ! The artist-nature is qualified and in part constituted by a sensitiveness that is extreme.

Mr. Hunt would not be called a man of religious sensibility by such as identify piety with an observance of stated forms. Neither would John Milton be so characterized in his absence from public worship in the later years of his life. But as truly reverent as that sublime poet was our artist, although his worship arose like the incense from ancient altars on the open plain. The blaze was too pure to make any smoke. Yet the consecrated walls and sweet divisions of holy time might well have been for him a help and a guard ! But he was in every thing shy. He would fain hide especially his pangs, and show his best. He had a noble shame, which would not suffer him to obtrude what was sad in his condition on those about him. Therefore, as he appeared to them in health better than he was, they with the whole community were shocked at his so sudden decease. But his vital interior had

already been consumed, and he was ready to crumble
while outwardly he stood so brave and fair. Never
surely was metal more fine than in that golden bowl
broken and silver cord loosed!

Mr. Hunt is more in the portraits he drew of others
than in those he painted of himself, as Shakspeare is
more in the plays than in the sonnets that bear his
name. He is indigenous in most of the products of his
brush, and at the last peculiarly an American in art,
however his earlier manner was French. He was a
lover of nature and of human nature, and while making
the outline of Judge Shaw he said he "wanted to hug
the man." We feel that many of his individual or ideal
portraits could walk out of their frames, pass through
our streets, and wander over the world. The artist is
in the generous scope, vivacious familiarity, self-obliv-
ious disinterestedness of his work, so real and ideal at
once that we know we have him in what he does, and
while admiring the performance cannot help but love
and honor the man. For how *he* loved and respected
the business he was at, with a depth of devoted interest
that issued in and was perpetual work! His "Trum-
peter," that stirred beyond any live one's prowess the
nation to the field, also blew him on. The singers, the
lambs, the kittens, the kids, hens, or sheep, they were
his own being for the time and his very soul. He entered into them every jot.

Mr. Hunt never fails of meaning and unity in his picture or sketch, and can fill with his central point of interest the whole space of his work, as, in his "Spring Chickens," the sky seems to spread and the river to roll for the
little brood to which a child scatters crumbs on the green

bank. Nature is never without humanity in what he conceives, and the smallest creature wins his deft hand and
tender eye. How jealous, therefore, he was of the dignity
of his calling! If there was aught better here below
than to paint, he knew it not! If one had to be persuaded to sit, he said he "would not paint a cat if it
had objections, theological, superstitious, or any other,
to being taken." He offered to his subject his heart,
and did not want any shamefacedness or by-play, but
affection deep and serious as his own. Of the selfishness which he said "shortens life to a point," he had
not a·jot. We shall see him as long as cloth and
panel can hold the light and shade he disposed and
the pigments he used. Those were his features! All
that belonged to his mortality he spent on his task.
His palette was the rainbow he dipped his brush into,
till the nervous touch was worn out that had waited so
long and faithfully on his imaginative mind. On his
stints he lavished himself. His life-blood was in the
tint and splendid staining of those Albany State House
walls, and they are his winsome relics. His remains
lie outspread in those magnificent forms, surpassing all
in the same kind which this Western continent has to
show. There is his court, his reception-chamber, and
his tomb. He lies buried under the dome he adorned,
while far away in his native village rest his tired bones.
His country will cherish tenderly the recollection of such
unpretending yet religious consecration of unmatched
powers dedicated even unto death. For into his achievement for our delectation all that in this world was in him
passed. Figure of "Fortune" at the helm did he draw?
What fortune did the draughtsman have? We think of

how many a fortune, besides, which seemed misfortune in
the history of the genius that glorifies our race, of blind
Milton and deaf Beethoven, and with which, in the
diverse measure of the men, what was sad in his story
may be compared! Under that civil ceiling on the
banks of the Hudson, bent and reaching, like Michael
Angelo at his awful Sibyls, did he give in superhuman
size the cheerful figure of "Hope"? Into it went all
the hope of his own throbbing, suffering, but never-
complaining breast! The susceptibility which is the condition and constitution of genius makes it "a pilgrim
and sojourner on the earth." It is allowed mercifully
at last to leave the carnal lodgings it finds so poor.
To other and better accommodations does it not go?
Did it not shiver like a new-born babe when it came?
The "Flight of Night" is conspicuous among those
mural tablets in paint from the hand of Mr. Hunt. But
the night he indicated had begun to settle on his own
brain. Yet he sketched truly; for him, likewise, it has
flown! There is a charcoal sketch by Mr. Hunt of a
church in the evening dusk, with a crescent moon going
down in the sky. Underneath are his initials and these
lines, expressing, doubtless, his feeling, whether from
another's pencil or his own, —

> "BEYOND A SPIRE THE MOON;
> BEYOND THE MOON A STAR;
> BEYOND THE STAR, WHAT?
> ETERNITY."

When I condoled with a noble man on a great bereavement, he said, "It is no affliction; immortality
is the fact that swallows up all!" We know neither our
friends nor our mercies till they are gone! One said

of Mr. Hunt, "Some persons seem to think a great deal more of him since he was dead." Pictures of his that might have been bought for hundreds of dollars a year ago bring, under the hammer, as many thousands now. "He can paint no more," the purchasers say. How long, indeed, has been the waiting for full appreciation of the man and the work!

The artist is a fellow-pupil with the moralist, going to Nature to school. As she has an aim vast, minute, immediate, and remote, as she pursues that aim by means the most simple and fit, and as in her impenetrable interior, which none can enter, she lays her plans, having as much as any saint a closet of her own, so in morals or the art of duty, and in art which clothes in beauty the moral laws, there is an object, a method, and a sphere in common, although the direction and visible outcome be not the same. Nevertheless, that is righteous which the pencil makes winsome, and ethics become beauty incarnate as we incline to obey the beautiful eternal laws.

Genius is thought, like the child of Melchisedec, to come straight from heaven without human descent. But by the law of heredity there seems to be an ancestral deposit of poetry, law, medicine, and divinity in certain brains, as former skill is laid up in the head of a bee. A great gift of imagination in any one, when traced, proves often to be but an old fire, that slumbered for a while in a generation or two, breaking out into flame again. But Mr. Hunt inherited directly from one parent, at least, his taste and practical tendency for art; and so the new philosophy of experience and evolution appears to be vindicated in his case.

As an artist makes a memory sketch, or as one hunts about his house to find something which he has left or lost, so I have tried to draw the lines of my subject from my recollections and reflections as they came and combined in such order as they pleased, with poor resemblance or half and halting imitation of the method of that living subject himself, who mingled painstaking method with inspiration while he mixed his paints. My theme at least has been a worthy one. The love of beauty is part of piety, unless the beauty of holiness be a mistaken Scripture-phrase; and what a perpetual solace is the beauty of the world! There is in it sin, sorrow, disappointment, death, so much that the old Persian theology gave it over to the Destroyer as well as the Preserver with an equally divided claim. But there is no deformity in its frame. "He hath made every thing beautiful in its time." The comfort of the charm of nature is second only to that of the Holy Ghost, and he who sees and shows and reproduces this beauty is an ordained and anointed minister as much as any who pronounce the clerical vows. The spirit is the same, although we must not confound the spheres. If some make art their religion, others make their religion an art; but both religion and art are one in the worship of that Being who is the all true and good and fair. Never was votary in his own profession more zealous or sincere than Hunt. Many will miss his speech more than we do the brush that has left its splendor behind; while the humor that smiled, wit that sparkled, pathos that melted, imagination that blazed and lit up every subject, have their words preserved only in the little safes of individual recollection, to be quoted as his image comes into

many a private talk. I remember his condensing the
worth of freedom into an apothegm, — " You cannot
work with your. elbow bound." He was a child, declar-
ing " there are lots of fun on earth, also in heaven,
which we are sure to have." Some of us one evening
shivered at his description of the death of an acrobat in
France, falling from his lofty trapeze to the ground, all
the spectators rising without noise in the solemn hush
to go out. He was one of the men of genius of our
country and time, whom it takes so few of our fingers
to count, and whose orb we should not let vanish and
make no sign. He sought not high society; any company of his fellow-creatures was good enough for him,
and none, he declared, from which he could not learn.
He was genial, gentle, generous, outspoken, as well as
kind; it being very difficult for him to be reserved. The
sight of suffering he could not bear, but ran to relieve.
" Take the sick girl," he said, " out of the dark side of
the house, and put her into a sunny room." Of another,
who was weak, he said to the employers, " You know
not how a heavy weight feels to her." He would run to
hush a baby, or carry in his lap a barking, dangerous
dog in the car. Meeting a music-grinder out of town,
he changes hats and jackets with him, takes his organ,
goes to the door of the house near by, plays the tunes,
pulls off his hat when the people come, is recognized,
and gets six or seven dollars for the poor Italian. He
was not—better had he been—a church-goer, but went
to a liturgical service once, and said he had to look at the
gowns and bonnets of the congregation, as he took in
the sermon with the millionth part of his mind! Almost
everybody loved him. The last fit use of his unoccu-

pied studio at Magnolia was to receive the dead body
of a young woman swept away and drowned close by,
as he was to take his last gasp by a shallow reservoir.
His personal friends and the members of his class were
all ardently such, and would prompt a better tribute than
I can render here.

His mind was indeed good ground, and brought forth
abundantly to the honor of the great Landlord who put
it to him in rent; but the soil was exhausted how sadly
and too soon! Alexandre Dumas says Michael Angelo
is the only man to whom God gave four souls, meaning,
I suppose, painting, sculpture, architecture, and poetry.
We can claim but one of these for Mr. Hunt, although
he could model skilfully in clay, and, like that grand master who was his own delight and pattern, compose in
verse if he would. This man, with such gifts from the
Great Giver, has gone. Before his intellect was dimmed
of one ray of its brightness, he has faded from view;
and, as a cold shadow unexpectedly falls upon us as we
walk when a cloud blots the sun in mid-heaven, this
sad occultation chills a thousand hearts. The unerring hand has lost its cunning, the musical tongue its
matchless aptness to persuade, the eye is closed which
naught worth seeing could escape, the manner and
gesture of a grace and originality peculiarly their
own are dust, or glorified and transformed. This Oriental in the West has had his occident; this Arab,
lithe and supple, with nerves of lightning and fibre of
steel, so swift, so strong, has disappeared among the
desert sands. In company he had kept up wonderfully,
and seemed in good spirits, though so weak. When
one, to whom his health was a precious care, entertained

him with some piquant and merry tales, he cried out: "I
never heard so many wicked stories before in my life,
and I should think you would not like to be alone with
your Maker. The air," he added, "is full of wicked-
ness," and he took a tumbler, which he turned over on
the table, and affected to fill with air, saying, "If I
should take a lucifer match this would burn like fire and
brimstone." In the last exquisite photograph taken of
him he looks like a macerated monk or pillar-saint, his
skin drawn like parchment over the hollows of his cheek-
bones. What caused such an end? Not any particular
trouble, among his many griefs, but the misery of a nervous system hindering sleep and forbidding work,—work
which was his calling, consolation, home, and refuge
from every ill. When that failed the last string cracked
in that marvellous harp some angel played in his breast.
It was death to him to have to stop in his designs.
When hope died he died. When we cease we decease.
Had aught been said against him, dying was his only
reply; and death gives an enormous advantage to a man.
Nothing strikes like a dead hand or reproves like for ever
silent lips; but with what comfort we remember any
effort or sacrifice for the departed! We give life when
we give happiness, and we take it away when we diminish joy. The real diggers of graves and hewers of
monuments are not the workers in marble yonder or the
sextons with their spades. God grant us grace while
we live, and when we die, to heal and forgive! For the
lamented man or those who in any relation with him
mourn his loss, what room in our bosom for any sentiment but pity, compassion, sympathy, commiseration,
commendation to God alike of the surviving here and of

those *there* who live beyond us all, having, in the beautiful untranslatable French word, *trespassed* on immortality while the flesh fences us in. Who can lift a horoscope over a coffin? Yet Hope, which Paul writes is one of the three abiding things, stands with her visions beyond the last eclipse.

University Press: John Wilson & Son, Cambridge.